3000 800013 77616
St. Louis Community College

W9-DJK-336

FV

WITHDRAWN

St. Louis Community College

Forest Park
Florissant Valley
Meramec

Instructional Resources
St. Louis, Missouri

Music Education in
the United States

Music Education in the United States: Contemporary Issues

Edited by
J. Terry Gates

THE ALABAMA PROJECT
Music, Society, and Education in America

The University of Alabama Press
Tuscaloosa and London

Copyright © 1988 by
The University of Alabama Press
Tuscaloosa, Alabama 35487
All rights reserved
Manufactured in the United States of America

Library of Congress Cataloging-in-Publication Data

Music education in the United States.

Based on proceedings of symposia sponsored by the Alabama Project: Music, Society, and Education in America.
Bibliography: p.
Includes index.
1. Music—Instruction and study—United States—Congresses. I. Gates, J. Terry. II. Alabama Project: Music, Society, and Education in America.
MT3.U5M76 1988 780'.7'2973 87-5836
ISBN 0-8173-0369-3 (alk. paper)

British Library Cataloguing-in-Publication Data is available.

This book is dedicated to the
many graduate music education
students with whom I worked at
Alabama. They knew how to care
—about music, about their
students, about each other.
J. Terry Gates, General Editor

Contents

Foreword

In 1982 the School of Music of The University of Alabama began to benefit from an endowed chair, the purpose of which was to bring students and faculty into substantive contact with internationally recognized authorities in music theory or composition performance, music history, and music education. A five-year rotation of these areas, with performance occupying two years of the rotation, was begun in the 1982–1983 academic year with Ross Lee Finney, composer, in residence. During the following year, the pianist Natalie Hinderas was based in Tuscaloosa.

The initial planning committee for the 1984–1985 music education year consisted of J. Terry Gates, chairman; Merilyn Jones, chairman of the program in music education; Mitzi Kolar, Robert Nicolosi, and Sheryl Cohen, faculty members in the School of Music; Elizabeth Meese, assistant dean of arts and sciences; and Dennis Monk, director of the School of Music. The committee began its work in early 1982. In the intervening years, Dr. Nicolosi, Dr. Kolar, and Dr. Cohen were replaced by Frederic Goossen, Carol Prickett, and Scott Bridges. Roosevelt O. Shelton was selected as coordinator of the project's events.

In March 1983 Dr. Gates proposed that the endowment proceeds be used to support a series of three-week residencies, four symposia with presentations by additional experts, a concluding symposium, and a publication which would contain papers written by those invited for the residencies and symposia. It was proposed that each symposium focus on a different specialization but that all treat foundational areas of music education. The calendar as it actually took place appears below. It is substantially the same as that proposed by the committee in September 1983 and approved by the board of trustees in December of that year.

September 20–October 7, 1984: Charles Leonhard,
  University of Illinois at Urbana-Champaign.
  Symposium I—*Professional Methodology*—October 6–7
   Merilyn Jones, chairman, University of Alabama
   Charles Leonhard
   Gretchen H. Beall, University of Colorado
   Robert Glidden, Florida State University
   William Jones, Minneapolis, Minnesota
   Richard Graham, University of Georgia
November 1–19, 1984: Max Kaplan, sociologist, gerontologist, and
  music educator, Auburn, Alabama.
  Symposium II—*Sociology of Music Education*—November 16–17
   J. Terry Gates, chairman, University of Alabama
   Max Kaplan

Albert LeBlanc, Michigan State University
Barbara Kaplan, Auburn University
Joe N. Prince, National Endowment for the Arts
Peter Webster, Case–Western Reserve University
January 13–February 3, 1985: Clifford Madsen, Florida State University
    Symposium III—*Research in Music Behavior*—February 1–2
        Carol Prickett, chairman, University of Alabama
        Clifford Madsen
        Terry Kuhn, Kent State University
        Judith Jellison, University of Texas
        Harriett Hair, University of Georgia
        Cornelia Yarbrough, Syracuse University
March 17–April 5, 1985: Abraham Schwadron,
    University of California at Los Angeles
    Symposium IV—*Philosophy of Music Education*—March 30–31
        Dennis C. Monk, chairman, University of Alabama
        Abraham Schwadron
        Malcolm Tait, Cleveland Music School Settlement
        J. H. Kwabena Nketia, University of Pittsburgh
        Michael Mark, Towson State University
        Gordon Epperson, University of Arizona
        Charles Fowler, consultant, author, editor—Washington, D.C.
    (This symposium was held in Mobile, at the biennial convention of the
    Southern Division of the Music Educators National Conference.)
April 26–28, 1985, closing symposium: Max Kaplan, Charles Leonhard,
    Clifford Madsen, Abraham Schwadron, members of the committee, and
    graduate students in music education—Guntersville State Park, Alabama

The publication first proposed was a single book built around the symposium topics and containing papers written for it by the symposium members. Subsequently, a two-book plan was approved, with the second volume containing previously unpublished reports by twenty-six of the field's top experimental researchers. It was also decided that further papers would be solicited for the first book on certain topics not covered in Symposium I. Invitations to write on these topics were accepted by Amanda Penick, University of Alabama (on studio instruction) and Craig Kirchhoff, Ohio State University (on bands).

Music Education in the United States: Contemporary Issues, then, can be characterized as a foundational reference in music education. Sixteen major theorists and practitioners in the field of music education have contributed an essay on the topic of the symposium to which they had been invited, stating what issues confront the field currently and suggesting ways that the field should meet the challenges of resolving these issues in the near future.

Each was asked to treat the topic in "presentation style" at the symposia but to write for the publication differently. This, then, is not a book of proceedings. Each section of *Music Education in the United States* was edited by the corresponding symposium chairman in consultation with the project headliners. The companion volume, *Applications of Research in Music Behavior*, edited by Clifford Madsen and Carol Prickett, contains the papers read at a March 1985 meeting in Fort Worth, Texas, five of which had been presented at Symposium III.

It is fair to say that the Alabama Project not only reached students and faculty at the University of Alabama, in and out of the School of Music; it also touched teachers and students in school systems in Alabama. Through the divisional convention of the Music Educators National Conference (MENC), its resources were offered to music educators of the Southeast. Auburn University's Department of Music presented a lecture series by the four project headliners. The residencies alone accounted for more than 130 presentations, speeches, clinics, addresses, and individual consultations, as well as many informal meetings. The symposia added more. In the publications, the University of Alabama offers to the field of music education a needed current repository of exemplary theoretical writing and experimental research reporting from the United States.

With thanks to those who made this rare experience possible, and with gratitude to those many who made it work, we commend these publications to our colleagues.

J. Terry Gates
Project Director and General Editor

Music Education in
the United States

Part I
Sociology of Music Education

1 Society, Sociology, and Music Education

Max Kaplan

I

The responsibility of those invited to write about the sociology of music education for the Alabama Project was to relate music education to the larger world of human interests. Housed in academia, the project turned to a sociologist whose background included the arts, political science, and anthropology. The last, together with psychology and history, is best known to musicians as the link to the social sciences. It would be presumptuous for any one discipline to claim all the proper questions or methods relating to music education, to the arts as a whole, or to the links between the arts and other forms of thought, creativity, action, or symbolism.

History, aside from its contribution to the narration or ordering of human experience, has contributed to our understanding of creative individuals. It has wavered and followed fashions, at different times subscribing to Carlisle's "great man" theory of progress; to the "psycho-historical" form of analysis; to the "bio-social"; and to determinisms of economics, political systems, race, or the "spirit of the times." Some historians, attracting such specialized allies from the arts as ethnomusicologists, have traced the history of instruments, musical styles, compositional forms, systems of patronage, or the relations of art generally to types of cultures and social classes.

Anthropology has been the fountainhead for studies of the folk arts, as in the pioneering collections of Béla Bartók, Zoltán Kodály, Cecil Sharp, and Alan Lomax. A new discipline may arise from the synthesis of resources that will be available to the Third World cultures as they seek a reconciliation between modernization and folk tradition.

3

The "mind" and "life" sciences—*psychology* and *biology*—have learned from the arts and contributed to our understanding of them: the inheritance of special abilities, the working of the brain, the nature of emotions, learning, memory, the subconscious, the nature of symbolism, personality. Both biology and psychology tell us that much remains to be known.

The queen of sciences, *philosophy*, has served as the grand hostess of aesthetics. Such faithful servants as Plato and Aristotle, and such contemporary guests as John Dewey, Susanne Langer, and F. S. C. Northrop, have graced the halls of the philosophical mansion with their conversation on the nature of beauty, or on the arts as insights to the world and to ourselves.

Both *political science* and *economics*, often entwined, have commented on the creator and artist as worker and citizen (or dissenter), on such issues as freedom, responsibility, value, rewards, relations with foreigners, state subsidies, propaganda, social restraints, commodities in the marketplace.

Can *theology* be omitted, given the close ties of the arts to the church, indeed, to the Ultimate Creator, and given the enormous service of religion as aesthetic subject, sponsor and core of so much painting, sculpture, music, drama, literature, and architecture?

The list cannot remain static, for the current race between Japanese and American techniques of the microchip is to create computers that "think"; and whether they succeed or not, we may anticipate some contribution to the nature of mind and thought processes. And who can tell what new sciences or syntheses may arise from the application of drugs or other forms of stimulation to the creative process; or what "social engineering" will offer to the manipulation of genes, toward either destructive or creative purposes?

II

Sociology may serve music education as the meeting ground of all these past and anticipated contributions to our knowledge of the arts as social interests and influences. In sociology's own uncertainty of its academic perimeters we find both strengths and weaknesses. The evident difficulty is inherent in the pursuit of "objective" generalizations about social groups and institutions by persons who are themselves the product of such groupings and institutions. This has led to a variety of traditions in the study itself. While the origins of sociology are ultimately found in philosophy and history, strongly held positions about method and content present every graduate student of sociology with the prospect of weighing the relative insights of the positivists, organicists, formalists, symbolic interactionists, functionalists, activists, and others. These divisions of thought come to mind with the mention of such scholars as Herbert Spencer, Charles Compte, Georg

Simmel, Max Weber, William Graham Sumner, Emile Durkheim, Florian Znaniecki, Philip A. Parsons, Charles Horton Cooley, Georges Gurevich, Howard Becker, Vilfredo Pareto, Pitirim A. Sorokin, George A. Lundberg, and—depending on where lines between disciplines are drawn—Arnold Joseph Toynbee, Thomas Hobbes, David Hume, Niccolo Machiavelli, and Plato. (Some general histories and discussions of sociology for serious readers who seek an introduction to this field are Lazarsfeld, 1970; Parsons, Shils, Naegele, and Pitts, 1961; Bierstedt, 1957; Barnes, 1947; Simpson and Simpson, 1983.)

Yet, with these internal differences, one sociologist of discernment, whose historical description and interpretation of the field are among the most sophisticated, distinguishes his discipline as a whole from others:

> Like common sense, sociology is concerned with the everyday, the average, the ordinary, the recurrent social event. In this respect, it differs most widely from magic and theology. However, unlike common sense, sociology is not a discipline bound to uphold the ethos of some particular social order. It seeks maximum freedom from value suppositions. On the other hand, sociology shares with the various disciplines concerned with the extraordinary a speculative and intellectual intent . . . dominated by the concept of "natural" rather than the supernatural. (Martindale, 1960, p. 5)

Going further into a comparison of fields, Martindale notes:

> Like folk wisdom, sociology aspires to generalizations about social events; unlike folk wisdom, it seeks to abstract knowledge not bound by the normative . . . like philosophy, sociology aspires to a body of knowledge resting on intrinsic rather than extrinsic standards of validity—a knowledge formed into logically consistent wholes; unlike philosophy, it is empirical rather than social-ethical. . . . Like history, sociology aspires to a knowledge of the general rather than the unique, for, when all is said and done, sociology is a scientific organization of knowledge. (1960, p. 19)

The particular kind of "organization" that was brought to the Alabama Project was a synthesis of three of my works, two in published form, one submitted for publication. A 1966 book, addressed to music educators, presented the arts as one form of knowledge ("assumptive, analytic, aesthetic"); the several functions of the arts; the application of social role theory to arts educators; a social profile of creative persons; observations of audiences and arts in the community (Kaplan, 1966). Nine years later, a volume on leisure presented a far more systematic instrument, or model, for analysis. My intent was to place various social components into some logical and accumulative order. But equally important, the model was so devised that instead of leisure as the topic, other issues—education, science, religion, art, and so forth—could be substituted, for the external elements common to all (economic, political, systems of values, etc.) would remain as the potential variables (Kaplan, 1975/1982).

The third volume, tentatively titled *The Arts in Society: A Sociological Perspective* (submitted for publication) is a large application of the same model specifically to the arts. Section III below presents the highlights of the model.

III

Our task is to put the *social* roles of the arts—creator, distributor, public, educator—into some context so that we may proceed to see them in relation to those social factors that make up the total society, either to parts of it (family, education, the state, etc.), or to the whole (communities, nations, regions, historical periods, etc.). In psychology, some call this the gestalt approach. Sociologists prefer the term *holistic*. Information theorists like *systems*. Although there is disagreement on how best to construct and apply the resulting models, scenarios, or "holistic configurations," there is a growing consensus for the need to avoid bits-and-pieces analyses.

The need for holism is seen by policymakers as well as by academics. One may cite the case of the largest newspaper and magazine syndicate in England as it explored potential markets in the Third World. To do this, it began about 20 years ago to examine the communications revolution resulting from television, satellites, and computers. Before calling a sociologist into consultation, the corporation had already engaged an in-house philosopher-historian whose specialty was technological change; it had commissioned a private volume by an outside expert in communication trends; and it was preparing to publish a scholarly journal, to be called *Futures* (still being published in the 1980s).

Again, governments such as that of the United States of America, whatever their stated ethos or ideology about national planning, maintain special agencies precisely for such purposes, as the U.S. Office of Technology Assessment. In Denmark, every resolution introduced in its Parliament must be accompanied by a study of the social implications of the proposed change. In Warsaw, in 1977, a social scientist headed a task force of 300 persons associated with the Polish Academy of Sciences, all involved in an ongoing research study titled "Poland 2000 A.D." (This was prior to the period of martial law.)

The most recent example of holism comes from the field of computers. A somewhat amusing part of it is that the scientists—especially the Americans and Japanese—who are currently in the race to produce "thinking" machines, seem to be unaware of past efforts toward holistic integrations, so that a Columbia University scientist is quoted as saying, "We're at a pivotal point in computer history. Fifty years from now people will look back on this transition with almost mystical respect." The *New York Times* report containing his comment begins as follows:

> In their quest for computers that are superfast and supersmart, scientists are renouncing a principle that has guided computer design for a third of a century and are embarking on an entirely new approach. Instead of solving problems step by step . . . the new machines are meant to break apart computational puzzles and solve their thousands or millions of separate parts all at once. The revolutionary approach goes by the unassuming name of parallel processing. (Salvatore, 1984, pp. C1, C8)

Given the tardiness of "hard" scientists in coming to the holistic approach, we cannot be surprised when planning in the arts remains largely on the level of piecemeal analysis. For instance, when the National Endowment for the Arts met in Baltimore (December 7–9, 1977) to examine policy issues, Dr. Joseph Coates of the Office of Technology Assessment evaluated research in the arts:

> One of the things that is clearly absent is the question of the general system. What is the universe of discourse that we are dealing with? What are the parts, the elements, and how are they compatible? Who has force? Who has influence? Where does the money flow? Who controls the information? It is important to develop that system fairly early so that one has a ground plan for what's important in the way of research. (Coates, 1978, p. 2)

Other aspects of Coates's critique are worth noting:

> The future is now a credible area of investigation. . . . Human factors seem . . . to be a neglected element that have a potential to strongly influence the creative performing arts. . . . The social psychology needs to be understood. We know virtually nothing, as far as I've been able to determine, about the users, the patrons, the purchasers of art. (Coates, 1978, p. 1)

Dr. Coates's last statement indicates a serious gap in his own research, for there have been many serious studies in the social and psychological aspects of the arts; and only four years before his statements in Baltimore, the Ford Foundation had issued a significant study on many of the questions he asks (Ford Foundation, 1974). Yet, Coates is right about the general level of research in the arts and the need for comprehensive, systematic study.

Several years before Coates's comment, there were similar stirrings in the studies of leisure (within which the arts may be included). *Leisure: Theory and Policy* (Kaplan 1975/1982) was based on a comprehensive model which was designed to be useful in other fields as well.

The holistic model, using an idea supplied by Duncan (1957, pp. 482–497), consists of four squares, for a total of sixteen social factors, or components. The inner square, suggested by the string quartet as a classic blend of the one and the many, will consist of the creator, the distributor, the public, and the educator (see Figure 1.1).

The second group, Square II, consists of the clusters person-family, group-subculture, community-region, and nation-world (see Figure 1.2). The third, Square III, will be made up of the cultural components: energy system, social system, value system, and symbolic system. The outermost set of components, Square IV, includes the conquest order, the kilowatt order, the cogno order, and the cultivated order. The total visualization then appears.

Several preliminary observations must be made of the model in Figure 1.2.

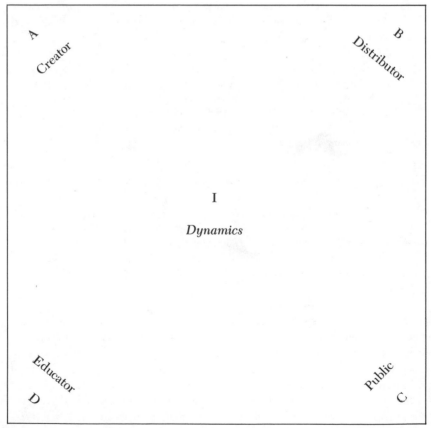

Figure 1.1 Societal Roles in the Arts

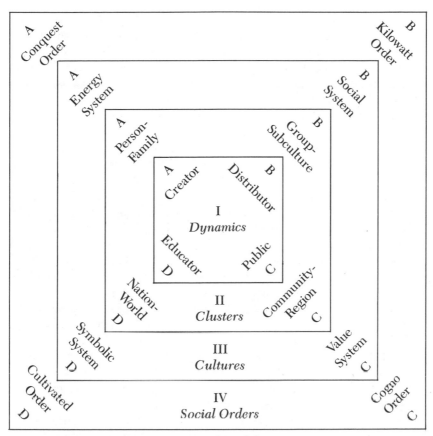

Figure 1.2 Arts Sociology Conceptual Model

1. So that the arts may be studied on the same level of seriousness and social analysis as other fields—science, education, the economy, and so forth—the outer three squares are the *constants*. The artist may, of course, use environmental resources differently, and the community will perceive the criminal differently from the way it perceives the artist. Still, all of us confront the same wars, the same changes in communications, the same climate of the day. Obviously, if the focus of study is different, different components will be isolated on Square I. For example, in leisure studies, for which the model was originally developed, the four were conditions, selections, functions, meanings (see Kaplan, 1975/1982, chap. 2). For a paper presented to professors of English literature, the components were inner-language system (linguistics), medium system of language (communication theory), systems in language use, and the systems of language as social control (Kaplan, 1972a). Again, for the 1973 UNESCO conference in Tampa,

Florida, "Cultural Innovation in Technological and Post-Industrial Societies," addressed to Third World nations that seek technology without de-
struction of their traditions, the components were tradition, innovation,
transition, and crystallization (see Kaplan 1974). For the special purposes of
industrial designers, the components were context for the design, conditions
of the assignment, the creation itself, and evaluations or critiques (Kaplan,
1972b; 1978, chap. 10). But in all of these particular studies, the same components for Squares II, III, and IV were those noted in Figure 1.2.

2. Since the model immediately provides a total, or holistic, view, we have
before us the smallest as well as the largest items to interrelate—that is, the
"microcosmic" as well as the "macrocosmic." Social scientists have recognized that the middle-range theory—the connections between the micro
and the macro—offer the most difficult problems in analysis. Indeed, the
model enables us to move freely in either direction.

An example of movement from the particular to the general might be an
exploration of the social class, ethnic background, and lifestyle of children's
families to find out why some children in a music classroom show tonal or
rhythmic sensitivity. Working in the reverse direction, beginning with the
general, we might consider the impact of technology upon social values, the
uses of mass media, changes in family life of varying social backgrounds, and
ultimately, what behavior patterns are brought into the classroom.

On a realistic basis, both directions may be employed simultaneously by
researchers and policymakers. Generally speaking, as policymakers in the
arts develop community programs, they tend to concentrate on factors seen
in Squares II, III, and IV of our model; teachers of the arts, artists themselves, and such distributors as museum curators more often start with the
interrelationships inherent in Square I. For example, the *Atlanta Consti-
tution* for August 5, 1984, carried a long article announcing the end of 70
years of activity by the Atlanta Music Club in sponsoring an "Allstar" series.
The report deals almost entirely with financial costs in advertising, rentals,
and the high fees of artists who can draw large audiences. We suspect that
had some of the artists been interviewed who are named—Pavarotti and
Horowitz, who ask for $50,000 per concert; Andre Watts, who asks $15,000;
or Alicia de Larrocha, who asks $8,000—they might have commented on the
values of a public that, precisely when the Atlanta series is discontinued,
pays scalpers $900 for a ticket to a Michael Jackson production.

3. The model is intended to suggest *relationships*, not to provide solutions, cause-effect processes, or simplifications of the subject. Further, the
relationships may touch on those of the aesthetic style or the product, but
these are not our primary concern. We seek, rather, relationships between
the social roles of participants in the arts and general social conditions.

From the entire model, two issues will be extracted: the roles and functions of the arts generally and of art educators in particular. Historically and

theoretically these issues may best serve the purposes of this portion of the Alabama Project.

IV

The roles and functions of the arts in all societies, at all times, are derived from a study of the society, that is, of those components noted as levels II, III, and IV on the model. This is not to say that artists are deprived of any voice or force about their own destinies; but the overwhelming forces that have swept the arts as well as education and other major interests along since the turn of the century have been social, technological, institutional. These have included major wars, demography, migrations of persons, scientific advances.

On the impressionistic, personal level, it is the advantage of a great-grandfather to be able to talk at first hand about social change. I do not go back far enough to remember that after the Civil War days the director of our U.S. Patent Office resigned with the statement that everything worth inventing had already been invented. But I was a lad during World War I, when a distinguished scientist wrote to our military to urge the need for more scientists; he was officially informed that they *already had one chemist*. Social change is dramatized by the knowledge that during my lifetime about 90% of all bona fide scientists who have ever lived are still alive. I recall seeing horse-drawn fire engines as a boy in Milwaukee. I remember the night when my two brothers and I wound wire around an oatmeal box, made a device to tune in the sound, hooked up a telephone receiver we had surreptitiously borrowed from a drug store, aimed it all into a glass fruit bowl for amplification, and tuned in to Chicago for our first radio reception!

One could go on to other changes in a lifetime: farm to city life, motion pictures of Charlie Chaplin the first time around, music videotapes, the great wars, the Great Depression, the jet airplane, walks on the moon.

There is little doubt that these social changes in one lifetime moved us generally toward greater complexity, more comfort, more speed, more impersonality. Some 14 or 15 megalopolitan areas have developed, such as that from Boston to Washington D.C.; we have greater freedom in the choice of family patterns; we also have some 4,000 communes and cults, based on dissatisfaction with mainstream values and religions; we are told that 4 of every 10 Americans are alcoholics or are close to it. Perhaps 40,000 teenagers attempt suicide annually, and 5,000 succeed. Such terms as *alienation* are common in our vocabularies. Even the discussion of abortion is subject to street demonstration; such clinics are now the objects of bombings. College students talk openly about nuclear holocaust and, in several universities, have voted for death pills in such an event.

On the less personal, more systematic, level of analyzing these changes, two major scenarios or projections of the coming social order have occupied our planners and futurologists. It is a worldwide concern. Academician F. Storm, president of the Czechoslovak Academy of Sciences, sets the tone of an inquiry undertaken in 1965 by the Institute of Philosophy there:

> The dynamic advance of scientific discovery in recent decades, together with the rapid development of the material base of human life, are assuming the magnitude of revolutionary changes that promise in the long run to transform the nature of civilization and open up boundless prospects for a new form of society. These considerations underscore the urgency of probing the substance of the scientific and technological revolution of our day—its social and human roots and implications. (Richta, 1969, p.11)

This potential conflict of technology and humanism has been put in many forms by many authors, even in the context of the underdeveloped societies. If the socialist societies claim to have a superior grasp of the issues—a thesis of the Czech document—the Western societies have discussed the issue with equal concern. There is a sizable library of evidence: official government documents in the United States, collaborative inquiries by such ad hoc committees as the Triple Revolution, reports by foundations such as the Twentieth Century Fund, innumerable commentaries by individual scholars, and entire conference proceedings. The main arguments are recalled by the mention of such writers as Jacques Ellul, Lewis Mumford, Hannah Arendt, Robert Heilbronner, Eric Fromm, David Riesman, Alan Touraine, and Joffre Dumazedier. Charles P. Snow (1959) touches on the issue, arguing two mentalities, the cultural and the scientific, as they impinge on insights of the world. A whole field, the "sociology of knowledge," originating in Germany, traces the social and ideological context within which forms of knowledge, including technology, are perceived. In between these poles—the originating mentalities and the recipient cultural conditions—this new issue has emerged: Do the facts show that technology has a momentum of its own that carries with it, modifies, destroys, or subordinates the so-called humanistic impulses?

Indeed, all the past analyses of the arts from the sociological perspective are rapidly becoming outdated because of the technological revolution now upon us. Computerization is the core of these changes. It has been said that anyone in his or her 70s has lived through more technological change than all of the accumulation of past history.

Here is the major theme of—or warning about—the task ahead of us. Whatever the problems of the arts may now be—finances, acceptance, faddism, educational objectives—they pale beside the new issues that are arising as a new society emerges based on the silicon chip that can be held on the tip of a finger. This chip can already perform millions of operations per second, and its possibilities double every year. Computers will become as commonplace in our homes as the television set or stereo sound equipment. In the society as a whole there is no area that has not already been affected by this "preeminent tool of our age": banking and finance, business, manufacturing, communications, scientific research, education, even religion.

Computer technology is already applied to medical research and its national network of recordkeeping; perhaps one of its most intriguing applications is on the human body itself, making it possible for the disabled to walk. For the 1980 census, 4 *billion* pieces of information are on file. Robots are increasingly put to use in manufacturing processes and will eventually be used in both office and home to free us from manual and mental work. By now the sight of children in elementary classes (and in special computer camps) using the computer as a pleasant learning device is familiar. We may expect a wider use of the computer as a tool of therapy and growth for the elderly, putting to final rest the myth that older persons are hopelessly set in their ways.

Yet we are in a state of infancy. On the theoretical level these gadgets give us the prospect of more adequately understanding the body, as in tracing the elements of coordination between movement and the brain; the brain itself, still far more capable and miraculous than the most advanced computers, will be increasingly understood.

It would be ludicrous to assume that the arts—both as creative processes and social phenomena—can remain untouched. Nor do artists really want to be untouched, even if they had the choice. For example, dance choreography now has a precise notation system for the first time. Concert-goers have heard electronic compositions for decades, both independently and in compositions with live performers. Tenuous efforts to invent electric typewriters for use by composers have been replaced by processes in which the composer will compose and simultaneously hear his or her product in a simulated performance, even in the dimensions of a full orchestra. Large screens may become permanent equipment for symphony orchestras to perform blends of sound and visualization.

Thus, a major thesis for consideration by students of the arts is that *the four primary components of the aesthetic enterprise are all directly affected, in some cases dramatically, by the electronic, cybernetic, "post-industrial" network of devices and applications.* These components, noted earlier, are creativity, distribution, public participation, and education. No longer can they be understood without reference to the new technology.

A corollary of this thesis is that a significant new function of the arts is the responsibility to serve as *a dynamic link between the humanistic and the technological, or between the pre- and the post-industrial.* This new function, if understood and articulated by educators in the arts, injects a fresh argument for their cause to the effect that there is no conflict between art and technology; nor, indeed, can the future be understood without seeing the two in a unified, comprehensive, holistic perspective.

The arts are an area—education is another—that embraces both technology and humanistic or cultural impulses. Yet one may express some concern that the arts, especially through their educational proponents, have not fully entered the debate. The Tanglewood Symposium, convened by the Music Educators National Conference (MENC) in 1968, was a major move in that direction (Choate, 1968). But an ongoing discussion on the same level has not occurred in the years since then. We close with some thoughts toward such a discussion of functions.

V

It is necessary, first, to review hastily some major conceptions of functions in the traditional literature. We may pass quickly over such conceptions of the arts as "collective possession" (the national anthem), as a highly personal expression of the subconscious (Freud), as "self-actualization" (Maslow), as symbolic or moral (the church mass), as escape, as social statement (rock music), or as commodity incidental to profit and propaganda.

Each of these positions has its history and merit. Yet, strangely enough, the most pertinent position for the place of the arts within the technologic-humanistic dichotomy is none of these. Rather, it is the Platonic view of art as a form of insight and knowledge, as a form of truth, beauty, justice, love, or even God. Several forms of knowledge were outlined in an earlier writing:

> The *assumptive* source of knowledge is the kind that reaches into past generations. It is therefore believed, affirmed, legendized, poetized, dramatized, embraced with enthusiasm, prayed to, immortalized in song, reaffirmed in salute.
>
> The teacher, in such a case, is the transmitter, preacher, policeman, propagandist. He reveals, reminds, and orders what is already established. He is the guardian of the thou shalt's and the thou shalt not's. He has been delegated the authority of morality, ethical order, social control. Assumptions need not be without validity and immanent logic; they are highly important and, as far as possible, are indoctrinated to new and powerless generations of children. One thinks of religion and philosophy as pre-eminent models for the assumptive approach to life.
>
> The *analytic* source of knowledge is best illustrated by the sciences. It is a knowledge based on objectivity, evaluation, examination, doubt, tests, and experiments. Within this model one does not permit oneself to be totally committed to conclusions as does a fanatic believer; he is a sort of *Luftmensch*—

always stepping back from the world to look at it. Enjoyment is incidental to understanding, whether it relates to a flower, a woman, an idea, a political system, or a beautiful city such as Paris. The observer here cannot permit himself to admit "This is what I like," "This is satisfying." At least in his role as scientist, he must live out the questions: "Is it really so?", "What is it?", "How do we know?" The laboratory is one workshop for such questions, although men have made notes on the stars long ago. The case study and IBM code cards are familiar tools for the social sciences, although George Bernard Shaw did very well in his plays without either.

The educator in this type of knowledge is a fellow explorer, interpreter, midwife to the birth of new data among his students. He has no need to apply his knowledge, leaving that to his assumptive brethren; he is fundamentally an amoral man, as all social scientists must be. He is a subversive of this society and, therefore, of the educational system, for he takes seriously the half-belief that the student should be taught to think for himself.

The *esthetic* kind of knowledge is based on the essence of originality in putting together things, objects, ideas, sounds, forms, and time and space relations in ways that have not been done before, but on the principle of beauty. It is not that creativity alone deals in symbols, for the others do so. For example, we symbolize many aspects of life, as in the prayer (assumptive) or in the hospital's antiseptic smell (an image of the analytic). The assumptive way of knowing depends for its strength on conserving, stabilizing, repeating, and ceremonializing; the strength of analytic knowledge is therefore a shock to those who cannot afford to have their notions challenged. The esthetic attempts to view both stability and change in terms of a subjective norm through the creator's own perception and experience as a trained, sensitive, courageous, individualistic, and confident person.

Analysis and assumptions of many kinds enter into the esthetic or creative process. But it has added a third element—subjectivity—whose essence, by definition, is that it cannot lend itself to generalization or objective verification. The nature of the esthetic as an art is that it is undefinable in any other terms of communication or meaning known to man. This is its strength and reason for being. The educator in creative fields has the function of inducing the proper atmosphere of liberty and craft, imagination and restraint, originality, and respect. He displays the masterpieces of others. He systematizes the requisite skills. He finally evokes the unpredictable resources of his students so that they may exercise their own limited perceptions of the world and thus know themselves and the world in greater depth. (Kaplan, 1966, pp. 19–20)

Behind this conceptualization is an equality between these three "truths" and, indeed, a desirable overlapping. Each constitutes what Max Weber called an "ideal construct" (see Parsons, 1949, pp. 601–610). Nor is there an implication that, as science and technology move ahead rapidly, they will dominate the totality, reducing the place of the assumptive and aesthetic. To the contrary, it is the analytic that is far behind the others, historically, and is catching up. For the time, during this "catch-up" phase, the technological becomes a fad. We are coming to the point now when a letter not written on a word-processor seems old-fashioned.

Now, while it is true that there are elements of the aesthetic in science, and elements of science (such as logic) in the philosophical, a uniqueness of the aesthetic is that it is highly flexible, moving between stability and innovation. The others have no such claim to make. Religion, for example—the most stable of the "truths"—relies on its conservative nature for its primary strength. Science, while open to constant evaluation, is an accumulation, and only an Einstein or a Darwin opens the whole system to a reexamination. Similarly, the speculative efforts of theoretical sociology and philosophy are conscious refinements of prior thinking. The arts, on the contrary, contain a historical range that makes it possible for the same concert to include a Baroque composition and the sounds of a synthesizer; the same museum can house ancient Egyptian pieces and surrealistic art works.

If this is true of the arts in respect to styles, sounds, materials, subject matter, and other internal facets, is it also true that this flexibility as a link applies to its social elements? In short, if we focus on two kinds of change, in values (assumptive) and technology (analytic), what is the impact on the creator, distributor, public, and educator? The search for answers may help the music educator to arrive at a holism that is the goal of Part 1 of this book. The caveat must be added that what follows is intended only as elementary illustration of an issue that requires far more intensive study.

Creators

PROPOSITION: *That new creative segments in America will emerge from three groups in the next half century: black persons, women, and the elderly.*

The relevant social changes suggesting this development derive from the fact that each of these groups, emerging now from subordinate roles in the society, are learning how to create and use power. In 1979 I had noted the several characteristics that apply to all these groups in greater or lesser degree:

1. An unwillingness to accept and act by the perceptions held of them by others: thus, in respect to traditions of their appositions—men, whites, and younger people—each is now a problem group.
2. A developing skill in creating power for social and political action for themselves.
3. An ability to learn from each other how to use this new power in establishing goals, in attracting attention from an apathetic public, press, or poli-

tician, and in organizing their skills. A counterpart group in other parts of the world, albeit with different cultural nuances.

4. An increasingly distinctive literature, with sets of cultural heroes, and recognized spokespersons. (Kaplan, 1979, pp. 48–49)

Differences among these groups were also noted, and in their use of the arts toward self-statements, one may suspect that they will call upon different arts: The black community will predominantly use music, dance, and literature, with theater to a lesser degree; women will employ literature; the elderly, some growing use of literature, and surprisingly, perhaps, the theater, arising from the use of oral histories.

The humanistic factors in these situations come from changing values in the society toward blacks, women, and the elderly and, more important, more positive attitudes by these groups toward themselves. The technological factors will center on communications, with mass media as a multifaceted channel for group solidarity.

Distributors

PROPOSITION: *That a new infrastructure will emerge, calling upon the joint participation of creative elements with traditional distributors (museums, theaters, clubs, churches, etc.) in experimental and innovative patterns of nonprofit, profit, private, and public structures.*

The relevant social changes suggesting this development will be part of current trends toward networks in all areas of services and cultural agencies such as health, education, housing, and recreation due in part to a rational arrangement of community resources and in part to tighter budgets. The humanistic factors will be based on attitudes of growing frustration with profit agencies on the one hand and inefficient government on the other. The technological factors will arise from computer-related gadgetry that now permits ready records and from the processing of data in those records.

Publics

PROPOSITION: *That there will be a dramatic rise in the arts of all kinds and styles among all strata of the population and a renaissance of preindustrial crafts, family creativity, and ethnic or neighborhood organization for the arts.*

Relevant social changes include the demographic shifts in population, particularly the growing number and proportion of elderly and the dramatic growth in the Spanish-American minority, of cultural as well as of economic importance. Evidence from Gallup polls as late as 1984 suggest a greater willingness to pay taxes for more subsidy of the arts, even in time of inflation (Macarov, 1980, chap. 9). Need for the arts is also related to the greater complexities of life and therefore to personal anxieties. It may be that if there is a counterreaction to the widespread use of drugs among all age groups and sectors, other forms of reality—including the arts—might gain adherents as a substitute. The humanistic factor will accompany the greater cry for leisure, as work becomes increasingly unsatisfactory, boring, and secondary in our lives. The technological factor of greatest importance will be the growing application of technology such as computers and robotics to the workplace, as well as the increasing popularity of "flextime," with the reluctant admission by American industry—as it learns from central Europe and Japan—that workers are most productive when they have greater control over time and function.

Educators

PROPOSITION: *The arts educators, in or outside of the school context, will increasingly find a wider range in the ages, backgrounds, and interests of their students, including larger numbers of retirees or part-time workers, and innovative structures of various age groups within the same educational context.*

The relevant social changes will include the modification of familiar family patterns, so that more flexible work time and more flexible school time will create innovative patterns of educational activity. A larger proportion of adults will seek educational nourishment, partly because of wider access to a variety of television experiences and, with home computer consoles, a relative ease of access to information. An increased elimination of reading will also enlarge the substitution of visual, electronic signals. The humanistic factor will center on the fuller integration of the arts into one's total life; the technological factors will be electronic, as noted above. The success and vocabulary of these electronic resources will not be automatic but will depend on the preparation given to these developments, such as adequate programming for instant use.

VI

We turn now to an expansion of the last proposition, the issue of the roles and functions of the educator in the arts.

The educator's role is, paradoxically, the clearest and the most confused among those that comprise the aesthetic process. It is also the role most misunderstood by society. Its ambiguity derives not only from the issues thrust in the face of all educators but also from special considerations about the creator, distributor, and the consumer, or public.

The arts educator today faces several dilemmas: Is the educator's role primarily to transmit the traditions and skills of the arts in a manner that has no reference to the lives of the students; or is it to use the child's life as the starting point and to use whatever values and skills that are inherent in the arts as one modality among others for goals established by the cultural system? In either emphasis, how much attention should be given to the more gifted in the arts—either in discovering or in developing them—in proportion to the benefits of the total group of students? In the educational research realm, how can arts researchers learn about the processes of creativity from other disciplines? How can they contribute in this regard to other disciplines? How can they best cooperate with other disciplines?

Is the educator's role to serve both the institution and the community as a distributor of the arts, providing space, funds, and time of staff and students for exhibitions, concerts, or other forms of presentation? What are the implications for the school resources if such a link is developed?

Is it the primary responsibility of educators in the arts to reflect the contemporary tastes of the society—the "popular arts"—or to serve as a guardian of traditions, even if held by minority segments of the population? Can a middle position be found that does not compromise the arts? Can tastes be related to a variety of traditions, and each be respected within the curriculum? Are there uniquenesses about childhood responses to the arts that have been established by research; and, if there are, how are they affected by maturation and the lifestyle of the adult? Conversely, are there uniquenesses of older adulthood, and if so, how independent are they of teachings and experiences established in youth?

These are the major issues that all educators of the arts confront in their period of training and every day of their careers in classroom, studio, museum, or community center: their goals, their techniques, their relationships to other subject areas, their responsibility toward innovations and contemporary movements vis à vis traditions. Books, symposia, conferences, and endless discussions are held on each of these.

This translates into the human dimensional duality which emerges between *essence* on one hand and *techniques* on the other. By *essence* we mean art itself: its sound, its colors, its inner structure, its emotional meaning. For the child it is the song, sung for the joy of expression. By *technique* we imply not only the steps, strategies, materials, and methods that may be required to enjoy the essence but the social apparatus that the sociologist or administrator speaks of: the organization of the school or the community center, the funding problems, the support of the home.

The training of teachers in the arts, most often when the potential teachers come from the general background of education with a minimum of art
experience, is often mired in techniques. As in some schools of education,
methods take over, whether in preparation for teaching science, reading, or
art. Yet the essence of music is music. The result is sometimes a subversion
of the arts; that is, the young music teacher may believe that music education is the teaching of eighth notes and staves. If we view this from the position of the social scientist, the appropriate term for essence is *creativity*,
the core of the arts. Unless the music or art educator is concerned with the
meaning and the search for creativity as the pervasive goal and end of teaching, the ultimate distinction between the arts and other areas of educational
and social interest is lost. Again, without the extensive analysis that the
model above entails, let us come to some general observations that are suggested by it and seek in the end to apply it to the thrust of the Alabama Project and its publications.

VII

Our greatest difficulty in drawing connections between creators and personality is that, even if there were to be a reasonable consensus on the nature of creators (which, of course, there is not), there is as little agreement
on the nature of personality. It depends much on the discipline that addresses the topic, yet even within the fold of each of the social sciences there
are schools of thought and varying traditions. Court trials occasionally highlight the opposing testimony of psychiatrists about the same defendant.
Graduate students know the whole range of commitments from the Freudian to the humanistic psychologists.

Four major psychological viewpoints on personality, which make up the
core of a volume by a team of midwestern scholars, illustrate the scope of
the relevant issues. Calling it their "scientific construction system," Wiggins
et al. (1971) build their entire discussion around these conceptual emphases:

> *Biological*, dealing with "early experience genetic endowment, and evolution-
> ary background"
> *Experimental*, dealing with "uniform learning, perceptual, and higher
> processes"
> *Social*, dealing with the "social models, cultural roles, and . . . cultures
> themselves"
> *Psychometric-trait*, dealing with "behavior observation, self-report, and the
> indirect assessment of underlying traits"

Each of these mainstreams of the past century find their beginnings in
the work of Charles Darwin and Sigmund Freud. Each is applied by the au-

thors to a quartet of topics: dependency, aggresssion, sexuality, and competence. A full chapter is devoted to the psychoanalytic theory of Freud and his followers—a theory that has been significant in the study of creators. "Social theory learning" is explored through the work of Clark Hull, J. Dollard, N. E. Miller, A. Bandura, R. H. Walters, and other pioneers. The cognitive-developmental theory applies biological principles to personality, with particular attention to the work of Donald Hebb, Heinz Werner, and Jean Piaget. Finally, the authors discuss the "self-theory," a distinctly philosophical rather than behavioristic view of man; among its major pioneers were Gordon W. Allport, Carl R. Rogers, and Abraham H. Maslow (Wiggins et al., 1971).

Maslow's broad view of creativity was not limited to scientists or artists but included all who are open to "experience" going beyond the expectations of most persons. Perhaps the best known of Maslow's contributions is his hierarchy of our needs as persons, proceeding from basic survival up to "self-actualization."

The only direct discussion of creativity in the volume by the four psychologists noted above takes place in connection with "self-theory," which "accepts freedom for action as a characteristic of human personality" and creativity as "the natural expression of man's inherent structure" (Wiggins et al., 1971, p. 555).

According to another psychologist, although the views of that discipline on creativity begin with Freud, there are contradictions in his central position, for "if at one time he claimed that the work of art could be reduced to the artist's neurosis, at another he claimed that it could only be understood as the product of the artist's neurosis *plus* his art, the latter being beyond the reach of analysis altogether" (Skura, 1980, Spring, p. 130).

In her brilliant summary of the subject, Meredith Skura reviews the theories of Freud, E. Kris, and the psychoanalytic-psychological contribution. Her own approach is to trace our knowledge of creativity to the process of thinking in general and its origins in infancy. She concludes that creativity

is not just retreat into the inner world of unconscious material but, rather, a way of combining inner and outer worlds. . . . All activity, of course, must combine the two worlds, from the most private subjective fantasizing to the most public objective perception and behavior, as well as the artistic activity that lies between the subjective and objective worlds. In every case, however, either a fertile meeting in which imagination informs fact, or a paralysis in which they clash or are frozen into a sterile compromise. Here, psychoanalysis promises to reveal most about creativity, not simply by telling us again that it draws on the inner world cut off from consciousness, but by studying specific cases to see how unconscious thinking meshes with conscious thinking and under what circumstances. (Skura, 1980, Spring, p. 134)

Skura distinguishes between fantasy and reality for the artist, who is less likely than others to separate the two. "The artist can live with contradictions, both between himself and the world, and within himself" (Skura, 1980, Spring, p. 137).

The private fantasies of the artist are often fed quite consciously by the way in which he or she prepares the immediate conditions in which productivity might be induced: the right room to write in, the time of day or night, the right pen, the habit of standing in full dress as one composes (as was Haydn's out of respect for the Creator, whom he only represented), or the need to smell rotting apples as one wrote (as did Schiller).

A recent attempt by another practicing analyst is Sylvano Arieti's volume *The Magic Synthesis* (1976). In his highly critical review of Arieti, Richard Gilman, a fellow analyst and writer on the drama, agrees with Freud that psychoanalysis "can do nothing toward elucidating the nature of the artistic gift, nor can it explain the means by which the artist works." Arieti's efforts at explanations, according to Gilman, are as "thin and dubious as ever." He continues:

> When Arieti writes that "we cannot offer quantitative measurements of the various elements that enter into the world of art, as exact science would require," he isn't simply being modest but revealing the basis of uneasiness and trepidation. . . . The creative act, Koestler wrote, "is the defeat of habit by originality." It's as simple, unsentimental, and mysterious as that. (Gilman, 1976, August 1, Sec. 7, p. 4)

Finally, an important contribution was made to the explanation of creativity by the Canadian psychologist Henri Peyre. In a paper entitled "Anxiety and the creative process," presented at Wayne State University in October 1962, he noted the high levels of both creativity and insecurity in Greece in the late fifth and early fourth centuries B.C., "an age which was far more ferocious than ours perhaps has ever seen." The Middle Ages, likewise, was an age of "quarrels, of catastrophe, . . . persecutions, crusades"; thus he demonstrates that all ages have had their problems but that paradoxically they have been "most creative when they were most anxious and most insecure." He contrasts the post-Hitler sterility of the Germans with their enormous artistic productivity between 1795 and 1812 (Goethe, Schiller, Beethoven, etc.), and between 1919 and 1930 (Kafka, Rilke, Thomas Mann, Brecht, etc.). Turning to America, Peyre notes the great literary production in the Deep South, perhaps because it has "more of a sense of history, more of a sense of tragedy, perhaps more anxiety . . . and the guilt complex about slavery." This would not have been the case if creation and art and literature "merely depended on prosperity, security, and wisdom."

How does this apply to individuals? Peyre (1962) notes the clusters of such persons: "While creativity is an affair of individuals and nothing else, it can also be fostered by a common spirit in certain groups where there is an atmosphere which also proves serviceable or opportune." Contrary to such writers as Jane Austen, Wordsworth, George Meredith, Flaubert, and Chekhov—who were somewhat removed from their time—there were hundreds of creators who "were afflicted by tension, who were impressed by a terrifying chaos around them, and whose purpose in creating was to put a little light into their own inward chaos."

Highly critical of Freud, more sympathetic to Jung, Henri Peyre (1962) concedes the neurosis of many an artist but observes that what is significant is "*not* that he may be neurotic—so may be his sisters or his brothers who don't create anything—but that he refuses to come to terms with some of the immediate demands of reality. He creates another, more prophetic, truer reality, a more inspired reality, and receives consolation thereby." Essential for all this, of course, is an ability as a craftsman, "to put some order into that chaos, to bring it all to the light of clarity."

In a somewhat bizarre recent attempt to explain creativity, Ernest Hartman, psychiatrist at the Tufts University School of Medicine, linked it with nightmares. Dr. Hartman studied 50 men and women of the Boston area who reported having at least one nightmare per week since childhood. Their personalities, he discovered, are "markedly open and defenseless," easily hurt, unhappy as children, with a huge incidence of schizophrenia among relatives. This proneness to mental illness "has allowed many of them to pursue the arts actively, such as painting and music." Many of them, says Dr. Hartman, "thought of themselves as artists even if they were currently supporting themselves in some other way." This comes close to both Freud and the inner world as seen by Skura (Goleman, 1984, October 23, pp. C1, C2).

Finally, the view of the journalist-science historian Arthur Koestler is that

> the conditions for original thinking are when two or more streams of research begin to offer evidence that they may converge and so in some manner be combined. . . . All decisive advances in the history of scientific thought can be described in terms of mental cross-fertilization between different disciplines. (Koestler, 1967, pp. 231–232)

Koestler provides an illustration in which important advances in neurophysiology were derived from astronomy. One finds wisdom in his admonition:

> But I must add to this a word of warning . . . the integration of matrices is not a simple operation of adding together. It is a process of mutual interference and

cross-fertilization in the course of which both matrices are transformed in various ways and degrees. . . . When Einstein bisociated energy and matter, both acquired a new look in the process. (Koestler, 1967, pp. 232–233)

VIII

Thus, both from a psychological approach and from others (including philosophy, political science, fiction, or the vernacular world), we get many classifications of personality "types," including some that are loosely applied to creative persons. Among such listings are C. G. Jung's "introvert" and "extrovert"; E. Kretschmer's "schothymic" and "cyclothymic"; V. Pareto's "rentieri" and "speculatori"; Znaniecki and Thomas's "philistine," "bohemian," and "creative"; David Riesman's "inner" and "other"; and Sorokin's "ideational," "sensate," and "intermediary" types. Among the terms that have sought a link between personality and creativity we have such examples as "spontaneity-creativity" (J. L. Moreno), "creative intuition," and "divine madness" (Plato).

The sociological approach to personality—therefore, to creativity—concentrates more on relationships among persons than with inner qualities. Sorokin, for instance, following the general explanation of behavior based on social roles, notes:

> When we interact with our families, we think, feel, and behave like father, mother, sister, brother, son, or daughter. Our ideas, standards, emotions, volitions, as well as our overt actions are of a certain kind well known to all of us. (Sorokin, 1947, p. 356)

In some detail, Sorokin then speaks of the "plurality of organized groups" to which each of us belongs, the harmonious as well as the conflicting values that may exist between the groups as they influence the person; then, in terms that the younger generation of sociologists would studiously avoid, Sorokin heads a section "The Cultural Content of the Souls of the Individual as a Reflection of the Cultures of His Groups." Note that in this section his explanation of creativity is somewhat less satisfactory.

> Finally, the individual's culture depends upon his *selectivity and creativity.* No individual can absorb all the cultural elements of his milieu. . . . Every person selects, combines, and sometimes even creates, and he is to that extent an active agent in the cultural process. True geniuses display great creativity. . . . Most of us display but little genuine creativity, but nonetheless . . . people are not *tabulae rasae*, on which society writes its cultural teachings. Whether their selection and creativity depend upon biological constitution or upon something more subtle and intangible which we can designate as the

transcendental soul or as the "creative X" (which hypothesis appears to be reasonable), this problem remains open. What is fairly certain is the importance of the social role of this X-factor. (Sorokin, 1947, p. 356)

All of the preceding theorizing, largely from psychology, is relevant or suggestive to sociologists. We are less inclined to deal with creativity (or "goodness," "beauty," etc.) as an essence, a something that exists inside one's skin. About the emphasis on the subconscious and the Freudian approach as a whole, many of us are agnostic. Among the others mentioned above, Koestler and Peyre appeal to me the most, but I am unsure whether because of sociological thinking or personal background. Koestler's "bisocial" theory is compelling to one who comes from the dual background of music and sociology. Peyre's view of anxiety as a basis for creativity is, again, interesting to the son of immigrant parents because of the social marginality that characterizes such families. When Maslow's conception of creativity is applied to the innovative housewife as well as to the artist, he takes us away from creativity as an essence to an evaluation by others. Indeed, a work of "genius" in one culture may pass entirely unnoticed in another. And who, in the most imaginative of biological fantasies, can imagine the number of potential poets, painters, mathematical giants, or composers who remain forever undeveloped, submerged in the ghettoes, tribes, desert villages in all parts of the world, or who were destroyed in Hitler's concentration camps?

Our primary interest as sociologists lies in such issues as the cultural identification of innovative persons and social images about them; with legends, myths, and stereotypes about such terms as *talent, genius,* and *creative*; with the profiles of such persons; and with those social factors (political, social class, family life, education, religion, etc.) that seem conducive or destructive to the arts.

What, then are some sociological positions on creativity, as the present writer sees them?

1. Societies define or identify those actions, attitudes, or products that fall into the realm of arts, as they do for science, religion, or education.

2. Societies also develop the relationships of social roles, values, symbols, and norms that make up the institutions, infrastructures, or organizations that are grouped as arts, sciences, and so on.

3. No *one* factor—age, sex, religion, wealth, or poverty, "talent," "will," degree of inner "conflict"—can alone explain creativity but, rather, combinations and interactions of social and biological elements that are unique to particular persons, places, and times.

4. The content, style, and techniques of art works as a whole or of specific persons and their products arise from the interplay of presently unexplained qualities or attributes of the creative person within (or in reaction to) tradi-

tional and emerging values, aesthetic trends, social currents, ideologies, movements, and the level and characteristics of the cultural life.

5. In developed, commercial societies, perhaps in others, creative works are identified to some degree with temporality and territoriality, that is, originality and group possession or pride.

6. Creativity in the arts may be evaluated differently within the same society at different periods and different regions, depending on traditions, fads and fashions, the influence of distributors, or political and social needs and controls.

7. Creators can be fully understood only within the total complex that includes distributors, the public, and educators.

8. Given the subjective values of creators and the social settings within which they function, it is possible to develop personality profiles as clues to their uniqueness.

9. Creators in the arts feed on communications with other creators or their work, confirming the theses spelled out by Plato for ancient Greece and by Teggart for contemporary America: That is, the necessity of multiple and conflicting values as the basis for intellectual and cultural life (as in the seacoast areas of one and the new frontiers of the other).

10. Finally, the ultimate "nature" of creativity can be taken as fully understood only when its ingredients can be so manipulated or "engineered" as to predict correctly the emergence of creative persons in specific instances or areas. The biological sciences seem to approach the possibility of an even more elusive goal—the creation of life itself—and, therefore, may in the future be able to create creators in given skills or in a general approach to problems. The models for such a breakthrough may emerge, if at all, from electronic sources; if "thinking" robots or computers develop, notions about "creativity" will be debated even more hotly than now, with unpredictable consequences.

Although the general thrust of these statements may seem to eliminate or minimize the factors of personality or family, it does not, since the sociological imagination and technique does not draw sharp lines between nature and nurture, or person and society. Each is within the other, like the dualities of matter and energy to the physicist or the moral qualities of *yin* and *yang* to the Oriental.

The most direct illustration of the sense of these propositions is the profile of creators below. It emerges from historical images, fictional accounts, autobiographies, the field of education, counseling, and—as in the present case—from intensive interviews of 50 persons, men and women, students and world-renowned performers, and from written questionnaires from many more.

The creative person:

1. is intensely attached to aesthetic values and minimizes the social implications or functions of his work.

2. is a social idealist, seeking a society in which his values will prevail widely.

3. will display little consistency as to his chances for success, alternating between cynicism and optimism.

4. is relatively unconcerned with social class rank, finding his own position in society an uncertain one. He is possibly more aware of social distinctions around him and is inclined to be disdainful of them.

5. is realistic as to the difficulties that the artist faces in our society.

6. is relatively independent of the norms and values of religious, political, and economic life, unless he can relate himself as artist and teacher to these values.

7. finds in his art a way of life sufficiently broad to satisfy his questions about such concepts as inner search and purposes of life.

8. finds art a bond that ties him strongly to others of similar outlook and interest, regardless of differences with them that the society thinks are important.

9. is relatively impatient of protocol or administrative procedures in such structured settings as schools.

10. defends, within the university circle, the standards and necessities of professional training and tends to fight the intrusion of academic subject matter upon the time of his students. (Kaplan, 1966, p.110)

Several case studies lead up to the profiles, as well as data on social class, attitudes toward factors of success and failure, and central values of the occupation.

Beardslee and O'Dowd (1960) sampled American college students and found the art student to be intuitive, rash, changeable, and impulsively expressive, with moods that are often dark, depressed, and pessimistic. Similarly, in a study of 189 male and female art students in four art colleges of Great Britain, Peter Stringer of the Lancaster College of Art and Design concluded that compared with other university students his subjects were individualistic, more likely to reject the accepted social values, less submissive to authority, and generally less conventional in outlook; the males are less concerned about "order" and less interested in amassing personal possessions. Women exhibit these characteristics even more than men but with greater emphasis on seclusion and independence (Stringer, 1965, October 7).

Yet, even such profiles and surveys, useful as they may be, do not tell us how such persons really *create*. Of course, the answer is that we do not know. I doubt that we will ever know about how creative minds wrestle with ideas—developing, rejecting, modifying, embellishing, being consumed by them. Max Weber, as keen a mind as any in history, wrote honestly:

> Ideas occur to us when they please, not when it pleases us. The best ideas do indeed occur to one's mind in the way which Inering describes it: when smoking a cigar on the sofa; or as Helmholtz states of himself with scientific exactitude: when taking a walk on a slowly ascending street; or in a similar way. In any case, ideas come when we do not expect them, and not when we are brooding and searching at our desks. Yet ideas would certainly not come to mind had we not brooded at our desks and searched for answers with passionate devotion. (1958, p. 136)

I would suggest a hope that the full explanation of creativity (or love, or truth, or beauty) will never be known. Science must be secure enough to admit that there are areas of life, thought, emotions, and "flashes of insight" that remain awesome and mysterious. Was it Croce who said that as he grew older he realized that he need not fully understand the art he loved?

An additional proposition relates creative persons with the time and place in which they happen to live: *Creative persons, considered abstractly by some standard that has nothing to do with visibility, may be found everywhere and anywhere; their recognition, opportunity for training, acceptance and status as creators depend heavily on the social structure of the society, its stage of economic and social development, its educational structure, family life, its collective values and needs.*

We cannot ignore biological factors, such as those emerging from the current research of the left and right brain or even some relationship to left-handedness. A whole body of knowledge about hereditary factors cannot be waived aside. If, indeed, human genetics research moves ahead as predicted in reputable circles—and a rapidly growing industry is banking on this emergence—we may learn much in the next few decades about predicting and producing certain kinds of abilities and personalities.

As someone has said, there would be no Beethoven symphonies without Beethoven, but would there as likely have been a Beethoven without the combination of circumstances of his time and place, including the concentration of wealth and the cultural atmosphere in Vienna?

One may, with only slight imagination weave a mountain of "ifs": *If* the black children under the policy of apartheid could be exposed to the same advantgages enjoyed by the white children of Johannesburg; *if* the millions who died in the concentration camps had grown up in a pre-Hitler milieu. Alas, there is no cosmic balance sheet that matches potential abilities with favorable social conditions in the arts or any other creative area. The best we can do is to provide a set of democratic practices, so that in the same society, at least, there is an equity of opportunity based on abilities and desires rather than on chance.

For reasons that take us into areas of pride and symbolic "territoriality," creativity is associated with temporal priority—with being the "first." Arthur Koestler has noted that genius is more than the perfect exercise of a technique; it is the invention of a technique. Once something is invented, imitations come and go. Sometimes the imitations are mistaken for the real thing, as during a dress ball in Monte Carlo, when twelve or more guests competed to imitate Charlie Chaplin, and *he* got third prize. We recall the embarrassment of art galleries, including the Metropolitan Museum, when famous pieces were found to be forgeries; or the classic case of the Vermeer imitations in Europe, when the experts refused to believe the forger even after his confession. Why, then, are not the imitation and the original of equal worth, economically and aesthetically?

A similar issue has recently emerged in the United States with the revelation that many designer's clothes are being imitated and sold for high prices. Apparently the owner perceives a work differently, knowing—or assuming that he knows—it is the original. Even in the scientific area, a long list has been drawn of "parallel" inventions, when the issue is not imitation or forgery but the honesty of both parties and the rare occurrence of simultaneous accomplishment. It is the honor of being the first that sometimes drives scientists down the road of fierce competition.

A final proposition may be useful: *the creative personality will be ever more dependent on the family environment if, as seems probable, the society moves toward more technology, or greater impersonality in the transactions that maintain and give color to the society.* John Naisbitt, in his influential *Megatrends,* argues that projections for the future are not realistic if they follow the familiar linear extrapolations. "Wherever new technology is introduced into society, there must be a counterbalancing human response—that is, *high touch*—or the technology is rejected." As an example, he notes that at the time that television was introduced, the group-therapy movement emerged, "much of both in the bellwether state of California" (Naisbitt, 1982, p. 35). Similar analogies can be found in the Oriental view of yin-yang, or the physical duality of up-down, or the revolution in the field of physics when it turned simultaneously toward explorations of the smallest as well as the largest of elements and theories.

IX

The discussion of theories on creativity cannot pretend to crystallize answers for the music educator. He or she will continue holding the view that talent "will out," at times forcing itself upon us. There are, as we noted earlier, several questions. Will this talent, latent or self-evident, be recognized by the teacher? What seem to be the most favorable conditions—in school, family, community, subgroup, the general society—for the appearance of such special abilities? And, what should be done with persons identified as talented?

We look back upon the discussion for clues to each.

Clue 1. The nature of the family environment is of such importance that teachers may need to incorporate a study of families represented among their students; this could be as important a part of their preparation as the subject area of music. No clear principles can be spelled out. There are obvious surface indications of family lifestyle, such as the presence of books in the home, reading materials; or more important patterns in influence, either from other persons or such penetrations as television. Those who pursue this line of inquiry will be helped by studies of family leisure, such as "time budget" studies. (Among many excellent studies of leisure, see the works of Dumazedier, 1967 and 1974; de Grazia, 1962; Pieper, 1962; and Neulinger, 1974. Two classic studies in time budgets are Lundberg, Komarovsky, and McIllney, 1934; and Szalai, 1972.) Many data are available on time use, including access and use of community activities in the arts. There is sufficient reason to know, through studies of audiences, that early exposure to the arts, outside as well as inside the home, develops taste at early ages. For example, a natural affinity for gospel singing is a blend of many elements, including the force of the church setting, religious belief in earnest, the family closeness, ethnic identity and pride. The white teacher in these settings, perhaps in the inner city, who looks down upon or ignores such traditions lives in a false conception of the students' world (see Kaplan, 1970).

Clue 2. One wonders, throughout a consideration of the "favorable social conditions" for the teaching of the arts and for a wider acceptance of the arts, whether the teaching profession has a commitment to the encouragement of *social* changes in the neighborhood or the community as a whole. Many years ago, a large hospital in a poor section of Chicago, observing the apparent relationship of the physical environment to ill health, became itself a unique agent for the rehabilitation of its surrounding area. Nurses and physicians could be seen in strategy planning sessions, engaged eventually in political battle with the official planning agencies of the city. In contemporary music education, can the music teacher reasonably take the time and make the effort to involve adults with special abilities or backgrounds in the school program? Should the raising of funds for an arts program in the neighborhood community center, for instance, be credited as official time for the arts staff? How sympathetic will school administrators be in these directions?

Clue 3. Again, one wonders, as a "profile" of creative persons is drawn, whether we are, in fact, begging the question. We surely cannot, even with the most optimistic scenario in behavior modification, hope to develop such persons. They seem to emerge from the earliest years. Can we do only so much as to look, as God's spies, for such persons? Shall we be reduced to counting on school counselors to give tests, ask questions, and consult their private specifications for various abilities needed in one field or another?

There is a further complication if, as I advocate here, the art and education worlds develop some concern for the latent penchant for creativity among such groups as the blacks, women, and the elderly. Adults in any of these groups have fully developed personalities. Would they, too, as "students," give evidence of similar creative qualities? At Boston University, in the early 1960s, a program was developed whereby young university music students, mostly those preparing to teach the piano, were put into teaching situations for a period of 18 months with older persons who had no prior musical instruction (Kaplan, 1966, pp. 155–158). Analysis of the project's careful records revealed that in almost every case the "love affair" between the students, all age 65 or more, and their pianist-teachers, in their early 20s, contributed to a measurable growth and clearer understanding of music by the "grandparents." Assuming that the young teachers themselves gave evidence of creative learnings on a high level, what special kind of contagious bonding took place here?

Clue 4. If, indeed, my thrust has been well placed in its emphasis on social change, and the thesis is tenable that music and the other arts can be a dynamic link between tradition and technology, does this imply that the innovative aspects and influences upon the arts should be minimized—that the profession of music education can absorb new gadgets for teaching while at the same time there is a systematic attempt to discover, uncover, enjoy, and celebrate the songs and folk materials of one's history and culture? One of the papers by a guest scholar for the Alabama Project Symposium on Sociology and Music Education (B. C. Kaplan, 1985) observes the present state of the Kodály approach in the South. Those who hold that there still is a South that remains intact even through the eruption of the Sunbelt will be interested in the uncovering, through Kodály's disciples, of the area's musical heritage. The investigation of the folk art of this region would seem to be a high priority at a time when, with one foot in the past and one in the future, our aim is to achieve a cultural as well as a historical rhythm. Direct questions arise: What is the relationship in such transitions, geographic and historical, that can be established between music education, assisted by musicology, and the current state of anthropology and regional or state history? Research by Driskell (1985) and others is a beginning. Again, can administrators and funding sources be made aware of the need for such joint study?

There are, undoubtedly, many other issues that can be flushed out with the model in Figure 1.2 or with other ways of relating musical activities in the culture to the social sciences.

A funny thing happened on the way to Symposium II of the Alabama Project: the totally unexpected sequencing of papers that were presented by the visiting scholars. Each not only fell into the parameters of the model above, but they came in a precise ordering according to the levels in the model. Albert LeBlanc opened with observations on methodology—his views of social theory as it applies to his studies of musical taste (Figure 1.2, I-C). Barbara Kaplan reported on her results in Alabama, applying the Gordon *Music Aptitude Profile* to children of various social and racial backgrounds (Figure 1.2, II-A, B, C, D). Joe Prince traced the history and impact of government on the arts (Figure 1.2, IV-A, B, C). Finally, Peter Webster described the responses of children to problems in creativity that he set out for measurement (Figure 1.2, III-D).

Perhaps what happened there was more than chance; it may have been an augury that there are innate, rational meanings or directions in the significant concert of cultural and social tendencies. Planners of the Alabama Project have nurtured this event and are deserving of applause by the national community of music educators.

2 The Culture as Educator: Elements in the Development of Individual Music Preference
Albert LeBlanc

In this chapter I will develop the sociological aspects of a global theory that attempts to explain how people learn their personal values in music (Le-Blanc, 1982). The theory is graphically summarized in the theoretical model presented in Figure 2.1. An ongoing program of experimental studies (LeBlanc, 1979; LeBlanc, 1981; LeBlanc & Cote, 1983; LeBlanc & McCrary, 1983; LeBlanc & Sherrill, 1986) is being conducted at Michigan State University to test the efficacy of some of the variables identified in this theory of music preference.

The theoretical model (Figure 2.1) shows the influences involved and the process followed by an individual in making a single music preference decision. The model is hierarchical, with input information entering at the bottom (Level 8) and progressing upward in a decision-making process until the final preference decision is made (Level 1).

Three primary influences are identified by the model: the music, the environment, and the listener. Two of these influences, the environment and the listener, function as aspects of the overall culture in which we live. The repeated sampling loop, which becomes an available option in Level 2 when no immediate preference decision is made, always involves further exposure to the influence of the culture. Even if the listener chooses to pay attention only to the music when carrying out repeated sampling, the culture will make its influence felt through the cultural characteristics of the listener.

Two dictionary definitions of *culture* are especially pertinent to the theory being developed here. *The American Heritage Dictionary of the English Language* gives a definition of culture as "the totality of socially transmitted behavior patterns, arts, beliefs, institutions, and all other products of human work and thought characteristic of a community or population." That

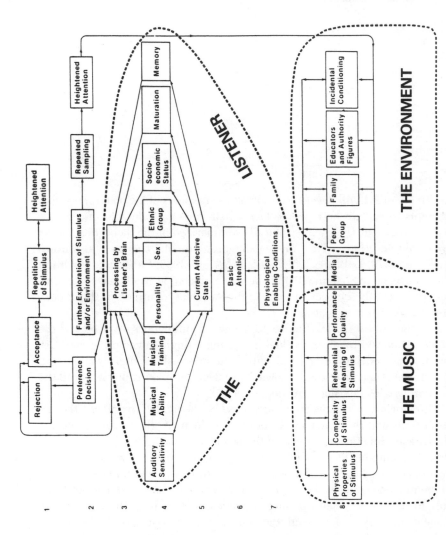

Figure 2.1 Sources of Variation in Music Preference

definition will be accepted here and will be referred to as a definition of "*the* culture." *Webster's Ninth New Collegiate Dictionary* presents another applicable definition of culture as "enlightenment and excellence of taste acquired by intellectual and aesthetic training." This definition is pertinent because it illustrates the aesthetic striving that seems to be shared by all cultures. For clarity "the culture" will be defined here as the individuals, the institutions, and the affiliation groups that interact to try to shape a set of values they consider to be the best. "Culture" will be defined as the resulting set of values. The main focus of this chapter will be the activities of "the culture" rather than any particular set of values.

Three elements of the theoretical model actually function as the culture. They are the environment, the listener, and the media. The environment functions directly and obviously as the culture for those people who live in it. The influence of the environment is manifested through two affiliation groups, the family and the listener's peer group; through educators and authority figures, the agents who represent societal institutions; and through the psychological process of incidental conditioning, which occurs when the individuals who constitute the cultural environment present their own choice of music to the listener in a setting that may have pleasant or unpleasant associations.

The listener functions as the culture indirectly, through his or her own sex, ethnicity, maturation, and socioeconomic status. Each of these listener characteristics will lead the listener toward an affiliation group with its own predetermined interests and values. The communication media also function as the culture indirectly, through their agents' opportunity to select the specific music and the specific environmental influences they will present to the listener.

What Activities of the Culture Influence Individual Music Preference?

To understand how the culture influences individual music preference, we must consider some activities of everyday life. Few generalizations are possible in the systematic study of music preference, but it is safe to say that almost all of the culture's influence comes through various affiliation groups to which the listener belongs. Chronologically, the first of these affiliation groups to have a significant influence upon the listener is the listener's own family.

From the first days of a listener's life, the family will control the music that is presented to the young listener. For practical purposes, this control is almost total, because the very young child is unlikely to spend significant amounts of time away from the family. One exception to this rule would be the case of young children who spend time at day care centers. In such a case, the day care center would share some of the family's influence.

Although the family has considerable influence over what the young child hears, it does not necessarily follow that the family will exercise its influence in any systematic way to shape the child's music preference. The most likely scenario is one in which the family simply continues its own listening habits regardless of the presence of a new baby. In many families a radio or television set is kept on throughout the day, and the favored radio or television station will actually select the music the young child hears. The family's influence is felt only in the choice of station and the decision to turn it on.

If teenage siblings are present in the home, the choice of music may be sharply different from that which would be favored by the parents if they were alone. It is thus possible for siblings to have distinctly different music listening experiences within the same family—an adult-oriented experience for the first children and a teenage-oriented experience for later children. Siblings of all ages can have an influence upon music heard in the home, but teenage siblings will exert the most obvious influence.

Family members of any age can influence the music heard in the home. Resident grandparents or great-grandparents can have an influence, especially if they bring their own record collection from the days of their youth. A family member who is a professional musician can influence the music heard in the home through his or her own teaching and practicing at home.

Careful research is needed to document the precise nature of the music listening experience of young children, and to measure the effect of that experience upon the concurrent music preference of those children and upon their preferences in later life. I have discussed the development of music preference in children in LeBlanc (1987).

The influence of the peer group will come into play after that of the family in the typical listener's life. For many young listeners, a day care center will present the first peer group experience, but at this point the peer group will be too young to influence the choice of music very much. In the area of music preference, the influence of the peer group tends to lie dormant until the onset of adolescence, when it begins aggressively to challenge adult values. In fact, some writing in the field always refers to the peer group as the "adolescent peer group."

When a listener reaches adolescence, the peer group begins to dominate music preference unless other affiliation groups challenge it. A listener's membership in a close-knit and select affiliation group, such as a high school wind ensemble, might successfully challenge the generalized influence of the adolescent peer group. Upper-class socioeconomic status would present another powerful affiliation. In each of these cases, a smaller and presumably more select affiliation group is competing for influence with a larger and more generalized peer group. The listener may feel closer to the smaller affiliation group, and choose to conform to its values. In terms of theory, it is important to note that other affiliation groups that successfully challenge the peer group could be called peer groups themselves, and one could then argue that the effect of the peer group is all-pervasive.

The peer group remains an influence on music preference throughout adult life, but it is doubtful that its power ever exceeds the level it enjoys during adolescence. When evaluating the influence of the peer group, it should be noted that a listener can function as a member of many affiliation groups at any one time.

A listener in our culture will typically encounter the influence of educators and authority figures only after the family has had an early opportunity to make its own influence felt. Educators tend to have a more direct influence than authority figures, at least in terms of personal contact. This contact can begin as early as a young child's day care experience, and music-loving parents will often arrange music lessons for their children. The Suzuki approach to music instruction is intentionally targeted to young children.

The influence of educators is not limited to those who are specialists in music. Most school systems mandate a certain amount of music instruction to be provided by classroom teachers if music specialists are not available. The typical activities of public school music educators are well known and will not be repeated here. The effect of music education is greatly magnified for students who elect additional music instruction beyond that which is routinely provided to every student. The most typical form of additional instruction is that provided to members of schools bands, orchestras, and choruses.

Not so easily discerned as the influence of specialist music teachers is the influence of other individuals and institutions in the educational system. College professors influence their own students and they influence elementary and secondary school students through their role as the teachers of current and future elementary and secondary school teachers. Boards of education and accreditation agencies determine curricular policy, whereas school administrators are charged with enforcing it. Educational evaluators try to determine how well policy is being carried out, as well as whether or not the implemented policy is having the desired effect upon student learning.

Church authorities stand somewhere between educators and authority figures in the way they influence listener exposure to music. Most faiths have very distinct policies on music. These policies will determine the relative emphasis given to music, and they will establish the listening experience of members of the congregation when they attend worship services.

Changes in church policy can have wide-ranging impact upon the members of a faith, and one example of this would be the changes in the liturgical music of the Roman Catholic church after the Second Vatican Council.

The authority figures who can influence music preference are a highly diverse group compared with educators. These authority figures include private citizens as well as government officials. One type of authority figure is the person who is in a position to determine what kind of music will be created. No one has absolute control over the creation of music, but when one kind of music will earn money for its creator and another kind will not, composers will be tempted to persist in the behavior that gets financially rewarded.

Government funding agencies and private donors can play an important role in determining which composers receive commissions, and funding is also a crucial question in deciding which new compositions will receive public performance. Government and philanthropic funding plays an especially vital role in the creation of contemporary art music, which will not normally pay back the expenses of its creation and dissemination with commercial sales income. Legislators play a role in this process through the level of appropriations they make to support the creation and dissemination of music, and they also exert influence through their ability to influence educational policy, particularly the relative emphasis given to music in the schools.

Once music has been created, it must be disseminated before listeners will have a chance to appreciate it. Influential conductors and soloists are two kinds of authority figure who can determine which music will be performed. Endorsement by a famous conductor or soloist can do much to assist an unknown composer in getting his or her music before the public. Endorsement by well-established artists can also make it easier to get new music recorded. In the field of popular music, the record companies tend to fill the role carried out by funding agencies and conductors in the case of art music.

The music critic is one type of authority figure who seems to be shared by the creators of art music and popular music. A strongly negative review that arrives at a crucial time can stymie the dissemination process for a piece of new music. By the same token, a favorable review can be most helpful. Record sales are very important in the field of popular music, and reviews published in influential places can have a strong influence on record sales. In popular music, the media are extremely important in the overall dissemination process, and the influence of the media is recognized under its own heading as an important element of this theory of music preference.

Educators and authority figures have a great deal of room for individual discretion in deciding how far they will go to influence individual music preference. Once again the cultural mores will do much to determine the level of effort that an agent of the culture will expend to bring individual values into conformity with the culture's values. American educators tend to be very meek in advancing the style of music they prefer. The American government may be less subtle than its educators, but the observer must turn to foreign educators and governments to see the strongest efforts made by educators and authority figures to influence music preference. Totalitarian governments will usually provide the most striking examples.

Finally, the psychological process of incidental conditioning has an influence upon individual music preference. Incidental conditioning is a process that occurs when music is heard by a listener in social situations that already have pleasant or unpleasant associations. Because it is paired with this situation in the listener's mind, the music will take on a pleasant or unpleasant meaning.

It is doubtful that the agencies of the culture engage very often in the deliberate planning of incidental conditioning experiences, at least in the United States. At first glance, it appears that the choice of background music is usually left to chance. But a closer analysis will disclose that although the choice of background music is not usually a matter of deliberate planning, it is usually in the hands of a specific element of the culture that will behave in a somewhat predictable and definitely nonrandom way. It is helpful to consider some typical examples of incidental conditioning experiences.

Perhaps the strongest example of incidental conditioning in ordinary life is the case of the married couple who have "their song." "Their song" is usually a song that was popular at the time of their courtship, and it was usually brought to their attention by the broadcast media. In this case the media were the agency of the culture, and the courtship was the pleasant experience that became associated with the music heard at that time. In this case, selection of the music was not accidental; the music heard was the music being presented by the broadcast media when the couple tuned in. The couple would be able to interact with the influence of the culture through their choice of broadcast station, but the culture would have already acted once to determine what stations were available and again to determine what kind of programming was offered by these stations.

The peer group is probably one of the most frequent providers of music for incidental conditioning. In the adolescent peer group, choice of music for the junior or senior prom appears to be one of the more important music decisions to be made by the group in the course of a year. The result of this choice is usually an excellent reflection of the musical values of the peer group. Restaurants and hotels select music for activities and settings that could become involved with the incidental conditioning process, the government selects the music for its most important ceremonies, and the church selects music for its own ceremonies, which include highly memorable occasions such as weddings and funerals.

Muzak Corporation is a commercial provider of background music. There may not be a specific plan to associate this music with pleasant or unpleasant experiences, but the company does assert that its background music will contribute to worker productivity, consumer buying, or the general good mood of listeners exposed to its music product. In this case, Muzak Corporation and the managers responsible for selecting the type of service will function as agents of the culture who select the music that is made available.

It would be rare for any person intentionally to associate music with an unpleasant experience, but the association can happen unintentionally, as is the case when a worker hates his or her job and associates the music heard at work with the disliked job. Perhaps a better example of negative incidental conditioning would be the association formed between music heard at the dentist's office and a particularly painful dental procedure.

A larger effect to consider than the influence of individual activities of the culture, is that in which these activities blend together to act with the unity and power needed to influence the behavior of individuals. This overall effect can be summarized in four statements of how the culture acts upon the people who listen to music and upon those who create it: (a) The culture provides a model for the appreciation of the music that it favors; (b) the culture rewards individual conformity with its own views about the value of different styles of music; (c) the culture greatly influences selection of the music people hear; (d) the culture influences the style of music created in the near future. The specific mechanism through which these four effects are felt should be apparent from the explanation of how the family, the peer group, educators and authority figures, incidental conditioning, and the media influence the music listener.

There Is More than One Culture

Experienced music teachers will testify that there is definitely more than one music culture in the United States. In some localities different ethnic groups are sufficiently well established to function as their own music cultures, but most music teachers will experience the effect of multiple cultures in terms of the competition between the "high" culture and the "low" culture. The competition between these two cultures is intense, and music teachers will be forced to take a position regarding the two cultures quite early in their careers.

The high culture will be familiar to music teachers because it is the culture in which they are trained. This training is appropriate, because the art music of the high culture has stood the test of time, amply demonstrating its potential to offer aesthetic satisfaction to those who make the effort needed to understand and appreciate it. For most music listeners, considerable effort will be needed.

Compared with popular music, art music is more complex, its works have a much longer duration, and many of its conventions require study before they can even be perceived. Self-instruction is difficult, and many aspects of art music can be probed only with the help of an experienced teacher. While this characteristic explains the appeal of art music to professional music teachers, it also shows why the people who prefer art music are usually in the minority. In essence, it is simply more difficult to appreciate the art music of the high culture, and that is why fewer people appreciate it.

In contrast, the popular music of the low culture is simple; its works are short and they are usually very easy to perceive. Most listeners can understand and appreciate popular music with no help needed from a specialist teacher. In everyday life it is often difficult to avoid hearing popular music. Virtually every student who comes to a music teacher will have already been exposed to the music of the low culture, and most of these students will be predisposed to like the music of this culture.

The terms *high culture* and *low culture* are used here as a matter of convention. There is nothing inherently wrong with the music of the low culture except for the fact that it will usually not provide intellectual or aesthetic stimulation equal to that offered by the art music of the high culture. Music teachers are wise to cultivate a preference for high-culture art music in their students, but they are unwise if they allow themselves to be unduly discouraged when they discover that most students come to them with a well-established preference for popular music. Teachers must realize that the overwhelming preponderance of influence from the culture will come from that segment of the culture that favors popular music.

Music teachers must also guard against another problem occasioned by the inevitable conflict between the high culture and the low culture. That problem is the mistaken notion that popular music has no value at all. The ragtime music of Scott Joplin, which was once considered unfit to be heard by the high culture, is now the topic of articles and books authored by respected musicologists. Within the overall genre of American popular music there is a wide range of potential musical value, and the professional music teacher should be open-minded in assessing that value. It will often be advantageous for teachers to accept the initial preference most of their students have for popular music and use this preference as a building block to lead their students into the discovery of high culture art music.

The Educator as Agent of the Culture

How can the professional music educator function most effectively as a member of the culture? The task of the educator is made more difficult by the fact that he or she must expose students to the aesthetic values of the high culture, whereas most students will begin school with some predisposition toward the music of the low culture. Fortunately, research indicates that this bias is at its lowest strength in the earliest years of schooling.

This suggests an important tactic for the music educator: Begin the child's music education as soon as the child enters school. The years between kindergarten and fifth grade may be crucial, yet many music programs begin only at the fourth or fifth grade. This is often the case in school systems that offer instrumental and choral music but no general music. It is vital that the school system offer a comprehensive program of general music throughout the elementary school years.

Usually music educators must enlist existing cultural influences to support the kind of music they are attempting to teach. These influences are already present in the culture, but the music educator must do whatever is possible to augment their strength. To encourage a preference for the art music of the high culture, the educator must identify those influences within the culture that already support art music.

It should not be overly difficult to find wealthy and powerful people from the community and nationally known figures who support art music. There is a long tradition of support of art music by wealthy individuals and by those who are generally aligned with the high culture. The educator can point to these people for an endorsement of art music in the same way that advertisers present images of wealthy and powerful ("successful") people endorsing an expensive product. Just as powerful individuals tend to endorse art music, the most powerful and dignified institutions of society—for example, the state and the church—also tend to do so.

In working to develop student receptiveness to art music, it is useful to point up this music's uniqueness. The longer duration of art music compositions can be explained in terms of the more ambitious things the composers of art music want to do with their compositions. They need more time to develop their music as they like to do. Art music is usually performed in concert halls of monumental architecture, and the teacher can draw an analogy between that architecture and music that is of monumental stature.

When endorsing a particular kind of music or doing anything else to expand student horizons, educators must function decisively as role models and authority figures. One teaching method that is often overlooked calls for the music educator simply to let students see that he or she enjoys the kind of music being taught. This enjoyment can be communicated nonverbally or verbally, and it is an effective way to make students more receptive to different styles of music. Teachers seldom realize the importance of modeling the enjoyment of good music because the good effects of this modeling require time to take hold.

Sometimes the teacher must act as an authority figure to ensure that students will give music the attention it deserves. The greater length and complexity of art music means that it will often need several repetitions before student listeners can begin to appreciate its value. A teacher who finds the students unwilling to give a piece of music the attention it deserves is well advised simply to demand that attention. The teacher should always remember, however, that this authority carries a corresponding obligation to all elements of the culture. In this pluralistic society it would be inappropriate for teachers to advocate a single style of music to the exclusion of all others.

It may safely be concluded that the culture is the single most important influence upon the creation and appreciation of music. Many of the difficulties experienced in contemporary music education stem from the failure of music educators to enlist available cultural influences to support their own work or from an unwise decision to oppose the influence of the culture when it ought to be left alone.

The culture preserves social order, upholds the values of society, and does much to introduce the young to these values and to the societal constraints that preserve order. The effect of the culture cannot be removed, and no wise educator will attempt to thwart it. The appropriate role of the music educator is to work to balance the influence of various aspects of the culture upon his or her students. Cultural input upon the individual will virtually always need balancing, and society maintains its teachers as agents of the culture to provide a positive and moderating influence upon the young.

3 The Community as Educator
Barbara Kaplan

The UNESCO conference held in 1973 on the campus of the University of South Florida under the sponsorship of the Leisure Studies Program was entitled "Cultural Innovation in Technological and Post-Industrial Societies." Consultants for the conference were grouped for committee work, and I was assigned to the committee called "Community," chaired by Rolf Meyersohn. The deliberations of the committee provided an awakening to the larger sense of the word *community,* a concept extending beyond the usual physical and social meanings to the philosophical connotation of common links that exist in the life of the mind, as in the use of the phrase *community of scholars.* Although not all the participants in Symposium II of the Alabama Project had met before the October 1984 session on sociology and music education in America, common interests and a certain community of thought brought this specific community of scholars together at this point in time. Only with this recognition of the twofold meaning of the word *community* may one approach the consideration of the community as educator.

Various facets of the American community, in its physical sense, and its relation to music education have been explored during the past four decades. Those that treat specific locales and their musical history or heritage include Buckner (1974), Dahlenberg (1967), Forbes (1974), Haack and Heller (1983), and Schrader (1968). Music education in urban or suburban communities has been the focus of research by Grant (1963), Hammond (1974), Lee (1970), Merritt (1967), and Sullivan (1975). Greene (1968) and Howe (1952) have dealt with aspects of the college-community relationship, whereas Farruggia (1969) and Lax (1966) have investigated community and school community factors in dropouts affecting instrumental music programs. Downey (1974) studied the role of leadership in community musical

44

activities, and Simon (1968) explored the propriety of the study of sacred music in the public school. Fain (1956), Harvey (1975), and Rabin (1968) have produced research related to the community orchestra, both adult and youth organizations.

In its more concrete sense, "community" appears in conjunction with region, nation, and world at the second level of Max Kaplan's model delineated in Chapter 1. Although it would be entirely possible to begin with the smallest unit of the four societal groups of the model and limit discussion to the role of agencies in the physical community, such as museums, art associations, organizations, cultural offices, and other institutions that provide active support for music education and equally possible to detail research carried on by such institutions or about them, there appears to be a more fundamental consideration. It seems important first to pose the question: Is there indeed a community of thought in regard to children and music? And a second question follows: If so, what is the nature of the commonality? A third question in the sequence could be extrapolated from the question asked at the Alabama Project lecture on the Auburn University campus, Is there an "international music"? Instead, one might ask, Is there an "international" music education? In a 1945 lecture on Hungarian music education, the composer Zoltán Kodály commented:

> The road from Hungarian music to the understanding of international music is easy, but in the opposite direction, the road is difficult or non-existent. . . . Thus we need a Hungarian musical education. . . . The more Hungarian we are the more can we expect an international interest. . . . Without a Hungarian musical culture, our music teaching is nothing but finding lodgings for foreign art. . . . We must find the roads that lead to the freest and fullest expansion of our musical individuality. . . . At this point democracy means two things: one is to make the means of musical education available to everybody, and the other a full assertion of national characteristics. (Kodály, 1945/1974, pp. 154–155)

Kodály's thoughts about democracy and music education recall the 1950 statement of the Music Educators National Conference Committee on Resolutions, which has been referred to as the Child's Bill of Rights in Music. At least five of the six articles contained therein refer to the right of *all* children to such education in music as will bring them happiness and well-being, enable them to share music making with others, allow them to cultivate performance abilities in music, develop their music skills to the highest degree that their potential and their desire may permit, and sensitize and refine their spirit (Dykema & the Committee on Resolutions 1950, March).

Even closer to the home of the Alabama Project comes a third statement of the entitlement of young people to education in the arts and specifically in music. The recommendations made by the Alabama State Superintendent of Education Wayne Teague in *A Plan for Excellence: Alabama's Public Schools* (1984) included a specific recommendation:

> The basics for instruction in grades K–8 should be defined as reading, language arts, mathematics, science, social studies, computer literacy, art, music, and physical education, all of which should be taught by properly certified personnel. . . . The opportunity to participate in art and music programs should be provided to all students. Individual expression should be nurtured in every child. (p. 34)

Each of the three statements—one by an internationally renowned composer equally recognized for his interest in the musical education of young people, the second by a national organization that has represented leadership for music education in our own country for more than three-quarters of a century, and the third by an official concerned with the development of excellence in his state—emphasizes the idea of music education for all children. The overwhelming evidence of such community of thought in the world, nation, and state communities would imply that the thinking would be a part of the smallest level of community as well. The truth is that the diversity of practice and the inequality of opportunity for music education in our nation and state are shocking in their lack of consistence with our stated goals. In fact, the Five-Year Planning Document (1986–1990) of the National Endowment for the Arts (1984) states that the

> Endowment Survey of Public Participation in the Arts, based on data obtained in 1982, indicates that most Americans have never had any form of arts instruction: 53 percent have had no instruction in music; 76 percent, no visual arts; 91 percent, no theater; 93 percent, no ballet; and 82 percent, no creative writing . . . [and that] the higher one's family income bracket, the more likely one is to have had some form of artistic instruction, usually between the ages of 12 and 17. (p. 135)

I will consider first the range of opportunities in one state, represented here by Alabama, then move to the larger socio-musico-cultural context.

A nonnative or short-term resident of a state (such as I, who have lived in Alabama for only seven years) may write glowingly of its good qualities without being accused of chauvinism. Alabama is a physically beautiful state, with growing material assets, a warm and neighborly population, a rich and interesting history. It has been tempered in the fires of war, racial protest, financial stress, political struggle, and farm losses. It is blessed with generous patrons of the arts and burgeoning activities at the local level, ranging from arts and crafts fairs in communities of all sizes to symphony concert series in several cities of the state. It is the home of Tuskegee Institute and its famed choir; the composer William Dawson; the Mobile Opera; the Alabama, Huntsville, and Montgomery symphonies; a half dozen youth orchestras; and bands and choruses in the high schools of even the smallest communities. It is the home of Hank Williams and Kowaliga, the folk-song collector Byron Arnold, accomplished performers on dulcimer, the top entertainment group "Alabama," and enthusiastic square dance groups in nearly every area.

Yet at the very point in time when educators and parents are especially concerned with the provision of the best education for the very young because of growing awareness of the importance of these early experiences and of growing interest in the arts, state personnel lists reveal that Alabama employs some 164 music teachers for its 650 primary, elementary, and middle schools. Of the 164 Alabama elementary music teachers, 57 teach in Jefferson County (the Birmingham area) and another 41 in Montgomery (Perdue, 1983). A music specialist in Auburn teaches in 40 classrooms in 3 of the city's primary schools, and a Huntsville elementary music teacher covering 5 schools sees each child for 12 music lessons a year. In still another city a certified classroom teacher, with a good background in music but without certification as a music specialist, is reponsible for the elementary music program. Finally, approximately 300 schools in the state relegate the teaching of music to the classroom teacher, who generally has the minimum one or two music courses as a preparation for teaching a subject with a mode of thought bearing little similarity to the verbal and mathematical modes that made up the greater part of his or her college curricula. Even with state expectations and requirements, the autonomy of the individual school system, upheld as part of democratic privilege, may be the very factor that prevents the equality of opportunity, also an expressed tenet of democratic societies. Each superintendent and board of education has a particular set of values, often derived from experiences that did not include education in music.

The fact that Alabama or any other state is not alone in its inequality of opportunity does not relieve its citizens of the need to be advocates of music and its allied arts or of the task of finding temporary solutions to bridge the gap between the status quo and the anticipated "cultivated society," in which music education will be available for every child. In one Alabama city, some temporary solutions included the provision of several activity programs in music, organized under the auspices of a local arts association. Individual schools could select any combination of programs. The choices of activities were (a) a choral–general music experience for third graders, culminating in a concert by all third graders in their individual schools and a city-wide concert by children selected from the participating schools; (b) a series of artists-in-the-schools concerts by local artists, ranging from solo instrumental performers, a woodwind quintet, and a string quartet to a madrigal chorus from the local music club; (c) exhibitions of musical instruments and artifacts from various countries. Some schools chose two programs, and others requested all three. In other schools without music teachers, musician parents have taken the responsibility of teaching a limited number of classes while nonmusician parents provided baby-sitting services for them.

University student laboratory experiences represent still another solution for communities with access to cooperative public school–university programs. In one Alabama county located within easy driving distance of a major university, two schools have provided a home for university student laboratory teaching in music prior to the students' internship, making possible for the schools a music program of eight music lessons per quarter for Headstart classes through the seventh grade. The arrangement doubles for these children the opportunity for involvement with music, in contrast with that provided for children in many elementary schools, and makes possible a program of continuity and sequence. This kind of laboratory experience has proven challenging to the university students as well. One of the schools has found the music program so beneficial that it is considering the possibility of hiring a music specialist—a gratifying development, because the laboratory experience, or any other temporary measure provided by the community, should not supplant the services of a music specialist in a full-time program funded by the community. In both schools, the Gordon music aptitude tests (1979b) have been administered to the students to assist in identifying children with aural skills who might especially benefit from further music experiences. One of the schools was also included in a study that related aptitude test scores to community considerations of home and school environments.

Differences in Alabama School Communities Expressed through Music Aptitude Testing

The use of the Gordon *Primary Measures of Music Audiation* (PMMA) to identify children potentially gifted in music in three Alabama schools was made possible through an Auburn University research grant-in-aid study in 1980 (B. Kaplan, 1981, April). I initially undertook the study to determine the validity of the Gordon test, following its appearance in 1979, as a measure of music aptitude in rural Alabama and to determine whether variables in home and school environments could predict aptitude scores. Studies of the construct validity of the test had been reported in both the test manual and in a later monograph by Edwin Gordon (1980). The intention of the Auburn University study was not to replicate previous studies but to investigate the content and process validity of the PMMA for use with children who were strikingly different, educationally and culturally, from the children with whom the test norms had been established. Gordon's designation of the process of inner hearing as "audiation" was a relatively new concept; it was also conceivable that the ability to audiate might be a selective process, not only in terms of music aptitude, but also in terms of educational and cultural development. The study focused on the investigation of the power of educational and cultural factors to affect test scores, with test reliability reported only as a sequential step in reaching the conclusions of the study.

The three schools that participated in the Auburn University study exhibit marked contrasts in degree of heterogeneity and size of enrollment, of home and school environments, and of music curriculum, although all three schools are located within a 15-mile radius in eastern Alabama. School A, a Lee County school, is situated on a campus that children in kindergarten and primary grades share with students of Grades 9 through 12; the middle school (Grades 4 through 8) is several miles distant. Although there are instrumental programs in middle school and high school, classroom teachers of the primary school conduct music activities for the younger children, supplementing their music programs with laboratory teaching by music and education majors from nearby Auburn University. The school is racially integrated, with 23% black enrollment. School B, a rural school in Macon County, approximately 10 miles from the town of Tuskegee, also depends upon classroom teachers and Auburn Unviersity students for its music program. This all-black school includes classes for children in kindergarten through Grade 7 and houses two Headstart groups as well. School C, with an enrollment in 1980 of children in kindergarten through third grade (now through fourth grade) functions within the Auburn City School System and has the regular services of a part-time music teacher, who sees all children in the school at least once each month. The school population is 40% black, with a fractional percentage of children of Far Eastern or Latin backgrounds.

Tonal and Rhythm Tests of the *Primary Measures of Music Audiation* were administered to 733 children in the three schools: 382 children in School A, 93 in School B, and 258 in School C. Of the 733, the results of 68 children's tests were not used because of missing scores on one of the tests. The total number tested is somewhat comparable to the group of 873 children used in establishing norms in New York. Although the results of the test indeed identified 194 children (29.2%, $N = 733$; Table 3.1) as being potentially musically gifted as defined by Gordon, there were interesting differences between the Alabama children and the New York children. It was

Table 3.1

Children Identified as Gifted in the Alabama Study, by Grade Level and School

	Grade K			Grade 1			Grade 2			Grade 3			Totals		
	No. ident.	% in individ. school (%)	% of grade in all schools (%)	No. ident.	Ind. school (%)	All schools (%)	No. ident.	Ind. school (%)	All schools (%)	No. ident.	Ind. school (%)	All schools (%)	No. ident.	Ind. school (%)	All schools (%)
School A	12	26.1	11.5	24	22	12.4	27	25.9	14.1	14	16.9	7.9	77	22.5	11.6
School B	1	7.8	0.9	4	16	2.1	3	12	1.6	1	4.8	0.5	9	10.7	1.4
School C	17	37.8	16.3	34	57.6	17.6	31	49.2	16.1	26	36.1	13.5	108	45.2	16.2
Totals	30		28.8	62		32.1	61		31.8	41		21.9	194		29.2

also evident from an examination of the percentage of children identified as gifted in each grade and from mean scores, school by school, that sharp differences were apparent among the Alabama schools.

A study of the mean scores of New York and Alabama children indicated that there were no significant differences in the Tonal, Rhythm, or Composite scores of the kindergarten children nor in the Tonal, Rhythm, or Composite scores of the other grades. In *t*-test comparisons, small differences did emerge in the Rhythm score means of the Grade 1, Grade 2, and Grade 3 children (2.9, 2.8, and 3.5) that were significant at the .05 level. In each case the Rhythm mean scores were higher for the Alabama children.

Although the reliability coefficients (.65 to .84) of the Alabama study, developed in the split-halves analysis using the Spearman-Brown formula, did not approach the .90 and .92 levels of the New York norms for Composite scores, they coincided in several instances with those of the New York tests. This close approximation occurred with Rhythm scores in kindergarten and Grade 1 and with Tonal scores in Grade 3. The reliability coefficients of the Alabama tests at no time fell below the .65 level of the kindergarten Tonal tests.

The Auburn University study attempted to deal with variables in the child's environment that were of a distinctly musical nature, first through descriptive statistics and then through a correlation of environmental variables with children's scores on the PMMA. Although several items on the questionnaire related to family occupations and length of residence in the community, the purpose of these items was description, rather than analysis of socioeconomic background for purposes of correlations with test scores. All identifications by race, age, and intelligence quotient were also eliminated in the effort to determine the effect of the musical variable alone; however, some contrasts emerged in terms of race because it was possible to compare School B, an all-black school, with the other two schools, which had integrated populations. Since the black children were not identified in the integrated schools, it would be essential to make such an identification and to include the scores of these children before attempting generalizations in regard to race for this sample.

Previous studies by Wermuth (1971) and Jenkins (1976) have discredited the theory that race accounts for significant differences in musical aptitude or musical development; however, if ethnic heritage is considered rather than race alone, it would be reasonable to attribute some development of rhythmic capability to the presence of home, school, or community experiences in the tradition of African and Afro-American polyrhythms, improvisations, syncopations, and dance. The developmental nature of music aptitude during this early childhood period suggests a second possibility— that of an earlier maturing of rhythm aptitude among the children of Alabama schools. The above studies notwithstanding, Young (1976, February), in a study of Texas children, concluded that the black children of the study showed later and slower maturation in tonal development than the white children; again, causes may have been cultural rather than racial. A similar phenomenon in reverse could exist in rhythm aptitude.

A third explanation of higher rhythm scores surfaced from responses to a companion questionnaire administered to teachers in the schools tested. The results indicated that all classroom teachers in the three Alabama schools worked with movement activities, whereas fewer teachers attempted to guide the development of tonal skills through ear training and singing. This instructional tendency could have contributed to the occurrence of higher Rhythm than Tonal scores for Alabama children, but it did not seem to explain the differences between Alabama and New York Rhythm scores. Still another difference in the two populations was the suburban nature of the New York community and the predominantly rural environment of the Alabama community. Could factors be present that might contribute more to the development of rhythm aptitude in the rural community than in the suburban? This seems unlikely, although Gordon's (1980) study of developmental music aptitudes among inner-city primary school children revealed a trend of systematically higher Rhythm test scores for the inner-city school children than for the standardization group. Finally, a survey of parents of the Alabama children tested indicated unexpectedly strong parental involvement in church-sponsored musical activities; this additional opportunity for guided musical experiences in children's choirs and so forth, may have been greater among the Alabama children than among the New York children, but it did not offer a clear explanation of why the significant differences occurred only in the Rhythm scores.

An interesting by-product of the effort to identify musically gifted children was a peak effect in the profiles of the children at School B, one of the rural schools in the Alabama study. In preparing profile cards for the PMMA, one profile emerged repeatedly (Figure 3.1a and b), caused by the ascent from a comparatively low score on the Tonal test to a distinctively higher score on the Rhythm test, followed by a descent to the Composite score. This profile had a companion rising effect (Figure 3.1c) in which the Rhythm score brought the Tonal score to a higher Composite score. Furthermore, these two types of profile were present with 85.7% of the children in School B, with the inverted profile and low Rhythm score occurring in only 14.3% of the children in all grades. The effect did not appear to be related as much to grade level as to school, indicating that there might be variables in school or home environment or background to which the effect could be attributed. Similar profiles appeared in School A and School C but not in the same startling proportion to the number of children tested as in School B.

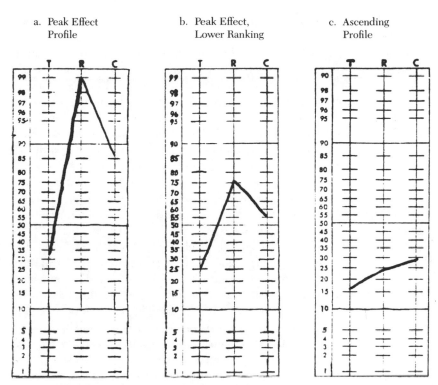

Figure 3.1 Effect of PMMA Rhythm Scores on Composite Score, as
Apparent in Selected Kindergarten Profiles, School B

Environmental Factors Predictive of Music Aptitude

Previous studies relating musical attitudes, musical achievement, or musical aptitude to variables in the child's background have emphasized intelligence quotient, age, sex, socioeconomic status, race, or community size. Crawford (1972) dealt with the relationship of socioeconomic status to attitudes of children in the fourth, fifth, and sixth grades toward school music, out of school music, and home musical interest, concluding from the study of children's attitudes that relationships did exist between socioeconomic status and rhythmic aptitude, age, and home musical interest. Walls (1973) considered race and socioeconomic environments in relation to the identification of musical concepts. The study of seventh-grade children in Arkansas and Mississippi (Dunlap, 1975) revealed socioeconomic status, race, and the father's presence in the home as significant factors in musical achievement, whereas community size appeared to be influential only in specific circumstances. Tapley's (1976) research revealed sex differences in achievement based on musical training in auditory perception for first-grade children.

Various researchers have focused on musical aptitude and its relation to environmental factors. Among them Wermuth (1971) treated the relationship of aptitude to family and student activity in music and to socioeconomic status as well as to student interest in music and to intelligence; however, the research was limited to middle school students. Holman (1973) concluded that intellectual skills necessary for the development of musicality were limited in lower socioeconomic status elementary school children, although creative thinking and memory in these children appeared to be as great as or superior to those of middle- and upper-class children. Moore's (1973) study of the effect of early musical experiences on the pitch and rhythm abilities of five-year-old children encompassed musical motivation in the home environment as well as sex type and socioeconomic status. Jenkins (1976) indicated that the musical home environment, as represented by the product of the experiences of adults in the home and the availability of musical items and activities, has the strongest relationship to the musical development of the young child; an analysis of socioeconomic status and ethnicity in the same study revealed no statistically significant differences. More recently, Gilbert's (1980) report, assessing motor music skill development in young children, again examined the relationship of test performance to age, sex, race, community size, and previous musical experience; in this study, race, community size, and previous experience appeared unrelated to performance.

In the concern over inner-city problems and urban environments, comparatively little research has been directed toward the patterns of musical environments in rural communities and the possible effects of these environments upon the musical development of children. Among studies of the rural community and music that do exist are Carpenter's (1969) account of the role of the Stephen Foster Memorial as a sociocultural force in a rural community and Watson's (1968) treatment of musical attitudes in relation to environment among rural students in central Oklahoma, again with particular emphasis upon the socioeconomically deprived. No previous studies have specifically related music aptitude to the rural community and only a limited number of studies have been concerned with music aptitude prior to the middle school years. Undoubtedly, this gap in information can be attributed in part to the developmental nature of musical aptitude in those early years, as it is described by Gordon (1979a), and in part to the previous dearth of reliable instruments for the study of music aptitude in the early childhood years.

To determine independent variables in the musical environments of home and school that might be predictive of variance in scores of the 733 rural Alabama children tested on Gordon's *Primary Measures of Music Audia-*

tion, questionnaires were administered to parents of the children tested and to the teachers of the schools participating in the test. With responses from 84.4% of the teachers and 45% of the parents, a multiple-regression analysis was made using Composite scores on the test as dependent variables and the items of parent and teacher questionnaires as independent variables. Seven variables of the teacher questionnaire appeared predictive of 33.2% variance in Composite scores, and the parent questionnaire provided 11 variables predictive of 35.2% variance. Contributing to variance in the scores were parent's musical preferences and teacher planning of lessons that included the development of concepts in music. Although the combined effect of the 11 variables of the parent questionnaire appeared significant at the .01 level, the combined effect of the 7 variables of the teacher questionnaire was not significant.

According to the questionnaire responses, parents attributed the strongest musical influences on their children to church music, school music, mass media, and themselves. Five percent did not respond and 3% listed factors such as rock groups, gospel quartets, and specific instruments such as guitar and drums.

A final question to parents dealt with the musical abilities that they would like to have developed in their children. Only 1 respondent of 330 said "None"; other responses included listening for enjoyment, developing the ability for unselfconscious expression, developing specific ability for church music, and the simple statement, "as she wishes."

The second questionnaire, directed to classroom teachers, dealt with the nature, amount, and purpose of musical activities conducted by the classroom teacher and with the preparation of the classroom teacher in music in terms of instruments played, participation in musical activities, and formal class study. Although all respondents indicated that they planned musical activities for their classes, there were varying degrees of frequency: 20% of the teachers planned daily activities; 8% planned for activities three times weekly; 16% twice weekly; 32% weekly; and 24% planned for occasional activities. Forty-eight percent of the teachers spent 30–45 minutes weekly on musical activities; 24% spent less than 30 minutes; 16% spent 45–75 minutes; 8% spent 75–100 minutes; and one teacher spent more than 100 minutes. Singing and movement were the most frequent activities (96% each), listening was emphasized by 92% of the teachers, and musical games by 60%; 20% conducted activities related to playing instruments and to creating music, and only 12% dealt with reading music. Although the teachers in Schools B and C, in varying numbers, used all types of activities, no teacher at School A listed playing instruments, creating music, or reading music among planned activities. Although 56% attempted to develop singing, moving, playing, improvising, creating, and listening skills, only 40% planned activities for sequenced conceptual learning.

Teacher preparation for conducting musical activities in the classroom seemed more diverse than the actual planning and direction of such activities. Of the 25 teacher respondents, 32% indicated that they played no instruments with confidence or played with minimal ability only. Those who did claim instrumental skills most frequently listed piano as the instrument played. As was true of the parents, the musical activity in which the greatest number of teachers (68%) participated was the church choir. Second on the list were high school instrumental and choral organizations, 32% of the teachers having been members of bands and choruses. Sixty percent held education degrees with two music courses, 20% held education degrees with one music course, and 20% held education degrees with more than two music courses. The private study of a keyboard instrument was part of the preparation of 36% of the teachers, and 8% had studied other instruments privately. Twenty percent had been active in attending workshops in music.

Relationships between Environment and Music Aptitude

1. The parents' expressed preferences for specific types of music, contributing to 25.7% of the variance in the children's scores, appeared to be the strongest factor of the 82 possible independent variables of the parent questionnaire. Although more parents expressed the belief that they themselves and the music of church, school, and mass media had the strongest musical influences upon their children, there was a higher correlation between the scores and the parents' belief that the private music teacher influenced the child's musical life than between the scores and the other variables expressed by the parents as influential. The influence of church and mass media appeared in the equation, but at less than the 1% level. Six other independent variables contributed to variance at the 1% level or above. The single most significant factor contributing to variance in children's scores was the parents' expressed preference for gospel music, which may be an indicator of the presence of musical experience in the child's early years, not only at home, but possibly in the church environment as well. It is important to note that the variables of this study are expressed in terms of parents' perceptions for the purpose of exploring the musical background of the community as well as parents' attitudes toward the musical environments that surround their children. As perceptions and, in some cases, beliefs, there must be less significance attached to the relation of scores to parent questionnaire variables than might have been the case had such yes or no questions as Does your child study music privately? been asked. The factual answer would produce a less troublesome correlation than an answer involving preference, particularly when a complex set of preferences appears to exist, as is the case in this study. To obtain a more effective set of predic-

tors in a replication of the study, a future experimenter could limit preferences to specified choices. In this particular study, the responses to all appropriate choices produced a more interesting community description.

2. In the teacher questionnaire, three variables contributed to 24.3% of the variance in scores. These variables included the planning of classroom activities to stimulate conceptual learning in music, and the teacher's musical background—specifically the study of instruments other than keyboard and the inclusion of more than two courses in music in the education degree. The preparation and the activity of the classroom teacher in music appeared to be potential contributors to variance in the child's developmental music aptitude scores; however, the F ratios of these variables were not significant, either individually or in the aggregate, possibly because of the relatively smaller teacher sample.

3. Although 48% of parents indicated that they would like to have their children develop music reading skills, only 12% of the classroom teachers acknowledged efforts to develop such skills. Since there was no separate category for indicating work with music reading readiness, the teachers may have been emphasizing, appropriately at this early childhood developmental period, activities designed as readiness skills. If there had been no effort in this direction, then it would seem that the failure to include music reading skills in the curriculum represents a lack of response in the school music program to the expressed desires of the community for its children. Such a gap between expressed community objectives for children and school programs may exist because the objective has not previously been articulated clearly. Other possible reasons for the discrepancy may have been the hesitation of the classroom teacher to work with music reading skills or the pressures of a curriculum oriented heavily toward the so-called "basics"— reading, writing, and mathematics.

4. For this particular community, and perhaps for this general type of stable, semirural community, the influence of the church choir appeared to be a recurring factor in the musical experience of both parents and teachers. Since there is wide variation in the educational objectives of church choirs, increased emphasis on the educational aspect of both adult and children's church choirs could perhaps contribute to the improvement of developmental music aptitude scores during an important period of the child's life—directly, through the musical experiences of the children, and indirectly, through the enhanced experience of the parent or teacher, whose preferences and skills in music may be producing an effect upon children's scores.

5. This study did not deal with the prediction of variance as it might possibly differ from school to school or from grade to grade. A grade-to-grade analysis of data might reveal changing factors as the child's experience broadens from home to school to the wider community, whereas a multiple

regression carried out with individual schools might produce more specific predictions for each school community.

The diversity of environmental factors and the diversity in music education practices within one state "community" are illustrative of the problems with which a country like the United States must deal in planning educational opportunities for all facets of the society—particularly in terms of arts education. A very different microcosm exists in Hungary, roughly comparable to Alabama in physical size. Many citizens of the country speak from two to eight languages, but there is one identifiable mother tongue that everyone shares and a musical mother tongue that is likewise shared and understood by all who have been educated in the public schools of Hungary. Although parents can choose between a music primary school (45-minute general music classes taught daily in grade K–8) and a normal primary school (45-minute music classes taught only three times a week), there are statewide expectations of musical competency and provision for music teachers to achieve such competency. Hungary's musically literate society, now into the third and fourth generations of school population since Kodály's earliest writings on music education in 1911 and 1929, may be attributed to the vision of a man who was as enthusiastic about what children could accomplish as he was involved in his own creative activities as composer and conductor and as concerned about the development of the mind and heart as the ear and hand.

The Kodály Concept as a Social Phenomenon

The Kodály concept of music education as a social phenomenon in Hungary represents a natural transition from community, region, and nation to the larger world, particularly a transition from its own unique music education to the influence it has had on the world. It does not seem necessary to delineate here the details or the principles of Hungarian music education that evolved from Zoltán Kodály's thought, for this has been done in a number of publications (B. Kaplan, 1985). Kodály's philosophy of the best in music education for the young people of his country manifests itself daily in the lives of the Hungarian people. The visitor to Hungary finds an informed awareness of music education programs and an obvious valuing of music in the most unexpected places—a taxi driver's intelligent responses about Kodály and his effect on Hungarian schools, or a policeman's personal radio tuned to the music of a string quartet as he mans the doorway of the local police precinct. Another evidence of the social outreach of music education appears in the public participation in music seen in the extensive audiences for concerts, the filled halls of two major opera houses in Budapest alone, numerous orchestras and choirs—school, community, and industrial— throughout the country, and music clubs of various kinds for young and old.

Kodály's belief in music for all reveals itself in the ability of a student majoring in English and Russian to notate in solfege several American folk songs that I sang for her later use in teaching her own students. The focus upon a musical mother tongue, with a musical language as important as a verbal language, represents a stimulating facet of music education, too little explored in our own country in the past. The international response to the logic of the Hungarian program and to the magnetism of its master teachers undoubtedly arises not only from the obvious musical literacy of the children but from the Hungarian goal of the development of an integrated personality through music. Finally, the bonding of those who have experienced the Kodály philosophy, in a desire to continue sharing their experiences, represents an important social tendency.

To see something of Kodály's impact on the world at large, it is necessary only to peruse several volumes of the *Bulletin of the International Kodály Society* for articles from Canada, Armenia, Great Britain, Israel, the Netherlands, Australia, France, Japan, Czechoslovakia, Italy, and Poland, to enumerate only a few. The diversity of observers in Katalin Forrai's Csobanc utca óvada (the Hungarian equivalent of the nursery school–kindergarten) ranges from classes visiting regularly from Finland, Sweden, or Germany to a French minister of culture, the wife of a Japanese embassy secretary, an American professor, and an Argentinian priest. The influence of Kodály's teaching in Japan has been widespread enough to prompt a group of 40 nursery school teachers, not music specialists, to travel to Hungary to observe in the schools, participate in music education seminars, and place a wreath at Kodály's grave as a symbol of their honor and respect for his impact on their own teaching.

It was never a part of Kodály's thinking that the principles he espoused and materials he composed for young people would simply be transplanted to another nation, there to grow and flourish as a "method." Rather, he advocated no compulsory guiding principle in method but the choice of a method and the best of procedures. He felt that it was indispensable to know the essence, progress, and momentum of the selected method as well as the student's personality and the nature of the material in order to adapt to the group and to the teacher's personality. In regard to adaptation, Forrai (1983, pp. 18–20), a first-generation student of Kodály himself and later his respected colleague and a leading authority on preschool music education, suggests the importance of:

1. considering the characteristics of the educational system and the teaching concepts of the given country
2. differentiating musical material and the pace of development of musical activity with (a) children who may attend kindergarten over a period of several years or start only at 5 years of age; (b) children in one group varying in na-

tionalities, with different mother tongues; and (c) children who differ in kindergarten skill development of letters, numbers, and writing

    3. learning Kodály's principles in the original and applying them to music
of value

    4. adhering to continuous in-service training for teachers

In relation to issues of ethnicity in the United States, the 1975 keynote
address by Max Kaplan (1976) for the second national conference of the Organization of American Kodály Educators dealt with these considerations:

    1. The revival of pluralism as a national value

    2. The movement toward self-assessment by public school music educators
(the Tanglewood Symposium in 1967)

    3. The tendencies of young people to humanistic visions

    4. A renewed interest in the arts as a social influence, particularly on the
part of social scientists

    5. The bankruptcy of mass culture myths

These kinds of issues and, a decade later, the swing toward additional or directly contrasting social considerations hold implications for the choice of
method or for the approach to the use of method. In Hungary, for example,
folk song is more than local color; it becomes the foundation of a new musical
language. The precisely spoken Hungarian language contributes to the correct speaking, listening, and writing of the musical language.

As one writer puts it, "All languages are equal, but some languages are
more equal to music than others" (Vander Schoot, 1983, p. 22). In a nation
such as the United States, moving ever more constantly toward the necessity for understanding and dealing with cultural pluralism as well as developing a central focus for the "American" factors that unite our federation of
states, it becomes increasingly important to use musical and social judgment
in working with a cultural phenomenon such as music education. What does
"musical mother tongue" mean in this pluralistic society with enclaves of
Mexican-Americans, Italian-Americans, Spanish-Americans, Chinese-
Americans, Japanese-Americans, Jewish-Americans, Irish-Americans, In-
donesian-Americans, Afro-Americans, native American Indians of varied
dialects, all of these with musical languages as varied as the verbal
languages?

The Role of Analysis in Understanding Musical Mother Tongue

First of all, we must acquire an understanding of the music that we call
our own—the folk songs that originated in the New World, in the language
that is presumably a unifying factor in our culture. Although we have made

opportunities for bilingual teaching of children who required such help, one Cuban refugee father in Florida moved his auto mechanic shop from Miami to Ocala because he wanted his children to find it necessary to use English as their daily mode of expression. There is an American folk music literature that comes from the memories of the people of this country, even though large segments of the literature may be traced to sources in other nations. The analysis of our folk and composed music provides a basis for greater accuracy of performance, for greater understanding of style, for the explanation of cultural differences in a literate, objective, musical way. Once we have acquired an understanding of our own music, we may use it for the purposes of curriculum planning, of sequencing materials for the development of music literacy skills, of developing both reading and writing skills in music—the latter too frequently left to the high school or college freshman music theory course, rather than developed as gradually, consistently, and logically as are the skills of verbal language. The acquisition of such musical skills need not and should not destroy the characteristic individualism in the performance of folk song, formal or informal but rather should contribute to a greater understanding of folk-song variants. The third step is to use the understanding of our own music as a basis of comparing it to that of other traditions. The sound of a piece of music may have an immediate association for us—we know from the total complex of sound that it is indeed Spanish or Chinese or Israeli or American—but the characteristics of which that sound is composed exist in a unique arrangement that alters the totality of the sound. The major scale and natural minor scale use the same notes in a different arrangement to produce a completely different sound effect.

To illustrate further the concept of musical mother tongue, it is possible to contrast folk songs of the southeastern United States with folk songs of Israel and find striking differences even in a limited analysis. Table 3.2 lists scales found in an analysis of 511 songs of Alabama (339 songs in two collections) and Florida (172 songs) and 677 songs analyzed by graduate students in a Kodály class in Israel. By examining the percentage statistics in relation to the groupings indicated, one finds that there are marked similarities of occurrence in the scale types found in the music; for example, the unhemitonic pentatonic scales occurred with similar frequency in both Alabama and Florida collections—30.1% in Alabama and 31.3% in Florida, producing a combined 30.5%. In contrast, the Israeli literature contains only 7.2% unhemitonic pentatonic scales. Do hexachord scales are present in Alabama (15.6%), in Florida (15.7%), and in Israel (16.7%) to give fairly comparable numbers. The occurrence of major scales in Alabama (30.7%) and in Florida (29.1%) is similar; however, Israel shows only 17.1% of its songs based on major scales. On the other hand, Aeolian scales in the Southeast show only 1.2% in the samples analyzed, whereas they represent 23.5% of the Israeli songs studied. If a goal in music education is to understand the music of our

Table 3.2
Comparative Analysis of Folk Songs of Alabama, Florida, and Israel

Scale	Alabama	% of total	Florida	% of total	Southeast total	% of total	Israel	% of total
Bitonal	—	—	1	0.6	1	0.1	—	—
Tritonal	4	1.2	3	1.7	7	1.3	3	0.4
Tetrachordal	5	1.8	5	2.9	10	1.9	10	1.5
Tetratonal	12	3.5	4	2.3	16	3.1	18	2.7
Pentachordal	11	3.2	7	4.1	18	3.5	69	10.2
Hemitonic pentatonic	11	3.2	2	1.2	13	2.5	11	1.6
Unhemitonic pentatonic	102	30.1	54	31.3	156	30.5	49	7.2
do	86	25.4	44	25.6	130	25.4	11	1.6
re	1	0.3	1	0.6	2	0.3	9	1.3
mi	2	0.6	—	—	2	0.3	2	0.3
so	3	0.6	4	2.3	7	1.3	5	0.7
la	10	2.9	5	2.9	15	2.9	22	3.2

Table 3.2 continued
Comparative Analysis of Folk Songs of Alabama, Florida, and Israel

Scale	Alabama	% of total	Florida	% of total	Southeast total	% of total	Israel	% of total
Hexachord	76	22.4	30	17.4	106	20.7	157	23.2
do	53	15.6	27	15.7	80	15.6	113	16.7
re	—	—	—	—	—	—	2	0.3
mi	—	—	—	—	—	—	3	0.4
so	23	6.8	2	1.2	25	4.9	21	3.1
la	—	—	1	0.6	1	0.2	18	2.7
Major	104	30.7	50	29.1	154	30.1	116	17.1
Harmonic minor	2	0.6	1	0.6	3	0.5	20	2.9
Melodic minor	—	—	—	—	—	—	6	0.9
Modal	12	3.5	14	8.1	26	5.1	197	29.1
Aeolian	4	1.2	2	1.2	6	1.2	159	23.5
Dorian	1	0.3	2	1.2	3	0.5	19	2.8
Phrygian	2	0.6	—	—	2	0.4	6	0.9
Lydian	2	0.6	—	—	2	0.4	—	—
Mixolydian	3	0.9	10	5.8	13	2.5	11	1.6
Hypomodes	—	—	—	—	—	—	2	0.3
Combinations	1	0.3	—	—	1	—	21	3.1
N	339	—	172	—	511	—	677	—

Note: Dashes = not applicable.

own culture, then it follows that the most characteristic traits of that music are the factors that should be dealt with first. It is possible that a more extensive analysis, and such analyses are in progress, would reveal somewhat different statistics, but the approximation of Alabama and Florida statistics seems to indicate several tendencies for the Southeast with even a limited analysis.

During the eleventh conference of the International Society for Music Education in Perth, Australia, Charles Benner (1976) spoke of the concept of comprehensive musicianship for the music educator as necessarily diverse and sometimes exotic in a pluralistic and changing society. He indicated a threefold function of music instruction:

> (i) to acquaint students with the structures, the forms, the styles, and the societal forces reflected in the music of the past; (ii) to give students the understandings and skills that will enable them to analyse, participate in, and make judgements about the music of the present; (iii) to give students a basis for comprehending the music of the future. (p. 36)

In turn, this implies a special role for the leader in music education—the task described by James MacGregor Burns (1978) as "consciousness raising on a wide plane" (p. 43). Leaders in music education increasingly encounter the need for realigning values and reorganizing institutions to achieve a more desirable purpose, a transformational kind of leadership.

With the emphasis of the 1980s toward excellence in education, and with a growing realization on the part of individuals and institutions regarding the importance of the arts for a fuller life in a free society, the time is opportune for more than a community of thought, expressed in terms of ideals and goals. What becomes increasingly important is the physical community's assumption of the responsibilities that attend its role as educator: (a) seeing that musical activity is provided for all children as a part of general education, not only for those who may participate in bands or church choirs or study piano privately; (b) assuring adequate instruction in music for elementary school children, as well as requiring high school units in music and supporting a high school instrumental program because of its importance to the athletic program; (c) providing opportunity for young people to experience the many musics of the world; (d) being aware of segments of the community other than the schools that may be deeply desirous of guided musical experience and activity; (e) expecting competent instruction that will acquaint the community with an understanding of its musical language, both its folk heritage in the sense of "musical mother tongue" and its composed music; and (f) seeking breadth in the musical involvement available to citizens outside the schools as in the schools.

Although it is difficult to find in every community a leader with the conviction, stature, and transformational qualities of a Zoltán Kodály, there are many music educators who may help in forming a more humane and musically literate community of citizens who exhibit the security of the integrated personality. Ewald Nyquist, former New York State Commissioner of Education expressed such a goal in this way:

> To me, the arts can greatly assist in re-sensitizing us, in making us fully human, in helping us to find our common humanity. As a friend of mine once said, "The arts are what you need so that when you knock on yourself, you will find someone at home." (Fowler, 1984, p. 78)

In the academic community, the Alabama Project has assumed a leadership role in forging a chain of encounters and experiences that surely will have far-flung effects on all of the participants but particularly upon those young professionals who will be the moving forces for a more comprehensive and human ideal of music education in the communities of the future—musical communities of thought and action in which advocacy may no longer be required.

4 Creative Thinking in Music: Approaches to Research

Peter R. Webster

> One of my professors in graduate school, a brilliant but insidious fellow, once taunted me: "Why study creativity? The psychologists who have done so are a notably dull lot." He was right in a sense, because the list of individuals who have studied the creative process is distressingly long in comparison with the handful who have actually illuminated it. But my professor was just as certainly wrong. The greatest psychologists—from William James to Sigmund Freud, from B. F. Skinner to Jean Piaget—have all recognized the importance and the appeal of a study of the creative processes. They have all sought to explain how human beings can fashion comprehensive theories in science or powerful works of art. And if they have not fully succeeded in providing a coherent and cogent account of this most puzzling of areas, it is not for want of trying. (Howard Gardner, *Art, Mind, and Brain*, 1982, p. xi)

This chapter offers some guidance for those individuals interested in completing research on the subject of creative thinking in music. The topic remains one of the most poorly researched in the field of music psychology, yet it is among the most important for musicians to understand. For many, the words *creative, creativity,* and *creativeness* have been used in so many musical contexts that all real meaning has been lost. New life needs to be given to these concepts in the form of fresh, theoretical writing and focused research employing different methodologies.

Presently, the theoretical literature in music offers little help in guiding research effort. There are no models of the creative thinking process in music that are being actively studied. What literature we do have has been largely based on intuition and anecdote. Until recently, the empirical literature on this subject has not moved us forward in any dramatic way. Happily, this state of affairs is changing. Recent studies by musicians and psychologists have begun to have an effect.

Literature on Creative Thinking in Music

My search for literature on creative thinking in music followed the traditional lines. I used the period from 1950 to the present as a working time frame, but I also included some important writings dating from earlier times. I searched computer data bases such as the Psychological Abstracts, ERIC, and Dissertation Abstracts, using the appropriate key words. In those instances where the indexes did not meet the dates within the time frame or when important journals were not included in the data bases, I completed searches manually. I also reviewed the published proceedings of symposia in music education and monographs pertaining to the topic.

Requirements for item inclusion included the following:

1. The study must be in published form
2. The study must have a direct connection to creative thinking in music
3. The study must conform to at least one of the following:
   a. Major tenets must be based on a carefully presented theoretical groundwork (philosophical or psychological)
   b. Emphasis must be placed on practical application of the creative process in music teaching and learning, with at least some reference to theory
   c. Presentation of empirical data must support hypotheses about creative thinking in music

A number of fundamental questions confront the scholar of creative thinking in music. A list might include the following:

1. How do you define "creative thinking"?
2. Who is the judge?
3. How do we measure creative thinking in the first place?
4. Is creative thinking the same for each individual?
5. Do we study process or product?

As researchers approach this vast topic, the choice of which questions to answer, which research procedures to use, and what theoretical biases to endorse all play a key role. In her review of creativity research, Richardson (1983) established a three-category model that delineates nonempirical, empirical, and measurement studies. It might be instructive, however, to consider the measurement studies as part of the empirical category and to include the many writings on educational methodology as separate from the theoretical, nonempirical studies.

The three principal categories chosen to represent the literature most accurately are based on approaches that deal with *theoretical speculation, practical application,* and *empirical data.* Figure 4.1 displays a categori-

zation of the three major approaches and their subcategories. Works that fall
into these groupings are listed under the appropriate headings in Figures
4.2, 4.3, and 4.4.

Theoretical Speculation

Studies based on this approach seem to be divided among those that are
rooted in either philosophical or psychological considerations (see Figure
4.2). These studies present little empirical data and do not emphasize practical matters but do present evidence for a particular theoretical viewpoint
and often point to the direction of future research. Chapters such as this one
might also be cited under the subcategory of general review.

As an example of philosophical writing, Brown (1968) focused on creative
thinking grounded in pragmatic philosophy and Gestalt psychology. He presented his own philosophy of music education with creative thinking as a
central idea. Like other writers in this category, Brown also endorsed the
four-stage process of preparation, incubation, illumination, and verification
first suggested in the writings of Graham Wallas.

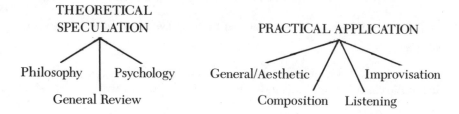

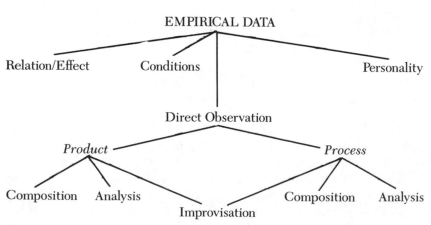

Figure 4.1 Literature Model, Major Categories and Subdivisions

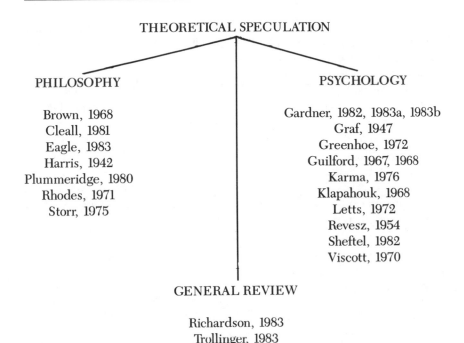

THEORETICAL SPECULATION

PHILOSOPHY

Brown, 1968
Cleall, 1981
Eagle, 1983
Harris, 1942
Plummeridge, 1980
Rhodes, 1971
Storr, 1975

PSYCHOLOGY

Gardner, 1982, 1983a, 1983b
Graf, 1947
Greenhoe, 1972
Guilford, 1967, 1968
Karma, 1976
Klapahouk, 1968
Letts, 1972
Revesz, 1954
Sheftel, 1982
Viscott, 1970

GENERAL REVIEW

Richardson, 1983
Trollinger, 1983
Webster, 1987

Figure 4.2 Theoretical Speculation Citations

On the psychological side, Greenhoe (1972) applied the Guilford Structure of Intellect model to a model of musical perception with creative thinking as a bias. She endorsed the notion of creative levels and, on the whole, presented a case for music education curricula based on a carefully reasoned psychological model. (It should be noted, too, that the famous case study by Revesz, 1954, and the more recent one by Viscott, 1970, also fall in this category.)

Practical Application

This category comprises those writings that emphasize the practical application of the creative process to the teaching and learning of music (see Figure 4.3). They often draw on both authority and empirical data research, but their primary focus is on practice. In some exceptional cases, the literature in this category is reflective of personal experiences in the creative process and tends toward the anecdotal. The inclusion of this literature in the model might be questioned by some who would contend that many entries represent an approach that is too informal. These writings do, however, represent a meaningful addition if a relationship to theory is either explicit or implied and if they are written by individuals with extensive experience in the creative process. Subdivisions here include: (a) general/aesthetic, (b) composition, (c) improvisation, and (d) listening.

By way of example, the monographs by Lasker (1971), Davies and Grant (1963), and Schafer (1976) are important. Lasker deals with traditional music composition and ways to encourage it in secondary schools. Both Davies and Schafer present strategies as well, but from the standpoint of twentieth-century composition. These books are important reading for teachers who wish to break with traditional class work and are looking for models to follow. A significant contribution by Feinberg (1973) for the teaching of creative listening must also be noted. The basis of his recommendations and practical demonstrations is rooted in psychological theory.

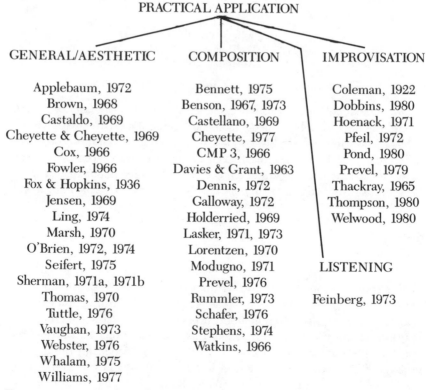

PRACTICAL APPLICATION

GENERAL/AESTHETIC	COMPOSITION	IMPROVISATION
Applebaum, 1972	Bennett, 1975	Coleman, 1922
Brown, 1968	Benson, 1967, 1973	Dobbins, 1980
Castaldo, 1969	Castellano, 1969	Hoenack, 1971
Cheyette & Cheyette, 1969	Cheyette, 1977	Pfeil, 1972
Cox, 1966	CMP 3, 1966	Pond, 1980
Fowler, 1966	Davies & Grant, 1963	Prevel, 1979
Fox & Hopkins, 1936	Dennis, 1972	Thackray, 1965
Jensen, 1969	Galloway, 1972	Thompson, 1980
Ling, 1974	Holderried, 1969	Welwood, 1980
Marsh, 1970	Lasker, 1971, 1973	
O'Brien, 1972, 1974	Lorentzen, 1970	
Seifert, 1975	Modugno, 1971	LISTENING
Sherman, 1971a, 1971b	Prevel, 1976	
Thomas, 1970	Rummler, 1973	Feinberg, 1973
Tuttle, 1976	Schafer, 1976	
Vaughan, 1973	Stephens, 1974	
Webster, 1976	Watkins, 1966	
Whalam, 1975		
Williams, 1977		

Figure 4.3 Practical Application Citations

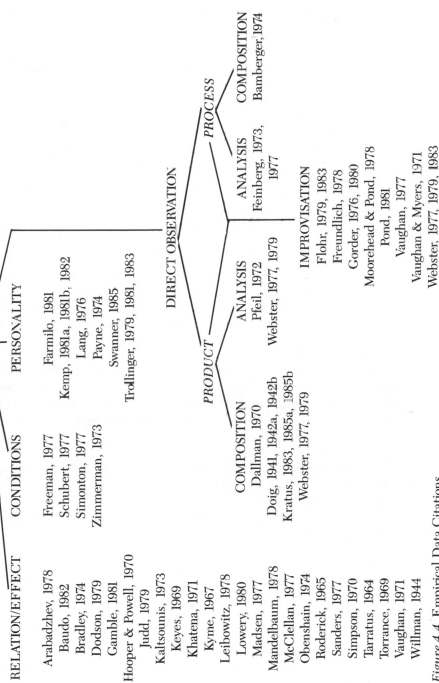

Figure 4.4 Empirical Data Citations

Empirical Data

The third major approach comprises studies that have investigated the topic in quantitative terms. The subdivisions include approaches aimed at (a) the possible relationship between creative thinking in music and other factors *and* the effect of creative-thinking variables on other factors, (b) the conditions under which the creative process exists in music, (c) personality factors that might relate to the creative musician, and finally (d) the direct observation of the creative process-product in a musical context. It is this last category into which measurement efforts fall. See Figure 4.4.

Relation and Effect Studies. Researchers have investigated the role of music experiences in stimulating general creative potential. Simpson's work (1969) is a good example of this type of study. He found that music experience did significantly affect general creativity in a positive manner. This finding seems consistent with other experimental studies of this type.

The relation between certain general creativity skills and musical skills in college music majors has also been a popular topic. Roderick (1965) investigated such relationships and concluded that creative-teaching ability is not related to musical aptitude, musical achievement, or general scholastic ability. This finding is in line with psychological theory that supports a separate factor approach to these skills.

Studies in this area are interesting in their own right and offer evidence for a model for creative thinking in music. It should be noted, however, that such studies do not deal directly with the measurement of creative thinking in music and must be viewed as premature until the profession reaches some agreement about the criteria question.

Conditions. The small amount of research that we do have in this subcategory reflects the findings of the general research literature on creative thinking, especially concerning proper incentives, materials, and personal encouragement. Freeman's study (1977) matched musically and artistically talented students with peers and discovered a number of distinguishing environmental characteristics. Simonton's biographical study (1977) of classical composers is also of interest from a historical perspective. Researchers interested in this area of investigation should be warned that little has been done in music, although many excellent models for this type of research exist outside the discipline.

Personality. The investigation of personality traits of the creative musician is a most difficult area. It is made complex not only by the problem of criteria for musical evaluation, but also by the complexities involved in measuring personality, especially in children. A set of interesting studies by Kemp (1981a, 1981b, 1982) directed toward the student and the adult performer and composer are worthy of note. Using bipolar questionnaire items evaluated by factor analysis, Kemp noted traits linked with introversion, pathemia, and high intelligence. A preference for complex stimuli also seems to be a recurring theme, as noted in Lang (1976). Trollinger's work (1981) with creative women musicians is worthy of note, especially in light of the growing literature on sex stereotyping.

As with the research on conditions, formal studies of personality traits in musicians are scarce. As the development toward more generally accepted measures of creative thinking continues, such studies will increase. At present, we know very little about this important topic, especially in terms of children.

Direct Observation. The organized study of the process-product dimension of creative thinking in music, in empirical terms, has been slow to develop. The problems surrounding this type of investigation are legion. The fundamental questions cited earlier are at issue here and require the researcher to adopt creative approaches to the problem and to be willing to take risks. It is heartening to see that much of the more recent study in the whole field of creative-thinking research is focused on this area. One possible reason for this is that many professionals are beginning to realize that before much progress can be made in *any* of the categories described thus far, the problems associated with the measurement of creative thinking must be met head on.

As Figure 4.4 indicates, research in the Direct Observation subcategory might be best viewed in terms of the way composition, analysis, and improvisation behaviors interact with process and product. It is possible to view both composition and analysis (writing and listening) in terms of musical process and musical product. Because of its singular nature, improvisation can be viewed as residing in both process and product, acting as a bridge between the two.

Surprisingly, we have little organized study of student composition from the standpoint of the finished product. This may be a function of the music teacher's lack of emphasis on original composition in the classroom or perhaps a reluctance by researchers to face the difficult problems of analysis in this area. Webster (1977) asked high school music students to complete a set of composition tasks that were evaluated with factors borrowed from the general creativity literature but defined in musical terms. Traditional notation and student-defined graphic notation were encouraged. More recently, Kratus (1985a) used a portable Casio keyboard to engage grade school children in compositional activities. Children were first asked to improvise but then were forced to refine their music until they were satisfied with their compositions. These final songs were then used as the basis for research study.

In terms of creative analysis from the product side, the study by Pfeil (1972) is noteworthy. His measure of creative-listening analysis, designed for college-level nonmusic majors, is itself a model of creative thinking and is quite applicable to younger subjects. The approach deserves more study and refinement, especially if considered with the process-centered work by Feinberg (1973).

Shifting to the process side in terms of composition and analysis, we discover an astonishing lack of study. Admittedly, the problem of recording the process of either written analysis of music or listening approaches to music is difficult, but the task is not impossible. Structured interviews, protocol analysis, and video tape study are all possible ways that can be considered. Certainly the approaches to creative listening that Feinberg (1973) discusses can be extended and refined through measurement studies.

With respect to the process analysis of composition, Bamberger's almost unknown study (1974) using compositional tasks that are monitored by computer offers a fascinating angle on this aspect of musical behavior. Her study is an excellent candidate for replication and extension using modern microprocessors. The study of both children and adults during the compositional process should be possible with protocol techniques and with certain unobtrusive measurement strategies (see the final portion of this chapter for additional comment on future research methods).

Improvisation activities have received the most attention by researchers. Some of the efforts have been directed more clearly toward the evaluation of the completed product, including the early work by Vaughan and Myers (1971) and the more recent studies by Webster (1977, 1979, 1983) and Gorder (1976, 1980). In these studies, children were asked to improvise while the researcher recorded the sounds on either audio or video tape. A carefully defined set of criteria was then used to evaluate the improvisations, usually by a panel of judges. Although the findings are tentative at best, they do suggest that assessments of such behaviors are not an impossibility, and the possibility of conducting more extensive research with this strategy is likely.

The work of Pond (1981) and Flohr (1979) are examples of improvisation study that seem to place more emphasis on *process*. In these studies, children are observed during improvisation, and musical decisions are studied in a developmental context. Here, too, the results are formative, but interesting musical patterns seem to develop at certain ages. These data, together with the findings by Kratus (1985a, 1985b), offer exciting avenues for future work.

Building Blocks for Theory

One fact that emerges from the literature outlined above is that there are no comprehensive, published models of creative thinking in music that serve as the basis for research and professional debate. What would be some of the assumptions for such a model? What would be its content? In order to generate possible answers to these questions, one might consider: (a) the involvements of man with music as art, (b) the enabling skills that are needed for creative thinking in music, (c) the nature of the thinking process itself, and (d) the enabling conditions.

Involvements

Few would argue that there are three principal ways that man involves himself with music as art:

> 1. *Composition.* The conception and recording of sound structures for presentation at a later time
> 2. *Performance-Improvisation.* The transmission of sound structures that are either composed previously or actually conceived by the performer at the time of performance
> 3. *Analysis.* The process of understanding and explicating sound structures in written, verbal, or (in the case of active listening) in mental form

Many who have studied and written about creativity in general argue for a distinction between creativity as *process* versus *product.* This is a legitimate distinction particularly if one is concerned with more singular matters of measurement, teaching strategy, or aesthetics. In generating overall theory, this distinction also plays a role in one's understanding of man's involvement with music, although the distinction in this case is more blurred. Composition, performance-improvisation, and analysis can be considered at the outset of creative thinking as goals of the creator—as *products* of the creator. At the same time, they define subtle and not-so-subtle differences in *process.* Any model that attempts to clarify creative thinking in music must start with the clear indication that the choice of involvement on the part of the creator implies both a product and a process.

Enabling Skills

With the involvement established, the author must rely on a set of skills that allow for the thinking process to occur. These skills form the basis of a *musical intelligence* and can be grouped as follows:

1. *Musical aptitudes.* Innate abilities to perceive auditory information, often measured by aptitude tests
2. *Comprehension of musical materials.* Cognitive facts that comprise the substance of music and often measured in achievement tests
3. *Craftsmanship.* The ability to use factual information in service toward specific musical tasks
4. *Aesthetic sensitivity.* The shaping of sound structures to capture the deepest levels of feelingful response, often referred to as *musicalness* or *musicality*

These enabling skills are used in slightly different ways, depending on the involvement of the creator. The composer, the performer, and the listener must all possess an understanding of the materials of music—rhythmic, melodic, harmonic, and timbral concepts. Craftsmanship and aesthetic sensitivity are, in turn, necessary for the composer and the improviser as the sound structures are shaped, organized, and woven into a formal whole. The performer who is interpreting written music must also be mindful of the aesthetic sensitivity found in the score, using the technical craftsmanship at hand to produce an artful interpretation. In order to make solid judgments about the music's content, those who listen and who analyze music must not only recognize the musical materials but also be mindful of the way the music is crafted to capture feeling.

Much of this is rather obvious and has been discussed by others in various ways before. In fact, the educational enterprise in music has been devoted almost exclusively to improving these enabling skills for each of the musical involvements. What has not received much study or attention by educators is the process by which these skills are used in creative thinking. What are the thought processes involved? Can they be taught? Observed? Measured?

The Creative Thinking Process

One key to understanding the creative-thinking process might lie in the psychological literature that addresses global intelligence. In his Structure of Intellect model, Guilford (1967, 1968) speculated on the existence of divergent and convergent production skills. Divergent thinking involves the generation of many possible solutions to a given problem—a kind of personal brainstorming. Convergent thinking, on the other hand, involves the weighing of those several possibilities and "converging" on the best possible answer.

In divergent thinking, imagination plays an important role, along with knowledge of the material itself. The obvious is noted, then placed "on hold" in favor of other possibilities, often without regard for tradition or common practice. At some point, however, this thinking process must cease in favor of a more convergent filtering. The mind must sift through the mass of possibilities in order to "create" a final solution.

It seems reasonable to consider that the composer, performer, and listener follow these paths with musical materials. This ability to move between convergent and divergent thinking is at the heart of the creative process for a musician. For instance, the composer may "hear" a musical idea, notate it, then form several possible alternatives for its musical permutation. Some of these possibilities will be rejected, some accepted and worked on more fully. Before the final version of the composition, many more musical ideas will be needed. Obviously, the enabling skills play an important role here, since the musical quality of the divergent and convergent thinking depends on the levels of aptitude, knowledge, craftsmanship, and aesthetic sensitivity. It is this interplay between creative thought process and skill that is vital. This creative process becomes a kind of "structured play" or "informed choice" that is driven by the level of enabling skill and the projected final product (involvement).

Of course, few people possess equally high levels of all the enabling skills. It is also true that many individuals are skillful with divergent operations but lack the ability to converge. For others, the opposite is true. The clearly creative person may be the one who possesses high levels of skill and who can move easily from divergent to convergent thinking in service to a musical goal.

Enabling Conditions

As the teacher and the researcher consider these possible bases for theory, other variables that are *outside* the creative process itself must be considered. Environmental effects would be included in this set of enabling conditions, as would a host of personal characteristics that are apart from musical substance. Such a list would include:

1. Motivational drives (both external and internal)
2. Personality factors (risktaking, spontaneity, openness, perspicacity, perfectionism, etc.)
3. Environmental conditions (financial backing, instrument quality, sound system, concert hall, etc.)
4. Subconscious and preconscious imagery

These variables mingle with enabling skills in delicate and profound ways that directly affect the thinking process. Such relationships vary from person to person and take different forms, depending on the involvement with music. A composer might be extremely motivated by commissions or dead-lines. A listener may be internally motivated by a desire to understand mus-ical structure. The performer's creativity might be influenced by a desire to understand musical structure. The performer's creativity might also be in-fluenced somewhat by a desire to perfect a technical passage or to try dif-ferent interpretations from the ones prescribed by a teacher. A supportive work environment for composers and performers is a clear example of ena-bling conditions of importance. Of course, such conditions are not absolute requirements for creativity but must be considered nonetheless.

Summary

A possible theory of the creative-thinking process in music might best be focused on a synthesis between divergent and convergent thought produc-tion. This synthesis is enabled by certain skills, innate and learned, and cer-tain personal and environmental conditions that are external to music. These bases for a model raise a number of interesting questions that can guide fu-ture paradigms:

1. Can these bases be explained in more detail and diagrammed in the form of a graphic model?
2. What specific differences would one postulate based on different product intentions? In other words, what differences are there between the crea-tive process employed by composers versus performers *versus* listeners?
3. What role does education play in this model? Can divergent thinking in music be taught?
4. Can the following be assumed?
   a. Creative process is measurable
   b. There are no gender differences
   c. Personality plays some role
   d. Cognitive intelligence is related to creative thinking in music, but not significantly so
   e. There are no racial or socioeconomic differences
   f. Creative-thinking ability in music is not significantly related to tradi-tionally measured music aptitude
   g. Creative-thinking ability in music is not related significantly to creative thinking in other fields

Future Directions

To answer these questions and others like them, continued research on the highest levels is needed. Theoretical discussion is important, and many competing theories should be forwarded. Such theories should be rooted in psychological and philosophical argument as well as informed practice and empirical study.

New approaches to data gathering are also important and should be combined with traditional experimental and descriptive methodologies. Two approaches that hold special promise for the future are ethnology and music technology.

Ethnology

The word *ethnology* has its roots in the classic study of anthropology. The *American Heritage Dictionary* defines ethnology as "the anthropological study of socio-economic systems and cultural heritage, especially of cultural origins and of factors influencing cultural growth and change in technologically primitive societies." The parallel in music that immediately comes to mind is the work and the stated mission of the ethnomusicologist. However, in terms of behavioral science in general and music behavior research in particular, the term has come to have a larger context than cultural heritage and includes study of technologically advanced societies. The topics of study might include such diverse concerns as children's play, music teaching style, musical affect, and—most important for this chapter—creative behavior.

What does an ethnographer do and how is the research accomplished? Ethnographers immerse themselves in a single or small number of settings for an extended period of time, collecting as much data as possible about what is observed. There are few preconceived ideas about what is supposed to be observed and there are often no stated hypotheses that are established before data collection. The system for data collection varies and is sometimes unspecified until the initial stages of observation. Typically the researcher uses a log or journal, audio and video tape recordings, or photographs. This information is summarized at the conclusion of the research and reported in expository style with a minimum of quantification. Theoretical implications for the research are considered as part of the ongoing process and are compared with existing theory on the topic.

For those whose primary research training and experience has been rooted in highly positivistic techniques, all of this may seem quite unacceptable. Behavioristic models that are highly structured, such as techniques of interaction analysis or other strategies based on behavioral intervention, use quite different techniques and assumptions about research design. The disadvantages of ethnographic research are clear for the positivist: lack of control, fuzzy methods of evaluation, no apparent basis for inductive logic, and little chance for exact replication. For the ethnographer, these shortcomings are understood but are seen as acceptable in light of the advantages:

1. More "humanistic" approaches to describing phenomena because of the nature of the actual experience being observed, preserved, and explained
2. The immediacy of the behavior observed, the reliance on first-hand observation of natural actions rather than performance on a written measure that might be obtrusive
3. Compatibility with the diversity (complexity) of the arts experience; stated another way, the ability to explain the richness of aesthetic response in a descriptive manner

These advantages hold special importance for research in creative thinking and behavior. Moorehead and Pond's work (1978) is probably the best example of this methodology in action. Using classic ethnographic techniques during a time when such strategies were not codified, Pond observed children improvising music in a natural, unstructured setting. The chronicles of these observations still provide a rich source of hypotheses for other forms of research today. Other examples include the more recent work of Flohr (1979), Webster (1983), and Kratus (1985a and b). Although these later projects do not employ all of the ethnographic procedures that are noted above, they are concerned with either natural settings, carefully designed (sometimes nontraditional) measurement techniques, or complex artistic response.

This line of investigation holds special promise for understanding creative thinking. Such studies may become more numerous in the coming years as this approach gains more acceptance and as technological advances continue. The use of sophisticated recording techniques that use advanced video tape machines will play a vital role. Microcomputers that can both generate stimuli and record the response to this stimuli will also be commonplace.

Computers and Technology

Computers, in their own right, will play a significant role in the future study of creative thinking. Microcomputers allow us to (a) present the user with creative, musical problems to solve; (b) record the reactions to and the solutions of these problems; (c) suggest alternative solutions; and (d) record and analyze these results in a number of ways.

Within the last two years, a method of interfacing a computer with a music keyboard has been developed, largely for the purposes of professional music studios and performance groups. This universal interface (known as

MIDI—Musical Instrument Digital Interface) holds great promise for research.

Imagine a young student seated at the music keyboard (perhaps a synthesizer) with a computer screen as his score. A fragment of music is played by the computer and a message requests that the student use this fragment to compose a short piece of music. The student experiments with this fragment until a version is completed. The computer displays the score and plays the completed version. The student experiments further until he or she is satisfied with the result. During this entire process, the computer keeps careful track of the composition process. At a later time, a researcher can "call back" the process and study it. Similar experiments might be considered for the performer, improviser, and listener.

These techniques are made even richer by the developments in laser technology for massive data storage and retrieval. The possibility for sensitive data gathering and analysis of complex music behavior is nothing short of spectacular.

The challenge is to recognize the strengths and weaknesses of the research and place what is of value together with other data as we advance theories and working models of musical ability. Music researchers *themselves* must be creative thinkers as they work with theories and research designs. This is not an easy task for many. The risks are great and the rewards may not always be clear. What is clear, though, is that few issues in our profession deserve a higher priority.

Part II
Philosophy of Music Education

5 Of Conceptions, Misconceptions, and Aesthetic Commitment

Abraham A. Schwadron

As indicated by a host of current reports from educational leaders and commissioned task forces at federal, state, and local levels, the national state of education—primary and secondary—is seriously threatened by qualitative and financial concerns.[1] Cited in this national debate are are several matters: mass illiteracy; lack of intellectual skills; grade inflation and decline in achievement; the need to attract talented teachers; the need for higher salaries and merit pay; educational improvements of conditions urged on by demographic changes; improved curricular directions in general, vocational, and college preparatory programs; advocacy for both public and private schooling; funding, budgets, taxes; basic learning; conflicting ends of practical skills on the one hand and scientific knowledge on the other; and inevitably, the place of educational "frills."

In the face of grand efforts to reform and improve schools, the demise of music and other arts education is once again imminent. At the least, it is in danger of extreme cutbacks in teachers and programs. In many locations, general music and basic art education is said to be on the brink of extinction. Since warnings about the state of music education have been issued over the past two decades, none of this should be surprising.

Still sounding are the signals sent out during the sputnik-initiated curriculum reform movement of the 1960s. What rescued music education then was a rethinking of its place as an essential entity in American education. Aesthetic values in the philosophy of music education were recognized as ends; aesthetic inquiry was recognized as means. For whatever reasons, neither the philosophical nor the pedagogical implications were examined rigorously enough for sufficient understanding and implementation (see Schwadron, 1973).

In many recent reports the "pro-arts citations" still address the concerns of aesthetic studies; of values and appreciation; of artistic experience and expression; of transcendent goals and uniqueness—"the potentiality for doing through the arts what cannot be done readily through the other fields" (Bolin, 1984, p. 12).

Statements of concern for music in education refer to its central place in the curriculum for its embodied values and approaches to knowledge—aesthetic knowing?—and humanizing experience—aesthetic experience? (Gardner, 1984). Similarly, others point up the intrinsic values that illuminate the human condition, the artistic impulse, the quality of aesthetic experience, and the responsibility of formal education for aesthetic inquiry and an appreciation of the arts (Lowry, 1984).

The statements are indicative of aesthetic essentials to qualitative living. They do not suggest the need for marching bands or for more and better performance. They view public accessibility and availability of the arts programs as essential. They refer not to passive concerns of entertainment but to active concerns for heightened experience; not to just liking or enjoying but to valuing (see Schwadron, 1985).

If the thrust of the present search for excellence is considered seriously, it should be clear that once again we are being challenged to examine our academic and musical goals and pedagogy, our deepest beliefs and current programs—all these, in view of a philosophy of music education supposedly already rooted in aesthetic inquiry and value. If the response of music educators, nationwide, is to be constructive, rather than defensive, then it must be recognized that our fundamental aesthetic commitments have not been met. There is evidence of philosophical inconsistency between what ought to be done and what is done; between desirably conceived educational purposes and actual programs and practices; between intramusical and extramusical understanding; between music education by media fallout and by public school instruction.

The winds of change are blowing stronger. Although they threaten, they also transmit a timely summons for philosophical and practical reconstruction. My purpose in this chapter is to consider several selected yet interrelated issues in music education that show confusion and conflict in matters of musico-aesthetic awareness. No polemical jeremiad, no panacea to rescue music education or proposal for a "new" philosophy is implied. Rather, the intent is to provide a better intellectual grasp and a revivification of that aesthetically charged philosophy of music education posed during the 1960s— one which is of inherent import to the collective conscience of musicians and music educators as well as to those supporters who have expressed themselves to the point in educational and public sectors.

I

The plain fact is that music continues to be important to American life. Any argument for the support of music education removed from that fact is naive. It would be difficult, however, to show that formal education (music instruction in the public schools) has been directly and responsibly involved with the shaping of the nation's musical tastes and values. I refer here to the lack of consistency between a relevant philosophy of music education upholding a desirable image of the musically educated and the prevailing curriculum of instruction toward this end.

On the other hand, the values of informal education (namely, the influence by exposure of mass media, MTV, Muzak, and electronic technology in general), concerned primarily with commercial rather than with aesthetic concerns, have been successfully realized in the dynamics of the marketplace. Here music is utilized as popular entertainment, as diversionary activities of industry and politics, in dentists' offices, elevators, and phone delays. Such nonart music has passed into the hands of the private music industry and consequently has become a public problem—one that has not been responsibly identified in music education. Although the effectiveness of teaching in formal education must be recognized, it must not be confused with the educational role of formal education.

Conventional (perhaps hopeful) thinking would have it that formal education is doing what cannot be (or is not being) done in informal education. Assumed in the former is an accessible (to all students, musically talented and otherwise), rigorous, systematic program of instruction in and about music—a balanced combination of knowledge, analysis, and creativity; of aural, perceptive, and performance skills; of music history, literature, criticism, theory, and philosophy-aesthetics. One would expect K–12 outcomes of formal music education to include (a) a sensitive awareness of various musical forms and styles in Western European as well as global contexts, and (b) a critical understanding of values and valuing as indicated by the concomitantly expanding field of contemporary aesthetic inquiry. Accordingly, and with due regard for the academic mantle characterizing the educational basics, music performance and music reading would be viewed as handmaidens to larger ends; medals, uniforms, and high-stepping marching bands would require the judgment of priority and place within the balanced academic program.

Music in formal education should function as the logical social agency for the transevaluation of socioartistic values, for the development of both the musically talented and the sensitive, discriminative, liberally informed consumer. None of these basic purposes is necessarily dependent on financial support or budgetary fluctuations. They do stand as a strong and vital educational need in response to the eccentricities and commercialism of American pop culture—the realm of informal education—where art is bought and sold as a commodity. Now, this is not to say that there need be a mutual nonassistance pact between formal and informal education. As a matter of fact, the technological potential of mass media, MTV, and satellite television, for example, for extending the benefits of formal education nationally and internationally, is rich and, by and large, remains untapped (Schwadron, 1976, pp. 21–29).

II

Behind the prevailing national effort to reform and improve the schools is the cry for excellence. Reports on the national music assessments published in 1974 and 1981 indicated that conditions were far from excellent. That there was little reaction from or action by music educators following these reports is unfortunate. The national assessments indicated flaws, not in how well talented Americans were performing music, but in how the publically educated masses emerged as "musically educated." Although they were not pointed out, these inquisitive directionals must have been clearly recognized: What is formal music education doing for the masses of listeners, music consumers, nonprofessionals? The studio (private) applied music teacher in informal education has been highly effective (and ultimately, most necessary) as both a complement of and alternative to school instrumental or vocal instruction, but what educational choices are there for the general music students? Why are the curricular priorities in music education so arranged? Who should be musically educated and in what manner? Who is to be held accountable for decision making? The questions are not new, but they still remain basic. Collectively, they spell out the responsible expectation of formal music education to serve, with "excellence," the sociomusical needs of the majority and plurality of general students in the public schools. There is no necessary educational bind whatsoever in this responsibility (a) to satiate the desires of youth for "their music"; (b) to urge values on to "better" music of a "higher" order; (c) to teach music as catharsis for minority needs of a socioeconomic nature, or as some form of ethnic tokenism; (d) to use music education nonmusically—that is, to teach democracy, reading, mathematics; or (e) to encourage habits leading to good breathing or proper ethical and moral behavior.

If these ideas are acceptable, then formal music education will need to take on a strong commitment not only to develop the musicality of individuals in rigorously perceptive ways but also to meet the musico-aesthetic needs of society in critically discriminative ways. Unlike mass media, formal music education is not driven by commercial interests. Its underlying (perhaps hidden) purpose is to educate for a musically articulate and aesthetically informed society. In the American system of education, it can do this best by including *all* music in the curriculum and approaching pedagogy— essentially as explored in this chapter, by a process of inquiry—by way of a transevaluation of values, however varied or argumentative. No one has a premium on the truth about the "good" in music. What is important is that young people become aware of this.

The public classroom is the proper, the only, teaching-learning setting where such musico-aesthetic commitment can be generated. Immediate concern by music educators should be directed to the philosophical import of this task (the why of music education) rather than to the pedagogical (the how). If we can agree on the former, the latter should present no formidable difficulty. In this regard the initial curricular suggestions by the Central Midwestern Regional Educational Laboratory (CEMREL) are exemplary. Here children are led to perceive art (music) in different ways so that they come to recognize that the "correct" answers to questions of artistic attitude, value, and so forth depend strongly on the way they look at (hear) aesthetic objects (Barkan, Chapman, & Kern, 1970, esp. pp. 27–35).

As pedagogues we are aware of how important the preschool, elementary, and junior high school years are to the chronological and maturational development of basic musical capacities and talents. We are also quite in agreement as to the kinds of technical skills in musical perception that are most necessary and to the kinds of instruction most effective to the development of musicality. Aural acuity remains prerequisite to all other aspects of music education. There is also nothing new here. Carl Seashore's studies during the 1920s pointed to the psychological grounds; and in 1936, Prall concluded the case for aesthetics:

> Thus technical training is very largely aesthetic, and sound aesthetics is largely technical. To consider training for appreciation radically different from technical training, and to be separately cultivated, is one of the obviously misdirected attempts that helps explain the often total lack of intelligent relation to the arts among civilized people who have had what are called fine opportunities. *Learning the structure of the scale in its actual heard nature as intervals in relations will do more for an appreciation of music than all the lectures in the world* [italics mine] even with musical illustrations drawn from classic works. For the lectures [teacher explanations] will be devoted to the verbal transfer of intelligent powers of musical apprehension, which is, if not a flat impossibility, at least an apparently hopeless enterprise. (Prall, 1967, p. 204)

Although Prall is stressing the problem of explaining the musical via the verbal (a matter also identified later by Charles Seeger in his "linguo-centric predicament"), his arguments for the education of skills in musico-aural perception are shared by studio teachers, professional musicians, critics, and astute listeners. Without aural acuity musico-aesthetic education is distant. We can and should be doing more in the elementary and junior high schools to develop both.

The development of skills in musical perception—for the general music student—has not been emphasized in the prevailing curriculum. Considering the assumed musico-aesthetic commitment of formal music education to the lay consumer, this development remains a sensitive point of inconsistency. Other matters of confusion in the general music program are already so traditionally rooted in practice that satisfactory solutions, within prevailing modes of and attitudes toward music education, are not likely to occur without difficulty.

For one, music educators have not demonstrated adequate and due concern for teaching excellence in respect to the needs of general music. The tendency has been to rationalize on weak musical footing and to compromise on frail educational grounds. To achieve the goals of mass musical literacy, discriminative values, and socioaesthetic sensitivity only the well-prepared music specialist will qualify. To invite the elementary classroom teacher to teach music for aural acuity is ingenuous. Consequently, one finds that curricular approaches tend to be tailored to simplistic levels of both teaching techniques and learning outcomes amounting to a better-than-nothing teacher attitudes and instructional outcomes. The standard college course(s) offered to introduce future elementary school teachers to music and music education (in methods? literature? theory? recorder?) has never been sufficient to the tasks as suggested here or to the host of already recognized creative curricular approaches—Contemporary Musicianship Project, Manhattanville Music Curriculum, Orff, Kodály. Nor is there any indication that certification requirements will change dramatically enough to provide for the prototypical musical and educational preparation necessary for any significant results.

Now, these arguments are not new. Given even a modicum of agreement on what ought to be the results of elementary music education, why are we not adamant in our stated beliefs and consequent actions? Why are we still teaching catch-all courses and writing more books on music fundamentals simplified for the classroom teacher? Why are we still preparing elementary music specialists when there is still a thread of belief that the classroom teacher is indispensable? When the position of the Music Educators National Conference (MENC), in 1972, was that "satisfactory instructional leadership can best be provided by [music] specialists," why do we persist in compromising, rationalizing, and procrastinating?

Another related issue, confused by statements of philosophical notion and actual teaching practice, is the very idea of a K–12 music curriculum providing for both the talented and the masses. It is clear that educational emphasis in music has been concentrated more on the former. General music classes, for the latter, are not offered beyond the eighth grade (in many locations, not beyond the seventh, if at all available in junior high school). Aside from questions of the quality of instruction and the lack of organized and sequential instructional musical learning at the elementary level, of critical concern is the increasingly obvious termination of music education at secondary levels for those students who do not sing or play an instrument. We are quite aware of the fact that there is little, if any, strong provision in the secondary school curriculum for a continuation of general music. Indeed, is anything now being taught geared to the sociomusical needs of the general music student that requires, or even suggests the need for, further study in history, literature, performance, theory, or musical creativity that presupposes sheer lay understanding (music appreciation)? Aside from the small, recently formed Society for General Music, who is disturbed about this situation? Who will produce a valid textbook for any of these areas to stand alongside the array of texts available in biology, English literature, calculus, and other basic studies? Indeed, given the lack of potential interest, who will publish such a text? Where is the registered concern among researchers and secondary teachers? Where are the exemplary programs?

Are financial and budgetary difficulties wholly to blame for the lack of a balanced and prioritized curriculum? Formal music education needs the benefit of enlightened thinking about its sociomusical responsibilities and philosophical-practical commitments to equality of opportunity—a basic democratic principle. The strongest case for general arts education programs is in its admirable aesthetic view and curricular purview: to serve *all* students in *all* grades, artistically talented or not. General music has not been successful in meeting these conditions (see Schwadron, 1982, pp. 175–192).

III

The role of performance—usually confused in the core issue of education or entertainment—warrants particular emphasis. Performance, per se, has become a highly successful branch of music education, one that flirts with professionalism, public relations, and director-conductor personality conflicts. Education in music via performance becomes so confused by way of contests, medals, winning awards, uniforms, travel opportunities, and so forth as to take on an inevitable nonacademic coloration—an educational frill. Its role has too often been defended as beneficial to good social, physical, and ethical development rather than for its own aesthetic-academic value. Conceptual ideation of such a value role by teachers, administrators, and parents tends to be faulty. Aesthetic understanding and related pedagogical refinement of the singular role of performance in musico-aesthetic education remain primary needs.

The concept of aesthetic education through performance stresses a laboratory rather than a mere rehearsal-concert approach to teaching and learning. The concept is based on the premise that the very making of music can be a valuable means of studying the aesthetic qualities of the music. The performance laboratory as the proper educational setting for this concept is envisioned as a prime opportunity for intimate contact with the actual shaping of and consequent sensitive interaction with sound properties. Conceptually it would allow (prioritize, it is hoped) curricular space in recognition of the unlimited potential for empirical understanding intrinsically characteristic of the aesthetic experience: feelingful reaction to music via syntactical relationships in the music (see Schwadron, 1982, pp. 187–189).

The concept is just as applicable to music education for student performers in general comprehensive high school programs as it is for those in high schools that center on the arts (music) for the talented. It calls attention to the selections of music for study purposes, for both musical and educational appropriateness. It focuses on musical expressiveness, aesthetic components in the musical structure, so often overlooked by the more obvious concerns with technical precision and concert scheduling (see Schwadron, 1969, pp. 109–122). A critical view at this juncture is imperative: The latter two, generally regarded as the reason for the place of music performance in education and the appropriate requirement of valuable rehearsal time, constitute a professional position.[2] The alternative, which would direct prime, valuable "rehearsal" time to laboratory activities for aesthetic inquiry, constitutes an educational position. The aesthetic alternative would also urge proper emphasis on ensemble music, put to rest the ills of band-feeder programs and conductor-teacher images, rationalize the education-entertainment dilemma, and allow for some vital reform toward a true equality of performance opportunity at all educational levels.

Because the laboratory concept needs the benefit of class time, actual concerts would require due limitation. From this perspective, public performances in education should be seen and heard not as entertainment but as capstone musical experiences, climaxing the aesthetic learning in the classroom (the performance laboratory)—ultimately a matter of value responses testified to not by the audience or the conductor but by the intrinsic, personal experiences of the students who are performing. To be sure, such a laboratory concept must be clear and acceptable to music educators and demonstrated by the most able in the profession so that exemplary approaches might emerge. It must also find its exploratory niche within the scholarly realms of academic research in music education.

But what is this method of "aesthetic inquiry" that provides the pedagogical key? Aesthetic knowing is nurtured by the very raising of questions—a process of inquiry suggesting that if we do not know all the answers to the meaning, value, expressivity, and so forth of music, why do we teach as if we do? The "right" questions expand conceptual understanding, imaginative inquiry, and intellectual curiosity. Further, they function to check dogmatic thinking and to direct inquiry not only to the musical object but also to the actual experience of the student. Some applications (for secondary school) can be gleaned from the following brief, generalized suggestions:

The aesthetic focus is on a piece to be "performed," "rehearsed," that is to say, studied. It is assumed that the aesthetic object (the piece of music) is educationally sound (playable, yet challenging) and of aesthetic value (of interest structurally and dramatically). In regard to the latter, it is the initial task of the teacher to answer the following: What can be learned from playing-studying this particular selection? Is the piece educationally and musically worthy? That is, is it a potentially important model for students to study (through directed performance and inquiry) for aesthetic properties such as these?

Expectation	Coherence
Delay	Ambiguity
Deception	Climax
Anticipation	Unity
Contrast	Stasis
Continuity	Dissonance-Consonance
Suspense	Tension-Release
Predominance	Norm-Deviation
Complexity	Emotions-Feelings

Pedagogical questions for teacher-student dialogue emerge accordingly:

Is this a "good" piece? Can the piece be "right" yet uninteresting? Why? Do you like it? Would you value it? What criteria—sensuous and structural—are involved in matters of liking and valuing? What in this piece is of tonal, textural, dynamic, temporal interest? In what ways?

Is there evidence of the aesthetic principle of economy of means? Of "less is more"? What is the artistic significance of this principle?

How is unity achieved? Is there evidence of variety? How does the introduction function? the principal theme and subthemes? the transitions? Why is contrast important?

What is expected by way of reaction in the climax? to the deceptive cadence? the anticipation, appoggiatura? the suspension? How can all these, as musical, structural terms, be performed so that they might be sensed more effectively?

Is there evidence of unity, variety, deception, suspense, expectation, tension, climax, and so forth in ordinary life experiences? How do these properties differ when they occur in musico-aesthetic experiences?

How do we explain the meaning of music verbally, if music is a nonverbal art? When words are sung is the result still music? How is the word meaning reconciled with the musical meaning? What is meant by patriotic or religious music? What are the intrinsic-extrinsic (primary-secondary, musical-extramusical, pure-functional, etc.) aspects that need to be considered?

What are the "right" answers? On what grounds? Are *all* reactions to music and descriptions of musical meaning shared? What conditions give rise to emotive reaction to music? Are these particular reactions inborn or learned? Are they universally shareable? Are feelings (general reactions like expectation, suspense) the same as emotions (specific responses like sadness, happiness)? Can music be sad? What criteria govern musical reactions, meanings, descriptions, taste and values? (See Schwadron, 1969; 1971; 1972; 1974.)

The query-based procedure is intended as a critical ground for probing fundamental aesthetic problems in and about music—not as a naive means of Socratic inquiry whereby immutable values are to be discovered by applying incisive questioning. In the performance laboratory environment, ideas, values, and reactions can be tested in unique contexts—in the very sounding, expressing, and study of the performance of and reaction to music. Important sections can be isolated; notes, tempi, cadences, and so forth can be purposefully omitted, altered, or otherwise focused upon—all for the express purpose of generating the aesthetic conditions basic to musico-educational activity.

Beyond the basic mode of inquiry directed to the aesthetic object under study are the larger concepts of the nature of music and the musical experience. These are uniquely suited to exploration in the performance laboratory environment, where sound materials can be sensitively manipulated to enhance discussion and evaluation of music. Matters aesthetically relevant to the music studied—stylistic, historical, theoretical—are quite admissible, for purposes of broadening the learning setting. In this respect, whereas personal biographies of composers or programmatic information would be questionable as relevant, understanding intrinsic to the aesthetic perception of the music under study would be essential. It is important in the laboratory study of the introduction to Beethoven's *Symphony No. 1 in C Major*, for example, to know the sociomusical expectancies of audiences in the composer's time to understand his adventurous deviation from the norm. To be theoretically cognizant of the subtle harmonic play—the deceptions and circuitous route to the tonic—is also necessary. But to perceive all this by way of one's participation in the musical event (which includes the further concern of dynamics and silences) is to invite a unique realization of that kind of experience called aesthetic. The uniqueness lies in the very aspect of performance.

Similarly, the teacher (director) might well introduce concepts, ideas, and arguments from the field of psychological-aesthetic theories of music—the fallacy of intention of the composer, psychical distance, play, empathy, cultural conditioning, expectation, musicality, virtual and literal time, aesthetic and ordinary experience, musical meaning and description, symbolism in music—and their significance in view of global man and his musics.[3]

When effectively realized, such an educational setting for music performance would be of high public regard. But reeducation of the public (the teacher too, of course) would be required. Administrative, parental, and school board personnel should be invited to exemplary laboratory classes so they might realize how music education via performance fulfills its necessary academic, aesthetic, social, and humanistic commitments.

What inhibits the realization of this conceptual approach? Beyond the personality complex (of the director-conductor) lies the more important problem of philosophic-aesthetic understanding. Given the theoretical and pedagogical field as stated, the need for an informed and sensitive teacher is evident; the need to correct extant misconceptions about the aesthetic underpinnings of music and education is fundamental. It is the lack of awareness that tends to confuse, oversimplify, and otherwise misdirect basic understanding, so that consequent action to direct performance toward its aesthetic-musical-educational commitment looms up as threatening or, at best, limited.

IV

In an earlier work I described the aesthetic-musical-educational complex as follows:

> The aesthetic function of music is inherently bound up with the uniqueness of the organization and deliberate control of sound, notated [as appropriate, culturally] by means of symbols, and characterized by the relationships of music to the human senses and intellect. Man's relationship to music becomes educational when succeeding generations are assisted in becoming critically intelligent about the social, emotional, and physical phenomena which characterize music as an art form. (Schwadron, 1967, p. 5)[4]

The passage suggests (albeit in summarized form, given its place in the original discussion) that an aesthetic commitment is intrinsic to education when music or art is the subject taught. As such, music education *is* aesthetic education.[5] It is assumed that the educational function of music in the schools is to teach music theory and to develop skills of musical performance not in isolation but in the aesthetic contexts of perception, meaning, reaction, criticism, experience, value.

The expression "music education *as* aesthetic education" emerged only gradually, following initial concerns raised in the now historically charged publication *Basic Concepts of Music Education* (Henry, 1958); in the report of the Yale Seminar on Music Education (1964); the Tanglewood Symposium (1967); and by a decade of concern over curricular reform. The expression is critically centered. It implies that music education has *not* met its aesthetic commitment and therefore needs to undergo revision; its nature and significance need to be reidentified and it must be rededicated to its educational purpose, namely, to help others to realize their own aesthetic experiences at increasingly sophisticated and subtle (hence, more significant) levels of response.

The meaning of the term *aesthetic education*, today has itself become confused within the welter of general arts programs.[6] The aesthetic thrust in music education seems to be contained in the argument about general arts programs. The latter are viewed as threatening because, if fostered, they might supplant some music programs, particularly performance. It is also argued that the problems in musical aesthetics call for instruction in the musical arts. To subsume them, however advantageously or theoretically, under multiarts education will not solve the primary charge identified in the aesthetic-musical-educational complex: Music education *is* aesthetic education. To delegate this educational responsibility under a generic arts umbrella is to water down the uniqueness of the musical arts in meeting its aesthetic commitment. But both the responsibility and the commitment require sensitive awareness, attitude, and professional decision.

It should be understood that what is suggested is not the teaching of aesthetics, per se, in any systematic sense (see Brameld, 1956, p. 235; Schwadron, 1967, pp. 61–62).[7] Rather, through the processes of study and analysis about the sensuous and structural content of music, the questioning of statements made about music, the discriminative perception of qualitative relations in the experience of each student—as applied to listening, performing, and composing—the field of aesthetics, as a broad philosophy of the arts in education, becomes properly engaged. It follows that teachers of music should have better than a nodding acquaintance with the aesthetics of music and the ways in which aesthetics and education relate.[8] Clearly, music theory and practice are so closely related that to rely merely on the latter would be oversimplistic. Too often the tendency to rely on the practical aspect alone has invited other modes of narrow conception resulting in the classic confusion between methods and music.

V

In the desire to put ideas into action, the aesthetic-musical-educational complex has been expressed in terse, formulated ways indicative of means and ends. Whereas a systematic synthesis of key terms relative to the realization of aesthetic value is helpful, naive interpretation can be wholly misleading. Bennett Reimer's concept that perception plus reaction result in value is a case in point. His reasonable assertion is simply that reaction is difficult to teach, particularly, when measurement and behavioral overtness are involved. When this becomes misinterpreted by conventional wisdom, such as "aesthetic reactions cannot be taught," confused mentation is suspected. Unfortunately, the very misconception has been cited in too many curriculum guides in reference to aesthetic approaches in music education.

The original statement must be understood in the context of a host of variables. Reactions (emotions, feelings—the hub of the musico-aesthetic experience) are learned, not inborn. They emerge from cultured conditioning. Where learning occurs some mode of teaching (e.g., conditioning) is in effect. Surely, reactions in a theoretical, psychological, and clinical sense can be programmed and learned, hence taught. (Obviously this approach is removed from reality and also most undesirable.) The commercial marketplace of mass media can also function as a teaching-learning environment bearing on mass reactions to music. Here, exposure—both powerful and problematic—is the teaching methodology. Thus, reactions as well as popular tastes are learned in informal education—the result of some manner of teaching, however indirect, yet effective. Mere exposure can breed parochialism and contempt; lack of exposure can inhibit adequate understanding. Yet either can function to influence liking of some kind of music. Because mere liking is an insufficient condition for valuing, neither would be acceptable for discriminative levels of musico-aesthetic knowing and truly individualized modes of value making.

There is no reason to believe that music educators in the context of formal education cannot be centrally and directly involved in the development of musical value criteria as well as in the shaping and refining of musico-aesthetic reactions. Students can be taught to identify shared reactions as well as those that are highly subjective. They can learn to differentiate primary (musico-structural) from secondary (extramusical) meanings in music. They can be taught to discern intrinsically generic feelingful reactions to music

(tension, anticipation, suspense, deception, etc.) from extrinsically parti-
cularized emotive ones (love, fear, sadness, joy, etc.) and, consequently, to
become further involved with music, critically and introspectively, that is,
with their own, individual reactions. Although exposure theory may suggest
something else, informal education in the American pluralistic society cannot, in good conscience, force-feed predigested value assumptions and attitudes about the musical arts—including reactions. But its aesthetic
methodology embraces the transevaluation of ideas—a setting where the
environment of musical reactions (experiences, etc.) should be argued sen-
sibly and sensitively refined. And such a setting is bound to tax teacher attitudes and understanding in engaging ways.

Expertise and connoisseurship are expected of the music teacher. He or
she is sure to have personal tastes, values, and reactions; and herein lies the
rub: Considering the teacher's position on the musical "good," the pluralistic
values evident in American democratic society, and the lack of any fixed
agreement in representative aesthetic theory, what sanction is there to teach
musical values, reactions, and so forth in the public schools from any singular point of view? The challenge to formal music education posed by the
idea of the transevaluation of values, however, does charge the teacher with
engaging young people in the reasoned determination of their own musical
value criteria. As such, personal values of the teacher should be placed "up
front"—along with the host of choices—so that these too can be demonstrated and "tested."

If a teacher believes that Bach and Brahms ought to be preferred over the
popular array of rock and country alternatives, he or she must make the case
for this clear, leaving the ultimate value decision to the student. The development of appropriate criteria for judgment and judicious analytical applications—the means toward discriminative values—remains, however, the
educational responsibility. This is not to say that the desirable educational
goal may well be a broad acceptance of a variety of relative values and musical reactions unmarred by egocentricities, ethnocentricities, dogmatisms,
and parochialisms.

The musico-aesthetic education of values and the concomitant shaping of
reactions places a heavy burden of responsibility on the public school
teacher not to dictate one aesthetic position but to expose alternatives; not
to avoid one's personal position but rather to introduce this in the teacher-
student process of aesthetic inquiry into the very search for values—a key
concern in current criticism of formal music education.

In short, aesthetic reaction can be and is being taught and learned in both
indirect and subliminal ways. The kind of teaching and the effectiveness of
the learned outcomes are questionable. Music educators would do well to
avoid the errors of oversimplification and address themselves to the chal-

lenge of grasping the nature of the musico-aesthetic experience and helping students to understand, hence refine, their reactions—a principal source of tastes and values.

Similar confusion exists with the desire for the objectification, quantification, and ultimately, the accountability of the aesthetic. Neither the religious nor the aesthetic experience can be tied to any fixed formula: "1-2-3-thrill!" The experience called aesthetic (and the aesthetic high) has been testified to empirically by a sufficient number of people to warrant its subjectively valid existence—whether explained intuitively, spiritually, or pragmatically. Some believe that what makes art great is the very thing one cannot explain or even preplan. Others hold that because such experience cannot be manifested overtly, and hence measured, it does not exist. In the latter regard, there is a strong inclination to lean toward Bennett Reimer's observation: "I have little doubt that some people who measure attitudes and tell us they are measuring subjective aesthetic reactions have simply never had an aesthetic experience" (Reimer, 1971, p. 85; see also Arnstein, 1966, and Swanwick, 1974).

VI

Inevitably, serious contemplation of musico-aesthetics in formal education must lead to philosophical considerations. Any philosophy of American music education marked by an emphasis on aesthetic perception and inquiry (sparked by the goal of discriminative value criteria) should then embrace the socioethnic plurality that so characterizes American democratic society. It follows that any notion of philosophical monism[9] should be defensible on pluralistic grounds reflecting a diversity of values—tutored and untutored, Western European and globally inclusive. As such, a monistic philosophy, democratically and pluralistically conceived would embrace cultural relativism and a transevaluation of that broad realm of attitudes and postures characterizing the musical behavior of man, worldwide. Inconsistent with this would be the dictation or insistence of any one particular set of absolute standards characterizing the musical "good." Severely questioned would be the utter philosophical (as well as historical, cultural, musical, and, of course, educational) determinants in support of such manner of monism.

A number of questions signal the confused grounds of conception: Do music educators stand philosophically united in regard to the musical "good"? about educational ends and means? Is there sufficient agreement on "enlightened cherishing"? "cultivated connoisseurship"? "great books"? musical "universals"? "international musicianship"? the musical and the extramusical? What and whose values are recognized as worthy of educational nourishment and development in formal instructional settings? How are these questions to be decided in the democratic society?

The aesthetic emphasis in contemporary philosophy of music education shows the broad influence of Meyer (1961), Langer (1953, 1957), Broudy (1958), Schwadron (1967), Reimer (1970), and others. One strong theory of musical meaning and value, based on Meyer's aesthetic posture of absolute expressionism and adapted by Reimer, still prevails. It should be understood that, aside from its validity in Western European music (principally as applied to common practice), absolute expressionism is simply not universally applicable. It is also important to note that following a reconsideration of non-Western European music, Meyer did modify his earlier views. (See Meyer, 1960; Schantz, 1983.)[10]

As a theory, however important and even applicable in its own right, absolute expressionism should be viewed as limited; relative, not absolute; Western European, not global. Its educational significance must also be considered with cogent concern for its appropriate application. The large bulk of music, worldwide, calls for musical understanding (of meaning, value, etc.) on other grounds, more contextual and even extramusical.

However argumentative, music educators in various parts of the world understandably are guided professionally by indigenous sociocultural particulars that are indicative of certain understandings, values, and educational outcomes. Philosophical positions are directly related to and influenced by political systems. In the United States, public school music educators are not obligated, legally, politically, or artistically, to accept any one set of beliefs about either the purpose of education or the nature of music. In fact, aesthetic theories like absolute expressionism (which appears to be set forth as fundamental to the prevailing idea of philosophical monism) are neither properly understood nor seriously practiced, if they are noticed at all. Nor has there been any recognition of or serious concern registered as to any need for philosophical monism. Organized research agencies such as the Special Research Interest Groups (SRIGs) sponsored by the Music Educators National Conference have not even identified the place of philosophy per se within its designated structures.

What seems to be suggested by the concept of monism is rather a loosely conceived philosophical consensus of recognition and consistency of beliefs about music and formal education within the framework of the American democratic pluralistic society. Given the inherent complex of problems involved, it is doubtful that monism will ever be realized in a fully acceptable and practiced sense. What remains is the desire and need for at least a valid, agreeable basis for a philosophy that would (a) recognize the aesthetic nature of music as the core of means and ends; and (b) allow for the transevaluation of values, value systems, aesthetic theories, and sociocultural factors that bear on these. The rationale for such a philosophical position in formal music education lies within the kind of premise posed by Stolnitz:

> No single theory of art and aesthetic experience is completely adequate and comprehensive. . . . Each theory asks different questions about the art-object and throws light upon different aspects of it. Each theory lends itself readily to the analysis of a certain kind of style of art. . . . We should accept and indeed welcome the plurality of theories of art. (Stolnitz, 1960, pp. 201, 205–206)

The statement is sociologically, musically, and educationally logical. It is defensible on democratic, pluralistic, and globally inclusive grounds. It upholds the importance of aesthetic inquiry, informed awareness, and attitude. It implies an educational obligation to explore value systems and the environment of musico-aesthetic preferences and theories. From such a base of common understanding, the potential for revitalizing an aesthetic philosophy of music education is hopeful and still promising.[11]

VII

Most recently, an alternative to *aesthetic philosophy* (a new, redundant term—since aesthetics is a branch of philosophy—now on its way to coinage along with *aesthetic education*) has been introduced in music education by way of utilitarianism. The latter involves a rationale that has guided music school music from its acceptance into the Boston school system in 1838 until the advent of John Dewey's reconstructionism (1957) and the revitalization of the aesthetic (Henry, 1958). What has actually emerged is the old and labored argument over utilitarian versus aesthetic purposes (see Mark, 1982. For contrasting arguments, see Coates, 1983; Elliot, 1983; Knieter, 1983; Phillips, 1983). Although this dispute deserves full attention, comments here will be limited to essential, current ideas in dispute.

The reactionary utilitarian view proposes a retreat from the aesthetic commitment in education to the functional: patriotism, good citizenship, national pride, team effort, racial understanding, improved reading, good breathing and posture, proper social and moral habits. A more conservative position suggests that aesthetics and utility be embraced in a new, corrective philosophical alternative. Reasons for both the reactionary and the conservative positions seem to be drawn from historical and contemporary determinants: respectively, the utilitarian roots in American music education and the current demise of music education in many of the nation's public schools. Both tend to offer loose discourse in place of aesthetic understanding; hyperbole and understatement, rather than keen insight and analysis. In summary, the major arguments for utilitarianism are these:

1. The aesthetic emphasis in music education has not assumed a societal responsibility
2. An aesthetically based philosophy of music education stresses music for music's sake; it is valued for its purposefulness and lack of utility
3. The aesthetic position does not provide a useful theory for maintaining music in the curriculum
4. Aesthetic education is founded on a philosophy of art rather than on a philosophy of education
5. The aesthetic de-emphasizes the role of music performance
6. The utilitarian concepts—intellectual, moral, and physical—employed throughout the history of American music education are better understood (by teachers, principals, and school boards) and, therefore, should be employed to save the music curriculum

The arguments overlap. Collectively, they reveal misconceptions and nebulous understanding about the field of aesthetics and its relation to music. Beyond, they make little reference to problems of formal and informal music education or to the attendant concerns about musical values. Although the basic points in contention have already been addressed in the foregoing discussion, some additional comment seems appropriate:

1. Modern musical aesthetics can be agreeably interpreted as "the study of the relationship of music to the human senses and intellect" (Apel, 1972, p. 14). Within the purview of the field, questions are raised about the nature, expression, value, and so forth of music and musical behavior and theories posed (indicative of some positions, e.g., heteronomous or autonomous) in regard to the questions. One is quite apt to find that there is no singular aesthetic problem, theory, or position that is acceptable as *the* most important. Ergo, "art for art's sake" as an aesthetic concept of considerable substance is only one—within a wide gamut of ideas, problems, theories, and subtheories equally as complex and intriguing. Its direct counterpart is that of music (art) as functionalism, contextualism, or utilitarianism, that is, "art for our sake." Both are subsumed under the generic aegis of aesthetic inquiry. In contemporary American education all such problems, globally inclusive, are admissible. To teach on the basis of art for art's sake is, then, to accept the one aesthetic point of view. Is this *really* observable in American music education? Educational philosophy in the Soviet Union, for example, blanketing music education, is socialist realism—a politically inclined theory of art based on aesthetic values of the masses. This theory applies to all Soviet education and is truly "accepted." Have we truly accepted art for art's sake in theory and practice?

Now, the archenemy of aesthetics is not utility, or function, but the boring, the toilsome, the humdrum, the work-laden—in other words, nothingness. The aesthetic issues remain open; the debate over aesthetic theory continues, as it should with any lively art.

2. Confusion becomes evident in the naive interpretations of such sloganized statements as "music for music's sake," valued for "its (extramural) purposefulness." Neither of these is literally acceptable. On the contrary, it should be understood that the aesthetic functions foremost to serve the individual and, inevitably, the betterment of society. Concern for the individual musico-aesthetic experience is fundamental in theory and educational practice. The ultimate disposition of the sociomusical estate of humankind is involved in an inextricable relationship of human beings to their musical environment, notably as contributing members of society.

Theoretically the idea of music for music's sake itself can be regarded along a continuum running from a pure interpretation of sound in isolation, at one end, to a more expressively centered position on the other. As discussed, absolute expressionism is one prevailing theory that is, in effect, a rationalization.[12] Far from lacking purpose in music education, it does underscore the need for aesthetic awareness, the significance of the heightened musical experience, artistic quality, values, and the attendant development of perceptive skills. Logically, all these are qualified by the theory itself. But the outcome direction should be clearly understood as purposefully pointing to the individual—the shaping of *his or her* aesthetic and musical reactions—to *his or her* values and the eventual benefit to society in general; not to some abstract or isolated or dehumanized concept of music.

The aesthetic argument "art for *our* sake" suggests that art cannot be isolated from ordinary matters of life: "Art after all, like the Sabbath, was invented to serve man, and not the other way around. . . . If beauty is to enter our lives . . . it must do so within the context of use" (Morris, 1961, p. 239).[13]

The educational implications in this consideration are *not* wholly removed from the artistic (aesthetic, musical); rather, they are directed to artistic concepts of utility and function that may range from improving the aesthetic environment in school to supporting the marching band.

The argument concerning the intrinsic and extrinsic purposes of music as art is likely to occur, for instance, over whether the school orchestra is deemed more valuable (in terms of financial, curricular support) than the marching band. The separation of the utilitarian and the aesthetic becomes more pronounced, however, when educational purposes are admittedly identified as nonmusical (extrinsic); for example, the excitation of fans at athletic events.[14] Any conservative conception blending aesthetics and utility will need to show the critical degree of compromise; in many affairs of life and music the line between the two is dotted.

3. To suggest any philosophical alternative that would isolate music education from music (or to attempt to move the wheels of history back to Lowell Mason's time) is sheer folly. Too often, the haste to implement new, vaguely understood ideas has been characterized by faddishness and simple conformity—possibly for the sake of survival—with the changing pressures governing educational reform movements. Viewed from the aesthetic commitment, musical principles should not be sacrificed on the altar of political, financial, or educational expediency. In spite of the historical accounts of utilitarianism in music education, a hidden, yet discernible premise of musical (surely, aesthetic) integrity has always been present.

To the extent that music, for whatever educational purpose, becomes removed from its aesthetic nature, it becomes something other than music education. Whereas the values attributed to the aesthetic experience per se are upheld as musically intrinsic, other values associated with or in reference to patriotism, ceremony, good social habits, and so forth are generally regarded as extrinsic. Learning a second language through singing may be an enjoyable way to learn the language, but it is not the best way to learn music. The critical matters in this regard involve the focus of instruction, teacher expertise, and the very need for a program of public instruction in music.

Accordingly, the question of whether the marching band is "musical" suggests that this organization (in its popular form) flirts with the extrinsic—that is, the extramusical. To use music as a pleasant, even safe way to induce sleep—something testified to by a good many people—is one thing. To teach for this outcome in formal education is something else. If alternatives are to be considered they should be sought within an aesthetic framework where the educational focal point remains the matter of intrinsic musical values. For example, if the concept of a transevaluation of values is more acceptable than any one value system, then relativism would be better than absolute expressionism as a theoretical basis for a philosophy of music education. [15] Nor is it impossible that both can coexist successfully in mutual and appropriate accord.

What is most puzzling in this stream of thought is that it is the music educator who is suggesting a reversion to the utilitarian—the nonmusical, the nonaesthetic—so that music education might overcome its current problems. Better wisdom suggests that what needs to be sanctioned is keener comprehension of musico-aesthetics and its educational implications. Most recently, contemporary educational leaders (like Mortimer Adler, Ernest Boyer, and John Goodlad) have expressed the unique roles for the arts in education: to address questions of value, beauty, and goodness; to challenge and extend human experience; to develop the skills essential to hear acutely and feel sensitively via nonverbal symbol systems like music; and to nurture aesthetic appreciation—an enlightened understanding of the processes of decision making and valuing in music and the arts. It is important to note that utilitarian values such as good citizenship, improved reading scores, and sheer need to release emotions are not cited by foremost educational scholars as substantive reasons for supporting music in the public schools. (See Bolin, 1984.)

Notwithstanding the views of educational leaders, some music educators (not parents or principals) still tend to bypass the aesthetic uniqueness of music for its tenuously (and questionably) functional uses. Music in the schools has also been deemed necessary because of its value to education in other academic subjects. Whatever the underlying reasons for all this (and the grand suspicion is that of shaky grounds of personal belief in and experience with music), it is very often the school music teacher who advises (convinces) the principal of the philosophical and practical "good." No amount of theoretical discourse on the philosophy-aesthetics of music will be effective without the intelligent, sensitive, and effective teacher who recognizes music for what it is and is not. If for no other reason, those responsible for the preparation of future music teachers must find ways to attract superior, talented students to the profession. *Res ipsa loquitur* (the thing speaks for itself).

Postlude

Will music education survive the present crisis? If so, with what philosophical perspective? With what course of action? With what ultimate impact?

For some, the foregoing discussion will give rise to a sense of déjà vu and perhaps a bit of frustration. Almost 20 years ago Harry Broudy said:

> The existence of powerful mass media able to shape the values of multitudes possessing political and economic power but untutored taste is as explosive a threat to rational democracy as an unlettered public was thought to be 50 years ago. Aesthetic illiterates are just as dangerous as intellectual ones; perhaps even more so, considering how closely choice and feeling are related to each other. (1966, p. 17)

Clearly, Broudy's observation remains not only timely but, considering the already established impact of contemporary technology in communications, also formidable. We are now living in an acculturated "global village." There is hardly an airport in the world that does not greet visitors with some form of pop music. At the 16th biennial conference of the International Society for Music Education, Tatsuko Takizawa (a Japanese official in public communications) spoke of the impact of Western acculturation in Japan since the Mejii Restoration of 1968. Western music was adopted in the Japanese public schools and remains impregnated in music education and in mass media. The latter do not offer the necessary programming to balance this with traditional Japanese music. Although there is evidence of some bimusicality, notably among musicians in the Shinto temples and the Imperial Household, music education (either via the public schools or public communications) is not involved. According to Takizawa, a resulting gradual erosion of value for traditional Japanese music, particularly in the younger generation has taken place. The average Japanese student (similar to his or her American counterpart) spends an amount of time viewing television equivalent to or more than that required in his formal schooling.

More than ever, young people today need to know when and why they have accepted certain value judgments. They need to develop sensitive aesthetic attitudes and discriminative value criteria. They need to differentiate between likes and values. Who will help them? What kind of educational setting will allow (indeed, urge) the teacher to maintain (and defend) his or her position, and to examine value alternatives removed from the dangers of dogmatism? In no minor way do the musical arts, so deeply related to the biological core of humankind, loom up in their potential importance to the education of values.

In his philosophy of social and educational reconstructionism, John Dewey recognized the dynamics of sociocultural change—in crisis and tension in human affairs—and suggested that philosophy should indeed be connected with, not removed from, such change. To be sure, the challenge of formal music education—particularly in view of its potentially aesthetic, value-centered perspectives—has been extended once again. Perhaps from the current search for educational excellence fresh opportunities for understanding, introspection, and commitment will occur.

New guidelines for recognizing arts electives in high school graduation requirements and university admissions programs have already been developed in some states and are under serious legislative consideration in others. Concomitant with these adoptions are the expectations that the music (and other arts) courses will show substantive improvements in the quality of "aesthetic education." The curricular actions are being taken not as token expressions of interest in the arts but because of the scant attention given to the "aesthetic education" of all secondary students—whether or not they are preparing for higher education.

Typically, in California the focus (at least, theoretically) has been on liberally educated students and their needs: "aesthetic perception," "creative expression," "arts heritage," "aesthetic valuing." Arts courses, to be worthy of acceptance are expected to nurture a broader [than the mere completion of an isolated project] aesthetic vision through the development of perceptual differentiation, critical insight, understanding of a particular art form within a cultural and historic context, as well as techniques for artistic production of performance. (Stewart, 1984, p. 2)

Courses in the visual and performing arts (dance, drama-theater, music, and visual art) are to show applicability to such fundamental art components as perception, criticism, creativity, and history. Further, the California guidelines state: "Courses which are primarily recreational, athletic, or body conditioning are not acceptable visual arts and performing arts electives" (University of California, 1984). It is most interesting to see just how the course proposals meet these conditions and to compare them with proposals made to a similar end elsewhere.

The latent impact of (state and national) legislation—for critical redirection at all levels of music education—is unprecedented in history. But philosophy is a means of effecting change by persuasion, not legislation. The implications for change—for a coherent, sequential K–12 program, for aesthetic realization in performance, for teacher expertise—are persuasive and dramatic in scope. The aesthetic direction is positive: a renascence inviting creative thinking. The transevaluative possibilities of cross-cultural aesthetic inquiry, for example, are yet to be explored.

Is it not possible for children to "test" the hypothetical universality of aesthetic principles, e.g. economy of means (and its postulate, "less-is-more") . . . with various musical examples? Is the Western notion of unity in variety so far removed from the Indian concept of variety in unity? (Or the Western notion of music as sounds in motion, from the African, motion in sounds?) Can children not perceive the drone functions of the Indian *tambura*, and the Chinese *sheng* or the fundamental in the Bulgarian *gaida* . . .? Can children not perceive, understand and respond aesthetically to the logical and artistic ways man has organized his music, e.g. Javanese coltomic structure, Indian *alap* and *gat*, Western sonata-allegro? Can we not explore *with* children musical and extramusical ideas of aesthetic sensibility so that liberal realizations of human commonalities and differentiations serve to extend and to refine personal experience and, hence, to educate for "international musicianship"? What avenues of research are necessary? (Schwadron, 1974, p. 10)[16]

Philosophical and practical decisions on such ideas—considered now—may well affect the status of music in the public schools. Will music educators, at all levels, accept the prevailing challenge as an opportune time to clarify thought and, accordingly, to modify the unique role of formal music education? In speculation, former MENC president Robert Klotman stated:

Today's schools will not fit tomorrow's needs. . . . We are going to have to find ways in music education to resolve the issues of today or there may not be a

role for music education in 2025. Our major obstacles are inertia, compla-
cency, smugness and general satisfaction with our current state of affairs.
(1976, pp. 19–20)

Klotman's "obstacles" are recognized as descriptive of the status quo.
With some effort and much hope, they need not prevail. There is sufficient
documentation in the brief history of music education in the United States
to demonstrate that music educators are not intransigent. In fact, adapta-
bility within the dynamic mainstream education—apart from the sociomusical arguments raised here—has been the characteristic posture. Music
education is poised for change. We can begin by challenging our conventional wisdom and making fundamental reforms in our thinking and curricular practices.

The gut question becomes increasingly more crucial: Should music education take its lead from the external dynamics of educational change or from
the internal nature of music itself? And there are related questions: What
are we doing? What should we be doing? What kinds of understanding—
musical, aesthetic, utilitarian, societal, educational—are fundamental to
music educators as well as to principals, parents, and the general public?
How is aesthetic sensibility in a technocratic world to be preserved? What
is the real confusion between education and society? between formal and
informal education? between aesthetic and ordinary experience? between
the general classroom teacher and the special music teacher? What really
inhibits a K–12 music curriculum? Why is there a gap between what researchers are studying and what teachers are doing? Are our conceptions of
music education really misconceptions—indicative of faulty constructs of
theory and practice? If so, why?

The questions are hardly exhaustive. In the present format they serve to
introduce individual presentations and studied views by those invited to
participate in the philosophical sector of the Alabama Project: Music, Society, and Education in America. However varied in either scope or direction, the topical papers are mutually inclusive. They are posed as processes
of critical inquiry rather than scientific conclusions. They should be received as potential ideas functioning to open and clarify avenues of philosophical thought and also as recommendations addressing needs for
practical concerns and exemplary models. The kinds of questions raised, in
all likelihood, will anticipate no final answers. But they should serve to indicate contradictions and confusions and thus to allow for valid, dependable
guidelines to beliefs underlying actions.

They also function to remind us that perhaps philosophizing is not something that can or ought to be done *for* the music educator. All things considered, one's philosophy of music and music teaching is quite personal. When

rigorous self-inquiry is applied, important and useful answers do emerge for the individual and, in time and with hope, for the profession.

No one ever said that philosophizing was easy. Suffice it to recall an old Yiddish saying: "The truth leads a hard life."

Notes

1. This is not to dismiss two recent critiques of higher education, calling for more emphasis on the liberal arts and for a concentration on excellence in teaching and research. Reports from both the National Endowment for the Humanities and the National Institute of Education warn of the stultifying emphasis on professional training and of the need for liberal education characterized by knowledge of the common threads of civilization offered in the humanities and the liberal arts.

2. The technical levels of professional quality achieved by some junior and senior high school instrumental performing organizations are remarkable. In many cases, private instruction (in some, similar brand instruments—to avoid tuning problems) is required for membership.

3. This is not to suggest that philosophical theories in music are not worthy of inclusion. In the context of the Beethoven example, the ontological question—where is the *real* Beethoven *Symphony No. 1?*—should serve to whet appropriate inquiry as to musical reality, memory, imagination, as well as to related matters of notation, interpretation, and authenticity.

4. As understood today the statement will stand firm for Western European traditions. From a world view, some points—e.g., those indicated for notation—require the benefit of qualification.

5. I can recall vividly the reaction of some of the music faculty at the University of California, Los Angeles, fifteen years ago, when I proposed the establishment of a new course, "Aesthetic Education." My colleague Mantle Hood responded with the cogent and rhetorical question: "Is not *all* music teaching aesthetic education?"

6. The flood of terms descriptive of "aesthetic education" include: arts in general education, allied arts, related arts, integrated arts, integrated art studies, fine arts, combined arts, performing arts, arts programs, comprehensive arts, humanities, interrelated arts, interarts programs, correlated arts, complete arts, unified arts, multiarts programs, and multidisciplinary arts. No firm distinctions, of category or limitation, prevail.

7. The possibility of a high school class in aesthetics—the study of theories, problems, social practices, mass values—is worthy of curricular consideration.

8. Such a course of study required in the preparation of the music teacher would be ideal. Although much can be gained by personal, intensive, reading in the critical literature on the aesthetics of music, sources treating the practical and applicative aspects of music are not readily available.

9. Assumed by this term is a mundane meaning associated with professional solidity and unity of thought about and approach to music education, rather than the ontological view of ultimate substance or other ideas of the unitary organic whole.

10. Schantz reports on a research interview with Leonard Meyer at which time Meyer commented on some changes in his thinking, namely about musical value: "I have become more relativistic with respect to value. Value depends more on context than I thought. It is related to richness rather than to mere complexity" (1983, p. 203).

11. The seminal directions for an aesthetic philosophy in music education were initially brought forth in two major works: Schwadron, 1967, and Reimer, 1970.

12. The theory obtains from Meyer (1961) under the premise, applicable to the absolute-referential continuum, whereas "almost all referentialists are expressionists, believing that music communicates emotional meanings, not all expressionists are referentialists" (p. 3). That is, musical expression (meaning, reaction, and value) is to be centered in the intrinsic experience of a subject with the music itself (absolute, formalistic—intramusical) rather than with referential ideas removed from the sound structure (extramusical).

13. The quotation also points up the need for a firm understanding of distinctions between aesthetic and ordinary experiences.

14. This is not to say that some other, nonartistic, quasi-aesthetic idea might not be served—for example, one based on the emotional high sought out by football (particularly home team) enthusiasts. Whether this end is acceptable as a valuable outcome of music education is in contention.

15. I dealt with relativism as a speculative philosophical position for contemporary music education in an earlier work (Schwadron, 1967). Given the acceptance of world music cultures—art, folk, popular, ritual, hybrid—in the American public school curriculum and the liberal recognition of globally pluralistic aesthetic values, the case for relativism becomes increasingly strengthened and unavoidable.

16. For a summary of my publications on this topic, see Schwadron (1984).

6 Aesthetics and Utility Reconciled: The Importance to Society of Education in Music

Michael L. Mark

Historical Aspects of Music Education Philosophy

Since the middle of the 1950s the literature of the music education profession has been supportive of a philosophy of music education based on aesthetic principles. It seems reasonable to state that the need to base the teaching of music on its own inherent aesthetic content, rather than on a utilitarian or instrumental justification is obvious to virtually all music educators who are familiar with the literature and have seriously examined the subject in their own minds. It is to be hoped that every music educator, regardless of whether he or she is familiar with the literature of music education philosophy, has undergone a self-examination of basic beliefs in a profession that offers gratification to the heart and soul but provides only minimal economic satisfaction. Why would one spend a professional lifetime teaching music if not for the belief that music is of such profound importance to his or her fellow humans that knowledge of it is worthy of a lifetime commitment? There must be a philosophical commitment to music and music education for one to dedicate a lifetime of meaningful work to the profession.

The phrase *profound importance* identifies the aspect of music education philosophy that has supported and kept viable the profession of music education throughout Western history. It is related to the term *utilitarian,* which refers to the profound importance of music education to society, rather than to the promotion of such benefits as described in the historic report of the Boston School Committee (1838), which stated that music in the schools would satisfy the threefold standard against which all school subjects must be measured: "Is it intellectual—is it moral—is it physical?" (p. 123). Although music education probably still satisfies that threefold standard, we are beyond such unsophisticated justification. We recognize the intrinsic aesthetic value of music to human beings and base our philosophy of music education on it. *Utilitarian*, therefore, means not the extrinsic benefits gained from the study of music but the value of aesthetic development to the individual and, by extension, to society. It is the individual whom we educate in music, not society, and not ensembles of students. The study of music leads one to self-expression, self-fulfillment, and self-development. These are benefits to the individual, not to the public. If a large proportion of citizens in a society is capable of self-expression, self-fulfillment, and self-development, we would expect such a society to have been influenced by the educational system that prepared people to take responsible, fulfilling, and satisfying roles in it. Music education plays an important role in preparing such citizens. Society supports music education because it serves society through its influence on the individual. Therefore, a purely aesthetic philosophy is not an adequate foundation for the profession, and it does not help the public to understand why we insist that music should be an intrinsic part of the curriculum.

Aesthetics is the basis of the human response to music. If music did not stimulate an aesthetic response in humans, it either would not exist or it would be a relatively unimportant activity. The philosophy of music education, however, is not a philosophy of music. It is a philosophy of education. To be credible it must reflect the aesthetic aspect of music, but as an educational philosophy it must also recognize the benefits to society of having an aesthetically developed population. Charles Leonhard and Robert House (1972) wrote:

> Indeed, where music education has flourished, it has always contributed directly to social unity and development. Its objectives were specifically drawn in terms of values important to society. The Greeks supported music education because it attempted to produce a rounded individual—one of strong character and intellectual grace. In America, music was admitted to the schools for the specific purpose of establishing a common music literacy, useful in the sacred and secular life of the time. (p. 74)

Although the philosophy of music education has provided its rationale for thousands of years, it has undergone profound change during the second half of the 20th century. Prior to that time, going back to the time of Plato, music was taught not so people would know its beauty, and therefore value it, but because people who knew its beauty and valued it were expected to be different kinds of citizens in the society that sponsored music education. To Plato (*Republic: III*) the educated person was one who had achieved balance between body and soul. To him, the true musician could recognize the "forms of soberness, courage, liberality, and high-mindedness, and all their kindred and their opposites, too" (p. 656). The purpose of educating such citizens was to populate Plato's ideal society, described in the *Republic*, with people capable of supporting its idealistic social structure and worthy of receiving its benefits.

Philosophy is easy to discuss but most difficult to prove, as anyone who has given the matter serious consideration knows. Interestingly, Plato's thoughts on the balance of gymnastics for the body and music for the soul are borne out, if not actually proven, by another well-known writer who attempted to create his version of an ideal sociey. This writer did more than just put his thoughts on paper and teach those students willing to study with him. Adolf Hitler wrote in *Mein Kampf* (1939):

> The folkish State . . . has to direct its entire education primarily not at pumping in mere knowledge, but at the breeding of absolutely healthy bodies. Of secondary importance is the training of the mental abilities. . . . A people of scholars, when they are physically degenerated, irresolute and cowardly pacifists, will not conquer heaven, nay it will not even be able to assure its existence on this globe. . . . What makes the Greek ideal of beauty immortal is the wonderful combination of the most glorious physical beauty with a brilliant mind and the noblest soul. (pp. 28–30)

He goes on to justify the need for more physical training, especially in boxing, in order to develop "a society of physically superior people, intensely loyal to the state, and capable of conquering other peoples." He acknowledges and confirms what he considers the rightness of the Greek concept of education but then proposes an educational system that promotes physical strength and aggressiveness rather than a balance between body and mind. In other words, Hitler adopted half of Plato's educational system purposely to create a society of aggressive and dominant people. The establishment of such a society, based in part on a distortion of Plato's ideal educational system, lends credence to Plato's idealistic balance of body and mind.

There is no need to discuss why Hitler proposed and supported such an educational system, except to say that his ideally educated citizen had very different attributes and motivations from Plato's ideally educated citizen. Plato's *Republic*, which continues to live in our classic literature, is still respected and worthy of study and probably will continue to be a classic after two more millennia. Neither Hitler's *Mein Kampf* nor the Third Reich survive except as memories of horror that the civilized world hopes never to see again. Hitler's failure does not provide absolute proof that Plato was correct because his ideal Republic never actually existed. One would like to think, however, that the evidence is strong. Acceptance of the evidence lends credence to the theory that the correctness and effectiveness of a philosophy are proven, or disproven, only by the events of history.

Another indication that philosophy is borne out by historical events is the use of music in religious instruction. Regardless of whether one believes in a particular religion, or any religion, it is difficult to argue with the success of music education as sponsored by religious authorities throughout history. If the purpose of including music in religious instruction is to deepen one's belief in a particular religion or denomination, thereby extending a particular set of beliefs to future times and perhaps to other geographical areas, then that purpose has been proven effective. Much of the large body of Jewish and Christian liturgical music is ancient. Religious educators have served the synagogue and church through the ages by educating their believers in music. Having developed basic musical skills and attitudes in children, education has then continued with the use of music. The primary purpose of religious music education was never to assist individuals to develop a love for music but to bring musically knowledgeable people into closer union with religion by virtue of musical training and experience.

The use of music to bring people closer to a common ideal serves political as well as religious purposes. Dmitri Shostakovich said in an interview,

> We, as revolutionists, have a different conception of music. Lenin himself says that "music is a means of unifying broad masses of people." Not a leader of masses, perhaps, but certainly an organizing force! . . . Good music lifts and heartens and lightens people for work and effort. It may be tragic but it must be strong. It is no longer an end in itself, but a vital weapon in the struggle. Because of this, Soviet music will probably develop along different lines from any the world has known. (Lee, 1931, December 20)

Despite his declaration of the nature of Soviet music, years later Shostakovich found himself in trouble with the Soviet political authorities when his music was no longer perceived to be supportive of Communist and Soviet ideals.

The 1984 international tour by the New York Philharmonic brought evidence that national leaders both recognize and fear the ability of music to represent political beliefs. When Sri Lankan officials refused permission for the orchestra to perform the work of Ernest Bloch subtitled "A Hebrew Rhapsody" because a Moslem nation could not permit such a perceived honor to Israel, the Philharmonic canceled its concerts in that country. Actually, it was neither the religion of the composer nor the music itself that caused the controversy but the word *Hebrew* in the subtitle. Nevertheless the power of music to influence the leadership of a nation was demonstrated once again.

Limitations on Music Education Philosophy in a Democratic Society

One need not agree with Plato, Hitler, various religious leaders, Lenin, Shostakovich, or the cultural arbiters of Sri Lanka to recognize the strength of their beliefs and their individual and collective impact on history. Although we sometimes have trouble agreeing specifically on an appropriate philosophy of music education, few of us would wish to adopt any of the above tenets as the basis of current music education programs because we live in a different age and a different kind of society. Our music education philosophy cannot be based on religion in a democratic society, at least not in the public schools, and the use of music to develop nationalistic feelings and loyalty is now considered a side benefit of music education. What is it, then, that we feel we need from music so much that we spend our lives performing and teaching it and defending it against educational decision makers who often wish to use their limited resources to support other educational disciplines, to the detriment of music education?

A simplistic answer might come from a less complicated time in our history, when perhaps it was easier to agree on such things. Years ago the state of Florida mandated music in its schools and specified its aim. The Florida school law during the second decade of this century, stated:

> The pupil should learn how to sing and to memorize a large number of sweet, simple, rote songs, in order to gain some appreciation of the artistic in the home. Once a day throughout the whole school life, the pupils shall have a period set aside for rote singing. Technique is not recommended. These songs shall consist of melodies relating to home and farm life, and shall be of a character to increase the love of singing and ability to sing.

This simple statement summarizes both the philosophy and method of music education in the state of Florida at that time, at least as expressed in the state code.

Perhaps it is more appropriate in our modern technological society to take our cue from an organization that has proven its ability to provide music in an effective way for large masses of people—Muzak. The aesthetic philosophy of that successful company was articulated by the chairman of its board of scientific advisers (Keenan, 1984, December 10): "Muzak promotes the sharing of meaning because it massifies symbolism in which not few but all can participate." It would be unusual to hear a philosophy of music education stated in such slick terms, but it does have a certain logic as a support statement for a profession whose goal is to bring music education to the masses.

A simplistic statement like that of the Muzak adviser hardly provides a rational basis for music education. The needs of our profession require a more complex and sophisticated philosophical foundation than that of a corporation whose success is measured by its profits. Also, we have matured as a society to the point where we are legally obliged to recognize and respect racial, ethnic, and religious differences and points of view. More important, we have made significant progress toward the social acceptance of all our people and all points of view as a moral obligation.

One of the very interesting manifestations of our legal and moral progress is that public school music education is not supposed to be a tool of religion. Still, in addition to its artistic functions, it is also generally recognized to be an effective vehicle for the development of understanding of religions. In other words, we do not use religious music in public education to support religion but to help students understand religions other than their own. Every public school music teacher has had to deal with the issue of the use of religious music during the Christmas season, and most have experienced a certain amount of discomfort because of it.

The Music Educators National Conference (1984) recently adopted a position statement on the use of religious music in schools. MENC is to be commended for dealing with a prickly problem for which a solution that satisfies all public schools constituencies does not exist. The position statement offers guidance to teachers based on a commonsense approach. It recommends that teachers, when selecting religious music for use in their programs, ask the following questions:

> (1) Is the music selected on the basis of its musical and educational value rather than its religious lyrics? (2) Is the sharing of the traditions of different people and respect for these traditions stressed? (3) Is the excessive use of sacred music and religious symbols or scenery in the programs avoided? (4) Is the role of using sacred music one of neutrality, neither promoting nor inhibiting religious views? (5) Are all local and school policies observed regarding religious holidays and the use of religious music? (6) Does the literature selected maximize musical and artistic skills? (p. 28)

It is unlikely that the satisfaction of these criteria truly keeps the celebration of religion out of the schools. It is not a coincidence that religious music is used around the time of religious holidays, and most of it is appropriate for the holidays because of the religious nature of the texts. Indeed, if it were not used, it is likely that serious complaints would be raised in communities across the country.

Most of the public school students in this country are Christians. The use of sacred music just prior to Christmas does not teach them about Christianity. They have learned that from their families and churches. Insights are offered to students of other religions, however, who are usually in the minority. Some schools sincerely attempt to balance the use of church-oriented music with Hanukkah music because Hanukkah and Christmas usually occur during the same general season. Hanukkah, however, is a minor Jewish holiday, and the use of children's Hanukkah songs in conjunction with Handel's *Messiah* hardly represents balance. If the goal is really to share traditions, then the important holidays of all religions must be marked by the use of appropriate religious music. Such might be the case in some isolated situations, but it is certainly not the usual practice.

Music teachers are relieved of the problem in an ever-increasing number of states and/or local school districts, where the use of any practice that suggests a leaning toward a particular religion is forbidden by either policy or statute. In a legal sense, fairness is achieved for all students. Unfortunately, students suffer a cultural and aesthetic loss if religious music is not permitted a place in the curriculum.

More needs to be said about the issue of religious music in public school music programs. We must ask about the validity of its purpose when used for any reason other than the revelation of its aesthetic content. We have ample reason to believe that music education practices aimed at helping people develop religious beliefs and feelings were successful in many times and places. Does that mean, however, that the use of religious music in contemporary programs, intended not for the practice of religion but to help students understand other religions better, is effective? A Catholic student who hears a mass in general music class identifies with the music because he or she hears it every Sunday during a religious service that is an integral part of life for that student. The same is true for a Jewish student who listens to a recording of cantorial music in class. He or she is familiar with it from having heard it in the synagogue since early childhood and identifies with it as an innate aspect of life experience. It is most unlikely that the Catholic student would feel a sense of identification with the cantorial music, however, nor the Jewish student with the mass. Both would miss the emotional significance of the music. Therefore, one must ask whether hearing the music, even if accompanied by an explanation of its meaning, will help the student develop anything other than the shallowest intellectual acquaintance with a different religion. Although such exposure to the music of other religions is probably quite beneficial, there is little evidence that the practice achieves the rather lofty goal of helping students develop a better understanding and appreciation of people of religious backgrounds other than their own.

The same question can be applied to the use of nationalistic music. Lacking the sense of identification that foreign people have for the music of their own countries, we do not know that it is actually effective with American students. In any case, it is most unlikely that religious and national music hold the same significance for people brought up with that music, and those who are introduced to it as part of a body of educational material. Graham Vulliamy and John Shepherd (1983), of England and Canada, respectively, discussed the topic as follows:

> It is not to be denied that we can elicit significance from the music of other cultures. The crucial question, however, is whether the significance is true to the culture and the music. Even within our own society there is ample evidence of the way in which the members of our culture can misinterpret the music of another, even when the interpretation is well-intended and sympathetic. (p. 192)

The practice was protested by the eminent American musicologist Archibald T. Davison (1926) in his book *Music Education in America*. Davison bitingly criticized music education philosophy, policies, and practices for reasons that still exist in many music education programs. He wrote about the use of music education to develop nationalistic feeling:

> We would, of course, not wish to follow the German ideal of exclusive devotion to the folk songs of a single country—even our own, did we possess a sufficiently large body of such melodies to occupy all the musical attention of our children—for music education should concern itself primarily with beauty and not with nationalism. (p. 49)

In reality, there is little argument with the use of music as a tool for the development of understanding of other societies and cultures. It is considered to be effective and is generally respected. It should be recognized, though, that such usage of music is actually utilitarian. It is an attempt to convey the aesthetic significance of music to students for a social purpose.

The Justification of Music Education to the Public

We have arrived at a time in history when it is necessary to justify, and not just explain, music education in order to maintain support by school administrators and boards of education. Paul Lehman (1984), president of MENC, pointed out that every major figure in Western history who has written on education has regarded music and art as basic to the curriculum. He discussed the dilemma created by the entertainment aspect of performing ensembles, which, although not necessarily reflecting the fundamental values of Western civilization, are considered necessary by some music educators. One of the strengths of music is that it is enjoyable. Because students and other community members want to enjoy music, it is not surprising that music education is often treated as a vehicle for entertainment, rather than for aesthetic education.

A similar dilemma was faced in the 1880s, when school leaders became suspicious of music in the schools because they perceived it to be more enjoyable than educational. The solution to that problem was to require students to learn more about music by changing from rote methods to approaches that helped students develop music reading skills. We have learned an important lesson from the 1880s: The problem was actually an opportunity that provided music educators the means for continuing long-term growth and development. Problems with which we are now dealing should also be viewed as opportunities, and we need to find ways to use them to our best advantage. The fact that music reading ability in students is now commonplace suggests that the problem of a century ago was indeed turned into an opportunity for professional growth. Often, though, there is little that can be done to make pure entertainment activities more educational.

The reason that we find ourselves obliged to justify music education in the schools after at least 2,000 years of success is that our society is unlike any that has existed before, and its relationship to art as cultural expression, entertainment, recreation, and therapy is different. The philosophical basis of an art form, and its extension as a branch of education, must bear a supportive relationship to the society in which it exists and from which it draws moral, economic, and other forms of support. Music education flourished throughout Western history because its relationship to society was, in great part, its reason for being, and that relationship influenced its practices. It, in turn, helped the citizenry develop the musical skills and appreciations needed to participate in society in the way that was expected. For that reason, societal leaders, including civic, intellectual, religious, and educational figures, supported music education by publicly articulating its rationale, leaving no doubt in the minds of most people that it was a necessary and important aspect of education. Since the middle of this century, however, the strongest spokespersons for music education have been music educators, either speaking as individuals or through professional associations. The music education profession has many articulate and convincing spokespersons, but when one serves as an advocate for his or her own profession, the impact is dulled by the fact that the speaker has a vested interest. Although our societal leaders do occasionally speak up for our profession, such statements are often not persuasive because there is little agreement on how music education serves society.

Ironically, one of the most influential voices for the profession in recent times was not that of an individual but of an industrial foundation. The Ford Foundation, in its role as founder of the Contemporary Music Project, affected both the profession and the public. A foundation with sufficient wisdom and money can do such things. The November 16, 1984, issue of *Time* magazine carried a large advertisement entitled "Art for the sake of . . . children," placed by the Mobil Corporation. It described the positive effects on children of exposure to, and participative experiences in, the arts. Mobil placed the advertisement to request that other corporations make grants to Young Audiences, Inc., to make possible more arts experiences for children. A high official in the Mobil Corporation recognized, or was persuaded, that arts education provides a societal benefit worthy of support by means of corporate funds that are also actively sought by numerous other worthy potential recipients. Other corporations have assisted arts education by direct grants or through their foundations. It would be irresponsible to state that the most significant external support received by music education and other arts education fields comes from corporations now rather than from societal leaders. Corporations provide enough support, however, to indicate a trend that deserves the attention of arts education leaders. An irony that should not escape observation is that the purpose of the Mobil advertisement was to support a private corporation that brings music to schools. Although music educators might well praise Mobil for its support of arts education, it is to be hoped that in the future Mobil will share its financial resources with school arts programs as well as with corporate educational programs.

A Historical Perspective on Aesthetic Education Philosophy

The development of the post–World War II technological society required a new kind of commitment by the entire educational establishment and by each individual discipline. The 1950s and 1960s saw several attempts by music educators and other musicians to find ways in which music education could serve contemporary society. One of the earlier attempts was the publication of *Basic Concepts in Music Education* (Henry, 1958), a book that still offers nourishing and enriching food for thought. *Basic Concepts* helped to focus attention on music education as aesthetic education. Other writings of that time also reinforced the need for an aesthetic philosophy of music education. The statement that probably best sums up the basis of an aesthetic philosophy of music education was written by Charles Leonhard (1966):

> A music program in the school is justified only when having a music program makes a significant difference in the student's conception of music, his understanding of it, and his competence with it. The purposes of music education are achieved only when it results in musical learning that would not take place without a music program. (p. 21)

Leonhard's statement summarizes what most music educators have known for many centuries. The difference was that the new movement toward an aesthetic philosophy was to have the effect of disassociating music education from societal goals, at least in the minds of many music educators. Music educators do not argue with a statement like Leonhard's. Indeed, they are music educators because they agree with it. However, the utilitarian aspect of music education philosophy, that is, the part that conveys to the public its value to society, was missing. This lack characterizes the difference between the aesthetic philosophy of music education that developed in the late 1950s and the philosophy that had existed previously. Although writings appeared after that time that linked music education philosophy with societal needs, the general perception of the profession, as articulated in articles and at conferences, has often appeared to be that music education exists in a social vacuum, isolated from the requirement to fulfill a societal need.

We must ask why such a perception developed. What happened at that time in the history of our profession that caused our intellectual leadership to propose a purely aesthetic philosophy of music education after thousands of years of utilitarian philosophy? The answer lies in the historical events of the United States since World War II. During the chaotic period of the late 1940s and the 1950s the attention of the public and of most public leadership figures was focused on the recovery from World War II, the Korean War, the cold war, technological advances that were changing the everyday lives of most people, and other fascinating and urgent topics that had implications, as yet unarticulated, for American education. Although no one knew exactly what the implications were, it was obvious that the role of education at that time was not satisfactory, and that it, like many other aspects of American society, would have to change. As the intensity of the cold war increased, and especially when our supremacy in space technology was overtaken with the launch of Sputnik I, Americans wanted to see more innovation in the schools, especially in the teaching of English, science, mathematics, and foreign languages. Other subjects received too little public attention, and it was feared that they would be relegated to a weak second place as the favored subjects received ever-increasing resources to enable them to rise to the challenges of modern society. Music was one of the "have-not" subjects at that time.

Again, adversity was turned into opportunity. The events of the 1960s were actually helpful to music education, thanks to the imagination, creativity, and hard work of a great number of music teachers and administrators. Strong factors in the modernization of the profession were the Contemporary Music Project, the Yale Seminar on Music Education, the Tanglewood Symposium, the development of new curricula (with support by government and/or private foundation funds), the new emphasis on behavioral and psychological research, and the growing recognition that music education must change both philosophically and practically in order to continue serving American education. By the term *modernization* I do not mean to imply that the profession suddenly became relevant and effective in every way. Rather, there was a generally acknowledged recognition that the nature of society had become more dynamic than at any other time in history and that music education would have to reflect that dynamism in its philosophy and practices.

In a time of fast and radical change a service profession such as music education cannot make specific plans for the distant future because accurate prediction of the shape of things to come is not possible. Although professional leaders did not know just how we would serve in the future, they had no doubt that music education would have a place in educational structures. In order to ensure a relevant and respectable role for the profession in the future, the Tanglewood Symposium was held in 1967 to analyze the nature of modern society from the viewpoint of music education, to predict as well as possible what society would be like in the near future and the role of music education in it. The symposium produced the Tanglewood Declaration (Choate, 1968), which was actually a set of principles to support the profession during a period of change. Curricular decisions would have to be made in relation to prevailing conditions in specific times and places, but the principles agreed upon at Tanglewood offered guidance to the profession and to the Music Educators National Conference, which was to provide leadership.

The Tanglewood Declaration (written by Allen Britton, Arnold Broido, and Charles Gary) was supportive of aesthetic education. The first article of the declaration stated: "Music serves best when its integrity as an art is maintained." It is a simple, honest, and direct statement, and entire music programs can be built upon it. It is significant that the writers had the wisdom to recognize that they must also justify the societal value of music as an art. The introduction of the declaration states:

> We believe that education must have as major goals the art of living, the building of personal identity, and nurturing creativity. Since the study of music can contribute much to these ends, *we now call for music to be placed in the core of the school curriculum.* The arts afford a continuity with the aesthetic tradition in man's history. Music and other fine arts, largely nonverbal in nature, reach close to the social, psychological, and physiological roots of man in his search for identity and self-realization.

This is an excellent statement, one that relates music education to the needs of the society it serves, whether in a time of relative calm, or of fast-paced change when the relevance of things and institutions can be short-lived. It addresses a major problem of contemporary life, which is that it is entirely too possible for an individual to lose his or her unique identity to the collective identity of the mass. As one individual in a society of hundreds of millions, we are sometimes served by, and sometimes controlled by, the technology upon which we have come to depend. People are more than the names and numbers used by computers to distinguish one individual from another. The benefits of music education that were discussed previously—self-expression, self-fulfillment, self-development—are the means by which individuals aspire to the goals identified in the Tanglewood Declaration. The art of living, the building of personal identity, and the nurture of creativity are achievable through education in any field of study. The search for identity and self-realization is conducted by some in the realm of the sciences, by others in the humanities, and by still others in such activities as travel, the crafts, vicarious experiences through reading, and so on. Virtually all people, however, can also conduct the search for identity and self-realization through the arts. The Tanglewood statement offers a rationale for music education that explicates the benefits of aesthetic education. It is inconceivable that society does not benefit from having a large proportion of citizens who have been brought closer to their "social, psychological, and physiological roots" through the study of music.

It must also be recognized that it is a utilitarian statement that firmly identifies the role of music in American education. It does not say we must study music for the sake of music or art for the sake of art. It identifies a need that can be filled by no other curricular subject and establishes a strong justification for music education. In other words, the Tanglewood Symposium, by means of the Tanglewood Declaration, provided a brilliant utilitarian basis for an aesthetic philosophy of music education. By doing so, it supplied a justification that could be accepted by the general public, by those members of the public who serve on boards that make decisions about education, and by school administrators who have authority over music programs.

Another excellent example is the statement of the American Association of School Administrators (1959):

> We believe in a well-balanced school curriculum in which music, drama, painting, poetry, sculpture, architecture, and the like are included side by side with other important subjects such as mathematics, history, and science. It is important that pupils, as a part of general education, learn to appreciate, to understand, to create, and to criticize with discrimination those products of the mind, the voice, the hands, and the body which give dignity to the person and exalt the spirit of man. (pp. 248–249)

Schwadron (1972) analyzed the statement and pointed out the operative words and phrases that make it what he termed "a statement of functional values." He wrote:

> Here is a statement of functional values which could provide an aesthetic framework for the advancement of music education. "To understand, to create, to criticize"—these are the essential ingredients of aesthetic education. The "dignity" and exaltation of "the spirit of man" are humanistic concerns, reflecting both naturalistic needs for values and aspirations for loftier goals. Here, too, there is scholarly room to explore many kinds of music, to probe into the meaning and nature of the musical arts, to understand the unique function of music among the arts in general, and to develop the power to "criticize with discrimination." The resolution also emphasizes the need for music education "in a well-balanced curriculum . . . as a part of general education." As it stands, the statement signifies a potential set of beliefs for an aesthetically-oriented program. (p. 73)

Unfortunately, it seems that many music educators have overlooked or forgotten those words that explain so effectively why students must be educated in music to gain appreciation of its aesthetic aspects. Instead, it seems to be the general feeling among music educators who discuss the matter that music should be taught for the sake of music. That approach is contradictory to what we know of the history of music education. Throughout Western history music has never been taught "for the sake of music." Also, such a statement is probably unacceptable to most members of boards of education, who must vote on funding matters that affect music education programs.

It would be more correct to say that music should be taught not for the sake of music but for the sake of children, as was stated by the Mobil Corporation in its magazine advertisement. That simple statement, followed by a concise and coherent statement like those offered by the Tanglewood Symposium and the American Association of School Administrators, sends a message to educational decision makers that music education serves American society and does so in a way that cannot be done by any other discipline. Our effectiveness in conveying this message, and in living up to it, might determine the future of music education in this country.

The music education profession is fortunate to have such eloquent and persuasive leaders and spokespersons in the area of philosophy as Charles Leonhard, Abraham Schwadron, and Bennett Reimer. They have expressed views on aesthetic education that provide both the foundation of a profession-wide philosophy and a basis upon which serious music educators can develop a personal philosophy of music education, operating principles, and methods and techniques of teaching. Certainly the writings on music education philosophy have not ignored the relationship between society and music education, but neither have they always provided a rationale that makes it understandable and acceptable to educational decision makers who are not musicians and/or artists. Such a rationale is often viewed negatively by music educators, many of whom do not differentiate between such nebulous extrinsic benefits as health, moral development, and effective use of leisure time and the solid utilitarian relationship between music education and society. As we have seen from the words of the Tanglewood Symposium, if a utilitarian statement of belief embraces both the aesthetic aspect of music and the societal need for aesthetic education, utilitarianism can be a positive force.

Current Music Education Practices

Since the time of the Tanglewood Symposium, music education has functioned on an eclectic basis. We have accepted, and even embraced, methods and materials that were considered unacceptable to the majority of the profession not too long ago. The use of all kinds of popular music in the curriculum and the new methodologies define a profession that has broadened its outlook to enable itself to serve a society that has established social equality and justice as priorities. It is not difficult to match our eclectic practices with an aesthetic philosophy. There seems to be little disagreement with the idea that popular music, folk music, jazz, and other kinds of music have aesthetic impact, and the use of a variety of curricula and methods reflects a diverse approach to helping students develop aesthetic sensitivity. The problem now is not so much with genre of music but in the selection of individual pieces. The recognition of aesthetic content in all kinds of music does not grant equal respectability to every piece of music. Davison (1926) echoed Plato with a statement similar in content to one offered by the Yale Seminar in 1963. He wrote:

> When taxed with the obviously poor quality of school music, the common refuge of many supervisors is the statement that in educating children to love good music one must employ inferior but, to the child, immediately appealing material. In other words, to ascend Parnassus one must first tunnel under its base. No more vicious educational fallacy than this was ever uttered; the way to right is never through wrong, and it is infinitely harder to create in children a sense of the beautiful in music when once they have associated with mediocrity. There is nothing more uncontaminated, more receptive, than a little child's musical taste. He will accept whatever music is supplied him, but if his experience is inaugurated with the type of music used in most American kindergartens, there is not much to be anticipated by way of later enthusiasm for good music. It takes an unusually strong superstructure to survive a weak foundation. This assertion that children must be wrongly educated in order that they may be rightly educated is a simple admission on the part of school musicians that they do not themselves really understand or love the best music, for this music exists in the simplest forms, suited to individuals of all ages from kindergarten through college, and has been in many countries, including our own, accepted and loved by children. (p. 49)

Eclecticism is one of the aspects of contemporary music education that distinguishes us from our long and successful historical precedents. Prior to this century, when music education was practiced for the purpose of supporting civic and religious institutions, materials and methods were quite standardized compared with current practices. There is no one right way any more. It is probably safe to assume that there are still wrong ways, though. There is no assurance that every teacher, or every school district that supports a music education program, accepts an aesthetic philosophy. Regardless, educational philosophy is determined by individual teachers in many cases and by boards of education in others. It is wise to remember that the individual teacher's philosophy usually has more profound influence on students than does the philosophy expressed by boards of education in their official publications.

The fact that so many excellent music programs exist in the United States is evidence that aesthetic philosophy underlies music instruction in all sections of the country. It is equally probable that music programs that contribute little or nothing to the aesthetic development of students also exist in all sections of the country. In every case where boards of education continue to support music education programs, however, there must be a perception on the part of the board members that such programs have some utilitarian value. Music educators who have not clarified the reasons for their programs beyond the barest statement about music's being worthy of study for its own sake may have difficulty in persuading boards to maintain support. In those places where boards have been told that music has such utilitarian values for students as health, development of patriotic and religious values, and effective use of leisure time, there is danger of challenge by board members who sincerely wish to fulfill their public trust by spending public money wisely. It is logical for them to reason that the same benefits can be gained from other disciplines. If such benefits are the major values gained from music instruction, then the music program might be cut because children can continue to derive similar benefits from social studies and physical education. The programs that probably have the best chance of continuation of support by board members and administrators are the ones for which statements of the relationship between aesthetic development and personal benefit, which in turn benefit the community, have been articulated.

The Role of Higher Education in Teaching Music Education Philosophy

If it is agreed that an aesthetic philosophy of music education, supported by a rationale that relates the subject to societal need, is proper, then who is to articulate it? As mentioned before, music education in our time is spoken for mainly by music educators, with infrequent assistance from public figures. This being the case, it is imperative that music educators speak well for themselves. Although their work speaks louder and more eloquently than words, much understanding of music education programs comes about at public meetings of boards of education, at parent and teacher meetings, in teachers' lounges, and in other places where words are the medium of communication. Ultan (1984) points out that this can be problematic:

> Questions which we, as music educators, must ask of ourselves are whether or not we have fully recognized the profound implications and significance of our

art; have we served it, and, through it, our society well; and have we the knowledge and skill necessary to articulate the philosophical premises that forcefully place music in the forefront of those disciplines that should be required in the education of our youth? . . . Regrettably we have not been generous in including in our self-defined diet of professional deliberation substantial study and debate of such philosophical issues. We have been the pragmatic practitioners who have developed considerable skills but may have lost sight as to why we have cultivated them. (p. 13)

How do music educators learn what an aesthetic philosophy is and how to present it in support of their own programs? Probably that is the responsibility of music education faculties in institutions of higher education. We have proven that we can teach students to become effective music educators, but too many of our students do not consider the "why" of the matter. Most people enter the profession because of a deep, although usually unarticulated, belief in music and its importance in their own lives. Belief and importance have led them to a significant act of altruism—becoming a teacher for rewards other than money. Such strong belief on the part of future teachers might be reinforced sufficiently to last throughout their careers by music education faculty members who should be knowledgeable about aesthetics and educational philosophy and who want their students to know that they are doing more than just teaching music performance and listening skills. Perhaps if all music educators believed that their work contributes significantly to the good of society and that the world would be a poorer place without their contribution, there would be less emphasis on the entertainment aspects of music education. Music literature and other instructional materials might be selected for their potential to further aesthetic education rather than for their ability to provide immediate gratification. Carried to its logical conclusion, music educators would be able to articulate a justification for music education that is irrefutable and for which boards of education could no more deny support than they could for English, mathematics, and science.

The logical time for music educators to begin developing such abilities is during their collegiate years, although it is really a lifelong developmental process. As one gains new experiences and matures, he or she gains new skills, refines old ones, and develops new insights into life's work. As one grows, change takes place, and, it is hoped, wisdom increases. If the beginning of the process is to be in the undergraduate curriculum, teaching methods must be expanded to the point where the question of "why" is discussed in relation to the "how" of every musical activity. At the graduate level, when the new teacher has gained sufficient practical experience to question seriously why his or her everyday work makes a difference in the world, the formal study of philosophy of music education can take place. It should include the study of history of music education. Rather than being limited to facts of who, when, what, and where, courses in the history of music education should include the philosophical basis for music education during all eras and in a number of societies. If graduate students learn that their field has held an esteemed place in Western history for thousands of years, and why it has done so, many of them are likely to feel the need to understand why music education is necessary to contemporary society. That could only be a healthy development. If a teacher does not relate his or her work to the society in which it is practiced, then it is unlikely that he or she will value the contribution made to society. Understanding of the strong relationship, at its many levels and in its many variants, might well provide the music educator with a sense of dignity and worth and could stimulate the need to explore aesthetic philosophy more deeply. That in turn could lead to revised teaching practices. The music educator who is convinced that society would be worse off if not for his or her particular contribution has good reason to examine very carefully what should be taught and the best way to do so.

It is not a simple matter to arrive at a solution to the problems of developing a profession-wide aesthetic-utilitarian philosophy of music education and disseminating it throughout the profession and to the public, but a start must be made. If American music education is ever to be based on a solid philosophical foundation, then music education faculties must themselves be aware of and believe in such a foundation, and they must expose their students to it with as much of a sense of mission as they have for teaching music itself.

Conclusion

The movement toward excellence in education of the 1980s has resensitized the American public not only to the need for individual students to be better educated but for education to be related to the needs of a changing society. These are not new concerns, but they have surfaced again with a new freshness and vigor. Again American education has reached a crisis point, and again music educators have the opportunity for long-term benefits by making the public aware that true education is more than just the training that is gained by the development of expertise in what are considered basic subjects. The development of skills in communication, mathematics, and science is important as a preliminary educational step, but it should not in itself be considered the goal of education. Those skills are tools to be used in gaining an education, rather than ends in themselves. Unfortunately, the American public sometimes loses sight of the fact that the purpose of skill development is to provide tools to help one become educated.

Music educators must understand, and must be able to make others understand, that one of the fundamental components of an educational system that provides not just training but education as well is an aesthetically based music education program. Such a program helps each student develop the aesthetic sensitivity to perceive profound meaning in music, to understand and appreciate his or her own heritage and those of other cultures through music, and to lead a richer life through a choice of music that is made on the basis of educated taste. In the words of the Tanglewood Declaration, "The arts afford a continuity with the aesthetic tradition in man's history. Music and other fine arts, largely nonverbal in nature, reach close to the social, psychological, and physiological roots of man in his search for identity and self-realization."

In the simplest of terms, the satisfaction and pleasures of music enjoyed by a musically educated population contribute to a higher quality of life. That is the utilitarian message, which needs to be integrated with an aesthetically based philosophy when it is communicated to the society from which we expect economic and moral support.

7 Toward a Democratic Art: A Reconstructionist View of Music Education

Charles B. Fowler

Philosophy, once the summit of educational respectability, now lies like a wasteland, suspect and downtrodden. As higher education turns increasingly to vocational pursuits, the study of philosophy appears more and more impractical, even useless. Whether or not it is presently out of vogue, philosophy remains of central importance to our search for wisdom, and wisdom remains the key to running human affairs satisfactorily. Philosophy is therefore critical to the human condition.

The Importance of Philosophy

As humans, we continually face the task of understanding our problems and formulating solutions to them. In such difficult undertakings, we turn to philosophy in our effort to comprehend the world and "to attain as unified, consistent, and complete an outlook upon experience as is possible" (Dewey, 1916, p. 378). *Philosophy* is defined "as the effort of any culture to become conscious of itself" (Brameld, 1955, p. 4), to face honestly its weaknesses and strengths, its failures and triumphs.

Philosophy expresses both the beliefs and the aspirations of a culture. It is, implicitly, "a recommendation of certain types of value as normative in the direction of human conduct" (Dewey, 1937, p. 122). *Direction* is an important term, for it reveals philosophy as a system for guiding and altering life, in line with cultural aspirations. In this sense, it is not simply a way to preserve and maintain but rather a means to direct the course of future action, to alter conduct. It provides a framework that permits us to reexamine our traditions and to seek new and more effective ways to proceed.

The Philosophy of Reconstructionism

Philosophies tend to divide between the conservative and the revolutionary. The tendency of some philosophies (e.g., idealism) is to preserve the values of the established order, whereas others (e.g., perennialism) harken back to values of the past. Reconstructionism stands for a rethinking, a reshaping, and a repatterning of the existing order of world civilization. It asks that education assume responsibility for cultural development.

Reconstructionism grew out of progressivism. The name itself derives from the title of one of John Dewey's books, *Reconstruction in Philosophy* (1920/1948). Theodore Brameld, professor emeritus of education at Boston University (and former professor of philosophy at the University of Chicago), formulated the foundations for social reconstructionism during the 1950s with the publication of several books.

The philosophy of reconstructionism is an attempt to meet the needs of an "age in crisis." Civilization faces the threat of self-annihilation. "An age sickened by crisis," Brameld (1955) maintains, ". . . is not to be cured by sophisticated apologias for time-honored structures and habits" (p. 202). The severe problems of our time call for new and more daring approaches.

While in many ways progressivism provided education with means, it did not adequately define ends. Reconstructionism views education as a mechanism for enacting a program of clear and precise social reform. Brameld asked his education students, What is the proper role of education—to transmit the culture as it is, or to function as an agent for constructive change? It was Dewey (1916) who said that:

> Education may be conceived either retrospectively or prospectively. That is
> to say, it may be treated as a process of accommodating the future to the past,
> or as an utilization of the past for a resource in a developing future. (p. 92)

The reconstructionist assumes the latter view. Culture is not inherited. It is transmitted and modified by each succeeding generation through education. What anthropology calls "enculturation" is the process by which every culture transmits and modifies its beliefs, customs, and institutions (Brameld, 1962, pp. 10–11). Education, then, is not simply a process for transmitting the existing culture to the younger generation; it is a process for altering culture as well. And with that altering, education creates a better world.

As an anthropologically centered philosophy, reconstructionism recognizes that culture is manmade and is continually evolving. In outlook reconstructionism is future oriented, and it is utopian in the sense that it asks us to envision, to formulate, and to achieve new possibilities for humankind. Culture is not something that is fixed and presented to youth as a given, as something to which they must adjust. In the process of transmitting the existing culture, then, students are not asked to conform to it but rather to engage in reformulating it.

The human being's abundant capacity for detached observation distinguishes humans from all other life. This capacity provides us with the ability to analyze experience and represent and convey it symbolically. And in that ability to construct systems of meaning, we attain the capacity to understand, to control, and to guide our own evolution. Thus, *homo sapiens* is viewed as "the unfinished animal" (Mumford, 1954, p. 214). Accordingly, Brameld (1962) views the human being

> as the evolution-directing animal—a definition that opens a vista of thrilling possibilities for shaping the course of life, and, by the exercise both of creative imagination and concerted social action, for constructing a higher and nobler civilization than man thus far has ever approached. (p. 16)

The way that the reconstructionist proposes to ensure improvement is to study and analyze our present problems honestly and evaluate possible solutions in order to come to agreement about a plan of action. The reconstructionist places great hope in the mass of people. Our responsibility to them is clear: "We should aim to build a social-educational program that will help to correct their weaknesses, heighten their morality, and release their creative potentialities in behalf of themselves and their individual members" (Brameld, 1956, p. 60). Brameld identifies two chief approaches to acquiring the habits, beliefs, and practices of the culture. One is "behavioristic," the other, "functionalistic." The behavioristic approach assumes that the primary work of enculturation is "to teach and learn by the process of conditioning; thereby each new generation can adjust *to* the given culture" (Brameld, 1950, p. 119). Here culture is viewed as something outside of people that they must acquire.

In contrast, the functionalistic approach assumes that, although conditioning is an important part of enculturation, in addition the student should be taught "how to function *with* the given cultural environment in such ways as actively to modify and remold that environment" (Brameld, 1950, p. 119). The functionalistic approach invites students during the transmission process "to engage actively and critically" in the events of the cultural experience and to evolve better ways to operate (Brameld, n.d., p. 7).

In Brameld's view, students should come to agreement about these better modes of operation through the democratic process of social consensus. It is important to realize that engaging students in the reconstruction of society is only begun in the schools. The process of determining the best values for humans to accept is lifelong, so the new order is continually evolving as more and better information is accumulated.

This very brief description of reconstructionism provides a philosophic perspective with which to survey the present state of music education, to establish goals, and to evaluate and reformulate priorities for the years ahead. (For a more complete overview of the philosophy of reconstructionism, see the writings of Theodore Brameld. For a more complete summary, see Fowler, 1964.) In the context of reconstructionism it is clear that music education serves the larger musical culture outside the schools. Its responsiveness to the realities and the needs of music in American society determines its purposes, its focus, its curriculum, and in many ways its value and its justification as an important subject in education. Therefore, it is essential, first, that we assess the present state of music in society and that we recognize and respond to those problems and, second, that we identify the obstacles in present-day education that thwart our achieving these purposes and then invent strategies to overcome them. In this chapter I apply the principles of reconstructionism to music education in order to begin the process of rethinking and reformulating music education as a force for cultural development.

Music in American Society

The arts in the totality of American culture constitute a vast terrain as diverse in its many styles and forms as our ethnic origins. Musical culture in the United States is all-encompassing. Our popular musical culture consists of such styles as rock, disco, pop, soul, country and western, reggae, bluegrass, jazz, gospel, ballads, musicals, folk music of many countries, and such older forms as blues, ragtime, and swing. Our classical musical culture encompasses solo and chamber music, symphonic literature, choral and operatic works of all historical periods and styles, from our own and other countries.

Given the enormity of the American musical soundscape, how do the schools choose what is to be passed on to the younger generation? What, if anything, is to be ignored, what to be savored? In posing that question, music education admits to being *value* education.

Ortega y Gasset (1932) argued that low culture, or *kitsch* (e.g., our popular musical culture), is a threat to a healthy culture and that it should be eliminated. He saw high culture and low culture as at war and spoke of how "the mass crushes beneath it everything that is different, everything that is excellent, individual, qualified, and select" (p. 18). But rock, pop, and music videos have not stopped opera and symphonic music; "Dallas" and "Falcon Crest" have not supplanted or suppressed *Hamlet* or *Death of a Salesman*. These varieties of theater exist side by side with no seeming difficulty. If anything, one might convincingly argue that popular and folk culture have nourished classical music. This is certainly the case with much of the work of Soler, Couperin, Dvořak, Janáček, Grieg, Bartók, Vaughan Williams, and, considering the influence of jazz and ragtime, of Copland, Stravinsky, and many other twentieth-century composers.

That our music is so diversified accounts for its richness and in many ways its vibrancy. These varieties exist to serve a multitude of needs. We do not dance to Bach, Beethoven, or Brahms. We generally do not worship to jazz or bluegrass. We do not socialize to Babbitt, Berlioz, or Britten. But, then again, we do not derive solace or inspired insight from rock. Our various types of music serve many purposes.

Should the schools, then, pass all the existing forms of music on as though all are of equal value? To the extent that all these kinds of music are part of our heritage, yes, they have a viable claim to a share of music education. The technique required to create and to perform popular music should be no less artful, skilled, and serious than that required to create and perform classical music. Virtuosity is not reserved for classical music alone. Composing popular songs or a Broadway musical score requires in-depth understanding of musical craft. The popular singer must be as artfully expressive as the singer of lieder. Both styles require considerable, though different, technique. Given this fact, conservatories, college music departments, and university schools of music might well consider providing curricula in music that would permit music majors to choose careers in the popular as well as the classical music field.

Musically, the United States is a microcosm of the world. Preserving the breadth and richness of that culture is one of the main functions of education. To these ends, music education is the irreplaceable conduit for conveying the musical heritage of Afro-Americans, Hispanics, Asian-Americans, and European-Americans to citizens in the next generation. For music education, this alone is an enormous responsibility, a national obligation.

To begin to undertake such a staggering effort, considering the constraints on time and resources, music educators are forced to make certain choices. What, then, do we choose to study? What do we pass *over*, what do we pass *on?*

First, let us resolve to develop skill and understanding within the widest range of music possible. Music education, like any education, should challenge students and provide them with new revelations in the form of ever-expanding personal ability and comprehension. This means that we do not need to stress in the curriculum what students already know and like. The current popular music that is abundant and ubiquitous and readily available to all young people outside the schools may not require as much attention in school.

There are great differences among children in what music they have been exposed to and what they have come to understand. From this standpoint, communities and schools will differ in what they need to emphasize. People should understand their own ethnic culture as well as the dominant culture of the society. The choice of music to be studied in education depends, at least in part, upon its accessibility. Young people do not need the schools to introduce them to popular culture. They quite often *do* need the schools to provide them with opportunity to understand their own ethnic musical culture and to introduce them to the music of other cultures, including the European traditions of classical music. If this music were not a part of music education in the schools, many American children would not have access to it at all.

A second criterion of delimitation and choice involves the degree of abstractness or difficulty of the musical "language." If a particular piece of music is easy to perform and readily understood, students may not benefit from studying it. Some popular and folk music is immediately decipherable. These musical codes, after all, are deliberately in the public vernacular. In comparison, understanding African or Hispanic rhythms, Asian tonal systems, or the intricacies of classical music traditions pose challenges comparable to learning a foreign language. To the listener or performer, these codes tend to be more complex, more highly structured and developed, sometimes more subtle, profound, or sublime in content. From this standpoint, they demand more *attending to* by education.

The American Symphony Orchestra League therefore does not recommend that symphony concerts for children include popular fare. It notes that there is "a superb body of time-tested music that is the mainstay of the orchestral repertoire," and goes on to say that "playing this music is simply what orchestras do. Giving children orchestral arrangements of Top 40 hits, therefore, is cheating them and ultimately doing a disservice to orchestras" (ASOL, 1984, p. 53). If classical music were not a part of music education in the schools, many American children would never be able, on their own, to grasp its meaning.

To understand Shostakovich's *String Quartet No. 8, op. 110,* or Mahler's *Second Symphony* requires not only acquaintance with a complex musical fabric but also knowledge of the world and the human condition. This puts an added burden on those who would decode such symbolization. It means we have to know *more* to get the message, like the extra trouble it takes to understand Shakespeare or Spenser or Milton. What I am suggesting is simply that every human being have the right of access to the knowledge needed to absorb these messages.

Yes, let us acknowledge our pluralistic culture, but let us not assert that all musical endeavors are equally excellent or deserve equal claim to a place

in the school curriculum. Why? Because every citizen should be provided
with the means to understand the apotheoses of human achievement in the
major traditions of American musical art, including classical music. We must
offer every human being in this society the right to climb those mountains.

Such transmission of culture is the responsibility of music education, not
its only responsibility, but certainly one of its main functions. This is strictly
a process of *maintenance*, a replication and revelation of American musical
culture with and for the younger generation.

Culture and curriculum may not be synonymous, but they are contiguous.
What is in the musical culture is what is in the schools but not necessarily
to the same degree. Schools need not waste time "teaching" those aspects
of the culture that are self-propelling. If access to understanding is being
provided by other means, say the media of radio, television, motion pictures, and recordings, then the schools do not need to duplicate these
resources.

In music education, it is a matter of emphasis. To understand fully and to
master the art of creating and performing popular, ethnic, or classical music
requires considerable study in any case. That some children have access to
understanding these traditions and others do not is antiegalitarian. What
must be maintained is the right of every citizen to have access to all our musical culture and the wherewithal to understand it. The role of schooling and
of music education is to open the doors that society might not otherwise
open. And we must open them to all.

The Problems of Classical Music

Music education cannot convey the values, meanings, and art of classical
music to students without becoming embroiled in conflicts with the tastes
and interests of the American public at large. Serious problems are now
being encountered by classical music in American society. The attitudes of
young people toward classical music are, perhaps, indicative of the greater
public. A recent survey of 6th and 10th graders conducted by the Association
for Classical Music (ACM) produced overwhelming responses describing it
as "boring sounds for old, rich people; soft, slow and relaxing; and heard in
hospitals and dentists' offices" (ACM, 1984).

The National Endowment for the Arts (NEA) has identified a number of
problems in the arts that directly relate to music and to music education
(NEA, 1985). Its analysis of the problems of music in society could give focus
to efforts within the music education field. Education still provides one of
the most potentially effective means to alleviate these problems.

The Status of the Arts. The "primary challenge" identified by the NEA
(1985) is "how realistically to internalize and articulate the centrality of the

artist in society" (p. 1). There is a "need to improve the status of the artist in society," the NEA says. "Should this be one objective of our efforts in arts education, even indirectly?" (p. 5) Should it be the objective of arts educators as well?

A recent survey of current trends in art education, conducted by the Alliance of Independent Colleges of Art, indicates that art teachers want assistance in upgrading the importance of art education and in assuring students, parents, administrators, and the community that art education can lead to a career. They also suggested "efforts to gain recognition and prestige for art and for art education" (Putsch, 1984, pp.29–30). One can conjecture that the situation is not very different in music.

It is no happenstance that the problems identified by the NEA in society and those identified by art teachers in schools coincide. The problems of the arts in society directly affect the arts in schools. And, similarly, arts education in the schools affects the arts in society. If improving the status of the arts and of artists is important for the arts in American society, then it is important for arts education as well. But in assuming this role, arts educators are immediately taking responsibility that goes beyond cultural maintenance. They are seeking to change prevailing societal views. They are actively engaging in a process of changing community values. To the extent that music education assumes this charge, it is reconstructionist in disposition.

How can music education act to better the status of the artist and of the arts in American society? One means is to introduce students and the community to musicians who are making a successful living at their art. Another is to provide opportunities for these artists to demonstrate that what they are contributing is of value to society. Still another is to show students the importance of music as an expressive vehicle in our lives. To be fully effective in this effort, we must reach the entire population.

Reaching a Larger Public. The status of the arts and of artists is just one of the problems. In spite of the enormous growth in audiences for music during the past two decades, the NEA's survey on public participation in the arts shows that 61% of the adult population in the year 1982 did not participate at all in attending live performances of music or ballet or in attending art museums or jazz performances. This amounts to 100 million adult Americans (NEA, 1985, p. 4). Of these, 29%—48 million—cited reasons for nonparticipation, including unavailability, cost, distance to travel, and lack of time. The startling finding is that 32%—53 million Americans—expressed no interest in participating whatsoever.

Of the 54 million who did participate in 1982, 13% attended live performances of classical music, 18.7% attended musicals, 9.6% attended jazz, and 3% opera (see Table 7.1). Many more people are participating in the arts via

Table 7.1

Percentage of Adults Who Participate in the Arts through Media and Live Performance and Those Who Want More

	TV	Radio	Recordings	Live performance	Want more
Jazz	18	18	20	9.6	18.1
Classical	24.8	20	22	13	18.1
Opera	12	7.2	7.6	3	3
Musicals	20.4	4.4	8.4	18.7	32.6

Note: Adapted from National Endowment for the Arts. (1985). *Audiences— Overview: 1987– 1991 Planning Document.* Washington, DC: National Endowment for the Arts.

television, radio, and recordings. The survey reveals that, in a comparison between percentages of those who attended live performances and those who participated in the arts through the media, "the mass media reach a wider arts audience—typically twice as large—than do live performances" (NEA, 1985, p. 5). Substantial numbers of Americans want more of these musical art forms. Surprisingly, the survey found that the greatest degree of "unmet desire" for arts performances is in the suburbs, next in central cities, and lastly in areas outside the metropolitan areas.

The survey shows that "enormous demand exists for the arts via media" (NEA, 1985, p. 14). It notes the large number of commercial radio stations devoted to classical music and jazz. It recognizes that opera depends greatly on television and radio to expand its audience. The survey also shows that, "as in attendance, higher levels of education and income are generally the strongest background predictors of using mass media to follow art" (NEA, 1985, p. 6). And the survey asks, "How can arts education be strengthened so as to build and inform future audiences?"

What is the message here for music education? First, there are enormous numbers of Americans who show no interest in jazz, classical music, opera, and musicals. Do we want it that way? Second, television has become the most viable means of reaching larger audiences with these forms. Considerable numbers of Americans want more of this music. Will generating increased public interest in this music create enough demand to warrant additional programming? Third, because classical music (including opera) is attended by such a small percentage of the population—a minority characterized as the "better-educated" and "better-off"—it suffers the taint of elitism. Should music education perpetuate this exclusivity? Fourth, the NEA recognizes the interdependent relationship between the health of the arts in society and the success of arts education. Our musical artists and our performing arts organizations are directly dependent upon the infrastructure of education to sustain them. They seem increasingly aware of this. But is music education aware of its responsibility to the musical culture?

In raising these questions, music education necessarily addresses the equity of balance between its goals of excellence and access. Building larger audiences means opening up more opportunities for the study of musical art to more students. It means that music education programs that now reach 15% of the students in a high school must begin to make inroads to reaching the other 85%. That will require some shift of concentration and energies away from the talented toward the greater mass of students.

But such social goals, however important to the well-being of our musical culture, must be translated in educational terms. As far as boards of education and educational administrators are concerned, audience development is not an acceptable goal of music education. One does not offer music courses in schools merely to fill the concert halls. But one does provide opportunities for all students to understand music as a basic form of human communication. If the main purpose of schooling is development of the mind, then students must be invited to exercise all of it, musical cognition as well. Students have a right to their musical heritage.

The point of any arts education is to provide people with the background they need to be receptive to and perceptive about the arts. Music education is the means by which we empower people to engage reactively with the art of music. One result of such education is to cause students to seek musical experience as an artist, amateur, or audience member. But the effect is strictly residual. The choice is up to the individual. Music education should guarantee the background, not its application.

And how can music education begin to reach more of the student population? By developing a general curriculum for all students that explores music as a wondrous human invention, a living history of eras and peoples, and a record and revelation of the human spirit. At the very least, our band, choruses, orchestras, and other performing groups ought to be enlisted in demonstrating these qualities to all students and the public at large. Music educators face a crucial choice: to offer music to the many or reserve it for the few; to maintain the status quo or to build a more inclusive, a more democratic, musical culture.

A Contemporary Art that Communicates. When it proved *not* to be a life-sustaining profession for many composers, contemporary classical music found a haven and a refuge in the academic world. This has had its good and its detrimental repercussions. In the universities many of our classically trained musicians and composers have managed to make a decent living. But the art that they render has become remote from the general public.

This has been the case for decades. As long ago as the early 1960s, Kenneth Rexroth (1963) decried the direction of modern music on the American campus. He said:

> Never a peep or a squeak, not even an electronic one, breaks the overpowering total roar of the dullest sounds ever emitted on the earth by man, beast, or machine. The academic sterility of a contemporary music contest must be experienced to be believed. (p. 123)

More recently, Michael Walsh (1984, September/October), music critic for *Time*, reiterated this breach. The second half of this century, he said, has been "marked by a decisive rupture between composers and audiences" (p. 24). One of the reasons, he suggests, is that "contemporary composers are faced with the unraveling of the serialist hegemony and the exorcism of the ghosts of Schoenberg and Webern" (p. 25). But he also speaks of the ivory-tower attitude prevalent among many academic composers today—"the idea that rejection is *prima facie* evidence of worth" (p. 26). It is as though, if art does not sell, it is somehow better art. Yet he maintains that this idea "flies in the face of historical evidence," and he offers Verdi as a prime example.

Walsh looks to Reich and Glass, the minimalists, and the new romanticists to replace the old orthodoxy. Whatever that promise, contemporary classical music is in trouble. It fails to present itself as a living art that speaks urgently and vibrantly to even the minority of classical music enthusiasts, let alone the American public. Christopher Lasch (1984), author of *The Culture of Narcissism* (1978), views this classical music malaise as the direct result of our proclivity for preservation of culture, what he calls our "custodial" orientation:

> If we look at the situation of contemporary music as a whole, what strikes us most forcibly . . . is the hostility of audiences to modern music, in Europe just as in the United States; the self-conscious, self-referential, and academic quality of most of the music now being written; and the endless recycling of masterpieces composed in the 18th and 19th centuries. The musical tradition in Europe has become as custodial in its orientation as the American tradition. (p. 14)

Lasch views this contentment with merely passing on the existing culture as the root reason why the great tradition of Western music still remains so little understood and appreciated in this country. Certainly music education programs that are content with simply passing on the culture *as is* tend to be prosaic and staid. Maintaining the status quo is not a particularly stimulating business. By steeping our young talent and our audiences in the standard repertoire, we sap the vitality of our art. In contrast, theater does not restrict itself to Molière and Shakespeare, nor visual arts to da Vinci and Rembrandt.

The crisis in music education, Lasch (1984) believes, derives "from its attempt to disseminate a tradition that no longer has much life." If classical music has become a dead language, then music teachers, like their Latin counterparts, will have "to save it from academic extinction" (p. 14).

In this important matter, obviously, the posture of music education is crucial. How composers and musicians and audiences are educated determines their musical values and expectations. Shall we allow the concert hall to become a museum? Our posture presents a philosophical choice. Shall we go on embracing preservation, or should we cast off the custodial blanket that smothers us and take up, with serious intent, the work of making the future what we want it to be?

And how can music education act to make classical music a living art that communicates? By encouraging more students to become involved in the creative process: learning to use sound as a medium for their own communication. Whether by exploiting the technique of improvisation, experimenting with the organization of sound with the help of computers and synthesizers, exploring the potential of the group creative process, or simply offering more courses in composition, music education can make music an art of *self*-creation rather than one totally of *re*-creation.

Involving students in the performance of one of their own original musical ideas can be instructive to all. In coming to terms with how one "says" with music, students will naturally come to value the musical creations of others. They will begin to grasp the "language" and the process of musical communication. At the very least, such efforts will develop increased respect for composers and will begin to produce an avid audience for new music. Given some years, music education could be successful in establishing an audience that will relish sharing the musical expressions of their own time.

This brief overview of music in American society presents a rationale for including all of the various kinds of music in American education but giving special priority to the troubled art of classical music. To solve some of the problems now being encountered by classical music, music education must act to improve the status of the arts and artists in American society, reach a larger public with the message of music, and attempt to create an art that communicates.

Emerging from this analysis is the first fundamental goal of music education: *to establish music as a vital and valued art in American society.* Since American education, particularly the public schools, K–12, constitutes the main system for attaining this goal, the function of music education within that system is crucial. What are the problems faced by arts education today, and how can we solve them? That is an essential question because those problems stand in the way of our attaining this first fundamental goal.

Music in American Schools

In many school systems, the arts exist on the fringes of educational legitimacy. It is generally acknowledged that the main purposes of schooling are to develop literacy and cognition. Most people do not perceive the arts as having a relationship to either. By and large, the arts are viewed as noncognitive, more to do with handedness than headedness. Music and its counterparts of visual arts, dance, theater, and athletics are categorized as recreational pursuits, studies that are often viewed as luxuries in this technologically based, business-oriented society.

Then, too, many Americans believe that education is not really essential to understanding the arts. The arts are viewed as play, as talent that one cannot learn, as something that can be picked up easily on one's own. There is little or no understanding that the arts are disciplines with a history and technique that require disciplined and structured learning (see Chapman, 1982, p. 7). When these attitudes are coupled with pressures for raising test scores, narrowing the concept of what constitutes basic skills, and increasing academic requirements, the arts do not fare particularly well.

For a number of years now, enrollments in elementary and secondary schools in the United States have been on the decline. Fewer students require fewer teachers. Schools budgets are directly related to per capita numbers of students. At the end of the 1978–1979 school year, for example, 900 music and 1,100 art teachers' contracts were not renewed because of budget limitations. These layoffs represent, respectively, about 1% and 2% of the teachers in music and art. Yet that same year, the fields of English language, mathematics, general science, social studies, and vocational education lost approximately 1% of their teachers as well (see Steinel, 1984).

Although these layoffs in music represent curtailment of some programs, they are not apparently disproportionate. The situation in art may be more serious. In the AICA survey cited earlier, it was shown that

> as of June 1984, nearly 70% of the schools [surveyed] had experienced reductions in faculty positions, course offerings or program budgets for the teaching of art over the past three years. In addition, 40% of the schools anticipate additional cuts occurring between 1984 and 1987. . . . Probably the most important single point to be derived from the data is that overall, *sixty-seven percent (67%) of the 1,164 schools reporting experienced reductions in at least one category of the inquiry.* (Putsch, 1984, pp. 26–27)

A problem of morale has resulted. Responses to the survey indicate that "60% of the art teachers feel pessimistic, uncertain, and insecure about their professional futures and the future health of their art programs" (Putsch, 1984, p. 28). Music education is incurring similar difficulties.

What can be done? Arts education is in need of a shot of adrenaline. The prestige and the status of the field must be raised. The importance of the arts—of music—in education must be reaffirmed.

The Arts as Basic Education

Fortunately, three of the recent educational studies and reports give strong support to the arts as a basic study in elementary and secondary schools. John Goodlad (1984) calls them one of the "five fingers" of human knowledge, and he says, "To omit the arts in the secondary curriculum is to deprive the young of a major part of what is important in their education" (pp. 286, 336). In a similar manner, Ernest Boyer (1983) maintains that "the first curriculum priority is language," but he goes on to say that "the second curriculum priority is a core of common learning—a program of required courses in literature, the arts, foreign language, history, civics, science, mathematics, technology, health—to extend the knowledge and broaden the perspective of every student" (p. 94). Then, too, the report of the College Entrance Examination Board (1983) proposes a core curriculum comprised of six "Basic Academic Subjects . . . English, the arts, mathematics, science, social studies and foreign languages" (p. 10).

The rationales in support of arts education provided by these reports have already been well documented in the literature of arts education (see Fowler, 1984, for a more complete account). What is significant is that all of these reports speak about "the arts" as a distinct area of curriculum. They present the arts as a generic part of education equivalent to the sciences, not as separate, unrelated subjects—art, dance, music, and theater. And they do it naturally, without providing any explanation. The enlightened education community is beginning to view the arts-in-their-totality as an enormously important area of human knowledge. Considering them collectively, instead of as independent entities, gives the arts far greater import. Viewing the arts comprehensively gives music educational clout.

Comprehensive Arts. The concept of comprehensive arts is not new. It became a reality for many arts people at a conference held October 17–29, 1974, at the John F. Kennedy Center sponsored by the National Council of State Supervisors of Music and Art and funded by the National Endowment for the Arts with assistance from the John D. Rockefeller III Fund. The Comprehensive Arts Planning and Development Conference/Workshop was attended by 165 arts education leaders, representing 42 state departments of education, arts educators, state arts council leaders, community arts leaders, artists, and officers of the major arts education organizations. They met to develop plans for comprehensive arts programs at the state level. (See Fowler, 1975, February, for a more complete report of this historic meeting.)

At that meeting *comprehensive arts* began to mean working jointly—all the arts together. To this collaboration among the arts was added the idea of using arts resources beyond the school. The term was also applied to the breadth of the arts program—a curriculum consisting of all the arts and one ranging from discrete arts to an infusion of the arts into all the various subject matters of the curriculum, to arts programs for special students—the handicapped and the talented. The efforts of the Rockefeller III Fund in perpetuating and defining this broadened way to think about arts education must be acknowledged.

All 42 of the states attending that meeting opted to create a state plan to achieve a comprehensive arts education program. True, some states were already well on the way. But no state opted out. The progress during the past decade has been remarkable. Many state legislators, state education leaders, school administrators, classroom teachers, arts teachers, parents, and students have been persuaded to view arts education in this larger framework. But many music educators have not been moved.

In the unity of the arts we gain strength. Joining forces—the idea of *inclusion*—is a winning one. The arts, not music alone, can be viewed as equivalent in importance to social studies or the sciences. But the idea of inclusion has other important ramifications. It means that the ever-present opposing idea of *exclusion* is being resisted. Inclusion can erode the elitist attitudes that have plagued the arts.

To achieve true collaboration and inclusion and to establish a truly comprehensive arts education curriculum, music educators must relax into less protectiveness, less autonomy, and less concern with territoriality. To achieve this larger curriculum of the arts requires that those in each individual art form practice the art of relinquishment, of letting go, of forming new alliances and alignments and partaking in new kinds of transactions across the arts and between artists and arts educators, principals, classroom teachers, parents, and educational leaders in colleges and universities and at the state and federal levels. The idea of comprehensive arts necessitates—and initiates—political activism.

Music education as it has existed is an educational cul de sac. The exercise of autonomy and territoriality will ensure that music stays right where it is. Regeneration requires more. It means joining forces to achieve a new presence in the schools, a new outlook, and new ways of operating. And that requires an informed sense of dissatisfaction with what has gone before. The concept of comprehensive arts is a key. As Cynthia Ozick (1974, December), the novelist and literary critic, once said: "The difference between barbarian and civilized expectations is the difference between the will to dominate and the will toward regeneration. To dominate, you must throw the rascals out; to regenerate, you have to take them with you" (p. 36). One of the ways, then, to reconstruct—to revive—music education is to join forces with the other arts. Immediately, that places music on firmer ground in the curriculum of American schools.

Equality of Opportunity. On the surface, at least, an analysis of course offerings and enrollments in the arts in American secondary schools prepared for the National Center for Education Statistics (NCES) in 1984 presents a rosy picture. A majority of the 1982 high school seniors (69%) enrolled in at least one arts course between their freshman and their senior years. The highest enrollments were in music and fine arts. Cultural appreciation courses in art and music were offered at about one-half of the secondary schools. Over 18,500 (94.1%) of the 19,704 secondary schools in the United States offered one or more courses in the arts during the 1981–1982 school year. Schools offered a total of 223,000 courses in the arts, with an average of 11 distinct course titles per school. A total of 93,000 music courses were offered for an average of 5 per school. Music instruction was offered by over 90% of the secondary schools.

The study found that students earned an average of two credits in arts during their high school careers and that "arts credits represented about 10% of the total credits that students earned." Also, "students earned slightly more than one credit in the arts for every credit earned in mathematics and one and one-third credits in the arts for every science credit." Surprisingly, "about 13% of 1982 high school seniors had concentrated in the arts during their secondary school careers." A "concentrator" is defined as a student who earned a total of more than three credits in any combination of courses in the arts. This means that there were approximately 432,000 seniors in 1982 who were arts concentrators among the 3,265,189 seniors that year. "In comparison," the report tells us, "277,000 students concentrated in mathematics and 306,000 students concentrated in science" (National Center for Educational Statistics, 1984, p. xviii).

These statistics sound amazingly good until you turn them around to see their negative implications: During the 1981–1982 school year, 31% of high school students did not even take one course in any of the arts. This means that more than 1 million seniors had no instruction whatsoever in the arts during their four years of high school. No wonder we have so large a disinterested public. Then, too, almost 10% of our high schools do not even offer a single course in music; 15% offer no instruction in the fine arts; more than one-half provide no instruction in crafts or dramatic arts; and more than two-thirds of the high schools offer no creative writing, graphic and commercial arts, dance, and design courses. Even though these statistics are not nearly as bad as we may have thought, they are certainly bad enough.

Looking beneath the study's surface, we find that our courses are not so well subscribed. "Arts enrollments were 70% of mathematics enrollments, and 94% of science enrollments" (NCES, 1984, p. 25). We have ample courses in the arts in some schools but fewer people in them. A study conducted by the Southwestern Regional Educational Laboratory (SWRL) in California for the same 1981–1982 school year that sampled 20 of the larger urban and suburban districts in Southern California shows that "there are not many high school students and teachers actually in the fine arts departments." This study also found that the largest percentage of fine arts courses are dedicated to "general, popular courses such as band, chorus, and basic art with just a smattering of other, more intensive course offerings" (SWRL, 1984, pp. 3, 7).

Who are we actually reaching out there? The National Center's study found that "the percentage of schools with above-average numbers of offerings in the arts . . . was greater when over one-third of their students were in an academic program" (NCES, p. 44). It also found that

> in general, the percentage of schools offering arts courses decreased as the percentage of students in a college preparatory program "decreases. . . . . and" cultural appreciation courses were offered more frequently in schools when the percent of students expected to go to college exceeded 75 percent. (NCES, p. xvi)

According to these statistics, then, the arts excel where intellect does. College-bound students tend to take more arts, even though colleges do not generally require these courses for entrance.

This study shows that music education programs are reaching the brighter students—the talented. It coincides—and confirms—the survey on public participation in the arts conducted by the National Endowment for the Arts in 1984, cited earlier, that found that those who attend concerts had attained a higher level of education than those who did not attend. Is this because these are the only people music educators teach? Parents may well convey their values to their offspring, or the survey may just affirm a natural affinity between the arts and intellect. But, then again, arts teachers may have a preference for working with the brighter students and deliberately or unwittingly seek them out.

Whatever the case, what does not appear in any of these findings is any evidence of music education providing courses of substance in the arts for *all* students. Is this the case because music educators are not equipped to provide such courses, because they do not have the time or inclination, or because they believe the students would not take them anyway? One fact is certain: Until all students are provided with high quality learning experiences in the arts, the arts will not enter the mainstream of American life but will remain the domain of the educated elite. What kind of cultural future do we want? Importantly, the cultural future will be determined, at least in part, by the philosophical choice that music educators make.

A New Rationale for Music Education. American schools are reorienting themselves to the mind. Pressures to refocus education on more academic pursuits are reflected in the current attention being lavished on Scholastic Aptitude Test (SAT) scores, by the back-to-basics movement, and in all of the recent educational studies and reports. The report of the National Commission on Excellence in Education (1983) is typical. The NCEE's first recommendation states:

> We recommend *that State and local high school graduation requirements be strengthened and that*, at a minimum, all *students seeking a diploma be required to lay the foundations in the Five New Basics by taking the following curriculum during their 4 years of high school: (a) 4 years of English; (2) 3 years of mathematics; (c) 3 years of science; (d) 3 years of social studies; and (e) one-half year of computer science. For the college-bound, 2 years of foreign language in high school are strongly recommended in addition to those taken earlier.* (p. 24)

Another study declares that "where nonessential and peripheral courses have invaded the curriculum, school systems must have the courage to put new emphasis on core academic subjects and must devote more time to them." The goal, this task force says, is "to eliminate 'soft,' non-essential courses" and to enliven and improve "courses not only in mathematics and science, but in all disciplines" (Education Commission of the States, 1983, p. 38). One is left to ponder the task force's intention regarding the arts; that is, whether these subjects are considered to be academic disciplines and therefore worthy of a place in the curriculum or soft, non-essential courses that should be eliminated.

Evidently, to many of those who call for the schools to be more academic, the arts are mindless. That misconception must be corrected. Fortunately, a new rationale supporting the arts as a major form of cognition is already in place. It derives primarily from the fields of visual arts and psychology. Howard Gardner (1983b) in his book *Frames of Mind* presents proof for his theory of multiple intelligences—that music is a separate form of human cognition. Indeed, music is one of six basic human intelligences that he has identified (there may be others), four of which relate directly to the arts. The human intelligences are: linguistic (literature and drama), musical, logical-mathematical, spatial (visual arts), bodily-kinesthetic (dance), and the personal intelligences that permit us to understand ourselves and others.

We use our senses and our mind to analyze our world, to interact with it, and to understand it. And we record these impressions in a variety of symbolic systems that we have invented precisely for these purposes. We need all these systems because some forms of human experience are better expressed through one means than another (see Eisner, 1982). We can, for example, convey something of the size and shape of the Great Pyramids through representing their mathematical dimensions, but a photograph or painting might provide equally as revealing concrete knowledge. Science can explain a sunrise, but the arts can convey its emotional import. In the third part of the ballet *Daphnis and Chloe*, as the light of dawn gradually fills the stage and birdcalls are heard, Ravel's musical score evokes the glorious exhilaration of daybreak. The expressive character of a sunrise is also an important aspect of its meaning, and this aspect can best be conveyed through the arts.

We need both the scientific and the artistic view if only because no one means can say it all. As Herbert Read (1949) reminds us, "Art is the representation, science the explanation—of the same reality" (p. 11). Both tell us something different. Elliot Eisner (1982) points out that "*every* form of representation neglects some aspect of the world" (p. 49). Collectively, all these symbolic forms ensure our survival, for they constitute the means by which we pass our knowledge from generation to generation. We manage this transmission, Gardner (1983a) observes, "through the invention and dissemination of various kinds of symbolic products—books and speeches, pictures and diagrams, musical compositions, scientific theories, games, rituals, and the like" (p. 48). Gardner (1983b) points out how important these systems are in our education: "Of course, the introduction and mastering of symbolic systems is not just a matter of theoretical speculation. It is a major burden of childhood and might even be regarded as the principal mission of modern educational systems" (p. 302).

What is important here is that the arts are *acts of intelligence*. Music *is* cognition. It is a unique form of human consciousness. And, as humans, we apparently need to shift our means of looking at the world, if only to refresh ourselves. We see this need manifesting itself in the rebellion of students from the dull routine of curricula that stress only the linguistic and logical-mathematical intelligences. Students alter their consciousness through rock music, motion pictures, television, and drugs. Their beings seem to demand that their entire minds be used. And their minds encompass their musical intelligence.

Because the human mind is partly musical and music is a form of human cognition, music education has a very legitimate claim to representation in the curricula of American schools. It stands to reason that every student should have the opportunity to develop all of his or her intelligences to the fullest. Eisner (1982) says it this way: "When we define the curriculum we are also defining the opportunities the young will have to experience different forms of consciousness. To have a musical consciousness, one must interact with music" (p. 52). One of the major responsibilities, then, of music education is to provide opportunities for all students to exercise their musical minds. To abnegate that responsibility is to deny students their cognitive potential and to neglect and delimit their intellectual competence and fulfillment.

The Importance of Creativity. All symbolic systems invite people to form new representations of the world. Einstein's general theory of relativity, couched in the formula $E = mc^2$, expresses truths about space, time, matter, energy, mass, motion, and gravitation. But that kind of creative breakthrough in science and mathematics is generally possible only on the highest educational levels. On the K-12 level, mathematics and science curricula do not, by and large, allow for much invention. Students must first learn the rules. This is particularly the case with grammar, punctuation, and spelling. When it comes to the facts of history and geography, there is no room for creativity.

The arts, too, require some technique before these symbolic forms can be used for the purpose of conveying personal impressions, even if the process is as simple as applying crayon to paper. What is different is the amount of acquaintance students must have with the preestablished symbolic system before they can use it for their own expressive purposes. Depending upon the way they are taught, the arts invite students to experiment immediately with personal representations. In their play, children quite naturally express themselves by creating their own pictures, dramas (i.e., Cowboys and Indians), expressive movements, and songs. Eisner (1982) says, "What the arts make possible—indeed, what they tend to elicit from those who use them—is an invitation to invent novel ways to combine elements" (p. 64). In the arts, he says, "ingenuity is considered a virtue." This is decidedly not the case in spelling.

There are those in music who would argue that the symbolic system of musical "language" is just as extensive and complex as mathematics. To understand the codes of music requires years of study to master musical notation; the rudiments of music; the rules of harmony and counterpoint; knowledge of melody, rhythm, and form; and such necessary devices as orchestration. In this view, music is no different from science. The students can become creative only when this highly codified system is firmly in tow, and that is apt to take many years.

This need not, however, be the case in any subject. Science fairs deliberately invite students to apply the scientific method to their own experiments designed to reveal some understanding about the world. Mathematical principles are applied by students to solving new problems; in a sense, they are asked to invent a creative solution based on what they know about logic and mathematical constructs. Of course, such creative approaches depend upon how a subject is taught.

The same holds true of music. Certainly students can be asked to spend years learning the symbolic system with no opportunities provided for using these codes for purely personal musical expression. But this need not be the case. Music is not nearly as prescriptive as the codes of mathematics, science, and language. As Eisner (1982) points out, the rules of music "do not lead, as they do in spelling and arithmetic, to uniform solutions to common tasks or problems" (p. 64).

Inventions in music do not lead to right or wrong answers, correct or incorrect solutions. Thus, Eisner (1982) says, "it is not surprising that the arts should be commonly regarded as providing optimal opportunity for personal expression, for cultivating creativity and for encouraging individuality" (p. 65).

In music, the choice of whether the students are invited to invent and to express is a pedagogical decision. Some music teachers are so saturated in the rules of musical notation that they insist the code be mastered before the system is applied expressively. They themselves often believe that they have not yet attained the level that gives them the license to create. They use the system primarily as a means of re-creation, as a way of decoding what others have expressed musically. They tend to forget that musical creation happened first, and then a notational system for it was devised. Tribal peoples are often very creative musically in spite of having no way to write their creations down. Their musical codes are totally aural.

Those music educators who tie creativity to notation deny students the opportunity to develop an important aspect of their musical intelligence— the ability to invent their own constructs of sound to express their spirit, their feelings, their musical "thoughts." In the hands of such teachers—and there are many—music becomes a secondhand art. As Eisner (1982) reminds us, "children who are given no opportunity to compose music are unlikely to secure the meanings that the making of music makes possible" (p. 55). They will be unable to use their musical intelligence to interpret themselves and their world musically.

The development of creativity is an important consideration in many of the recent education studies and reports. It is viewed as an essential factor in enlisting education in the economic battle to keep America competitive in global markets. For example, *A Nation at Risk* states that "our once unchallenged preeminence in commerce, industry, science, and technological *innovation* is being overtaken by competitors throughout the world"

(NCEE, 1983, p. 5; italics mine). The report of the Education Commission of the States (ECS) declares that "our faith in ourselves as the world's supreme *innovators*—is being shaken." Increasingly, this task force says, jobs that offer upward mobility will be "those which require the *creative* use of technology" (1983, pp. 13 and 14; italics mine).

Yet, with so much expressed concern in these reports for the development of innovation and creativity, it is ironical that they do not make the obvious connection to the arts. The reason may well be that arts education does not make that connection in its own practice. Goodlad makes this observation in his study. He found that arts classes "did not convey the picture of individual expression and artistic creativity toward which one is led by the rhetoric of forward-looking practice in the field." He indicts the arts for not living up to their expressed purposes and goals. Arts education often justifies its value in education on the basis of its importance to self-expression and creativity (among other qualities), but it does not deliver on those promises. Goodlad (1984) says, "A funny thing happens to the arts, too, on their way to the classroom" (p. 220).

As these studies make clear, America must invest in the creative development of its young minds. Music education could encourage students to be innovative and to value their creative selves. Is such an objective nonmusical or extramusical? Let us admit that just as students do not study mathematics primarily to become mathematicians, neither should they study music primarily to become musicians and composers. If music is one of humanity's *systems of meaning*, then learning to use music to convey meaning must be part of what an education in music is about.

But let us not delude ourselves either. We do not know the answers to creativity in music. In this sense, curricular problems in visual arts and music are exactly opposite. The visual arts have always been taught primarily from a creative approach. But they have emphasized this to the neglect of developing technique, a structured curriculum, or teaching aspects of art history and criticism. In contrast, music educators have been notably successful in developing students' technique. They have taught something of the history of music and its literature and have developed a highly structured curriculum, particularly in the elementary grades. But we have neglected creativity.

Incredibly, it is widely possible in music to get a doctorate without taking one course in composition. Yet composition is the heart of the art. If one is in visual arts, it is commonplace to paint and sculpt; if one is in theater, to study playwriting; if in dance, to choreograph; if in writing, to write. We deceive ourselves into thinking that interpretation (artistry) is the equivalent of creativity in music. If we allow that there are major decisions in the process of performing music that do invite some creative choice, it must be acknowledged that, for the most part, these decisions are made by the teachers and presented to students as a *fait accompli*. At the very least, music educators could do less telling and invite students to exercise more judgment in the performance class: Play it angry. Sing it velvet. Choppy. Connected. Faster. Arched. Which do you like best and why?

The creative act explores the essence of musical art. Maxine Greene (1985, January) maintains that "imagination releases us." It instructs us from the inside out instead of the outside in. As Greene says:

> There is no human being, no matter what the age, who cannot be energized and enlarged, when provided opportunities to sing, to say, to inscribe, to render, to show, to bring through his or her devisings something new into the world.
>   But there is more. It is largely through some immediate involvement—"making," or if you like "creating"—that individuals who are not themselves artists can begin to get a sense of what is demanded by what might be called artistry . . . to know something of the craft, the long trying, the self-reflection, the rehearsing, the remaking, and even the doubting. (p. 3)

Without the realization of its potential for creative self-expression, music education reduces its importance in the schools. It is precisely in the creative process that the arts elicit the development of the higher forms of human intelligence, and this is what schools and education are primarily about. Creativity requires the exercise of judgment, of estimating possible outcomes, of weighing the result of particular choices, of deciding among unlimited options, and of taking action based upon such estimates. This is not a matter of following rules or of memorizing procedures. It is problem solving of the most difficult order, far more akin to the kinds of problems adults face at home and on the job than the true–false, yes–no, right–wrong problems children encounter in most of their "academic" courses. In this regard, Eisner (1982) asks: "How do we prepare children for life by posing problems to them in which ambiguity is absent and the need for judgment rare?" (p. 74)

When we ask students to use sound to convey an emotional state, there is no one correct answer. When we write, we literally begin with that part of the unabridged dictionary that we know and work in. The choices are staggering. How do we decide when a painting is finished? It was said of a poem, "It is never finished, it is abandoned in despair." (This was attributed to John Ciardi by Harry S. Broudy in a lecture, February 17, 1971.) In the creative process, the arts ask students—require them—to exercise the highest forms of cognition. This alone qualifies the arts for a central place in education. Musical intelligence is not just the capacity to interpret or to master the technique of playing and singing. It is also the ability to create and to use sound as a means of self-expression and communication. No education in music can be adequate, and certainly not complete, without development of the creative ability. It is simply indigenous to what musical intelligence—and humans—are about.

An Infusion of Music. Another way of making music more basic in education is to infuse it into the entire curriculum. Many music educators resist this notion. They see music per se compromised when it is used as a device for teaching other subjects. It is as though the autonomy of music as an art were somehow debased when it is put in the service of nonmusical objectives. These people argue "music for music's sake." Their justification for the study of music is based upon its own intrinsic qualities.

But what are music's intrinsic qualities? Is music just about music? Are paintings just about painting? Is theater just about theater? The subject matter of the arts is as broad as life itself. The arts sometimes do speak of themselves (e.g., the musical *A Chorus Line* is about the theater), but largely they are about nonarts.

What music educators seem to forget is that all the human systems of symbolization, the arts included, function as both the means to express understandings and to acquire them. We use all these various means to transmit knowledge. What we learn about life from reading a good novel does not malign the purity of literature. Certainly, we may study a great book to understand literature as an art, just as we learn to play an instrument to gain knowledge of music. But every art, every system of symbolization, conveys knowledge and understandings beyond itself.

What is music about? Much has been written on this subject that space does not permit to be reiterated here. Susanne Langer (1953) calls music "significant form." Its "import," she says, is the feeling, life, motion, and emotion that it conveys (p. 32). It can evoke the appropriate spirit of a holiday, a parade, a wedding, a coronation, a victory, and a death. It can portray our sense of nature—the seasons, the sea, the planets, and space. It can express, awaken, and reinforce our religious nature. It can clarify our feelings of lost love, loneliness, joy, peace, and tragedy.

But music "says" much more. It is among the most distinctive ways that people have used to characterize their lifestyle. It is one of the primary means by which human tribes identify themselves and give coherence to the group. It is such an exacting conveyance of cultural character, in fact, that, with considerable frequency, we can actually hear music and tell what culture it represents.

Music also evokes its era or time. It is a repository of historical understanding. In a sense, style is character. The style of music that is baroque, classic, romantic, modern, ragtime, or rock inscribes a particular period.

Mozart's music is a reflection of the eighteenth century just as surely as Stravinsky's evokes the twentieth. Gary Sudano and John Sharpham (1981) state it this way:

> Art objects inform about the past and serve as a measuring stick of human progress and concern. Reflecting not only the aesthetic spirit and sensibilities of their creators, but the aesthetic, religious, intellectual, and social spirits of the time in which they were created, such objects yield important information about the forces that have shaped the world. (p. 50)

Music is a natural adjunct to the study of history and peoples. Its very nature dictates that it have a place in those studies. Indeed, it is difficult to understand how social studies and history can be taught effectively without incorporating the arts, because these symbolic systems can evoke periods and peoples in a way that words alone cannot. Rather than corrupting its integrity, such a use of music *realizes* its intrinsic qualities.

Infusion, however, has other positive ramifications. It necessitates transactions between music teachers and classroom teachers and teachers of other subjects. It provokes other people—whole schools—to become involved with music and to understand its meaning and its educational potential. It places music, quite obviously, in the service of education. It demonstrates clearly that music is a vehicle for transmitting knowledge and understanding that cannot be conveyed as effectively any other way. That makes music enormously valuable—an important part of basic education.

This discussion of music in American schools suggests some ways to make music more central to the educational enterprise. Emerging from this analysis is the second fundamental goal of music education: *to establish music as a significant force in American education*. If music education is going to realize its responsibility to the culture at large, it must acquire greater power in the schools. To reconstruct music in American society, music education must revitalize its place in education. There can be no doubt about the arts being basic.

For years, music educators, sometimes in league with our colleagues in the other arts, have engaged, however tentatively, in the business of reconstituting culture. We have recognized that we want to alter the aesthetic values of American society. We are not content with American musical culture as it is. What, then, has gone wrong? What thwarts us?

Music educators, by and large, have only the vaguest notion of their power to reconstruct American musical culture. One of the basic hurdles is in conquering our own philosophical conflicts. On the one hand, we are not entirely satisfied with the present state of music in society or in the schools. We believe that its educational value and role is underestimated. But on the other hand, our relentless training in the conservation and preservation of musical art—of learning to accept culture as a given, as something fixed out there that we must take upon ourselves—conflicts with the idea of taking a more active role in remaking the culture. Our own musical education tends to orient us to cultural passivity and to creative paralysis.

The two fundamental goals of music education—to establish music as (a) a vital and valued art in American society, and (b) a significant force in American education—call for sweeping changes in American values and American education. They envision an ideal that has been only barely glimpsed. And they demand a major revision of the way music education itself is conducted. Reconstructionism is an invitation to partake in the process of developing and improving culture. It brings an exciting—and challenging—new dimension to music education and to all the arts.

One postulate appears certain: Music will not attain its potential vitality and value in American society—nor will it become a significant force in American education—until it makes peace with the great mass of people. At a minimum, every American could enjoy a symphony concert in the park, own a record or tape collection that includes some of the classics, and know with some justification who his or her favorite classical composer is. They could understand and enjoy a broad range of music, including the ethnic and popular music around them.

The concept of a democratic art is not unreasoned, nor is it unattainable. We must make music part of our common experience—a shared communicability. The means is at hand. Music education could achieve such strides by joining—and leading—a more visible and powerful comprehensive arts curriculum, providing ample opportunities for *all* students to study *all* kinds of music, promulgating wholly new reasons for music education that revitalize the curriculum, stressing the importance of music as a creative art, and infusing music into the larger educational curriculum so that it permeates the entire fabric of the school. That is an agenda that could bring music education in sight of its two fundamental goals during the first half of the twenty-first century.

8 Further Reflections on the Language Connection
Malcolm J. Tait

The novelist and composer Anthony Burgess begins his book *This Man and Music* (1982) as follows:

> Because we think in words, the semantics of literature does not offer insuperable problems, though none of us understands the nature of a poem, play or novel as well as he thinks. With music the whole question of understanding fails for lack of the right expository language: we fall back, as in wine-tasting, on metaphor and analogy. And yet we hear music every day of our lives, and sometimes every hour of every day, without raising the questions of its intelligibility. The question has to be raised sometimes, nevertheless: we have to examine our aesthetic sensibilities as we have to examine our consciences. (p. 1)

The relationships between music and words have challenged the best minds of every age, and the current age is no exception. Critics, musicologists, and music educators try to use words to make sense out of music, and yet it seems to be something of an uphill battle. We have not yet found the key.

At the National Symposium on the Applications of Psychology to the Teaching and Learning of Music held in Ann Arbor, Michigan, several psychologists and music educators battled over the language connection. Roger Brown had this to say:

> Emotional language comes nearer than other languages to conveying the musical experience. Perhaps technical musical language is more precise, but it is only known to a relatively small community. There must be some affinity linking emotional and musical experience that causes non-musicians, at least, to use the former as metaphor for the latter. It did not arise from any conspiracy of the enemies of music, if such there be. Eventually, I would guess, we shall

156

find a new sort of terminology that suits both emotional and musical experiences as well as some experiences that are now thought of as "purely intellectual," a terminology far more precise than is now offered by English, French, German, or Italian. (Music Educators National Conference, 1981, p. 242)

The question is not whether we should use language in music education, but rather, what language should we use and for what purposes? No one questions the validity of words such as *rhythm, harmony, tone,* or *concerto*—words that constitute a vocabulary capable of describing the elements and forms of music. Similarly, words such as *legato, vibrato,* and *pizzicato* are widely used and understood because they describe generally accepted methods for producing musical sounds. In recent years, because of an increasing concern for aesthetic education, we have come to use words such as *line, shape,* and *design*—words that characterize aesthetic properties and qualities within a composition.

All of the words in the list below are employed to describe what might be called tonal phenomena, and together (with many others of the three types listed) they constitute a professional vocabulary. They are words that highlight audible qualities or, more simply, identifiable sound characteristics.

Physical Properties:	articulation, attack, bowing, diction, duration, embouchure, fingering, intensity, intonation, legato, marcato, pitch, posture, release, reverberation, staccato, timbre, vibration
Elemental-Formal Properties:	accent, binary, coda, crescendo, dynamics, fugue, harmony, melody, phrase, rhythm, rubato, sonata, symphony, tonality, tone
Aesthetic Properties:	balance, clarity, color, density, design, direction, line, pattern, perspective, shape, space, style, subtlety, unity, variation, variety

Music educators along with educators in other disciplines have become quite skilled in analyzing, defining, and categorizing the phenomena with which they work. The results of this process have come to represent the body of knowledge or discipline without which a student would not be considered to be educated. Furthermore, the phenomena have been organized into sequential processes, which, it is argued, assists learning. The words that describe tonal phenomena have spawned innumerable taxonomies allowing curriculum experts and publishers to flood the markets with new materials that identify and describe what we refer to as music.

But there is something wrong with this process in that it deals with only one-half of the educational equation. Although we have a sound academic base in a vocabulary that is descriptive of the tonal phenomenon, this same vocabulary does not begin to do justice to the ways in which we experience that phenomenon. And yet it is the experience that is educational. There-fore, if we are truly interested in children and the ways they experience mu-sic, we must employ words that deal with that experience.

It is one thing to describe the ingredients of a meal but quite another thing to describe the experience of eating that meal. It is one thing to de-scribe the formal or aesthetic properties of a musical work and quite another to share the experience of that work.

This is the point at which we enter a controversial arena. There are those who argue it is enough to deal with the sounds themselves. They argue we cannot hope to deal with the ways the sounds are experienced; that realm, so the argument runs, is private and inaccessible. "Stay with the cognitive processes and observable behaviors," they say.

On the other hand, there is a growing body of opinion that argues that our failure to motivate and our failure to educate have come about because we have failed to take the musical experience into account. The proponents of this argument claim a breakdown in the process of internalizing tonal phe-nomena. Confusion has arisen because words associated with tonal phenom-ena have been attached both to the experience and to the phenomena. It is time to address both areas. A successful educational enterprise depends on subject matter as well as students; it depends on a certain body of knowledge as well as a child's interaction with and contribution to that knowledge. Therefore, our language needs are at least twofold and they must not be confused.

Before examining language appropriate to the experience of music, we should consider another attribute of tonal phenomena or, in a broader con-text, an attribute of artistic phenomena. Jacob Bronowski (1978) observes:

> The work of art is essentially an unfinished statement. It presents you with this so that you will make your own generalization from it. And of what does this generalization consist? It consists of a statement which is not the same as the artist's and yet which could only come from him to you because, in the wealth of imagery that he employs, there is something which speaks to your inner lan-guage so that you re-form the poem or picture for yourself. . . . The work of art does not exist for you unless you also recreate it; you recreate the work of art when you see it, when you hear it, when you read it, because you enter into it, and the little words, the little images suddenly take off in you and it is you who remember about the tie or the token or something else which gives a direct path into your experience and suddenly makes you feel that yes, that is what life is about. Not my life, not his life, but just being a human being. (p. 143)

If Bronowski's view is accepted, then the experience of music involves a bringing to, and entering into, a sharing of self with sound, whether it be in terms of a creative initiating act or a consuming act. The concept of music as an unfinished statement minimizes the oneness and unanimity of the experience with a musical object while validating the desirability and the uniqueness of what each individual brings to the experience. Extended to music education, Bronowski's view encourages children to experience music on their own terms—in their own worlds, so to speak—as opposed to experiencing it on the teacher's terms in the adult world. "Interpreting" music for students, which some teachers do, substitutes a vocabulary about an object for a personal, student's vocabulary about the experience.

Other art forms have perhaps been more successful in encouraging children to invest their own thoughts and feelings in a particular artistic medium. For example, a group of young children (reluctant creative writers) was taken to the Cleveland Museum of Art to stimulate their writing. After looking at still-life paintings they were asked to describe five things that were special to them and that they would wish to select for a still-life painting. They were asked to write a letter to a friend describing a meal with the foods shown in one still-life. After the children visited the Egyptian Gallery they were asked to write five questions they would ask a sculpture or relief figure if it were alive and could speak their language. When looking at paintings of groups, the children were asked to imagine what the characters might be saying to one another and what they might be thinking. The outcomes of these exercises are not important to the current discussion; but, surely these are the kinds of challenging assignments that promote self-investment, self-exploration, and self-discovery. They also encourage more detailed, analytical, and descriptive abilities as the perception is heightened. With altered specific assignments—more applicable to the musical experience—this is the kind of engagement through which students in our music classes can grow more skilled at knowing and sharing their musical thoughts.

Admittedly, sharing poetic, visual, and literary images uses mechanisms traditionally within reach of the child. Furthermore, child drama, child art, and child poetry have been readily accepted in research, counseling, public exhibitions, and education as valid artistic statements of a child's world. But, there has been comparably little use made of child music. Is this because we have been opposed to the concept of child music on philosophical grounds, or is it because we have been unable to provide children with adequate tools to create such statements? Would parents accept their children's musical compositions in ways they have accepted children's paintings? Of course they would. And with the current availability of means such as cassette tape, recording synthesizers, graphic notations, aleatoric compositional techniques, and computer software, child music becomes a very real possibility.

But what would the starting point be for such an exciting development? In one sense music begins from silence and returns to silence; in another sense music begins in the imagination and returns to the imagination. The starting point for the creative act, as well as the concluding point for the consumer, is the imagination. And so we need to think in terms of access to a child's imagination.

The world of the imagination is one of sensing, feeling, dreaming, exploring, and so on. It is an intimate world that, when successfully tapped, becomes a vital and energizing force. Imagination can be verbal as well as nonverbal; when children enjoy *Peter and the Wolf* their imaginations are fired by both verbal narrative and nonverbal imagery in the mind's eye. Many children experience a feelingful response as well, depending on the characters they most easily identify with. These feelings may not be verbally identified; this, of course, is not unusual, because we frequently experience feelingful states but do not consciously label them with terms so specific as *anxious, invigorated, proud,* and so on. In fact, it appears that there are many feelings that we often have and yet fail to recognize. Here are 133 of them.

accepted	exhausted	peaceful
afraid	exhilarated	positive
aggressive	exuberant	pressured
agonized	explosive	proud
alive	fragile	refreshed
alone	fragmented	relaxed
angry	frantic	resigned
anxious	free	resolved
ashamed	friendly	restless
assured	frightened	sad
belligerent	frustrated	scared
bitter	gentle	serene
bored	good	soothed
calm	guilty	spontaneous
capricious	happy	stable
challenged	helpless	stifled
competitive	hesitant	stimulated
complex	honest	stretched
confident	hopeful	strong
confused	hopeless	stunned
controlled	horrible	suffocated
cool	humble	surprised
creative	humorous	suspicious
delighted	insecure	tense
depressed	inspired	tentative

despairing	insulted	terrorized
desperate	intense	threatened
determined	interested	tired
devoted	invigorated	touched
different	joyous	tremendous
disappointed	lazy	triumphant
disgusted	lighthearted	turbulent
disillusioned	lonely	undermined
disoriented	loving	unique
distorted	manipulated	upset
disturbed	moved	used
doubtful	mystical	vibrant
drained	negative	violent
dramatic	nervous	vital
ecstatic	nonchalant	vulnerable
elegant	okay	warm
energetic	open	weak
enthusiastic	organized	worried
envious	outraged	
excited	overwhelmed	

The question can be asked whether we know ourselves and our feelings more fully if we recognize our feelings. A reasonable answer is yes, and many support the view that music educators should address feeling processes as often as they address thinking processes. Certainly there is evidence to suggest that many behaviors are determined as much by feeling as by thinking.

When I say, "I imagine this," or "I feel thus," I am sharing an internal and personal response. I am not describing an external or objective phenomenon. Therefore, feeling and images belong not to music or tonal phenomena but to children, to students, to human beings. It is therefore inappropriate to say that the music is angry, the music is colorful, or the music is boring. Angry, colorful, and boring describe the experience of a particular human being; they illustrate a person's ability to identify a feeling he or she has experienced.

As music educators we have to ask ourselves whether identifying personal feelings is something to be encouraged in the music class. If the feelings of anger, colorfulness, and boredom are induced by the music, then surely they are relevant to the learning situation and should be considered. We all know that words about feeling are not the feelings themselves; but words about anything are not the thing for which they stand. The important point here is that all words—all vocabularies—can serve enlightenment if they are appropriately used. It is entirely inappropriate to use a feeling metaphor or an image metaphor to describe music as such; but it is appropriate on the other hand to use these vocabularies to describe personal experiences of music.

The reader may ask why we should be concerned with the student's personal experiences of the music, or, for that matter, with personal experiences of anything. My answer would be to argue that the tragedy of student apathy in schools today can be traced at least in part to an unwillingness or inability among many teachers to concern themselves with the personal experiences of their students. If knowledge is not personalized, it is not relevant. It is not meaningful. It is nonsense. If the arts are nonsense to large sections of the population it is because we have failed to link knowledge about art and aesthetic phenomena with ways in which these phenomena may be experienced.

Feelings are neither irrelevant nor superfluous in the arts; they are absolutely central. Therefore, we must deal with them positively and constructively. The arts should be providing opportunities for people to share their feelings rather than to ignore them, bury them, or allow them to explode. If we are to be able to do this, we must be willing to accept the primacy of feeling as well as thinking in the artistic process, and we must be willing to encourage the use of words that convey feeling states as well as cognitive states.

We are dealing with a controversy that will undoubtedly continue for a long time, for the issue is larger than arts education in that it addresses basic teacher accountability for educating the whole child. If music educators and art educators could accept this responsibility and spearhead programs to demonstrate an education of feeling as well as of thinking processes, their contributions toward educating the next generation of children could be truly remarkable. But we may not be ready for this. Many of us remain uncertain of our own feelings, unable to identify and share them or lead students into confident self-realization. There are dangers, too, in traveling too far too quickly in this direction. Our classes should certainly not switch from a perceptual focus to one of subjective indulgence. Thinking and feeling must balance and support one another.

As we come to accept the significance of human feeling in the educative process, we will undoubtedly come to understand more fully the range and quality of feelingful response. For example, there is an enormous difference between feeling angry or feeling happy and feeling moved. For, as Gaylin (1979) writes:

> It is a peculiar quality of being moved that even as we are being "lifted out of ourselves," we experience the greatest sense of self. It is as though being rid of specific feelings allows pure feeling to come through. Being moved then is the transcendental emotion that brings us a sense of what we are in essence, beyond measurement and specificity. This may explain why we experience it at its purest in the non-literary forms of the arts: in music, dance and fine arts. There is a feeling tone beyond cognition—unattached to ideas, thoughts or

perceptions. Being moved . . . is a deep and intense emotion and it rarely relates to a transaction between people. More often than not the feeling of being moved is in relationship to certain abstractions, events, concepts and sensations. It may well be that this lifting up expresses the feeling of our being lifted out of ourselves and characterizes that which is unique in this feeling. While so many emotions deal with our relations self to self or our relations self to others, this is the one emotion which tends to take us out of our struggle for survival and even out of our search for gratifications. It affirms our relationships above and beyond even the limits of our body. (pp. 197–198)

Most of us know what it is to feel moved; an aesthetic experience can be a moving experience. It is an intense and all-pervasive response in which music becomes a kind of super life-support system. When we are moved we are renewed and we feel better for having had the experience. There is a sense of inevitability about being moved that is more than the spontaneity of random feelings; there is a sense of structure that reminds us of our most fundamental human needs and characteristics. *Predictability, consistency, deviation, organization, growth, variety,* and so on—these words are analogs from the living process itself, the dynamic interplay of forces around us. Here are more.

action	deviation	order
adjustment	dimension	organization
alternative	direction	orientation
anticipation	distortion	pattern
balance	divergence	perspective
blend	duration	predictability
clarity	energy	probability
climax	excitement	quality
cohesion	extension	relativity
compensation	flexibility	satisfaction
complexity	frustration	similarity
conclusion	fulfillment	stability
consistency	gravitation	stimulus
continuity	growth	stress
contrast	inhibition	substitution
convergence	interruption	surprise
decay	length	tendency
deception	modification	unity
decline	momentum	variety
design	monotony	vitality

Some would say these words are more purely aesthetic terms, and they may be right. Certainly they bear an abstraction that allows broader usage than simple feelings. In any event, they represent a further vocabulary that is available to us in probing and clarifying our experiences with music.

It would seem there is much that can be done here to explore links between certain terminologies. For example, while we *describe* modulatory
passages, we may *experience* gravitation; while we *describe* a crescendo, we
may *experience* growth; while we *describe* a cadence, we may *experience*
resolution or deviation, and so on. In other words, we have two vocabularies:
one that is capable of describing tonal phenomena and one that captures the
experience or the potential experience of these phenomena. There are many
words yet to be identified that might be useful in this connection. Some may
have imagery or feeling connotations such as *surprise* or *climax*; others will
be broader and perhaps more complex—words such as *compensation, in-
hibition, modification,* and *distortion*. Nevertheless, all these terms have
educational implications that deserve exploration and research. They are not
words that will limit perception or destroy desirable listening or performing
habits built up over the years. On the contrary, they may well provide the
key to unlock many aesthetic mysteries.

It is appropriate to stress again the importance of context and function for
this experiential vocabulary. It is a vocabulary that is fluid and personal,
whether it be evocative of feeling, metaphor, image, or life analog. No taxonomies are intended here. Still, as we gain familiarity with the experiential
vocabulary we may indeed find an implicit developmental cycle—one that
moves from shared experience in more concrete imagery with little children
to feeling metaphors and life analogs with older children. Here is a starting
list of experiential terms.

Imagery:	animals, colors, events (domestic, foreign, martial, pastoral, patriotic, religious), landscapes, people, seascapes, shapes, space, sports, supernatural
Metaphor:	angry, calm, confused, disturbed, energetic, excited, flowing, frantic, inspired, lonely, proud, refreshed, reverent, scared
Life Analog:	cohesion, complexity, consistency, decay, deviation, distortion, expectation, extension, gravitation, growth, inhibition, modification, momentum, novelty, relaxation, stability

We now have considered two vocabularies in the language connection: a
professional vocabulary, with subcategories physical, formal, and aesthetic;
and an experiential vocabulary, with subcategories imagery, metaphor, and
life analog. We cannot stop here, for a third vocabulary is needed to draw
professional and experiential terms into interactive relationships.

When the behaviorists were "in full bloom" (so to speak) we became very
aware of behavioral terms, but they were largely limited to observable be-

haviors. Words associated with covert behaviors such as *imagine*, *feel*, or *sense* were suspect and undesirable (possibly even harmful). We were encouraged to shy away from anything unmeasurable, and we forgot that in fact these are the qualities that epitomize our humanness, our most profound and subtle behaviors.

If our language connection is limited to words such as *identify*, *describe*, *classify*, and *list*, we are emphasizing behaviors that focus on tonal phenomena, whereas, if we employ words such as *explore*, *imagine*, *sense*, or *feel*, we are more likely to be encouraging internal awareness. Obviously both kinds of behavior are part of the repertoire of an educated person and an educated musician. Self-knowledge assists knowledge-of; and knowledge-of assists self-knowledge.

The behaviors associated with music creation and music consumption are indeed complex, but in their most fundamental form they include a progression of imagining, producing, listening, and responding. It could be argued that the process has frequently been abbreviated simply to produce and listen. This truncated version affords further evidence of our tendency to remove, or at least underplay, the importance of the human component in music education. The internal behaviors of imagining and responding tend to be bypassed in favor of the more visible and perhaps controllable behaviors of playing and listening. After all, if we ask our students to imagine and respond, the conventional parameters are down and *our* vulnerability is increased. Nevertheless, if there is no time, no space, no effort to involve the imagination and the response, the creative fires will be extinguished and in their stead we may have athletic exhibitions and anaesthetic marathons.

Since we are social beings, as well as private individuals, it is not enough to think and to feel; we must also share. But who shares with whom, and what is to be shared? Customary classroom practice suggests minimal sharing on the part of our students; their thoughts and feelings about music are unlocked more frequently in the company of their peers than in the classroom. On the other hand, a teacher shares his or her thoughts about the music but less frequently his or her experience of the music. And so we have a traffic pattern that is narrow and one-directional. Teacher-dominated learning patterns inhibit the communal atmosphere of discovery and growth. They may be more efficient in the achievement of short-term goals, but their long-range impact is negative. We encourage certain behaviors by the use of certain words. If we always ask students to *describe* thus-and-so and never have them *imagine* thus-and-so we will have another generation of "describers" rather than "creators."

> The construction of knowledge, as distinct from the attainment of it, presumes freedom and skill in the sharing and use of controlled emotion and imagery.

We say then that the children are involved, are making the lessons their own, are aroused, excited, interested, original, inventive and so on. (Jones, 1968, p. 26)

Sharing in these terms closely parallels the concept of self-investment discussed earlier in this chapter. Opportunities to expand and complete, to vary, and, yes, to discuss, assist self-realization. Below is a partial list of behavioral vocabulary descriptive of thinking, feeling, and sharing.

Thinking:	analyze, classify, compare, compile, define, imitate, list, locate, recognize, relate
Feeling:	create, discover, experiment, explore, imagine, improvise, modify, react, respond, search, sense
Sharing:	accompanying, asking, conducting, expressing, interacting, moving, performing, showing, telling

When we consider the extraordinary breadth and vitality of music across cultures and generations, our classroom vocabularies do not do the art justice. The language connection we are making now is, by contrast, vague, colorless, unfocused, and unbalanced. If the situation is to change, we must accept the tremendous significance of language as an educational tool. We need to think at great depth about the three vocabularies discussed in this chapter and ways in which they may interact with one another so that music in education can become a more valuable experience for all.

One piece of music leads to many experiences; one teacher's experience with music should nourish many student experiences with that same music. More often than not, I suspect, we have told students what they should be experiencing. Students whose experience seems to them to be different think there is something wrong with them and may even believe themselves to be unmusical. By turning off self-investment, self-exploration, self-identity, and self-realization, we are turning off the music. In order to avoid such a catastrophe, using classroom language must not be the sole prerogative of the teacher, and it certainly should not be used to intimidate students. Language is in fact a common instrument for sharing knowledge and experience. Therefore, teaching behaviors that stimulate questioning are to be fostered—that is, using questions directed toward the music as well as the experience of the music should be encouraged. Some examples: What might assist cohesion in this performance? What do you experience while you play this passage? Where is the climax? Should there be a sense of gravitation toward the climax? How can this be brought about? These are questions that can motivate thinking in students and challenge them to fuse their thinking and feeling processes.

If the goal were to be classroom improvisation or the creation of a sound mural, we might begin with the following: Imagine a title for a musical adventure. Experiment with tonal qualities; project different qualities of feeling through the tones. How can you clarify or intensify the image? How can you extend or sustain it? If the program involves listening, we might ask if anyone sensed surprise or deviation in a given passage. Could students suggest reasons in the music for their particular responses? Could they share a gesture to typify the qualities of movement in a selected event? Could they designate a function for a particular piece?

> We need to keep before us constantly the fact that music becomes educationally significant only when it contributes to human development, that is, when learning takes place. We define learning here as a process of deriving meaning from experiences where meaning represents the interaction, the marriage of thinking and feeling. In music education learning takes place when a musical experience has meaning for a student; that is, when one's own thought and feelings are related to a musical event. (Tait and Haack, 1984, p. 116)

Students can and must be challenged to generate questions that will intensify their own experience of musical works. My aim in this chapter has not been to present a curriculum for music education but rather to call for a change in attitude toward the interaction of music and language. A new attitude will create a new ambiance in classrooms across the country. We must stop thinking of music and language as being essentially incompatible. We must also resist the ongoing temptation to associate language and music in shoddy and inappropriate ways. The language connection is here to stay. And rather than fight it, we should do everything we possibly can to realize its intrinsic power for music education.

9 E Pluribus Unum—Music Education for the One and the Many: Aesthetics and the Art of Teaching

Gordon Epperson

I

The Anglican Prayer Book carries this injunction: "Let us pray for the whole state of Christ's Church." I trust that it is not the purpose of this volume either to prescribe or proscribe prayer on behalf of music education, though a great many of us, I feel sure, are receptive to help in our endeavors from any source that may be regarded as legitimate. But the *whole state* of our vocation—whether that calling be regarded as a secular enterprise, a sacred trust, or both—is clearly the concern of this book, devoted as it is to an examination of music education in the United States. We are undertaking a critical and comprehensive look at what may be called the state of our art: the art of teaching music. This is what a philosophical investigation should be. I accept it as axiomatic that a (or the) philosophy of music education—or indeed any consensus of beliefs, precepts, or directives—could lead to a rigid orthodoxy and perhaps exact a pledge of allegiance. Still, the practice and teaching of music can flourish—can be vital—if exploration, adventure, and (yes) novelty, are not merely tolerated but encouraged and valued.

In an interview with Leopold Stokowski, Glenn Gould (1983) asked the maestro what he thought were the chief requirements for viable education in music. "Subtlety and elasticity," Stokowski answered (p. 163), enunciating ideals that were exemplified throughout his long career. There is no end to the making (and breaking) of laws; but certain concepts, widely entertained, are likely to contribute to growth and dynamism in the art, just as others may be restrictive or conducive to a static uniformity.

All musicians are theorists, insofar as we give expression to our aims, feelings, and aspirations. As active players, singers, teachers, we "compare notes" with one another in every kind of informal setting, demonstrating and verbalizing our ideas of "good tone," authentic interpretation, and the myr-

168

iad concerns of tempo, phrasing, pitch, and rhythm. When such talk is vig-
orous and frequent, it is indicative of a healthy and wholehearted
involvement in music as a vocation. Susanne Langer, a philosopher who took
practicing musicians seriously, described such talk as "studio metaphor."
She listened to it. She was amphibious, able to mediate between the worlds
of formal academic spokespersons and practicing artists. The day-to-day talk
of active musicians is not erudite or esoteric, although jazz players develop
a vocabulary that can be bewildering to the uninitiated; but it is theory
nonetheless. And whenever a teacher says, "Do it this way," or "Try this," or
"Please eliminate that ugly glissando," he or she has recourse to an implicit
"standard" that resides in his or her blood, brain, and bones.

Nothing is more empirical than the practice of music. Theory and practice
are interacting at all times, and should be mutually corrective. What was for
a long time called "method" is necessary, no matter what name we give to
it; but method—indeed, *methods*—must be provisional, because they may
prove faulty, in need of amplification or revision. We discover not the
"truth," but *truths*, in our teaching and in our learning. This is pragmatism
in the valid (because demonstrable) sense that William James gave to the
term. Through trial and error, through experiment, through persistence and
determination, we seek what "works," musically speaking. And now and
then we find it.

I believe that we who have written chapters for this book are in search of
the normative, that we seek principles on which productive argument is
possible and desirable, in order to unify and strengthen our professional efforts and thereby improve the state of music education. I see this as a salutary enterprise, provided flexibility, subtlety, and, I would add, *diversity* are
accorded a high place in any tentative agreement we may reach.

Music education cuts a wide swathe. Within its purview are all the students and teachers of music who are identified, impersonally, through statistics. The designation *music education* is troublesome and ambiguous,
although it is doubtless here to stay. What is the difference between a music
educator and a music teacher? Is the *educator* more likely than the *teacher*
to be an administrator? Of course the terms can be (and often are) treated
as synonyms; but the connotations are subtly different. The educator, surely,
is more remote, less personal, than the teacher. I suggest that *music education* is an appropriate term for the *whole state* of the art; but the individual
practitioner is a teacher.

II

It is the living person for whom music education has come into being; and
it is that individual, and the living teacher as well, who should be central in

philosophic speculation. I see these unique individuals, nowadays, in jeopardy, threatened with extinction on the counting boards of the numbers game. This is not to say that numbers are of no importance, or that they have no relevance to what we do. We need, surely, to know which "programs" are tenacious of life, well-supported, recognized, and valued. These serve as paradigms. Believing as we do that accessibility of instruction in music, and opportunities for hearing it, are essential components of education and culture, we must strive to safeguard their availability, secure and protect the rights of properly qualified teachers, reinforce and reward their dedication, and, indeed, inform the national community of the importance of their work. We cannot do this responsibly without recourse to facts and figures.

Organization, therefore, by those united in common cause, is necessary; and measurement is an important means for identifying—for locating, if you will—areas of danger and deprivation in music education and thereby challenging not only practitioners but (whenever possible) a larger public to remedial action. Such action, obviously, is political. Effective action calls for nothing less than the creation of environments that are *nurturing*, that give prominence to artistic undertakings, and that enlist the economic support and rewards that are the true tests of society's commitment.

I said that organizations are necessary; it is of some comfort, at any rate, to believe so. And I suppose that administrative superstructures, which seem to be multiplying like rabbits, must be tolerated. But I see these, in essence, as epiphenomena, providing *services* to practitioners. I think that teachers, once licensed and at large in society, should be allowed to practice their profession with minimal interference, so long as they do not engage in criminal activities or threaten their pupils, peers, or other professors. There are, today, entirely too many solemn bureaucratic pronouncements and directives; the quantity of redundant paperwork in colleges and universities is intimidating, to say nothing of formal surveillance and evaluation. This situation is endemic in secondary schools as well.

It seems at times that we spend more hours, and more psychic energy, in documenting our exploits than in performing them. Many of the required forms adopted in our institutions, such as particular ones I have examined that provide for student evaluation of their teachers, are supplied by independent agencies and scored by computer. These practices, intended to be "objective," put teachers on the defensive. As instruments for evaluating effective performance they are, for the most part, pathetically inappropriate. They promote anxiety, distrust, and conformity. Yet once adopted, they acquire a sacred aura. When such measurement becomes the rule, moreover, it is quite naturally regarded (after the initial protests have died down) as the name of the game.

William James said that it is the mark of an educated person that he can recognize a "good man" when he sees one! It seems to me that we are fully aware, in most teaching environments, of who is doing productive work—who, if you please, is a "good teacher." We have the living evidence all around us. And we know about the malingerers and the ineffectual teachers as well. Excessive documentation is a smoke screen. It sometimes provides camouflage for ineptitude. It tends to equalize disparate accounts of teaching and performance, because the data are abstracted from living situations. Almost everyone's vita "looks good." Most persons seem to be able to make out a good case for themselves on paper.

Excellence is being proclaimed throughout the land as though it were a concept altogether novel in the history of human endeavor. (One wonders just what else many of us have been trying to achieve all along; but no matter.) Excellence is not an ideal anybody is likely to oppose, and we need, in any case, to continue the exploration of its many aspects. But what kind of excellence are we talking about, and for whom? What are the possible means of ensuring excellence, and have we, indeed, the perspicacity to recognize its myriad manifestations?

Measurement, I venture to say, cannot take us very deeply into the question, its usefulness as a tool notwithstanding. Present-day research is addicted to it; "studies" by and large depend upon numerically defensible investigations that can be represented in charts and graphs, define a "problem area" with a high degree of accuracy, and give the progenitors of such studies the mandatory task of suggesting full or partial solutions. This is an approved, aboveboard species of scholarship, in which "findings" are presumed to constitute a contribution to knowledge. Productive, useful study has, to be sure, been conducted within this framework; but there has been, as well, an enormous amount of painstaking busywork in the service of what Jacques Barzun described as the "Ph.D. octopus." And when a particular mode of investigation is hallowed, admitting only topics deemed appropriate (according to the prevailing canons of measurement), "research" becomes a Procrustean bed; a great deal of priceless energy is devoted to documenting the mundane, the minuscule, or the obvious. How often do we speak of *exciting* research projects or hear such projects referred to?

Nevertheless, organized music education in this country has come a long way since the days—which I remember well—when emphasis was given to the social aspects and benefits of music study. *Participation* was paramount. A cliché that I often heard in my youth went like this: "We didn't play very well but we had a heck of a good time together." A good time, however, is seriously compromised by mediocre or poor music making. Good times become better when music is challenging to teacher and student and its real difficulties recognized and grappled with. This is not to say that a concern for musical values was absent in the 1930s and 1940s of our century, because we have had many gifted and dedicated practitioners in the profession throughout the history of school music. Many of my colleagues in string teaching had their start, as I did, in a public school program. The quality of such programs has always varied widely. The best ones I have had opportunities to observe have reflected the talents and prodigious efforts of individual teachers. Obviously, the availability of public funds and the support of administrators are of crucial importance. But the influence of one teacher can be enormous. When an enthusiasm for music is awakened in a student it is a teacher, most often, who is catalyst and role model. A special, indeed unique, chemistry exists between them. This is a *personal* phenomenon, recalcitrant to computation.

A salutary tradition of democratic idealism within the music education fraternity holds to the proposition that music should be widely available. This axiom, I believe, is *not* in jeopardy. It is no less democratic, however, to recognize significant individual differences among students and to place a premium upon unique abilities. For a long time the recognition of outstanding merit and achievement was, practically speaking, discouraged by many music teachers in the schools. When the charge of elitism is leveled against outstanding performance, it may be construed, I think, as an incomplete understanding of the connotations of *democratic*, if not a fear of *excellence* as well.

The ratings "superior," "excellent," "very good," and "good" dispensed at state and regional music festivals have reflected such leveling-down tendencies. Young people are quick to see that good is bad. One is reminded of *Alice in Wonderland*: "Everybody has won," said the dodo, "and all shall have prizes." The answer to the question "Are we training professional musicians and concert artists?" has long been a mandatory *no*. Many fine musicians, nevertheless, have had their start in the schools. Of course we are not training concert artists! But now and then one will emerge from the educational matrix, and that is not a bad thing. When I speak of the individual student, however, I am not thinking only of the gifted one but rather of every student for whose life music can be significant.

I said that music education has come a long way. A very heartening development in recent years has been the upsurge of concern for improving the quality (excellence, if you please) of the arts being studied in secondary schools throughout the United States and Canada. In music, the tenacious conviction that the values gained through participation in choral and instrumental ensembles were largely social—hence, extramusical—is giving way to a more widespread and explicit attention to the *kind* of music chosen and to the technical and artistic levels of performance.

Bennett Reimer's committee on aesthetics of a few years back, his and Abraham Schwadron's books, and many articles in the *Music Educators Journal* and other publications have testified to a growing concern for the affective and cognitive aspects of musical perception—*qualitative* perception. Aesthetic response to music is individual and cannot be otherwise. One has only to think of the diverse reactions various people can have to the same performance to realize how much of himself or herself the *listener* brings to any musical experience. There is, moreover, wide disagreement and disputation in any viable musical culture. Would we wish it otherwise? It is *because* we are making value judgments that such ferment arises; and again, we are *theorizing*. It is easy to say, in retrospect, that the outrage attending the first performances of Stravinsky's ballet music was mistaken; but the Parisian riot over the *Rite of Spring* demonstrated a passionate public involvement with music.

If there is now such a growing preoccupation with *quality* in music education, what am I complaining of? Excellence is proclaimed from the rooftops!

My complaint is that the proclamation often betrays an acceptance of the *word* itself as sufficient. And I am uneasy about the homogenizing effects of slogans, even in a good cause. Such terms as *excellence* and *quality*, like *love* and *nobility*, are abstractions. All of us like to think that we know a good thing when we see it, or hear it. But whether we do or do not have such clairvoyance, the terms are useful—make sense—only in the particular situation. (I recall here Susanne Langer's assertion that it is the business of philosophy *to make sense of experience*.) There is no excellence, presumably, in a void; and when a concept, unrelated to specific things, is repeated often enough, and *fortissimo*, it paralyzes thought. Any objection is then looked upon as heresy. Observe the uniform vocabulary of this fashionable bandwagon: *Excellence* is something everybody must be *committed to*. The lamp of learning often appears on official stationery that bears the motto. In the official pursuit of excellence many of us in the last two years or so have been enjoined to practice *entrepreneurship*, a vague if grandiose prescription that, so far as I am able to determine, is a euphemism for raising money. Or for recruitment. Compliance and uniformity are likely to result from the energetic prosecution of such (no doubt) nobly intended directives.

III

I think there is a way out of the dilemma. I return to Stokowski's suggestion of *subtlety* and *elasticity* as ideals for music education. These, too, are abstractions; but the moment we enunciate them, we are likely to think of *cases*: the trial and error of teaching as experienced, sometimes most poignantly, by ourselves; the limitations and frequent failures of formulas; experiments that succeeded or did not pan out; and so on. Every teacher with

vocation has engraved on his or her soul the record of interactions with individual students. Human encounters, especially profound ones, are a risky
business. The teacher is also a learner. Therefore our use of the expression
studying with is preferable to the equally prevalent *taking from*.

It is best in this context to speak from experience. Although I have done,
and continue to do, a moderate amount of classroom teaching, the center of
my work is the private lesson and what I believe to be its necessary adjunct,
the weekly performance class. After forty years of such teaching I have what
is called "experience" and maybe some kind of track record. But every lesson is a new beginning; there is perpetual uncertainty and, happily, perpetual novelty as well. We speak, in our educational jargon, of
competencies. Well, one hopes for competence; and, as Somerset Maugham
reportedly said in response to a critic who described him as competent, "At
any rate it is better to be competent than incompetent." Assessing competence empirically is troublesome. Statistics, like biblical quotations, can be
invoked for almost any purpose.

But until rapport is established with a new student, competence cannot
come into play. Learning takes place through dialogue: Each must give and
receive. The initial stage of such a relationship may require a few weeks.
Once established, rapport is likely to endure. Sometimes, to be sure, it
never comes; both student and teacher are then frustrated, and both may be
at a loss for an explanation. At *whatever* level of advancement we may be
working, not "concert artistry," necessarily, but "artistry" is what we aim for.
The studio atmosphere should be humane, supportive, serious, but not
solemn.

Every teacher is a practicing psychologist regardless of training or credentials. The teacher's obligation during a lesson, as in a classroom setting,
is to the task at hand; in my own domain it is cello playing. But one's resources of subtlety and elasticity are challenged at each meeting. Occasionally the impact of a head-on collision is needed. But, more often, oblique
techniques, even trickery, may be called for. After all, there is the element
of "illusion" in art, and we are illusionists. We want results; if they are mag-
ical, so much the better. Let me say, however, that the world of the private
music studio is as *real* as any other. And it has this in common with other
real worlds: everybody has *not* won; nor shall all have prizes. Yet failure, to
whatever degree, need not be a permanent state of affairs. If music, being
something more than a mere activity, deserves as secure a place in the curriculum as algebra or physics, it should be possible to fail, as well as to pass,
in music along with all the rest.

I remember hearing, very often in my younger years, the old saw that education consisted of Mark Hopkins sitting on one end of a log and his pupil
on the other. Hopkins, an alumnus, professor, and for many years president

of Williams College, was a prime mover in 19th-century American education. His chief concern was the nurture and development of the individual student.

Learning, in an art, offers a paradigm of education in its most intense and concentrated form. At the Third International Educational Conference, held in Heidelberg, August 1925, the general theme was "The Development of the Creative Powers in the Child." Martin Buber (1947), the great Jewish philosopher and sage, addressed the gathering. He remarked:

> Art is the province in which a faculty of production, which is common to all, reaches completion. Everyone is elementally endowed with basic powers of the arts, with that of drawing, for instance, or of music; these powers have to be developed, and the education of the whole person is to be built upon them as on the natural activity of the self. (pp. 84–85).

And further, "Real education is made possible by the realization that youthful spontaneity must not be suppressed but must be allowed to give what it can" (p. 88). The child, Buber goes on to say, is educated by *relationships*. (If he is right, it is surely pertinent to ask what the large-scale consequences of a burgeoning computer culture are likely to be.)

Finding the right *balance* in the teacher-student relationship is problematic, depending as it does upon the inevitable tension between freedom and discipline. "Freedom with order!" Pablo Casals proclaimed again and again; and it is not so paradoxical as it sounds. Expressive freedom requires a substratum of technical fluency that is, itself, evolving.

I was a young student in 1939 when Stokowski, then conductor of the Philadelphia Orchestra, formed the All-American Youth Orchestra, which was to tour South America and Europe. In setting forth the requirements for string players who aspired to play in the orchestra, Stokowski expected that they

1. Play with accurate intonation, rhythm, and singing sound
   a. at a very fast speed
   b. at a slow speed, with sustained legato
2. Go from *pp* to *ff* in a single bow
3. Go from *ff* to *pp* in a single bow and to maintain, as well, sustained *forte* or *piano* where required
4. Play with poetry and fire!

Provided the technical underpinning is secure, it is, of course, the poetry and fire of authentic performance that speak to the sensibilities of an audience—"move" the listeners—and justify the difficult acquisition of the craft of music making.

When these components are realized to whatever extent—"brought to-gether," as it were—the musician's individual style (and, one hopes, a sense of appropriate musical style as well), tone color, and phrasing will serve a joyous self-expression and, ideally, an active and well-developed musical imagination. I believe *imagination* to be the most important, and most ne-glected, element in our teaching of young students.

Like many of my readers, I have taken part in a great number of clinics and workshops. Invariably, in my experience, these have been given over to mechanical fundamentals: approaching and holding the instrument, deter-mining which fingers go down first, dealing with positions (on stringed in-struments), coordinating movements of left and right hands and arms, and so on. Since tendonitis is now of epidemic proportions among string players, tension receives, and deserves, a fair share of the time. All these things are important and require attention. But I often find that, in the welter of prob-lems being dealt with, music is likely to get short shrift.

When we hear a thrilling performance, do we remark on how well the art-ist has solved his or her problems, or do we surrender to the magic—the po-etry and the fire?

IV

If the concept of *making music from the start* is crucial, as I believe it to be, how do we (assuming that our own imaginations are active) stimulate the imaginations of our pupils? How do we inculcate style, variety of tone color, sensitive phrasing? Not, I think, by crying "Play with color!" or "Let's have some style!" or "Watch your phrasing!" and not, for that matter, by insisting that they play with poetry and fire.

I suspect that here—where so many verbally ineffable elements are in-volved, so much subtle nuance—we must transmit musical insights by sug-gestion and example, through osmosis, as it were, rather than by frontal attack; through *example* and precept rather than through precept and example.

All my remarks thus far may have suggested that teaching music is a sol-emn business—rigorous, anxious, even painful. The study of music is seri-ous, is demanding, but it need not (and should not) be a lugubrious affair. Its multiple "meanings," its varied contours, are life-enhancing. Great music is an unending source of delight; our appetites are never satisfied. Unless we as professionals are caught, as the years go by, in what Rabindranath Tagore called the dreary desert sands of dead habit, we play music, listen to it, and teach it because we want to. No one is obliged to become a musician; and most of our students in the secondary schools do not, to be sure, enter the profession. We want to bring the joy of music to all of them, if we can, and not only the joy of "great" music but good music of all kinds, each work to be appreciated and recognized for what it is.

Here the multiple choices are bewildering, and the question of musical *value*, inextricably bound up with musical meaning, is the most difficult challenge to the musician who teaches. Aesthetics seeks relevant criteria for evaluation, always acknowledging and attempting to define (if we are to be useful or reliable guides) levels of musical worth. This is not tantamount to elitism or snobbishness, for there are hierarchical levels in every culture, each level offering examples that may be good, or not so good, of their kind. Bach—and rock—have each their proper place. But they are not to be equated. And they are not interchangeable.

Discrimination is the finest attribute of the educated sensibility, whatever the discipline. Through discrimination—through educated choices—we can guide ourselves, and our students, toward the better, toward what we believe to be the "best." Discrimination and consequent *choice* make available a range of satisfying musical experiences that would otherwise be beyond reach, even if one were literally "plugged in," day and night. Susanne Langer has spoken of "the madhouse of too much art"; we can say the same of music. Teachers can hardly avoid making their own preferences clear, though quite unconsciously for the most part, simply in their capacity as role model, mentor, and surrogate parent. But in guiding students through the profligate repertory of music, they should allow and respect the students' choices. Is this not one of the ways in which taste is formed and a precious diversity of tastes encouraged and cultivated?

V

It is not necessary to invoke the hypotheses of game theory in order to see that the study of an art is done for fun, out of curiosity and desire. This fact does not diminish the passion or intensity of the game; on the contrary. Practice of an art does not originate in external social pressure. Parental insistence may, to be sure, impel study for a time, in the absence of desire. But unless, as sometimes happens, the child gets hooked, this study is not likely to last very long. We have all heard dozens of adults say, "How I wish now that my parents had *forced* me to practice the piano!" But this is hindsight.

I said earlier that oblique gambits, even trickery, may be needed to get a student's attention; getting and holding attention is how an effective teaching game is played. But is it really trickery (or to put the worst face on it, dishonesty) to offer music, somehow, in the guise of a game? Not, surely, if it *is* a game. Psychological studies in recent years have indicated that many of our common distinctions between games (however seriously they are taken) and the so-called serious pursuits of life are largely semantic. Nobody is going to play every kind of game, no matter how the term is defined. But any activity *regarded* as a game will be played only by choice, and according to the rules.

If the rules of the game (and for music let us say the rules are the essential disciplines) are ignored or abrogated, there is no fun, no joy. (I find, for example, that with music that is largely aleatoric, when anything goes, nothing much goes. It is simply boring.) New games, with new rules, do come into being: Serialism, partial or total, is illustrative. Particular games, or styles, may or may not be tenacious of life, or they may be viable for special audiences only. The study of aesthetics gives some perspective, offers some highly provisional criteria in this complex area.

When a concern for musical quality becomes central in our thinking, all the benefits of music study cited by earlier educators may be expected to appear in rich profusion: togetherness, having a good time, all the rest of it. *The old-time religion is back*, but with a difference: These undoubted goods are extras, by-products of attention to the music itself. The love of playing good music, and playing it as well as possible, characterizes the game. And let us not forget that all games have winners and losers.

The individual student and teacher are engaged in a game that can have the most far-reaching social consequences. Musical experience is realized only by living persons. Abstracted in numerical surveys, the fundamental importance of these living protagonists is lost sight of. Statistics, I have already conceded, are useful; but they do not communicate any of that human ferment and dynamism that may, under changed circumstances, yield quite different sets of figures.

The numbers game is here to stay, and dealing with group phenomena in music education is necessary, not least in the political arena. But unless the primacy of the student-teacher relationship is given explicit recognition, it will continue to suffer conceptual and, hence, actual neglect.

Part III
Professional Methodology

10 Professional Methodology: Introduction

Merilyn Jones

Methodology is generally defined as a set of procedures employed by a particular discipline. At the genesis of American music education, the procedures were exact and the goal was clearly defined. The objective of the singing school was to improve singing in churches, and the procedures of Lowell Mason sufficed—for a while at least. As the profession grew, so did ideas about teaching, goals, and materials. Music conventions brought teachers together to share these ideas, and publishers were ready with materials and workshops to instruct teachers in their use. Such were the beginnings of methodology.

Today we face a more complex situation in which the "what" and the "how" have been extended to include "when," "why," "to whom," and "to what extent." Methodology has been affected by a myriad of influences, including accountability, competency testing, back to basics, mainstreaming, and lifelong learning, to mention a few. It is time to take stock of where we are as a profession and where we need to go. The chapters here on professional methodology were conceived to guide our thinking and to provide some insight as to the state of the art.

Charles Leonhard lays the foundation for the writings on professional methodology by focusing upon the human values of music education. Leonhard states that the uniqueness of music lies in its "expressive import" and its appeal to the "life of feeling." He cites recent developments in music education that have shifted attention away from music itself while directing our efforts toward test scores, behavioral objectives, concepts, teaching strategies, and the like. As a profession we are teaching more about music, at the expense of the music itself. Leonhard challenges music educators to join forces with those who seek excellence in an educational program that embraces the arts as essential to humankind.

In a chapter directed to teachers of methods courses in music, Leonhard points out the all-too-frequent gap between theory and practice. Although students must have some exposure to theory of instruction, they must also have a model for the application of theory in practice. Leonhard believes that the instructor of the methods course must have an opportunity to practice what he or she preaches. The laboratory school would appear to be the ideal setting for this experience; however, as Leonhard points out, the laboratory school is now almost extinct. Included in the chapter is a detailed approach to planning the music methods course using behavioral objectives, experiences, and experiential objectives. The instructor of the music methods course is reminded that students learn to do what they do.

Methodology as it relates to music in general education is treated in the article by Gretchen Hieronymus Beall. Beall begins by establishing a context for general music methodologies, tracing programs and methodologies from the Hawes School in Boston through the influence of Orff, Kodály, and Dalcroze in the late 1960s and 1970s to the challenge of teaching methodology in the college classroom of the 1980s. Principles for music in general education speak to the role that music should play in the education of the general student: (a) the musical intelligence of every child must be developed; (b) social and entertainment functions of music must be addressed; (c) programs must allow for the development of creativity in the arts; (d) musical performance should continue throughout life; and (e) musical and personal needs should be met at each stage of life. Beall concludes with recommendations for music in early childhood, the school years, and for senior citizens.

Music methodology for exceptional children is presented by Richard M. Graham in a comprehensive overview of professional activity in music education and music therapy. Graham addresses first the changes in laws and educational practices in the past fifteen years that resulted in the inclusion of handicapped children in the regular music classroom. Following a discussion of what mainstreaming is and what it is not, Graham offers encouragement for the period of transition in which music educators learn to work effectively in mainstreamed classes. The author states that music educators who succeed in teaching exceptional children, handicapped or gifted, subscribe to a basic philosophy: The exceptional child, like all other members of society, must be provided an opportunity to develop his or her abilities. Graham concludes with descriptions of successful methodologies being used with exceptional children in the music classroom.

Methodologies in higher education is the subject of Chapter 15, by Robert Glidden. His discourse is organized around Charles Leonhard's definition of the processes involved in a program of music education—program development, instruction, administration, supervision, and evaluation. Glidden points out that our system of higher education is the product of a free society with comprehensiveness as an important objective. Although he states that there have been few major changes in college music programs in the past 50 years, he comments on those influences that have been felt in music programs in higher education. In his discussion of administration, Glidden describes the organizational aspects that characterize the collegiate music department, the school of music, and the college of music. Program evaluation, faculty evaluation, and accreditation are dealt with in the concluding section of the chapter.

Wind band pedagogy in the United States is dealt with by Craig Kirchhoff in Chapter 16. After a brief description of the historic role of the band in society, Kirchhoff analyzes the process of program development, beginning with the importance of philosophy. The author believes that many instrumental programs do not address the primary goals of music education. Kirchhoff further states that activity-oriented instrumental programs often seek goals that can be achieved through other activities—winning, entertainment, discipline, cooperation, and teamwork. Kirchhoff sees aesthetic education as the primary objective of the instrumental music program. In a discussion of current trends, Kirchhoff addresses problems associated with maintaining the program—competition, corps-style band, jazz ensemble, repertoire, and programming. Finally, Kirchhoff asserts that the key to a successful instrumental music program is the teacher-conductor.

The professional methodology associated with school and youth orchestra programs is addressed by William L. Jones. The author begins with a discussion of the orchestra from a historical perspective and moves to a description of orchestras in five categories: public and private schools, colleges and conservatories, civic and community contexts, youth orchestras, and professional contexts. The organization and administration of the youth symphony is treated in great detail. In a description of the methodology associated with the youth orchestra, Jones offers an alternative to the hierarchy of chairs resulting from the traditional method of auditioning. Also included in this section of the chapter are suggestions for score preparation, motivation, and rehearsal pacing.

Expanding the students' musical awareness is cited by Amanda Penick as the primary goal for instruction in the private studio. The student who is more aware accomplishes more in practice, is more enthusiastic toward progress, and has greater understanding of the music being performed. Penick focuses upon three areas of awareness: (a) visual awareness, (b) physical awareness, and (c) aural awareness, which includes theoretical awareness of sound. Each of these categories is carefully described, and suggestions are given for development of each type of awareness. Penick states that although students may perform at different levels according to ability, all students can experience growth in awareness with the proper guidance of a teacher who can offer imaginative suggestions and can translate symbols or concepts into sensation.

The chapters on methodology represent current thought in each of the areas of specialization addressed by these writers. Each writer has made a significant contribution to our understanding of methodology as it relates to mission. The common thread that binds these works together is the emphasis upon music teaching, and therein lies our mission: teaching music.

11 The Human Values of Music Education

Charles Leonhard

This chapter is cast within the framework of a broad definition of music education: *Music education encompasses all deliberate efforts to bring about musical learning.* Thus, the term applies not only to public school music and music teacher education but also to all types of institutionalized instruction in music at every level from early childhood through graduate education. It also applies to music instruction carried on outside the context of a school.

Definition of Terms

The term *professional methodologies* refers to the modes of behavior used by professional music educators as they play their adopted role in carrying out the processes involved in a program of music education. Those processes are program development, instruction, administration, supervision, and evaluation.

Program development is the process that involves making decisions about objectives, stating them in terms of behavior, and then selecting and describing experiences designed to enable students to achieve the objectives sought.

Instruction is the process by which the teacher arranges a learning environment that enables students to undergo the experiences growing out of the program development process. In both program development and instruction, experience with music must have the qualities of undergoing, doing, and being involved cognitively and affectively with the subject matter, which is music itself.

Administration involves providing the setting for learning. It includes provision of personnel, facilities, equipment, instructional materials, and budgetary planning.

Supervision refers to the expert technical service and leadership designed to improve instruction.

Evaluation is the process of determining the extent to which the objectives established in program development are being achieved.

Authors of subsequent chapters will treat one or more of these processes in their own area of specialization—general music; special education; orchestra and band education; and higher education.

The Human Values of Music Education

My role is to sound the keynote for the section on methodologies in music education. The keynote I have selected is the human values of music education. It is my thesis that emphasis on human values should pervade all of the processes at every level of the music education program from early childhood through the graduate school.

Emphasis on human values in music education becomes more essential with every passing day. It appears obvious that the contemporary world is becoming increasingly mechanized, depersonalized, computerized, and homogenized. Howard Johnson's, McDonald's, Burger King, and Wendy's are prime examples. Each of these chains not only has the same look but also has the same menu from Maine to Hawaii and beyond. Every passing year sees a greater premium placed on predictability, standardization, control, and rule-governed behavior, both within the school and without. The atmosphere of the school as well as of the society has become increasingly anti-aesthetic and anti-imaginative.

The role of the imagination, the uniquely human characteristic, has become more and more limited in the school, in children's play, in literature, and in the theater. Yet the need for imaginative experience persists in people. Madam Alexander cannot meet the demand for her dolls even though they have no moving parts and no tape to activate talking or crying. They are simply replicas of beautiful people that delight the senses and stir the imaginations of their owners. Witness also the sales of millions of copies of Harlequin Romances, which leave a great deal concerning male-female sexual relationships to the imagination of the reader rather than describing the act of sex in the concrete and explicit terms that has been the mode in much of contemporary literature.

Motivated by President Reagan's National Commission on Excellence in Education and its report, *A Nation at Risk* (1983), educators and others are making a mad dash to emphasize the basics in education. If the most obvious parts of that report were put into effect in American education, the school program would consist entirely of reading, writing, mathematics, science, and computer science, all monitored and controlled by standardized tests. Didactic and computerized instruction leading to rote and memoriter learning designed to enable students to remember information long enough to pass a standardized test would pervade the school. The tyranny of the test makers would become absolute.

We now hear rumblings from music educators, threatened by this educational climate, about students needing to amass more testable information in music. They want these objective data to establish the worth of the music program.

To do so would inevitably result in emphasis on the externals of music's structure and on the minutiae of music at the expense of its essence. I believe that we must stand, like Horatius at the bridge, and fight any move away from the human values of music education. We must, indeed, strive to enhance the human values in music. If we can do so, the music education program will stand like a beacon, shedding the light of imaginative and feelingful experience on a school and a nation dominated by standardization and quantification. It is for this reason that I stress the importance of musical experience and musical learning, which can serve as a spur to the imagination and a stimulus to the life of feeling.

Expressive Import

The strength of music as an art and the reason every society has nurtured and valued its music lie in the strong appeal of music to the life of feeling and to the imagination. The potential strength and value of the music education program lie in the development of responsiveness to the expressive import of music. Bereft of its expressive function and its aesthetic quality, music has nothing unique to offer to the education of children, young people, or adults. With consistent emphasis on its expressive function, however, music education can fill a unique role in the development of the human potential of people of all ages. This should be the dominant objective, the overriding end toward which we strive and toward which the entire program is directed.

Recent developments in education as a whole and in music education have occurred at the expense of the expressive import of music. The mania for quantification of results through test scores has affected the climate of the school adversely. Music educators have taken refuge in any one of a number of false havens: organized approaches to musical learning such as those of

Carl Orff and Zoltán Kodály, elaborate teaching strategies, elaborate notions about concept development, behavioral objectives, emphasis on technique, emphasis on the externals of the structure of music. We have become so involved with the strategy, the concepts, the behavioral objective, the techniques, and the externals that we ignore or give only secondary attention to the essence of music: its expressive import with its effect on the imagination, the sentient life, and the spirit of the people.

In children's early years and, perhaps, even in kindergarten, music is a source of delight, an avenue for self-expression, a spur to the imagination and a high level of feeling. As children move through successive years of the school, however, they find less and less in school music to feel good about and more and more about it to learn; and much of what they are expected to learn has little or nothing to do with the enchantment they found in music originally.

Music—that marvelous force that seemed so wondrous to children—begins to recede in their consciousness and that of their teachers. What once was a source of delight becomes increasingly a source of drudgery and boredom. Children are subjected to the trivia of music at the expense of its essence. They do not learn to shape a phrase, to project and respond to the expressive line in music, the real fundamental of music. They are not permitted to use their imaginations and let their feelings soar when performing and listening to music. They are expected, on the other hand, to learn technical trivia that they are usually not in a position to use and that they quickly forget if they learn them at all.

In listening the focus is on recognition of form, recognition of instruments, recognition of themes and facts about composers' lives, all of which come to intrude on children's imaginative responses to the expressive import of the music. Seldom if ever are they permitted to listen to music and respond to it in their own creative and imaginative ways without the encumbrance and interference of musical and technical trivia.

Little changes when children begin instrumental instruction. They drag through instruction books filled with exercises, scales, contrived melodies and tunes that have little or no expressive appeal. Little that they play has expressive import and, even if a piece they are playing does have such import, they are perforce so involved with technique that they are likely to miss that import. There is no time for listening to artistic performances on their instrument, no time to play by ear tunes they know and like, no time to improvise. There is only time for technical study and drill. The tremendous dropout rate in instrumental music should long since have alerted us to the fact that students are not gaining the musical satisfaction they expect from their experience with music. As a result we lose contact with the mass of students and leave their musical education in the hands of disc jockeys who do not interfere with the expressive appeal of country and western music and rock.

At the collegiate level the neglect of the human values becomes increasingly blatant as the music major pursues preparation for a lifelong career in music. Students are too often immersed in the "theory" of music with little attention to music itself. They are confronted with the task of memorizing detailed information regarding history compiled by Donald Grout and others, often with little opportunity to relate that information to music itself. In conducting courses the emphasis is on developing precise beat patterns with little or no attention to the real role of the conductor—revealing to performers the expressive line of music. In applied music the development of technique dominates both teacher and students at the expense of learning to project the expressive import of the music they perform.

In graduate music programs the neglect of human values reaches its apex. Specialized studies in musicology emphasize the minutiae of history, style, and structure of music in the European tradition with little or no attention to contemporary art music or popular and folk music. Music education professors and, as a concomitant, graduate music education students become involved with research, aesthetic theory, learning theory, computers, statistics, and measurement to the degree that they often forget that music is their subject, and the essence of music education, therefore, lies neglected.

The most damning aspect of music education lies in our consistent avoidance of self-expression through the creation of music by composing and improvisation. At no place in the music curriculum from elementary school through graduate school do students other than composition majors have the opportunity, motivation, or encouragement to use their creative abilities. Jazz bands have become stage bands, most of which adhere to the score as slavishly as the symphonic band or orchestra. The demise of the Manhattanville Music Curriculum Project and Comprehensive Musicianship is not just regrettable; it is a symptom of our lack of concern with human values.

Most of the graduate students with whom I have contact have, during their musical education and probably as a direct result of it, lost or buried their intuitive responsiveness to the expressive import of music—the very essence that grabbed them and touched them as children and motivated them to become musicians and music teachers. One of my greatest rewards from teaching is seeing that interest and responsiveness restored and the students' intuitive insight into the expressive properties of music undergirded with intellectual insight through a combination of courses in aesthetic theory and comprehensive musicianship.

Expressive import is the humanizing force in music; it is the source of the human values in music education. The human values of music education include growth of children and young people as thinking, feeling, imaginative individuals and as social beings who have made some aesthetic choices, who control the aesthetic quality of their own lives, who feel competent to do things with and about music, who are satisfied with their own abilities, who participate in musical experiences for their intrinsic rewards, and who are sufficiently attracted to music to establish deep involvement with it.

The Basics of Music Education

The time has come for music educators to return to the basics of music education, the true fundamentals of music: emphasis on the expressive import of the music we involve our students in and the cultivation of responsiveness to that import.

We must realize that the appropriate subject matter of music study is music itself. We must select music for study that is expressive and appealing to students, and we must emphasize that expressive import. We must begin instruction with the expressive import of the music we are dealing with, relate everything we do or ask students to do to that import and end with that import. Expressive import is truly the alpha and omega of music learning and music teaching focused on human values.

The primary role of the music program is to stimulate feelingful thought and thoughtful feeling, processes in which the imagination is freed, is stimulated, and takes flight. In this role, music education will be in a position to counter the sterility, the depersonalization, and the retreat into isolation that pervade contemporary society. In this role, music education will be valued and supported by students and by the public.

Happily, we do not stand alone in our quest for human values and our belief in the worth of the music education program in achieving those values. We find support in the reports of two prestigious bodies that stand in sharp contrast to the narrow and arid conception of education espoused in *A Nation at Risk* (1983). *The Basic Academic Competencies* (1983), published by the College Entrance Examination Board, places the arts on an equal footing with other academic subjects, a true first in the history of prestigious publications about American education. The statement concerning the worth of the arts in that publication has significance for all of us. In emphasizing the human values of the arts, the report says that the arts:

1. challenge and extend human experience;
2. represent a unique record of diverse cultures;
3. provide distinctive ways of understanding human beings and nature;
4. represent creative modes by which all people can enrich their lives by their own self-expression and response to the expression of others;

5. and [most important, in my opinion] enhance the quality of living, engage the imagination, foster flexible ways of thinking, develop disciplined effort and build self-confidence. (p. 6)

Ernest Boyer (1983) supports education in the arts with these words:

The arts are an essential part of human experience; they are not a frill. We recommend that all students study the arts to discover how human beings use nonverbal symbols and communicate not only with words but also through music, dance and the visual arts. (p. 98)

The Future of Music Education

I will close by establishing a few caveats for the future.

1. We must not dehumanize the music program by making it merely an academic discipline, a repository of information that can be quantified and tested objectively.
2. We must not fall victim to the siren call of the computer, which, with all its potential, can only serve learning as a sophisticated machine useful in drill on and testing of information.
3. We must glory in the fact that music is different from other subjects in the school and requires a form of evaluation different from objective tests of information accumulated by students. The questions with which we must evaluate programs are these:
   a. Do we provide opportunities for *all* students to participate in learning experiences with music?
   b. Do we develop usable skills: the ability to sing, to sing in parts, to read music, to play some instrument by ear and from the notation?
   c. Do we identify talented students and provide special opportunities for development of their talent?
   d. Does the music program result in the enhancement of the spirit of the individual student, the school, and the community?
   e. Does the program result in raising the level of students' self-esteem of their musical abilities?
   f. Does the program produce students who have a basis for making reasoned choices about the role of music in their lives?
   g. Do students use music as a means of self-expression in school and out?
   h. Do they value the expression of others?
   i. Do they seek further opportunities for musical experience in school, at home, and in the community?

Gathering evidence of our success in meeting these criteria will provide justification for the music program that will be convincing to school administrators and the public alike.

Human values should pervade each of the processes involved in the music education program. In program development we must establish objectives and provide experiences designed to reveal, in Angela Diller's words, "the hidden splendor of music" and to develop musical independence on the part of all students.

In instruction in all classes and activities at every level we must involve students in all the avenues to musical experience: feeling, performing, hearing, discriminating, knowing, and composing. We must strive for success for all students in doing worthwhile things with and about music that will enhance their self-esteem through expanding and helping them use their musical abilities.

In supervision and administration we must establish a setting and structure that provide for human values for every music teacher: recognition, reward, positive reinforcement, freedom to teach in a style that is consistent with his or her personality and value system. Unity of purpose tempered by an atmosphere that permits divergence in teaching style is essential.

In evaluation we must emphasize securing evidence that we are attaining the human values established by our statement of objectives. We must use objective tests only when and if their content is directly related to the objectives we seek to attain.

I charge all music educators with the mission of carrying the torch of human values of music education into the schools of a society that is becoming increasingly mechanized, depersonalized, and unimaginative.

If we accept this mission and put it into practice—if we realize that music education operates in the realm of feeling and can truly educate for humanness in an increasingly mechanistic and depersonalized society—music will no longer be considered a frill. Music can indeed operate as a core subject lying at the heart of the school curriculum. Music will truly be basic.

12 Methods Courses in Music Teacher Education

Charles Leonhard

The methods course lies at the very core of music teacher education. It is the basis for the claim of professional status for the music teacher educator. Without methods courses no music teacher education program can exist. The truth of these statements is self-evident, and I feel confident that no music teacher educator will disagree with them.

We must, however, recognize that our success in organizing and conducting methods courses has not been overwhelming. Surveys of the opinions of graduates of music teacher education programs consistently reveal an alarming degree of dissatisfaction with methods courses. The following opinions are common:

1. The courses are overly theoretical and unrealistic
2. They do not provide useful preparation for meeting current teaching problems
3. There is too much overlap among methods courses
4. They are uninteresting

Students typically rate ensemble experience as being more valuable in their preparation for teaching music than methods courses. Although curriculum decisions cannot be entirely based on the opinions of graduates of music teacher education programs, neither can their opinions be ignored. The situation behooves us to examine our methods courses and revise them so that they do accomplish what they are supposed to accomplish: provide a viable basis for each prospective teacher to develop sound and effective teaching competencies.

The Reconciliation of Theory and Practice

The task of reconciling theory and practice intellectually and operationally, in methods courses and in the music teacher education program as a whole, is one we have never accomplished satisfactorily. It is not an easy task. Students must not only encounter the principles that constitute a sound theory of instruction; they must also undergo instruction in which a theory of instruction is consciously and obviously applied in the teaching that takes place in the methods course.

At the present time there is almost a complete separation between theory of instruction and instructional practice in the music teacher education program as a whole and in methods courses in particular. Almost every curriculum requires one or more courses in educational psychology and general methods of teaching, but these courses are too often set aside in a theoretical compartment that bears little (if any) relationship to music methods courses or to the real world of music teaching. Having made a nod in the direction of theory, we then set out in our specialized methods courses to prepare prospective teachers with a few tricks of the trade that will help them survive student teaching and their first professional year. We too often ignore the task of applying generalizations from theory to practice in our own instruction. Not only are our students denied experience in such conscious application, they graduate from the music teacher education program without even the foggiest conception of the process of applying theory to practice. And many have serious doubts about the relevance of theory for the real world of teaching.

An example of our failure in dealing productively with the objectives of instruction may be enlightening at this point. Over the past 20 years or so, the wide use of Leonhard and House (1958/1972) and other books has brought the necessity for behavioral definition of objectives into the consciousness of most people involved in music teacher education as either students or instructors. As a result, literally reams of statements of objectives have been produced for all levels of the music education program from preschool through college. Some statements are admirable in their precision and comprehensiveness; others are startlingly inept. The problem is that those statements, whether admirable or inept, have rarely been used as the basis for selecting content, structuring learning experiences for students, and evaluating the results of instruction. We talk about the necessity for objectives in methods courses but rarely apply and demonstrate the relationship between objectives and evaluation.

Essentially we fail to provide a model in the organization and conduct of instruction for students in methods courses, a model that they understand and value as a basis for developing their own modes of instruction. In the absence of such a model, prospective teachers harken back to the most prestigious model they have encountered in their own musical education—usually a band director or choral director or, occasionally, an applied music teacher.

The truism that teachers teach as they were taught, not as they were taught to teach, applies vigorously to music teacher education. Our task, and it is a formidable one, is to serve as such a prestigious model that we can affect the changing teaching behavior of our students, change that they accept intellectually and emotionally and will incorporate in their own teaching practice.

Principles of Teaching and Learning

The theory of learning and instruction is not in a finished state, but it does contain a body of well-substantiated principles that are applicable to teaching and learning in all levels and specializations of music education. I hazard the opinion that few music educators would cavil at the soundness of such principles of teaching as these:

1. Formulate sound teaching objectives in terms of student behavior
2. Select valid subject matter and structure learning experiences that are relevant to the establishment of the desired behaviors
3. Provide for active participation of students in the learning experiences selected
4. Use a variety of devices to increase perception
5. Manage the learning environment to secure a high level of motivation

If such principles were applied consciously in all of the instruction that music teacher education students undergo and if the students were consistently engaged in analyzing the instructional process they are undergoing, promising benefits would inevitably accrue.

1. They would learn to analyze the processes involved in the instruction that they themselves carry on
2. They would value theory and its applicability to instruction
3. They would have a basis for evaluating instruction, both their own and that of others
4. They would develop the ability to draw on principles to initiate teaching rather than relying on the bag of instructional tricks we provide
5. They would be able to use analysis and evaluation in solving the instructional problems and educational dilemmas they are likely to encounter in their professional lives
6. They would develop cognitive skills usable in the development of effective teaching

In the utopian world, all the teaching that music teacher education students undergo would reflect the reconciliation of learning theory and instructional practice. What a difference it would make if instruction in music theory, music history, applied music, ensembles, educational psychology, and music education courses were organized consciously to engage students in experiences with the subject matter that were directly related to the achievement of clearly stated objectives! This may be achievable, or nearly achievable, in small departments in which most of the music faculty have done graduate study in music education. For most departments and schools of music, however, it is an impossible dream. Still, we should be able to achieve this level of quality in instruction in our own professional courses and activities in which we involve music teacher education students.

Once we have described the teaching competencies that a particular methods course is designed to develop, we are in a position to select and describe the experiences we consider productive of those behaviors and organize the learning situation in such a way that students are enabled to undergo those experiences.

Planning a Methods Course

The simplest and, therefore, most effective approach to program development and planning a course in music or music methods involves three factors: behavioral objectives, experiences, and experiential objectives.

Behavioral Objectives. The stating of objectives is not a new idea in music education. For years we have established and stated our objectives. The problem is that those objectives have been so vague and abstract that, although no one could disagree with them, neither could anyone teach from them nor tell when they had been achieved.

We are fond of objectives having to do with knowing, understanding, appreciating, and developing musicianship. These abstract concepts provide a starting point and can be useful as broad goals, but they cannot serve as instructional objectives in the methods course or any other course.

What we have to do is answer the question What kinds of behavior can we accept as evidence of the achievement of those goals? The answer lies in behavioral definition of the objectives. Defining objectives in terms of behavior requires that we use verbs descriptive of an observable behavior.

At the risk of redundance, I will review briefly the process of deriving and stating behavioral objectives. A behavioral objective must specify the *individual* who is expected to achieve the behavior. In the case of methods courses, that individual will be the prospective general music teacher, band director, choral director, or other type of teacher. Behavioral objectives force us to be concerned with the individual students and their achievement, not with groups or classes.

The *action verb* defines what the student is able to do as a result of instruction. The action verb describes an overt and measurable behavior.

The *content reference* identifies the subject matter with which the objective deals and toward which the behavior of the student is directed. We cannot equate the presentation of subject matter with learning it. The student can demonstrate that he or she has essential control of the subject matter only by doing something with or about it. Behavioral objectives specify what he or she is supposed to do.

For a behavioral objective to become operable, we must also establish the *conditions* under which the student is to demonstrate the behavior and a *criterion* against which his or her behavior is to be evaluated.

Thus, a well-stated behavioral objective is five-dimensional: (a) a description of the conditions under which the behavior is to take place, (b) a specific description of the individual involved, (c) a specific and observable behavior, (d) a substantive or content dimension toward which the behavior is directed, and (e) a criterion measure.

A behavioral objective appropriate for a course in choral methods would be: "Given an SATB score and two listenings to a recorded performance of the work, the prospective choral director will identify melodic and rhythmic errors in the performance with 90% accuracy."

You will find in developing instructional objectives for methods courses that many objectives are not amenable to a quantified criterion measure and are therefore defective. Often the criterion measure will be "to the satisfaction of the instructor." For example: "Given 15 minutes, the student establishes in writing a behavioral objective in each of the following categories: (a) knowledge, (b) listening skills, (c) performance skills, and (d) attitudes that fulfill Robert Mager's (1962) and Norman E. Gronlund's (1978) criteria for behavioral objectives to the satisfaction of the instructor."

Experiences. Each behavioral objective implies the types of experience that will be fruitful for the student in achieving that objective. When I use the word *experience* I use it in the sense that John Dewey used it—having a quality of undergoing, doing, and being involved with the subject matter. I suggest that in selecting experiences we heed the most potent principle from the psychology of learning that I know: *Students learn to do what they do.*

The choral methods sample objective given above would imply such experiences by the student as:

1. hearing tapes of two performances of a choral composition while following the score, one version with errors, the second without
2. marking on the score errors heard
3. identifying errors when he or she performs with or conducts the class in a composition

After undergoing experiences such as these, the promising prospective choral director should be able to fulfill the criterion measure specified in the behavioral objective. Those who cannot do so should receive remedial work in hearing or be discouraged from becoming a choral director.

Experiential Objectives. It appears obvious that not all the objectives of methods courses can be stated in behavioral terms and all cannot be measured within the bounds of a particular course. This fact necessitates the use of another level of objectives, which I choose to call experiential objectives.

The term *experiential objectives* refers to experiences, the result of which we can assume to be of value to the prospective teacher even though the outcomes may be long range and not amenable to measurement or evaluation during the course or even at the end of the total music teacher education program. Experiential objectives include such experiences as: (a) attending a competition festival, (b) observing an experienced band director's final rehearsal for a concert and the concert, (c) observing an in-service workshop of music teachers in a school system.

Context for the Methods Course

The optimum context for methods courses provides their instructors with the opportunity not only to preach but also to practice what they preach. The laboratory school was designed to achieve this kind of environment. Methods course instructors also taught music in the laboratory school and were able to establish a theoretical basis for their teaching in the methods course and to apply the theory in their teaching of children with the college students observing. There was, ideally, constant interplay between the content of the methods course and teaching and learning in the laboratory school. For a variety of reasons laboratory schools have all but ceased to exist, and where they are still in operation, the mode is for them to become increasingly independent and unrelated to the teacher education program.

A viable alternative is to attach a laboratory situation to each methods course. In some instances such a laboratory can be established in a nearby parochial or public school with the methods course instructor teaching children in that school. Such arrangements are often unfeasible, however, and this kind of arrangement cannot be considered typical nationally.

A promising substitute lies in adding one hour a week to the methods course to enable the instructor to practice what he or she preaches by teaching methods course students in a general music, instrumental, or choral class, using, not materials suitable for children, but materials suitable for the methods course students themselves. In the methods portion the students can be involved in identifying materials suitable for children and in adapting the strategies used in the laboratory to children's abilities and levels of achievement.

I have been fortunate over the past 30 years to be in a position to preach in two courses that involve philosophical considerations, program development, and methods of teaching and to practice what I preach in an additional course in comprehensive musicianship. As a result, students have been enabled to experience directly the result of the application of my principal philosophical, musical, and pedagogical tenets in what amounts to a laboratory situation.

In all three courses I provide students with behavioral objectives and experiential objectives—I describe the experiences they will undergo. As a result, students inform me that a true reconciliation between theory and practice takes place, and that they are enabled to adapt the resulting teaching insights to their own area of specialization in music teaching.

Such a context for methods courses can and should be established. Such a learning environment is decidedly preferable to having students do peer teaching with children's materials, which almost inevitably results in an artificial atmosphere that is not conducive to learning. Obviously, the classroom and laboratory experience must be supplemented by observation in school music classrooms and the opportunity to become acquainted with instructional materials suitable for children of different ages in all kinds of musical learning situations.

We must broaden our concept of methods courses to emphasize cognition regarding the teaching process, to develop insight into the art of successful teaching, and in addition, to establish a repertory of viable teaching behaviors growing out of these insights that will see the prospective teacher successfully through student teaching and the first professional year.

I have not advocated the adoption of any one theory of learning or theory of instruction. The theory or theories that one adopts represent a personal choice, although one may find assistance in the writings of Gordon Allport, Jerome Bruner, Jean Piaget, David Ausubel, Robert Gagne, B. F. Skinner, Abraham Maslow. The first Ann Arbor Symposium established, at least for the present, the futility of appealing to learning theories or learning theorists for an easy explanation of successful teaching of music and efficient learning of music (MENC, 1981).

The preferable route is for us, who should be and are the specialists in music teaching and learning, persistently to analyze the processes involved in both, to determine the different types of learning that make up the gestalt of music learning. Then we can appeal to an applicable learning theory as a source of greater insight into the processes of music learning and into the kind of teaching that will be successful in bringing it about efficiently.

Beginning systematic work on a single methods course represents an excellent initiation into the description of teaching competencies. Such an effort will not only lead to systematic improvement in your own methods course but will also inspire you to initiate an ongoing effort at total program development in the music teacher education program in your college or university.

A Professional Program of Music Teacher Education

Once we have learned to describe in behavioral terms the musical and teaching competencies of the graduate of the music teacher education program and to select and describe the experiences we consider productive of those behaviors, we will be in a position to make informed decisions about the courses and activities that serve as means to the involvement of students in those experiences. Only then will we have a truly professional program of music teacher education.

A consistent effort at program development would enable us to answer many of the questions that face us and for which we lack satisfactory answers. I will present only two such questions: How and when should entry to music teacher education be established? and When should early field experience be initiated?

A logical entry point would be through a course designed to develop the cognitive skills required to analyze and evaluate music instruction. Such skills would enable the student observing music instruction to determine the elements and factors at work that make the instruction successful or unsuccessful. This course must operate within the framework of revealed behavioral objectives and experiences that are genuinely related to those objectives. The cognitive content establishes the components of the learning environment that the student needs to identify when he or she observes music teaching. Those components include objectives, the relationship of learning experiences to objectives, motivational techniques, and provision for individualized learning.

This course would not be offered in the freshman year when the student is facing all sorts of personal adjustment hurdles; the sophomore year would be more appropriate. Such a course represents essential preparation for early field experience; and early field experience should be postponed until the student has developed the analytical skills that can make early field experience worthwhile. The student would then approach it from a perspective entirely different from that which is common—simply racking up enough hours of often mindless observation to meet certification or program requirements.

The presentation of the content of subsequent courses in the professional component would be based on the cognitive framework established in the entry course. Instructors serve as models who organize experiences directly relevant to the revealed objectives and encourage their students to analyze and evaluate the instruction they are undergoing. With this kind of organization the music teacher education program would epitomize a true spiral of learning experiences about which we talk so much and achieve so rarely.

This systematic approach to developing methods courses could lead to the day when teaching music methods and conducting the professional component of music teacher education are not routinely assigned to graduate assistants in large institutions or, in smaller ones, shoved onto faculty members as an addition to their other, more valued, duties. The day must come when meeting such responsibilities is recognized as an essential and valued professional role for specialists in music teacher education.

13 Methodology and Music in General Education

Gretchen Hieronymus Beall

Music in general education is the central task of the music education profession. The expressive power of music at every level of culture mandates our attention to it as a creative force in societal life and in general education at every level. General music continues, however, to have a tenuous hold in general education, more so in the eyes of the public than in the educational establishment.

Three trends in public education currently reinforce this fact. First is the paramount position given to science. The sciences currently hold ascendance both in the support of the public and the government; the humanities and the traditional social sciences are given meager support by comparison. Greater support and attention are needed to improve the access to cultural information through these "humanistic" fields. Future generations may then find it possible to understand and evolve solutions to economic and social problems and to create meaningful and productive lives for themselves.

Second, a great deal of attention is given to the education of the specialist, all in the name of excellence of education. Responsibility and respect are given to the "expert," and expertise is expected at a high level of functioning. Medical specialists, politicians, computer technologists, engineers, researchers, media specialists, and, yes, even entertainers—certainly specialists in their own field—accept responsibility for a level of functioning that takes years of concentration to attain. The amateur—the person who does something for the love of it—is losing out. There have always been great variances in levels of attainment; but our expectations, especially for the skilled amateur, have changed.

Finally, music and the other arts do not fill easily demonstrable, practical needs in life. The knowledges that the arts give us have little apparent ap-

202

plication, and the values are difficult to discuss. Yet the need that they fill is fundamental. Salieri, in *Amadeus,* entreats his "sharp old God" concerning music's power: "What is this? Tell me, Signore! What is this pain? What is this need in sound? Forever unfillable, yet fulfilling him who hears it, utterly!" Conditions in contemporary life force us into mediated, vicarious experiences. The arts, by their very nature, cannot really be known and experienced save by direct, personal involvement. Music education is personal education. It is a continuous process, beginning with the first awareness of sound and ending when life ends. In this chapter, I will consider programs and methods of teaching music in general education from early childhood through the school years and ending with senior citizens. First, a context for methodologies and programs will be discussed. Then, principles for programs and methods for music in general education will be developed. Finally, programs and methods will be described, based on research and current methods and focused on the ages, abilities, needs and cultural interests of each level of student.

General Music Methodologies: A Context

Music education has given a great amount of attention to programs and methods in general music. Concern has been confined largely to Grades 1 through 6, with periodic forays into early childhood and the junior high school or middle school and an occasional high school offering of music appreciation or music literature classes. Performance group offerings in the secondary schools are also sometimes seen as a form of general music education.

Both programs and teaching methodologies have evolved in form and content over the years. We usually trace the beginning of music education in this country to Lowell Mason in the Hawes School in Boston, where music was first recognized formally as part of the curriculum in 1838. (All historical material is taken from Birge, 1937 and Tellstrom, 1971.) Vocal music had been taught in schools for some time on the initiative of individual school principals. The earlier singing schools, which Mason considered to be the foundation of popular music education, actually were attended by a small and self-selected minority. Mason's goals on coming to Boston had been to raise the quality of singing school teaching and to improve the compositional quality and choir performance of church music material. The methods that he used in the Hawes School, and those that were used by the teachers that followed him there, were the methods of the singing school. The joy of singing, the skill of reading music, and some rudimentary theory content were paramount considerations. This was not yet general music.

Luther Whiting Mason may be more properly considered the founder of school music methodology. His *National Music Course* was not only the first completely planned course in music to receive national recognition, it was also the prototype of the many methods that followed. He formulated a music course for the primary grades. Most notably, he espoused a particular philosophy and methods for music reading based on the principle that children learn to read words with which they are already familiar. Therefore, they should learn to sing songs by rote first, and *then* learn to read them. Luther Mason focused on the use of modified Tonic Sol-fa notation—using numbers and the staff instead of syllables. Tonic Sol-fa, a moveable-do system, was being taught in England at this time (mid-19th century), and there were many efforts to introduce it in this country. But these efforts were never entirely successful with Luther Mason and his contemporaries. This was the first of many historic skirmishes with regard to methods of teaching music reading.

Following this period, in the 1880s, there existed a more concerted effort to introduce music in many school systems, and the focus remained on music reading. Music was taught by the grade teacher along with all of the other subjects. The *Normal Music Course*, written by Holt and Tufts, was published by D. Appleton and Company in 1883 and by Silver Burdett in 1885. Its use extended to every part of the country. The work had two purposes: first, to offer a large number of well-graded exercises and songs that the grade teacher could teach successfully and, second, to cover every problem so thoroughly that children could not escape becoming music readers. Charts to be used for drill on tone and rhythm were included with the elementary books. In the summer of 1884 Holt opened a summer school so that in-service teachers could learn how to use the course; soon afterward the school was expanded into one to train music supervisors.

Several music series followed late in the century. They reflected the dominant concerns of music in the public schools—music reading and the singing voice—so that, by the first decade of the 20th century, there had been three outstanding developments: It was found that almost all children could be taught to read music; the uniqueness of the child voice was discovered; and emphasis was placed on the individual singing child.

The teaching of music reading was of continuing concern, but there was also an accompanying cry for more "real music"—more songs with intrinsic beauty for use in the music lesson. The "song method" became *the* method of teaching music reading. Exercises that were used were developed from songs.

W. S. B. Mathews published a music appreciation text, *How to Understand Music*, in 1888. It was widely read and recognized as a new kind of music study. The real beginning of music appreciation in schools, however, came in 1911, when the Victor Company organized its educational department and placed Frances E. Clark in charge of developing educational uses for the phonograph.

Recordings were made of the world's music as well as of school songs, folk songs, and dances. Special educational records were produced to illustrate the sound of individual instruments, musical style, and musical form. Many books and other records followed. This methodology had a double aim: to teach a body of musical literature and to develop in the student an approach to and an attitude toward listening to music. Thus, listening lessons entered the music class. In the lower grades, song games and folk dances were also added to music activities.

Music classes had thus evolved somewhat from the singing class, with its focus on music reading, to a kind of general music class. However, private study values still dominated music education methods, and general music curricula were activities oriented rather than music oriented. That was yet to come. In *Human Values in Music Education* (1934), James Mursell staunchly advocated the teaching of music performance in classes, a real change in direction for the profession.

Following the guidance of Mursell, Lilla Belle Pitts, Gladys Tipton, and many other fine educators down to and including Charles Leonhard, the general music class for elementary schools evolved into the general music class at all levels. In addition, due to the influence of Leonhard and House (1958/1972), general music teachers looked to the study of philosophy and psychology to form music curricular structures and teaching methodologies. John Dewey, Susanne Langer, and Leonard Meyer focused attention upon the unique values of music for human life and gave us an understanding of music's structure and function as an art. Jerome Bruner's emphasis on the structure of cognition and the resulting "disciplines" movement influenced us to focus on the structure of music as material for study.

Jean Piaget, in his research and writing, gave us a greater understanding of the developmental process and the nature and sequence of learning, and, by implication, of musical development and musical learning. Ausubel's emphasis on the organization of the learning experience for the cognitive structure of the adolescent and mature learner gave us direction for ordering secondary school and college-adult music learning experiences. (For a more detailed discussion of how the writers mentioned above influenced music education content and methods, see Leonhard and House, 1958/1972.) These developments culminated in the notion that comprehensive musicianship was the proper focus for all music studies. An application of aesthetic education to music, this position grew to prominence in the third quarter of the century among music education leaders; but to say that it took hold as a force in curriculum goes beyond the evidence. Carried to its logical end, comprehensive musicianship may have proved too complex in content and concept for students and teachers alike, especially given the absence of the kind of attention given to teacher training in other methodologies. The teacher's task was to develop real musicianship and musical responsiveness in children—to have them sing in tune with good sound, to read music, to play a variety of instruments with good technique, to move expressively, to create music freely, to listen feelingfully, and to analyze music with a knowledge of its structure.

In order to accomplish the desired goals of instruction, regardless of the methodology selected, every general music teacher should then (a) be a fine musician, (b) have a real liking for children, (c) have both a theoretical and a practical understanding of child development and what it means for musical development, (d) possess a thorough understanding of the nature and sequence of musical learning, (e) have a solid knowledge of music literature that in its structure and value will complement the development and sequencing of musical learning, (f) have a firm grounding in how to organize this music into experiences appropriate for six or seven different levels and many more different groups of children, (g) keep an eye out for new methods and materials as well as for applications of current research into musical learning, and (h) be able to organize ideas and materials for more than 500 students each week. For teacher candidates we need the most intelligent and the best of the crop of young music students.

This complexity of challenge and task, without enough clear guidance, was responsible for and, perhaps, encouraged the growing influence of first Orff then Kodály and, to a lesser extent, Dalcroze methodologies in the late 1960s and 1970s. Alarming to many, all these methodologies attached themselves to what had been a long process of methodological evolution.

These developments have also had great appeal. Materials and activities learned in the Orff certification courses can be taken to the classroom and repeated without further translation. Since much of the learning is rote learning, the teacher can more easily control the learning situation and take fewer risks. The instruments give support to singing and movement. They also sound good, and voices sing in tune easily with the Orff accompaniments. Their simplicity is attractive, and the music itself is rather simple. Little attention is given to more complex music or to listening and analytical activities, and no risks need be taken, either in the necessity of extending the teacher's knowledge or in asking for students' responses to different kinds or levels of expression. And attractive too is the fact that there is very little theory at the most-used early levels—just practice. From the teacher's view, there are fewer problems with discipline, little need for research in either planning activities or locating materials, pretty good sound, and happier, more active kids. It is fun. Why not?

My chief criticisms of the Orff approach are just the ones implied above. It tends to encourage teachers to be simplistic, and the literature is very narrow. There is meager experience with the broad spectrum of music in our culture. Orff's purpose was the development of the creative potential of children. The methodology has the potential for meeting this purpose. As it is often developed, however, it remains rather limited in its orientation. One more thought: The singing and instrument playing of the teachers in the certification courses are always beautiful. There are no ugly sounds. It is the very rare teacher who attains anything like that sound quality with children. It is too special. But its memory seems to carry the teachers along from year to year until they are back in the course.

The Kodály approach seems concrete, too. The hand signs, along with rhythm and pitch syllables from the Tonic Sol-fa (moveable-do) system are good "handles" to sound. The pedagogy helps with planning and curriculum organization in specific, definite patterns. The method adapts theoretically to any folk literature. It uses a simple, not too analytical approach to listening to European art music literature—the most familiar pieces. The primary instrument, the voice, is inexpensive and readily available. In the certification courses a great deal of emphasis is placed on the development of the teacher's musicianship through the study of solmization and folk-song analysis, simple chamber ensemble performance, and other special musical activities that are very satisfying and productive for good teaching.

Like the Orff system, the Kodály one is a very special approach. Simplicity is essential so songs can be sung in tune—an important concept in developing the younger singer. The method does possess the possibility of developing musical skills and knowledge to a very high degree. My only negative reaction is an almost intuitive feeling that the method's uniqueness disconnects it from the broader culture. The challenge of contemporary life and new knowledge concerning child development are grafted onto the method. Music study should not be a retreat—it is a way of meeting and understanding life.

For most of us, Dalcroze means eurhythmics. Eurhythmics clothe in experiential form that musical element we most often teach abstractly: rhythm—beat, meters, specific patterns, syncopation, polyrhythms, phrasing, rhythmic notation. The approach is very expressive and very musical. The use of solfeggio and improvisational exercises have real promise; however, they are not often well enough understood to have much influence. The system is less known because it does not have a published, definite, sequential method. Learning about the Dalcroze method is more difficult because information and instruction are not as easily available.

The practice of Dalcroze has not spread as widely in the United States as that of Kodály, and Kodály not as widely as Orff, and none as widely as the so-called eclectic approach. This is true partly because advocates are not so numerous and partly because the demands of the unusually specialized training required in the named methods are great.

The three "European methodologies" hold one more appeal: identity. The general music teacher does not have the public exposure of the band, chorus, or orchestra director. There are lots of general music teachers, and they feel a need for closeness and identity within the profession. This need is often met for individuals by the adoption of an identifiable methodology.

Such methods can be very helpful. They must, however, be placed in a larger framework of understanding and supplemented with broader musical literature for performance and listening, with learning how to listen, with creating music outside of the limitations of the method's music, and with focusing on the expressive import of the culture's full musical range.

Those of us who are involved in general music teaching and in teacher preparation programs must learn from the appeal of these movements. At the same time we must remain on guard against subscribing to a method that is too alluringly simple. We must learn from their positive outcomes and use them to promote musical growth in a program that has an adequate theoretical foundation and that protects the teacher's responsibility for designing a culturally deep music curriculum for his or her students.

At this point, we need to turn to the aims of general music and their basis in foundational studies. The structure of the curriculum and the specific objectives for teaching and learning music will emerge from these. From this process the concepts and techniques of the methodologies can be assimilated into principles of method that meet the demands of those objectives. This process requires a clear understanding and careful analysis of methodologies—not just using the techniques or materials that strike us as appealing. Techniques must be selected carefully. They cannot all be used, and trying to do so would result in a confused approach to teaching music.

The difficulty in teaching methodology is that students must be able to think on several levels at once. Teaching a general music "methods" course involves (a) undergoing prior foundational studies in psychology, philosophy, and music, from which are derived the principles upon which goals to guide the work of general music study are based; (b) knowing the principles of organization of general music courses, and specifying objectives and learning experiences for every level of the curriculum; (c) having ways of developing techniques of teaching in students; and (d) learning and applying a large body of expressive literature exemplary of our culture's major styles. Students need to understand that materials and techniques of teaching are the most immediately relevant, because these will help the student during student teaching and for a year or two of teaching. Understanding the process of deriving objectives and experiences for teaching will be important and helpful for several more years. Foundational studies will serve for most, if not all, of their teaching careers to guide them in all of their professional work.

As early as 1934, James Mursell expressed concern about fads and fights in methodologies in *Human Values in Music Education*. He was still concerned two decades later when he wrote *Music Education: Principles and Programs* (1953). Methodology is certainly in a confused state today. The Orff and Kodály camps each take united stands on methods and materials. You can know what these positions are by reading books and attending courses. As to the direction of the eclectic methods, there is less agreement. At one time, it was possible to look at the music series books, the *National Music Course* or the *Normal Music Course*, to see where general music stood. The scope, direction, methods, and literature of the current series books are very diverse, but they all claim to appeal to the same audience.

The solution to the methodological problems in our general music programs cannot be simplistic. I do not believe that the solution lies in a new methodology written by the Music Educators National Conference (MENC) or even by the Alabama Project. Neither do I believe that the solution can come from any one scholar working with his or her research group and writing one method for us all.

I do believe that the solution might come from a concerted effort to agree on a methodology by those of us who are general music teachers and by those of us involved in teacher preparation. The solution depends upon fine preparation and professional concern. That approach would have several activities: (a) maintaining active professional scholarship and research in music and psychology, especially in musical development, music learning, and philosophical considerations of the aims and functioning of today's general music in society; (b) agreeing upon a set of principles for deriving objectives of music learning at every level and planning experiences to meet those objectives; (c) identifying and developing teaching techniques which are successful in promoting musical learning at all levels; and (d) identifying a body of musical exemplars that are aesthetically valid, that embody cultural values significant in our society, and that can serve as models for teaching musical expressiveness and structure.

Principles for Music in General Education

Music programs in general education ideally follow a model of the ways in which music, at its best, gives meaning, satisfaction, and enjoyment in life. Howard Gardner (1982, 1983b) has given us a new dimension for understanding the unique role that music plays in coping with our environment. Gardner utilizes a theory of multiple intelligences, one of which is musical intelligence. Music counts as a unique function in human intellect, a separate set of mental powers. It earns this designation on the grounds of its having a separate evolutionary history in cultures, a developmental history in individuals separate from other development, and a set of operations manifested in its own information processing system in the brain. It has its own encoding system—musical notation. Experimental psychology also deals with musical tasks that are specific to certain kinds of memory and perception. Specific forms of brain damage prove music's autonomy as a system: Amusia and other musical dysfunctions can result from damage to specific areas of the temporal lobe in either hemisphere. Finally, the existence of prodigies and individuals who have exceptional capacities in music unrelated to levels of other abilities are evidence of music's uniqueness as a symbol system (Gardner, 1983b).

Abilities in music develop in accordance with the music of the cultural environment similar to the way in which language abilities develop in accordance with cultural linguistic structures. Abilities vary widely. But musical abilities exist in all individuals in society as surely as linguistic abilities exist. They exist as surely as the other intelligences that Gardner (1983b) has identified—logical-mathematical intelligence, spatial intelligence, bodily-kinesthetic intelligence, and the personal intelligences.

The recognition that music exists as a separate intelligence, having its own process of development, leads to an important conclusion: Musical development must be nurtured from first awareness through the school years, and it must be extended as an imaginative and satisfying experience throughout life. Our society does not tolerate illiteracy, and one measure of a society is the extent to which it can eradicate illiteracy. Our society, however, *does* seem to tolerate a high degree of musical illiteracy; and this denies a measure of understanding, communication, sensitivity, imaginative projection in sound, and social enjoyment to a large proportion of the population.

From Gardner's work (1983b) and the caveat that musical development must be nurtured throughout life comes

PRINCIPLE 1: *Music is a unique ability in human beings. Musical intelligence is dependent upon the development, from the very beginning of life, of abilities to organize and perceive tonal organizations and upon the development of abilities to express individual understanding and feeling in sound images through performance. This development must be extended in a consistent system throughout schooling to help individuals achieve expression and understanding of values in the music of the culture.*

Musical intelligence functions across cultures. It also functions throughout life. Understanding how music functions in cultures can give music in general education another perspective for setting goals and developing programs. Alan P. Merriam (1964) proposes a set of concepts concerning the uses and functions of music in human cultures. Drawing on the writings of anthropologists and ethnomusicologists, he distinguishes between uses and functions. He emphasizes that music's uses refer to the ways in which music is employed and these extend into almost every part of human life.

> The importance of music, as judged by the sheer ubiquity of its presence, is enormous, and when it is considered that music is used both as a summatory mark of many activities and as an integral part of many others which could not be properly executed at all, without music, its importance is substantially magnified. There is probably no other human activity which is so all-pervasive and which reaches into, shapes, and often controls so much of human behavior. (p. 218)

Function refers to music's value in a culture—the broader purposes it serves. Merriam (1964) identifies 10 functions of music: (a) music as emotional expression, both of specific and general emotion; (b) music as aesthetic enjoyment; (c) music as entertainment; (d) music as communication; (e) music as symbolic representation; (f) music as physical response; (g) music as enforcing conformity to social norms; (h) music as a validation of social institutions and religious rituals; (i) music's contribution to the continuity and stability of culture; and (j) music's contribution to the integration of a society (p. 219ff.).

Music education frequently places great emphasis on some functions of music in society and neglects, in fact repudiates, other functions. The prevailing view of music education as aesthetic education ignores to a great extent the development of music as entertainment, as communication, as physical response, and, generally, the social and cultural functions of music. These functions *are* developed in secondary school with the show choir and the pep and marching bands, to cite the more obvious examples. Yet these very aspects are often denigrated by many music educators. Music education must extend its resources to include these neglected functions of music so that all positive values of music are developed. These functions, which we have often labeled "extramusical," contribute to the nurturance of musical intelligence and should be part of the system, not left to chance development.

PRINCIPLE 2: *All functions of music should be provided for in programs of music in general education. Programs should be structured to include, in a purposeful way, personal contacts with music's social and cultural influences, including the entertainment functions of music.*

Music provides creative, imaginative channels for symbolizing feelingful responses. It is unique in that it can do this without specific referents, as in those arts that use language or drawing as mediums. This imaginative projection can be observed in very young children. It exists to a high degree in a very few adults. The truly creative life is highly regarded in our society as an ideal, but it is seldom regarded as a desirable course in the institutions of our society.

> A totally creative society would be an anarchic society. The possibility of whole societies becoming self-actualized remains, nevertheless, slight, due to a persistent terror of original acts of all kinds. It is easier to remain Mr. Smith than to become Beethoven. (Schafer, 1976, p. 233)

Perhaps this is because creativity is regarded as too precious, too special. Perhaps we confuse creativity and genius.

> Humanity struck right down the middle may never be capable of appreciating the best of Bach and Beethoven, and most people could waste their lives trying to perform them eloquently. The genius syndrome in education often leads to a debilitation of confidence for more modest achievements. . . . I am merely trying to point out that music education, geared down to the average human intelligence, may have its own rewards; and certainly it would be more appropriate for schools where average human beings congregate. (Schafer, 1976, p. 224)

Bruner's (1979) view of creativity is attainable. Creativity in his view would appear to be an individual, unique response to life.

> There is, alas, a shrillness to our contemporary concern with creativity. . . . We had at best begin with some minimum working definition that will permit us at least to look at the same set of things. An act that produces *effective surprise*—this I shall take as the hallmark of creative enterprise. . . . [At] any level of intelligence there can be more or less of creating in our sense. Stupid people create for each other as well as benefiting from what comes from afar. So do slothful and torpid people. I have been speaking of creativity, not genius. (pp. 17, 18, 29)

The creative process as it occurs in children and adults can be observed. Gardner's (1982) discussion of artistic development, which seems to be the development of creativity, gives us further guidance.

> While mature artists have much better developed skills, far more control of their gifts, and superior abilities to experiment systematically and to choose deliberately among alternatives, much in their processes of creation is reminiscent of children. Both young children and adult artists are willing, even eager, to explore their medium, to try out various alternatives, to permit un-

conscious processes of play to gain sway. . . . But it is in the forms of expression allowed by the arts that the closest tie exists between the young child and the adult artists. For both, the arts provide a privileged and possibly unique avenue by which to express the ideas, feelings, and concepts of greatest moment to them. Only in this way can individuals come to grips with themselves and express in ways that are accessible to others their own vision of the world. In the end, the artistic achievement emerges as intensely personal *and* inherently social—an act that arises from the most profound levels of one's own person and yet is directed to others in one's culture. (p. 102)

The urge to creative expression exists throughout life. That music can afford this outlet to persons of all abilities and ages gives further direction to music in general education. Music educators have tended to confine their outlooks to the school years, leaving early development to chance. A growing body of research in this area now gives us greater understanding of early musical development.

University schools of music have not yet extended themselves within the university community to afford truly creative musical opportunities to students from all areas of study. Their offerings of music appreciation and literature courses are important, but without prior preparation other areas of study are closed. Responsibilities for satisfying creative experiences in music for people after they have completed formal education have been abandoned by music education and left to the media and to social agencies. Many social agencies—the churches, music clubs, choral and symphony societies, and community performing organizations— provide channels that are highly satisfying for a very limited number of people who have special abilities or opportunities. The commercial media have not provided access to music other than entertainment that is controlled by the commercial interests.

Music education has the opportunity to make music vital in the community by expanding desirable creative musical opportunities through various social agencies, such as the important, growing senior citizen centers. Senior citizens have the leisure to explore their creative, personal abilities. Research into this phase of music education is just beginning.

PRINCIPLE 3: *Opportunities for the development of creative, individual musical expression through composition and improvisation must be available throughout life. Music education must be active in offering programs that allow the development and expression of creative ideas through the arts at all levels in the community, for enjoyment as well as for understanding cultural values.*

Finally, human responses to music and through music are really quite simple in form: Humans perform music and they listen to music. Our knowledge sometimes pushes aside the directness that lies at the heart of musical expression. The sophistication level of the performance and composition of art music and of entertainment serves to make many of our students, from early life but more so in adult life, denigrate their own efforts and abilities. The tendency toward self-criticism sometimes causes people to leave this most personal of expressions to others. The tendency in music education to focus on aesthetic expression and on art music to the neglect of folk and popular music is almost tragic.

Folk music emphasizes individual interpretation and performance. It reinforces, expects, and rewards the individual's musical contributions. Its simplicity puts many people more deeply in touch with their own lives, values, and expressive abilities. Popular music offers many similar values. I do not mean to imply that music in general education must neglect the values available in art music. Art music, too, affords deep personal satisfaction and personal and cultural knowledge and understanding, unavailable in any other symbolic form. Including good folk and popular music in our programs makes it possible to provide full access to music important in our culture.

There are different developmental priorities and different personal, social, and educational needs at different times in life. Infants are just beginning to sort out tonal structures and to make them a part of their functioning—both in understanding and expression. Young children are highly creative in their exploration and development of symbol systems. The preadolescent child is concerned with "literal" interpretation of his or her world and with conforming to social norms. The adolescent is absorbed in the development of critical capacities, ego, identity, and value systems, as well as finding ways to function as an adult by making a living and contributing to society. The emerging adult is extending his or her abilities, especially in developing occupational and professional competencies, societal roles, family and personal ties, and cultural values. Finally, in retirement, our focus is on understanding personal and cultural values, continuing to make contributions to society, and enjoying our life's achievements.

PRINCIPLE 4: *Music in general education must plan programs and determine flexible enough methods to meet developmental and personal needs at each stage of life. Continuous growth and development of personal satisfactions, and the broadening of musical contacts, should be afforded to people of all abilities and ages. A variety of good music literature can afford a full range of values—the aesthetic and personal values available in folk music, popular music, and art music.*

In determining method, it is essential to examine dominant aspects of developmental theory, research in learning, and current methodologies. The literature is voluminous, and some aspects of methodology are highly developed, some very meager. Selection of research findings and of some methods will lead to recommendations for four levels of general education: (a) infancy and early childhood (0 to 7 years), (b) elementary school years (ages 7 to 11), (c) early adolescence (11 to 15) and adolescence (15 to 18), and (d) retired people.

Infancy and Early Childhood (0 to 7 years). Musical experience should conform to the natural developmental sequence of infants and young children. The teachers of infants are those who care for them—normally their parents. It is becoming more common in our society for two and three-year-old children to be placed in the social settings of nursery schools. Four- and five-year-old children are in preschools and kindergarten, and six- and seven-year-old children are in the primary grades. The preschool or nursery school teacher becomes the child's second music teacher, and the third music teacher may be either the primary grade teacher or a music specialist. Little coordination occurs among these levels, and there is little effort by the early childhood teachers to consult music education research to determine the procedures or sequence they will follow in teaching. (For a more complete discussion of the state of music in early childhood, see Gerber, 1982.)

Research and theoretical writings in this area have been extensive, making it possible to draw several conclusions concerning musical development. Infants' first aural discriminations in the jumble of sound that comes to them are the identification of the sounds of individual voices. This is accomplished by the end of the first month of life. The earliest aural discriminations are timbre, loudness, and pitch. Fridman (1973) emphasizes that early musical experience is essential for discrimination to develop, and she makes recommendations for the forms experiences should take.

> The little child who is not musically educated usually cannot differentiate pitches from timbre; this ability to differentiate comes from training. A child must be awakened through songs, rhythmical movement, and different timbres and pitches of sounds. (p. 267)

Infants explore the perceptual environment by perceiving and attending and by experimenting with their own responses. They center on dominant aspects of the sound environment and imitate them. The following paragraph summarizes Howard Gardner's (1982) description of the sequence of development of this imitation and play into song as it was observed in the laboratory at Harvard Project Zero:

A great deal of play with sound—both language and song—develops the discrimination and expression of young children. They move from the imitation of pitches and the vocalizing of indefinite melodic contours (12 to 15 months) to the production of discrete pitches (18 months) and spontaneous song (second and third year). Spontaneous song consists of short phrases made up of discrete pitches that are very loosely organized both tonally and rhythmically. Intervals of seconds and thirds and sometimes fourths are most common. Lyrics dominate. At the age of about three, rhythmic organization makes it possible for children to begin to reproduce learned songs. This is accomplished through their working with tonal fragments and combining them into small structures. During the third and fourth year, learned songs begin to dominate spontaneous song. Lyrics and surface rhythms are prominent, and tonal sense is only approximate. By the age of five, a total song can be reproduced with steady pulse, stable key, and accurate intervals in the melody.

Rhythmic organization develops more slowly than pitch perception, and the earliest organizations are serial. The child can vocally repeat rhythms successfully at ages three and four. The next accomplishment is playing the beat on rhythm sticks and clapping. The use of large locomotor responses—marching, walking, and running to the rhythm of music—are most easily accomplished after the age of five (Rainbow, 1981). The child of two does move expressively and very generally to musical sound, but it is movement for the sake of movement. The child gives shape to melodic contour and pitch by projecting them into real space (Zimmerman, 1982, p. 34).

Zimmerman, drawing on Piagetian theory, reminds us that action patterns and perception are the tools for thinking and that they are linked serially, not in structures, during the sensorimotor stage. (For a very complete review of developmental research in music, see Zimmerman, 1982.) Through action with their sound environment, children begin to build perception and action patterns into representational structures during the preoperational period of the concrete operations stage. Perception involves pattern recognition and the extraction of meaning from patterns. Conception—thinking in the sense of conceiving and transforming structures—is dependent on perception and develops later, although Zimmerman tells us that there is no magic age or stage when this shift takes place (p. 29). It occurs as structures are formed, as literal imitation is transformed into abstraction and symbol and then reproduced in the child's own symbol system.

What does the teacher have to work with in developing the child's musicality? A great deal of imitative vocal play through singing and chant and manipulation of simple instruments may be transformed into spontaneous song. Expressive movement will give a concrete form to song contours and responses to loudness, timbre, and tempo. Fragments of spontaneous song will give way to fragments of learned song. Spontaneous song can be encouraged by engaging in musical "conversations" with the child. After more play and experimentation, whole songs, tonally and rhythmically organized, can be mastered—at about the age of five. Chanting and playing very simple instruments will be the dominant response forms to rhythmic structure before the age of five.

Children of five can refine and extend their vocal, rhythmic, and creative capabilities through learning a large body of song literature, exploring the possibilities of creative movement, and dramatic and creative play with many kinds of sound sources. This is in effect a period of practice with the symbolic material they have mastered—practice with musical structures.

Appropriate songs will move from short, conversational phrases about the child's environment or story material to folk songs with short, repetitive phrases. Small intervals and many repeated tones will keep pitch organization within the child's reach. Rhythmic organization will at first resemble chanting, then move on to clear rhythm patterns. It is important that the total sound environment remain very rich and very broad in sound sources, so that the child's discrimination can be extended to many different tonal organizations and styles. Response to sound complexes in different styles is determined by perceptual discriminations formed early in life, probably before the age of eight.

The music education profession can influence music in the preschool, kindergarten, and primary years through further research, the training of preschool and kindergarten teachers, and the dissemination of excellent music education materials (Gerber, 1982). Methodology should focus on the developmental sequence. Barbara Andress, in *Music Experiences in Early Childhood* (1980), sets forth a method based on theories of Piaget and Bruner that generally follows the sequence of development discussed above, although there are some departures from research in her methods of promoting rhythmic development. There is a great deal of encouragement of imitation, spontaneous song, creative dramatic play, and expressive rhythmic movement. The songs are very appropriate and are excellent for use with very young children. The book is a fine resource for the preschool teacher.

The Elementary School Years. Development during the elementary school years, ages 7 to 11, may be viewed as a time of concept development, skill development, and learning to conform to social norms. Children are very literal, and in these years the loss of spontaneity and originality in speech forms and in artistic productions may be noted (Gardner, 1982, p. 94).

Musical development is a complex interaction of skill acquisition, concept formation, and the expression of feelings and emotions. In skill development there is a gradual refining of singing tone and accuracy as the perception of melodic structures is refined. Physical development that accompanies this skill development allows for extension of vocal range and accuracy. In spite of the difficulties presented by high student-teacher ratios in most primary grade settings, it is essential that a great deal of attention be given to *individual* development of singing accuracy and tone at the early stages from ages five to eight, before expecting conformance to group sounds through unison singing (Goetze, 1985).

The understanding of pitch organization can be further developed through the study of simple melodic instruments—keyboard, barraphonic instruments, and recorders. The use of sol-fa syllables, simple notation, and then complete notation in a well-structured sequence will accomplish the shift from perceptual to conceptual understanding of melodic structure. The emphasis in music reading is thus on understanding rather than on skill. When children can sing melodies in tune alone and in groups, more complex textures can be performed. Singing alone moves to singing in unison, then to singing with simple accompaniment, and finally to canon, simple two-part and eventually to more complex part songs. This is a long process of development and cannot be hurried. Pedagogical ideas from the Kodály system can be incorporated in this process to real advantage.

The perception of rhythmic structure can be refined through several means. Chanting speech rhythms, patsching the beat, playing the beat and rhythm patterns on rhythm sticks, and walking to the beat represent the structural aspects of rhythmic response at the beginning of elementary school. The young child will also move expressively, giving general form to melodic contour and phrase. Refinement of conception will take place as the child learns to respond freely to elements of rhythmic structure: beat, meter, patterns, phrase, direction, and contour through locomotor movements. The techniques of Dalcroze can be adapted to aid in achieving the understanding of rhythmic structure to great advantage. Later, the children can imitate animals, objects in nature, and the like as they move toward expressive dance. Singing games and "play-party" games can help in freeing the child's responses. Only after the child moves with confidence to structural elements should he or she attempt the disciplined folk dances.

The understanding of rhythmic structure will also be advanced through playing small percussion instruments, reading and chanting rudimentary rhythm notation, and then using complete notation.

The development of discrimination through listening is essential in these years of concept formation. This skill is an important foundation for developing strategies for listening and attitudes toward listening. The socialization process that occurs through the sharing that is involved in listening to music having great expressive import is also very important. Exemplars for listening should be chosen to reinforce the conceptual structure that is being acquired through performance. Melodic structures, tonal organization, textures, rhythmic structure, and formal structures can be studied and concepts extended through listening because children can perceive and understand more than they can perform or verbalize. Listening must be made concrete and active, however, through the use of iconic charts, expressive movement, call charts, line scores, simple scores, and other means that the teacher can devise.

Children can begin to perceive harmonic structure first through identifying harmonic changes, then through specific understanding of simple chord forms and the appropriateness of harmonies for accompanying simple melodies. Harmonic vocabulary can extend to chords within major and minor keys, and sometimes simple chromatic harmonies if approached in concrete terms.

Experimentation with sound and sound sources must be afforded throughout the elementary school years. The spirit of serious play focused on creative, expressive ideas will allow children to come to know their own ideas and express them socially. Creative activity can take many forms in the elementary grades: writing lyrics for songs; setting poetry to music; improvising simple instrumental pieces to express poetic ideas; improvising instrumental backgrounds for drama; creating movement or dance compositions; creating descants and ostinatos for songs; creating sound compositions in various conventional forms (two- and three-part form, rondo, theme, and variations); creating instrumental and vocal music using techniques of blues, calypso, country, and so forth; creating compositions on tape recorders; improvising melodies on different tonal bases: minor, major, pentatonic, created tone rows, and so forth; and improvising melodies to follow charted contours. (See Beall, 1981, for a detailed description of sequential learning in the elementary grades focused on the experiences of moving, singing, playing instruments, creating music, exploring sound, and listening.)

These years are very active years, and constant challenge and involvement are vital to learning at this level.

> Although the data are not conclusive enough for us to make any definite recommendations about music education, our results do show that even young children are capable of comprehending fairly complex musical concepts. Teachers may be doing students a disservice by teaching music too slowly. It seems that concepts such as inversion, mode, and rhythm pattern can be taught to children at ages lower than previously imagined. We think it is also important that music education involve more active participation and experimentation by the student. Too much of what passes for music education involves only very passive participation of the student and discourages any experimentation. Children should have the opportunity to create and experiment with music in a very active way, so that by their own creation and experimentation, they may learn that such aspects of music as tonal pattern, rhythm, tempo, and intervals are equally as plastic but immutable as clay. (Zimmerman, 1970, p. 14)

Early Adolescent (11–15) and Adolescent (15–18) Years. The early adolescent years are marked by a shift toward analytical thinking and self-critical analysis. The need for identification and ego development accompany profound mental, emotional, and physical changes. Musical learning during these years can channel analytical thinking, creative expression, emotional growth and identification, and value formation. The music program must be relevant to students' views of themselves and their culture. The music program must be highly involving. The music studied must encompass folk song, popular music, jazz, show music, country music, and art music of all genres.

It is unfortunate that contemporary middle schools and junior high schools have in large measure discontinued general music study for all students. This has been supported somewhat by the music education profession, in that they have followed the trends for exploratory education in the junior high school, rather than insisting on the importance of music as value education during those impressionable years. This trend leaves the music education of early adolescents to chance at the very time when students need effective arts education so that they can make informed aesthetic choices.

Analytical skills based on the understanding of musical structure can be developed during this period. Students can master ideas of tonal and rhythmic organization within styles—folk styles, popular music styles, jazz, and historical styles in classical music. They are beginning to understand cultures and cultural history. This understanding can aid in their understanding of musical styles; conversely, the study of musical styles can aid in their understanding of cultures and cultural history. Cultural contexts of music compositions should be studied—of folk music, of music of other cultures, of popular music, and of art music—to enable the students to grasp music's role in culture as well as in personal lives.

At this stage, general music classes should offer a study of singing and vocal development, especially because voices are changing and growing. The study of fretted instruments, recorder, and the keyboard can give students greater structural understanding, social involvement, and an expressive outlet. Theoretical knowledge should accompany the study. This theoretical knowledge should encompass scales and modes and elementary chordal structures within keys. Students should be afforded greater development of music reading skills to accompany advanced performing skills and understandings.

Students should be encouraged to improvise and create music within their performances, using many ideas from experience but focusing activities on creating particular structures, improvising vocally or on the instruments they play, creating poetry and music, creating dramatic and musical presentations, and creating movement compositions. The teacher must be very encouraging—confidence is easily lost during this period, and music can add to or destroy the confidence students have. An atmosphere of honest acceptance and success is vital if students are to develop the ability to express themselves freely in music.

In adolescence (15 to 18 years) students can study music of all genres with an understanding of structure and cultural context. Their knowledge can be deepened by concentrating on musical exemplars of a wide variety. This study can take place in general music classes, in music appreciation classes, or in music literature courses studying one phase of music; for example, American music, history of jazz, opera, operetta and musical shows, chamber music. Students' performance skills as well as reading abilities are developing. Individual vocal development can be studied in general music classes or in voice classes. The fretted instruments, recorder, and keyboard can be studied in classes for beginners or as an extension of earlier knowledge to give a personal expressive outlet and experience to students.

Music theory may be studied to encourage greater understanding of musical structure and greater independence. Music composition, improvisation, and arranging can be taught in general music classes, in theory classes, in chamber music groups, in jazz groups, or in any class where performance is offered. (For a full discussion of music education in adolescence, see Beall, 1982.)

Finally, late adolescence is the period when musical skills and social interests can focus on music as entertainment. Marching bands, pep bands, show choirs, musical productions, and jazz bands and choirs all provide a viable means to study music and also provide entertainment for students and the public alike. These forms of performance should be available to all students. They provide an entry into the community for the students who are leaving school. Still, students can become so absorbed in musical entertainment that those activities overbalance the rest of the music program and dominate the students' educational program. All aspects of music education as well as general education must be kept in balance.

Music for Senior Citizens. Professor Leonhard defined music education as all deliberate efforts to bring about musical learning in the school or outside of the context of the school; that certainly includes the provision of music learning experiences for senior citizens. More than one in ten Americans are over the age of 65. By the year 2000, 30 million Americans out of a total population of 310 million will be age 65 and older. The trend is toward retiring at an earlier age. For the average American, approximately 20 years, or one-fourth of his or her life, will be "free time" (Sunderland, 1974, p. 10).

Senior citizen centers have developed across the country to provide this growing public with programs to fit their needs and interests. The musical community and music education have responded meagerly with occasional programs offering bands, choirs, music appreciation courses, rhythm bands, and other similar groups. Some research has explored stated preferences for musical activities. Colleges and universities are beginning to offer special courses in communities where there are many seniors. Elderhostel is a special program on college campuses that provides programs in lifelong learning for senior citizens.

Musical intelligence and musical involvement are a part of the human response to life. Growth in musical response is part of lifelong learning. Programs for retired citizens who have the leisure time and interest in self-development should be a part of the community's and the music educator's responsibilities. A broad range of offerings should be provided to seniors. These students may then continue to expand their interests and their aesthetic expression and understanding.

Recommendations for offerings are based on general knowledge and on some published articles. Music is learned throughout life by means of performance and through listening. Those people who have played instruments earlier in their lives may wish to continue to play in community bands or orchestras, or in special senior citizen bands or chamber groups. Some may wish to begin playing instruments.

A performance outlet for beginning senior students might include playing in bell choirs or learning to play recorder, guitar, or other fretted instruments. Fretted instruments are especially appropriate because they may be practiced and played alone and also can function as social instruments when played in groups. Bell choirs require minimal music reading skills, and good ones are interesting musically and give a great deal of musical satisfaction.

Music appreciation and literature classes allow time for students to explore new music literature or to know better already familiar works. Tapes of works studied could be made and checked out to class members. Literature classes should be organized in short courses to accommodate busy schedules. Music of the 1940s, Great Jazz Musicians of the 1930s, Puccini's Greatest Operas, and Three Beethoven Symphonies are examples of literature courses that would be attractive to such an audience.

Related arts classes would allow students to explore the values in all of the arts and to know some works better. Classes in aesthetics could offer opportunities for discussion of values of the arts in culture and society.

Programs that provide opportunities to attend concerts could be accompanied by "meet the artist" sessions or by study groups to learn about the music that is performed. The barriers that sometimes prohibit concert attendance (lack of transportation, lack of a companion, going out at night, unsuitable programs, or reluctance to meet new situations) would be removed (Johnson et al., n.d.).

Classes should be structured to allow maximum involvement and discussion. The students' values are already formed; ideas about life and art are rich, and music affords a focal point for discussion. Opportunities for outside practice, reading, and listening should be provided so that students can be as involved as they like, but outside work should not be necessary to the class. The goal is involvement in creative expression and satisfaction in that involvement. Literature should be carefully selected to meet the needs and interests of the students.

Surveys can be conducted in local communities and senior centers to determine the type of music programs seniors would like. Gilbert (1982) found that elderly people have definite preferences for selected musical activities, and in the communities she surveyed, the enjoyment of music through listening or observation prevailed over active participation (p. 252). There were significant differences among activities that were selected by rural, urban, and suburban senior citizens.

In summary, musical learning occurs in two ways: through performing music and through listening to music. Music in general education will be successful if it derives its methods in performance and listening from the creative needs, the ages, the abilities, and the cultural interests of students. Music education must meet its responsibilities for music in general education for early childhood, children and adolescents in schools, and senior citizens in the community.

14 Music Methodology for Exceptional Children: Current View of Professional Activity in Music Education and Music Therapy

Richard M. Graham

Any current view of professional activity in the music education of exceptional children must take into account the changes in laws, attitudes, and educational practices that have taken place since the early 1970s. The changes in education for handicapped and gifted children have affected the roles of all teachers and administrators, and some knowledge of the pattern and history of these changes is necessary in order to appreciate fully the requirements being made upon today's music educator. This information gives us a more substantial basis from which to predict what may be in store for music educators of the future.

It became evident early in the 1970s that handicapped children would become a part of regular music classrooms and that all music educators needed some special training to prepare them to teach such classes better. The impetus for this movement came from the wave of judicial pronouncements concerning the right of any child to appropriate education in the least restrictive environment regardless of handicapping condition. The major legal precedent for these pronouncements resulted from the federal case of the Pennsylvania Association for Retarded Children against the State of Pennsylvania (*PARC vs. Pennsylvania*). The case was won by PARC. It led the state of Pennsylvania to undertake a search for all retarded children in the state and to initiate immediately programs that would provide each child with an appropriate education. In another landmark decision in 1975 (*Goss vs. Lopez*), the Supreme Court moved against school exclusions, expulsions, and suspensions of any kind by principals or teachers for any reasons but the most compelling ones and, even then, by careful procedures. One of the high points of the movement toward equal education for the handicapped was the passage by Congress of Public Law (PL) 94-142, the Education for

All Handicapped Children Act of 1975. This provided that no child be denied access to equal education on the basis of handicapping condition alone.

In the mid-seventies the gradual, then rapid, reduction in populations of state hospitals and the return of many formerly institutionalized persons to the community resulted in the obligation of local schools to serve many seriously handicapped children. About 1975, handicapped children began to appear widely in festival choirs, bands, and, occasionally, competing orchestras. The appearance of handicapped children in the elite performing groups of the high school reflected yet another movement of the mid-1970s—that of opening all programs, even the most select ones, to persons formerly believed to be uneducable. Most school systems had for some years offered segregated schooling for "educable" and "trainable" children, but the emotionally disturbed were sent to special institutions, as were the blind, the deaf, and the multihandicapped. The new trend became clearly established in the late 1970s with increased offerings in many subject areas, including music education, to those previously excluded; the hearing impaired, for example, were now included in the planning of music education programs and curricula.

The old boundaries between regular education and special education were becoming less clearly defined. Music educators and music therapists had their territories clearly defined at the beginning of the decade, but from the late 1970s to the present, one has seen and continues to see many handicapped children in regular music classes; consequently, the music educator must employ many music therapy techniques in order to effect meaningful music education to all children in the mainstreamed music class. On the other hand, the music therapist, who now finds his or her nonadult clientele restricted almost exclusively to the severely and profoundly impaired, must make use of sound music education procedures to meet the goals and instructional objectives of the typical individualized education program (IEP) developed for such children in whatever setting they are housed.

The decade of the 1970s saw the emergence of new support roles for special education specialists, who began teaming up with regular educators. To a certain extent, music educators and music therapists also began to team up. As fewer children with special needs were referred out of regular music classes, music therapists were found, for the first time, in "regular" school settings, working with the regular music educators to assess and plan programs for and to teach music to certain exceptional children.

The 1970s saw a greater participation of parents—particularly those of handicapped children—in assessment and planning and in the placement of their children. Whereas the better school districts had always considered parent participation good practice, it was now established as a right of parents of handicapped children under federal and state statutes.

A final important change of the 1970s was the serious objection of many parents and minority groups to the prevailing systems for testing, classification, and placement of children in special classes in the schools. There was at that time, and there continues to be, considerable resistance in some quarters to the use of standardized music tests to determine who will go into music in the middle or high school, for example. There is every possibility that the individual music aptitude tests will go the way that individual intelligence tests have gone in the state of California—that is to say, they will be discontinued.

Mainstreaming

The dominant theme of the developments leading to current practices in music education of the exceptional child today can be described by the term *mainstreaming*. This term, which came into common use in the early 1970s, was never clearly defined and even today has numerous definitional variations. It has caused particular difficulty in the area of music education.

In 1976 the Council for Exceptional Children, then a national organization with a membership of 60,000 special educators, described the school environment in which exceptional children should be educated in an official definition of mainstreaming:

> Mainstreaming is a belief which involves an educational placement procedure and process for exceptional children, based on the conviction that each such child should be educated in the least restrictive environment in which his educational and related needs can be satisfactorily provided. This concept recognizes that exceptional children have a wide range of special educational needs, varying greatly in intensity and duration; that there is a recognized continuum of educational settings which may, at a given time, be appropriate for an individual child's needs; that to the maximum extent appropriate, exceptional children should be educated with non-exceptional children and that segregation should occur only when the intensity of the child's special education and related needs is such that they cannot be satisfied in an environment including non-exceptional children, even with the provision of supplementary aids and services (Reynolds, 1976, p. 43).

It would appear that, to some administrators, mainstreaming means the return of *all* handicapped children from resource rooms to the regular classrooms at least for some part of the school day. Typically, this has been accomplished by putting large numbers of these handicapped children in music, art, and home economics classes with the remaining "academic" classes being open only to those students who "meet entrance requirements" for such classes. Some music educators interpret the term *least re-strictive environment* to mean "easiest possible classwork" and have carried out this interpretation by letting mainstreamed music classes become in-school discotheques where students bring their favorite records and tapes from home to play during the music class. Other reports tell of music classes that are little more than "gospel sings" or "hootenannies" in which the students "have fun" but really learn very little about music.

A State of Transition

There have been problems for music educators in changing from traditional band, chorus, and general music classes of normal and gifted students to classes containing handicapped children. The reasons for the problems in music were much the same as the reasons for problems in other subject areas. The music educators—much as their colleagues in other subject areas—were not prepared to teach children who, because of handicapping conditions, did not look or act like the typical, highly motivated normal child. Nevertheless, music educators in the 1980s have been presented with handicapped children in greater numbers than ever before. There is every indication that music educators will be required to teach more handicapped children in music classes in the future. The professional activity of the moment suggests that music educators are still in a state of transition with respect to acceptance of the concept and attendant practices known as mainstreaming.

The situation becomes all the more delicate when one considers that music educators are not being properly prepared to teach handicapped children—either in segregated or in mainstreamed classes. A cursory review of the methods classes in any music education degree program will reveal a set of assumptions roughly equivalent to the following:

1. All children at all ages love music and are highly motivated to study it.
2. All students are capable of, and desirous of, performing and listening to music in groups.
3. Music education means the development of performance skills.
4. Music is to be taught to groups of children in 20-minute periods in elementary school and in 30- to 60-minute periods in higher grades.
5. Elementary school music activities are planned around, and success is measured by, the acquired abilities to respond to musical sound in a linear (left to right) manner.
6. Comprehension of the generally accepted "basic concepts" of music is an essential prerequisite for aesthetic response to music.

7. Music education at all levels must be directed toward "musical literacy" for the education experience to be of immediate and lasting value.

Newly graduated music educators may suffer great frustration when they enter their first class of students to find that the basic tenets of their discipline prove to be, at best, tenuous. But what of those who make the best of the situation—those new music educators who succeed? What are some of the characteristics of the successful music educator of handicapped children in both segregated and mainstreamed classes?

A Philosophy of Music Education for the Handicapped

I am firmly of the opinion that those music educators who succeed in teaching exceptional children, handicapped or gifted, subscribe to a basic philosophy. This philosophy can be stated briefly as follows: The exceptional child, like all other members of society, must be provided an opportunity to develop fully his or her abilities. This philosophy requires that music education programs in public, tax-supported schools of the nation must adjust and adapt programs and offerings so as to meet a variety of needs.

Where this philosophy exists and policy is determined by it, one finds enlightened administrators and music educators striving to adhere to certain principles of methodology that permit effective music education of the exceptional child in mainstreamed and in homogeneous classes:

1. Music education, use of the singing voice, and experience with high-quality instruments, must be started as early as possible (i.e., during the preschool years).
2. Music education should continue through high school or as long as the exceptional student remains in school.
3. Minority or low socioeconomic status may present an indelible effect upon the child's musical taste and motivation to pursue music in school settings.
4. Individualized assessment, planning, instruction, and evaluation are absolutely essential and basic to any music education methodology with exceptional children.
5. Some handicapped children, particularly those with irreversible disabilities, may be better served by music therapists in special environments for part or all of the school music experience.

Successful Strategies in Today's Schools

To bring into better focus some of the successful methodologies being employed with exceptional children in contemporary music education settings,

I would like to present several vignettes—situations in which I have participated directly or that I have observed. Let us begin with the handicapping conditions.

The Speech Impaired

There are approximately 2,000,000 speech-impaired children in the public and private schools of the United States. Under most conditions there is no special intervention required in the music class for such children. Their instrumental experiences are, essentially, no different from those of children with normal speech. The speech problem may show itself in singing activities and in general music lessons where the student is required to talk about the music being studied. Although speech problems may be divided or categorized in a variety of ways, the music educator is likely to encounter three categories: (a) disorders of voice; (b) language problems; and (c) disorders of articulation, with the latter being by far the most common.

All teachers of the speech-impaired child are asked to support the work of the speech therapist by encouraging the child to practice drills developed for the child's particular problem. The music educator can offer support in the regular music class by following a few simple suggestions and by designing the singing curriculum to deal with certain articulation problems while teaching the required musical concepts at the same time. An example might involve articulation problems of the sibilant *s* sound being met while the student studies the minor tetrachord with the remainder of the class. The song shown in Figure 14.1 was conceived with just such a situation in mind.

The exercise permits the entire class to experience minor tonality while, at the same time, permitting the child with the sibilant *s* problem to practice the *s* sound and accompanying *s*-blends that might, otherwise, have to be

Figure 14.1 Song Emphasizing the Sibilant *s*

practiced alone, perhaps instead of participating in the music class. This is but one example of how music lessons and speech drill might be combined in a class where speech-impaired children are mainstreamed with normal speaking and singing children. Any effort to assist in alleviating speech problems of any type must first be thoroughly worked out with the speech clinician. In addition, it is advisable that some indication be made on the IEP form of support efforts by the music educator.

The Mentally Retarded

There are from 1,375,000 to 1,650,000 mentally retarded children of school age in the United States. Most of the mildly mentally retarded (formally called educable mentally handicapped or educable mentally retarded) have been mainstreamed into the regular class and are seen today in various settings in any given elementary, middle, or junior high school. Fewer of these children are seen in the upper grades than in the lower grades and *very* few are seen in the high or upper schools. For this reason, the problem of music education of the mentally retarded is almost exclusively an elementary and middle school problem.

The problem presented to the music educator is a music class of wide ranges of (a) reading ability; (b) language ability; (c) abilities to attend and concentrate; (d) abilities to generalize and conceptualize; and, of great importance for music and art educators, (e) play interests (with those of some retarded children virtually undeveloped). An example of the kind of highly individualized music instruction needed in a class containing both normal and retarded children is suggested in the following vignette.

The instructor presents a "reading song" to the class using the standard music education methodologies appropriate to the age and abilities of the class. To one seriously retarded child, the "reading song" is taught by letting the child play the rhythm of the words on a drum while the class chants the words. Another possibility would be to have the child beat the major pulse in each measure as the class chants the words to the song, accenting the first beat in each measure. The final product might be a total class "reading effort" while the retarded child accompanies the song on the drum. Such an approach to a "reading song" allows each child in the class to succeed at the level at which he or she is capable. Some will, no doubt, be able to read the entire song; others will "read" only the repeated refrain or phrase; still others will read only a word or phrase here and there. The mentally retarded child will play the drum, as accurately as possible, to the words being sung by the class.

The above activity assumes some ability on the part of the mentally retarded child to learn basic pulse and be able to coordinate his or her efforts with the more advanced accomplishments of the remainder of the class. Some mentally retarded students will not be able to function even at that level of complexity. The severely and profoundly retarded students may profit more from the specialized attention of a music therapist in a special environment conducive to teaching and learning the kinds of things the severely and profoundly retarded are capable of learning. More will be said about the special skills of the music therapist later.

The Emotionally Disturbed

The emotionally disturbed make up about 1,100,000 to 1,650,000 of the population of handicapped students in America. The number varies according to the manner and stringency of the assessment process. In most states emotional disturbance is described in terms of acting-out behavior on a continuum from mild verbal disruptive behavior through bizarre disruptive behavior. Most school administrators expect the music educator to be able to deal with discipline problems resulting from mild disruptive behaviors. The child is not considered handicapped, that is, emotionally disturbed for education purposes, until his or her behaviors can be accurately described as physically disruptive behaviors that occur with enough frequency to be threatening to the child, classmates, and to the music educator.

Music educators who have emotionally disturbed children in their classes must learn some of the basic procedures and principles of behavior management. When these are applied in the band, chorus, or general music class, the child is instructed early in the school year that he or she must be responsible for personal behavior and will have to suffer the consequences of any disruptive behavior. With that understanding, behavioral or classroom contracts can be made up that involve the entire class, including the emotionally disturbed. Having entered into such a contract at the beginning of the school year (quarter, semester, and so on), the child knows long before he or she is motivated to act out what the consequences of acting out behavior might be.

In addition to behavior contracts, the school environment should be structured to meet the needs of the emotionally disturbed child. Time-out rooms should be provided for the child who becomes overstimulated during music activity. The child is permitted to excuse himself or herself from any activity to go to the time-out room until he or she is relaxed sufficiently to return to the learning activity. Where such planning and provisions have existed, there have been far fewer outbreaks from emotionally disturbed children in high school classes and in lower grades.

Specific Learning Disabilities

The most recently developed category of exceptionality is that of specific learning disabilities (SLD). The number of children who properly fit into this category probably runs from 1,100,000 to about 2,200,000. Because of the special provisions for reading and mathematics tutoring of the SLD child, many parents and school officials have attempted to put children who were simply behind in reading or mathematics into the heavily funded SLD classes. In September 1984, the U.S. Department of Education issued to all states a directive that requested better monitoring of students placed in classes set aside for children with specific learning disabilities.

Music educators have seen learning disabilities in otherwise talented students for years, that is, the child who plays an instrument or sings beautifully but cannot learn to read words or music. The child who cannot handle basic arithmetic concepts can often execute intricate maneuvers with the marching band or improvise in a jazz or country-western ensemble. When such students are found in music classes, the music educator must deal with the difficult question of to what extent music learning will be dependent upon reading and number or arithmetic concepts. Successful teachers have built upon the strength of learning by rote or playing by ear to facilitate mainstreaming such a child into the band, orchestra, or vocal ensemble. The strong aspect of methodology with the learning disabled child is clear, concise modeling with occasional modifications in modeling behavior, such as mirroring the desired behavior. Because SLD children are almost always more like their normal classmates than they are unlike them, the music educators should strive to see to it that such children experience the joy and happiness that can be brought about only through successful dealings in music. Never make progress in music dependent upon reading skills alone!

The Visually Impaired. There are only about 55,000 children whose visual impairments are so severe as to warrant categorization as handicapped. Among this number only a relative few are totally blind; significantly more are "legally blind" and most are "visually impaired." Music educators have had a good deal of success in teaching visually impaired children over the years. Successful methodology must take into consideration age, level of musical achievement, intelligence, talent, emotional stability, and motivation to learn music. In this respect, like his or her classmate with a specific learning disability, the visually handicapped child is a good deal more like than unlike the nonhandicapped child.

For years the greatest problem in music education of the visually handicapped child was the great difficulty presented by printed information, including sheet music. As in every other area of teaching and learning, modern computer technology has made remarkable strides in dealing with the difficulties imposed by inability to read the printed score. For the visually impaired, the technology is the Opticon, an electronic scanning device that permits even a totally blind person to read sheet music. Opticon music reading makes use of a tiny camera to scan even the smallest printed notes and words and enlarges them five times. This transformation is done by setting some of its 144 metal rods into vibration. Sensing vibrating patterns with the tip of the left index finger, the blind music student can read music at a rate of from 20 to 100 measures per minute. The only difficulty presented is that of learning the shapes of notes and letters, which are usually unknown to the blind child who learns only braille.

The Hearing Impaired. The fact that music educators have routinely omitted hearing-impaired children from music study in the past is due in great part to a basic misunderstanding of the nature of hearing impairment and its relationship to music learning. A number of methods and techniques are available to the regular music educator that may be beneficial to the hearing-impaired student. Children with mild hearing losses (27 to 40 decibel loss) can hear practically everything that can be articulated in singing or by musical instruments. The child with the moderate hearing loss (41 to 55 decibels) can hear everything performed in music except, perhaps, the extreme pianissimos, even without the hearing aid that such a student will, in all probability, be required to wear. The child with the moderately severe hearing loss (56 to 70 decibels) can hear most of what is performed by large instrumental and vocal groups, even when these groups perform at their relative "piano" dynamic level, which is louder than the "piano" of a soloist. The student with the severe hearing loss (71 to 90 decibels) can hear practically everything that a concert band plays and everything performed by a rock band with electronic amplifiers. Even the child with the profound hearing impairment (91 + decibel loss) can hear recordings of music with the help of high-quality earphones (the Sony Walkman and the like), although he or she must turn the volume to a level that approaches the threshold of pain for most listeners.

A hearing-impaired student with personal earphones or one who is seated close to the speaker system of the performing group can take part in general music classes, music appreciation classes, and most other group music situations. It is up to the music educator to make the most of current technology in any and every methodology to permit the hearing-impaired student to share in music experiences with nonhandicapped children in regular music education settings. According to recent research on music listening, retention, and perception, an intelligent and highly motivated hearing-impaired student may be able to receive as much as 40% to 50% of the music coming from any sound source—about as much as that perceived by the unprepared, little-motivated student with normal hearing.

The Role of the Music Therapist

The music therapist is a specially prepared musician who works with atypical populations in treatment and rehabilitation settings. In recent years more and more music therapists have been retained by school systems to work with the severely and profoundly impaired students in the system. The music therapist is, by education and training, capable of assisting and directing the social and physical development of handicapped children as well as their musical development. The music therapist is always aware of the goal of building enough social and educational behaviors within the handicapped child that he or she might eventually be placed in a mainstreamed class. Until the child arrives at that state, however, the music therapist normally works with him or her in small groups (typically five to seven or less) in special classrooms, training schools, or in other types of residential settings.

The Gifted and Talented

It is not unusual for music educators to deal with and successfully teach talented children. Musically talented students have sought out performing groups for years, and traditional methodology has permitted such students to become "first chair" performers, student conductors, solo and ensemble participants in all-state festivals, and the like. This is individualized music instruction at its best for these talented youngsters. On the other hand, the academically gifted student may pose a problem to the music educator. Such students learn the standard curricular skills and content quickly and easily and need novelty and additional challenge to keep a high interest level. Continued rehearsal (drill) of the same piece (for all-state festivals or for any other reason) will hold neither the interest nor the attention of the academically gifted student. What is likely to happen after the third or fourth day on the same overture, show piece, or march is that the student will withdraw from the music class and get into a computer or science class that is of more interest because "there is something new every day."

Successful methodology with the academically gifted student (as with the mentally retarded student) depends upon intelligent individualization of instruction by the music educator. In almost every case, this type of instruction means at least three things: (a) acceleration of the pace at which all aspects of information are imparted in the music class; (b) introduction of important abstract concepts and ideas along with the skills of playing an instrument or singing; and (c) expansion of opportunities for independent study, not only through private studio instruction, but by discovery and synthesis of ideas derived from direct contact with creative persons such as composers, critics, and scholars (musicologists). The academically gifted student may never become as good a performer as the talented individuals in music classes, but a properly individualized methodology will permit that person to learn how to experience music on a fuller and deeper level in much the same way that he or she would experience the academic areas in which giftedness has been detected and properly nurtured.

The methodologies included here are only a few selected suggestions for serving children with special needs in regular music classes. Indeed, there are many methodologies for appropriate individualized music education. The purpose of these brief examples has been to show something of how the enlightened music educator deals with the exceptional needs of pupils in the regular music education environment.

Contemporary Issues and Trends

Trends during the 1970s were always more clearly perceptible than are trends during the 1980s with respect to education of exceptional children, generally, and in music education, specifically. During the mid-1970s, there was talk of massive new infusions of federal funds and regulations to implement Public Law 94-142, the Education for All Handicapped Children Act, and related legislation that favored mainstreaming and education of the handicapped. The pundits of that time did not foresee the austerity efforts or the general indifference to education of the Reagan administration. During the first two years of the Reagan administration, efforts were made to eliminate federal funding of PL 94-142. These efforts were largely unsuccessful because Congress was more sympathetic to the problems of the handicapped; but one thing was made clear to all involved in the education of the handicapped: the once-anticipated expanding partnership with the federal government was not to come about. States and local education agencies would have to manage on their own in much greater ways than they were prepared to handle.

The trend, which must be tied to funding, is for schools to do as much as possible with limited funds and limited personnel for the education of exceptional children. Mainstreaming as we know it in the mid-1980s may not change appreciably within the next few years.

The law remains with us, however, and greater numbers of parents of handicapped children become more and more aware of this law each day. For that reason, another trend will continue—that of parental participation

in the curriculum planning process in music and in other courses for handicapped and gifted and talented children. More active parental involvement
means greater numbers of handicapped children in regular schools. The
music educator can look for more and more handicapped children in music
classes. The number could reach 5% in most music classes by the end of the
century. This number will be higher in large cities and in lower socioeconomic neighborhoods and will be lower in the more affluent neighborhood
schools. Where the number of handicapped children is high, major role
changes for school personnel are inevitable. Music educators with handicapped children in performing groups and in general music classes must
learn to work cooperatively with specialists who understand handicapping
conditions (or giftedness and talent) and are experienced in general methodologies with the handicapped. In such settings, the music educator will
undergo major changes of opinion, attitude, and concepts. There will be serious challenges to the place of the traditional band and chorus programs in
high schools with 5% handicapped students enrolled. If music courses more
relevant to the needs of mainstreamed music classes are not created, the
public school music class may be put more seriously at risk than at any time
in recent history.

Persons associated with the discipline of music education can already de-
tect changing trends in the areas of measurement, expectancy, classification, placement, and grading. There is no certainty that this trend will lead
to the long-awaited answer to the question, What exactly does an "A" grade
in music mean? Perfect attendance? Good behavior in class? Seniority?
(freshmen and sophomores get grades below "A," juniors and seniors get
"A"). One final trend that should be mentioned in a setting such as this is
the increasing awareness of the existence of child neglect and abuse. Although the neglected and abused child has no officially designated category
of exceptionality as a handicapped child, I anticipate increasing sensitivity
to the problem and a concurrent increase in the need to develop effective
methodology in music and other classes in the schools of the immediate
future.

Problems for Research

The problems for research are inherent in the areas of interest and activity that have been described. The hypotheses stem from the belief that exceptional children can be taught and that exceptional children can learn.
Experimental designs will need to focus upon how this teaching can be
more effective and how learning can be more extensive. The problems do
not call for elaborate experimental or descriptive procedures. The research
questions are relatively simple: How can we best teach singing to the speech

impaired? How can we improve music learning for students who are more than three years behind in reading? Can music be taught in brief time periods to permit effective learning by the child with the short attention span? How can we best effect carryover of music learning into the post-school life of handicapped children? There are many other questions that cry out for answers if we are to make methodology with the exceptional child more effective.

The attendant, administrative problem of conducting "action" or "practical" research with handicapped or gifted children should be mentioned. The problem involves the great amount of bureaucracy that must be encountered to get "human rights clearance" for even the most simple kinds of research. In most states, clearance for research involving handicapped children must be granted on the state level. The time from the initial research proposal on the classroom level to the clearance on the principal's level, school board level, and State Department of Education or Human Resources level (or both) may be several months. The brightness of any research idea dulls after so long a wait to initiate collection of data.

There is the additional problem of research models for individual and small group study. The typical music education graduate student does not study such research procedures and must learn them while on the job or enlist the skills, time, and patience of a psychologist or scholar in special education who understands multilevel baseline studies and small group studies that employ nonparametric measures. Most of these measures have not been entered into local university computers and must be done by the investigator with hand calculator, pencil, and paper.

One final problem area for research involves the complex interaction between music educator and student, which is difficult to describe and even more difficult to study. This interaction has never been thoroughly examined, even with nonimpaired students, although it is an extremely important factor. It is perhaps doubly important to understand the profound influence that music educators have on the behavior and achievement of their handicapped students.

Music therapists have been more aware of the influence of positive interaction upon their patients and student clients, and attention should be given to the research that they have generated. Even that research is not as deep or extensive as would be desired, but music therapists learned long ago that the changes they effect in their clients are never by music alone. The therapeutic environment, posture, physical position, attitude, appearance, and methodology of the music therapist all bring about learning and subsequent change.

Certainly something near to the same situation exists in the mainstreamed music class. If a student is having difficulty in music and is withdrawn or acting out in class, we must consider a number of variables that may have an influence on his or her poor achievement or unusual behavior. Study of the situation must take into account the student, the music educator, the music or other materials being studied, and the learning environment. The kind of research that this situation demands is more qualitative than quantitative, more given to study by sociometrics and taxonomies than by linear or curvilinear statistics. The problem is a humanistic one and, consequently, does not lend itself to the kind of study one most often sees under the rubric of "discipline" or "behavior management" in current education and psychology journals.

A Vision of the Near-Term Future of Music Education for Exceptional Children

Music educators will see more and more handicapped children in their music classes in the immediate future. We probably shall not see the 10% to 12% handicapped students that were once predicted for the typical mainstreamed class because of the failure in the development of massive funding programs. Two or three handicapped children in a 50-piece band will not demand much of a change from the traditional methodologies, but 5 or 6 handicapped children in a 100-piece band will do so. When excellent performers who cannot march because of blindness or crippling conditions begin to appear in marching bands on a fairly regular basis, instructors will be required to make adjustments. Severely hearing-impaired children in a music appreciation class will demand new approaches. Hyperactive children in music classes in the elementary grades will force some changes in classroom procedures.

The pattern for the near-term future is already set for music education. Some school systems still persist in the old methodologies and build music programs around the performing elite of the school. Such activities will generally be denied to the handicapped, and that inevitable day when some parent or some child advocate forces the confrontation will be put off till later and will probably have near-disastrous effects on all involved. Other programs are presently being adjusted, usually in rather minor ways, to permit the mainstreaming of children with exceptional needs. In both cases, the music program is due to undergo change. These changes need not be for the worse and can be, in fact, changes for the better for all concerned—handicapped students, nonhandicapped students, and music educators. New ideas and new methodologies are needed. Although they will probably retain some of the old values, they must make use of new technologies and new alignments of education specialists, and they must be based upon positive interactions between the music educator and the handicapped student. To the extent that these new arrangements lead to better learning of music by all students, we shall have placed ourselves and our discipline well along the way toward the ideals and goals of the Alabama Project. For we shall have, at least in this one important aspect, dealt successfully with music, society, and education in America.

15 Music in Higher Education
Robert Glidden

It is not possible, of course, to discuss thoroughly all of the professional methodology of music in higher education in a few pages. However, Charles Leonhard's definition of the processes—program development, instruction, administration, supervision, and evaluation—will help both to delimit and to organize. It seems satisfactory for the purpose of this writing to combine administration and supervision; those processes will be addressed in that order. This report may fall into the category of "random commentary"; it is certainly not based on research, but it does derive from some years of observation of the field. It is, then, a general overview of the methodology of higher education in music from a personal perspective and may be, therefore, subject to the risk of overstatement or overgeneralization that can result from such an approach.

The sheer size of the enterprise, that is, music in higher education, is larger than many persons would suppose. The best statistics available are from the Higher Education Arts Data Service (HEADS), operated by the National Association of Schools of Music (NASM), and from the College Music Society (CMS). The HEADS Data Summary for 1982–1983 (NASM, 1984, Music Chart 1) indicates that approximately 75,000 students were studying music in some 400 accredited postsecondary institutions reporting during that year. Of that total, 62,000 were studying at the baccalaureate level, 10,500 for the master's degree, and 2,450 were in pursuit of the doctorate. The *Directory* of the College Music Society (1983, p. vi) reveals that during the 1982–1984 period, approximately 23,500 persons were teaching music in 1,500 institutions of higher education in the United States.

Program Development

The first statement that should be made about the development of programs of music in higher education is that the system in the United States is to a great extent the product of a free society, one that operates without the monitoring or interference of a centralized, controlling agency. In other words, no one agency in Washington (and in most states, no one state agency) has determined which institutions of higher education shall offer music programs, what the purpose or mission of those programs shall be, and therefore who *cannot* offer programs of any particular type. The result is a proliferation of programs for college music major students that are considered by their sponsors as both comprehensive and "professional" in nature, this being a result of competition with other institutions for students, attention, and so forth. Some people who have a relatively elitist philosophy (people usually associated with institutions that they themselves consider to be among the "elite") would argue that this is wrong, that we do not need more than a few truly "professional" schools of music in the United States, and that there should be tighter controls through accreditation or some such means. That will not and cannot happen on a national scale, of course, nor should it. If anything, we need more diversity in programs, not less, but uniformity is largely the result of competition and of institutions striving to emulate many of the same models in both performance and scholarship.

Comprehensiveness has been an important objective in American higher education for musicians. We have striven for performance skills and scholarly knowledge in each individual, for example. In fact, it might be said that great efforts have been made to blur the distinction between the practical and the theoretical in the study of music. In the European model, theoretical and historical matters are studied in the university, and the practical, or practice oriented, aspects of music—performance and composition—are dealt with in the conservatory. Such was the case in the United States until the early part of this century. Now it is the norm for theoretical and historical studies and "applied" skills to be taught in both universities and conservatories, and the differences between those two types of institutions have become less distinct with each passing year. It is difficult to say why this melding has taken place, why comprehensiveness has been so important to us. Perhaps it is a result of American common sense, along with the lack of governmental control over such matters in education. Or perhaps it is a natural part of the American dream of more and better education for upward mobility, or because much of American higher education in music has been involved with the preparation of teachers for our schools, for which both the scholarly and the practical are essential. Whatever the reason, the merging of scholarship and practice has been an important American development in the study of music at advanced levels.

Another observation about program development is that we have come to assume that most students begin the serious study of music in higher education with very little knowledge of the theory, history, and even the literature of their art. Their performance skills are generally very good, reflecting the emphases of the educational programs and private tutelage that prepared them prior to the college years; but compared with other disciplines, their knowledge of the subject is extremely elementary. This situation also is, after all, a result of a free market economy in which there is great competition for students. That is the reason we cannot arbitrarily set an absolute standard for what every student must know before entering higher education with a major in music. Our very survival as institutions is dependent upon enrollment, and we compete with one another for students. Few institutions are willing to set a standard that is beyond the majority of their entering students because if they did they would soon be without students to serve. Because the level of background knowledge is low, and because the development of skills in such areas as performance and aural acuity must be continuous, music curricula have been designed to begin the major area studies at the outset of the college career. The sequence of music courses is rigid in order to accomplish what might be termed remediation in some subjects, and this situation necessitates extending extramusical studies over the entirety of the baccalaureate program. Thus, another given when considering program development in music is that there is relatively little flexibility in dealing with the curriculum, particularly when we set out to meet an objective of comprehensive education in the field.

The Bachelor of Music has been the standard professional degree at the baccalaureate level since the 1930s, its core including studies in music theory and aural skills, history and literature, and performance. Elementary composition and advanced analysis have usually been assumed as part of theory instruction, and ensemble experience has been deemed an essential element (except perhaps for keyboard players) in performance. These, then, are the basic experiences that have been determined as most important in the comprehensive education of musicians at the college level. Generally speaking, there is relatively little variation from one institution to another in the way these core elements are treated. Institutions with a conservatory orientation or tradition tend to place more emphasis on the development of aural skills and sight singing, and those with a research orientation place more emphasis on history and literature. Students in a conservatory, for example, are expected to practice and continue to develop aural skills to a higher level of acuity through at least three years of study, whereas in other institutions that study may be required for only one or two years. Music departments or schools that are located in research institutions may require two years of music history in addition to one year of music literature. Institutions with a teachers' college background or whose enrollment today is largely in teacher preparation tend toward less emphasis on advanced theory and analysis than either the conservatory or research institution, because something "has to give" in order to make room for the teacher's professional education courses. These are generalizations that may not be entirely warranted, but those relative emphases do reflect the attitudes and interests of faculty members likely to be found in those respective types of institutions.

Regardless of type of institution—conservatory, research university, or institutions based on teachers' colleges—most music programs place a heavy emphasis on ensemble experience. Orchestras, bands, and choruses, and now jazz ensembles and musical theater, are regarded as showcases for the music school and often for the college or university as a whole. Thus, there is usually heavy pressure on students to participate, perhaps beyond that which is reasonable or essential for their individual development. Furthermore, if that experience is to be worthwhile the ensembles must be good, which requires balance and numbers. Music is one of the few disciplines in a college or university in which the quality of education for the individual is so dependent upon the capabilities of the entire group. Actually, quality of education for the individual depends also upon a particular balance of instrumentation within the group. The need for balance intensifies the competition for good students, particularly those on certain instruments and, therefore, necessitates a greater amount of scholarship funding for music students than is afforded most disciplines on the campus.

One could say that in many respects there have been few lasting changes in the core of college music curricula over the past 50 years. A valiant effort was made in the late 1960s and early 1970s by the Contemporary Music Project (CMP) to integrate the study of theory, skills, history, and literature and to incorporate performance study with all of that, and no doubt, some progress in that direction was made. CMP was funded by the Ford Foundation and administered by the Music Educators National Conference; it therefore had the funding and the constituency to have a significant impact nationally. CMP took over and followed the Ford-funded Young Composers Project of the late 1950s, which placed composers in schools to write for school groups in somewhat the same way that the court composers worked in the 17th and 18th centuries. The passion for integrating music curricula grew out of the experience of those composers, who had found that music teachers were not particularly well grounded in musical analysis, for example. CMP was founded on the belief that a more literate musical public would result only from more comprehensively educated teachers, hence the development of materials and plans for "comprehensive musicianship" programs. CMP's

Comprehensive Musicianship was the most organized attempt to revise college music curricula since the founders of NASM established standards for the Bachelor of Music degree in the late 1920s. A number of institutions revised their theory-history-literature courses into "basic musicianship" sequences, integrating the various components of the curriculum into one holistic study. This approach called for a great deal of breadth, and confidence, on the part of faculty members. Perhaps the greatest problem encountered was that too few faculty members were comfortable with that approach, some because they did not feel well enough prepared to teach in that manner and probably some because they did not trust the break with tradition. Many institutions that had adopted or experimented with the comprehensive musicianship approach have since reverted to teaching theory-skills and history-literature as separate courses in the curriculum.

The Contemporary Music Project had an important influence on music curricula, however, even though the comprehensive musicianship approach did not become the norm. The study and revision by the Music Educators National Conference (MENC) of music teacher education curricula about 1970 were influenced by the CMP, and that study subsequently influenced NASM's standards for all baccalaureate music curricula. NASM's Basic Musicianship statement (under "General Standards for Graduation from Curricula Leading to Baccalaureate Degrees in Music") begins with the statement: "Musicians share common professional needs; for example, each to some extent must be a performer, a listener, a historian, a composer, a theorist and a teacher." The NASM statement goes on to call for "a repertory for study that includes various cultures and historical periods" (NASM, 1985, p. 45). The recognition of the need for comprehensiveness in the first statement, and expansion of the curricula to include repertory from various cultures indicated in the second, were both important derivatives of CMP.

Recent years have seen increasing specialization in music curricula, as indicated by the titling of degrees. The NASM *1985–1986 Handbook* presently lists standards for nine specializations within the Bachelor of Music degree and twelve within the Master of Music degree, with guidelines for several others. Jazz Studies is one of the more recent additions to the list of recognized degrees, and guidelines are now provided for combinations of music, business, and/or arts administration, and music in combination with electrical engineering (for technologists, recording engineers, audio designers, etc.). Most of this degree proliferation has occurred in the name of greater specificity to serve the needs of the profession and society, but in fact it also reflects the intensity of competition for students.

The development of graduate programs has been in response to the increasing number of students who seek advanced study and the increasing reliance upon academic credentials in the society. A master's degree is no longer regarded as "special," perhaps because of the preponderance of doctoral programs in almost all aspects of the field. The development of doctoral programs, of course, is in response to the requirement of that degree by many institutions of higher education for tenure and promotion to higher academic ranks. Just as the need for comprehensiveness in the education of K–12 music teachers has had a great influence on baccalaureate curricula, so the need for doctoral degrees by college teachers has directed the program development of music schools at the graduate level. Thus, music program development has not followed any grand design derived from systematic planning or national policy, but rather it has responded to the marketplace—to the "needs of society."

Instruction

Music students receive rather special treatment in comparison with students in almost any other college or university discipline. They are afforded private instruction for 10% to 40% of their college credits earned at the baccalaureate level, and perhaps as much as 50% or more at the graduate level, depending, of course, on the curriculum they are pursuing, the amount of applied music required or allowed as elective, and the credit granted for applied study in the institution. The one-to-one mode of instruction has been accepted as the norm for many years, and most faculty members and music administrators do not seriously question its necessity. In the early 1970s, at the time when the higher education boom period was coming to an end and administrators were beginning to look systematically at cost factors, there was considerable discussion about the relative efficacy of performance instruction in small groups. Little has changed since then, however, and, in fact, there seems to be less discussion about the topic of group instruction today than was taking place a decade ago. That fact seems strange when one considers that costs are even more of a concern in 1985 than they were in the early 1970s. It perhaps reflects strength of feeling on the part of those who do the teaching, and perhaps it partly reflects the conservative nature and satisfaction with the status quo that marks our national mood at this particular time.

Group instruction in applied music has had a few strong proponents over the years. Professor Guy Duckworth of the University of Colorado is one who has championed that cause (and still does), not for beginning level piano or voice classes, but for advanced instruction in all instruments. A few others have espoused those beliefs as well, but most applied music teachers are firmly wedded to private teaching as the only possible mode of instruction that works. One of the problems with proposing change in this area is that the risk is great. If XYZ University were to initiate a program in which all applied music was taught by group, it would almost certainly observe a drastic and immediate decline in music major enrollment. Competing schools would take great glee in pointing out to prospective students that at XYZ University they could not get a "quality education" because they could not have private instruction, and the teachers of precollege students would issue similar warnings. It seems unlikely that any institution that values its music program will make an overall change in the mode of instruction for applied music in the near future.

According to the Higher Education Arts Data Service (NASM, 1984, Music Chart 40), music schools have a ratio of approximately seven students for every full-time equivalent faculty member, a figure that is certainly less than half that expected for institutions as a whole, and this difference is usually attributed to our need for one-to-one instruction. One-to-one instruction may not be the economic culprit we have assumed it to be, however. At Florida State University in the fall of 1984, although applied music study accounted for only 20% of the credits generated by the School of Music, it also required only 26% of the total salaries paid to faculty. It is reasonable to believe that the same situation exists in any university with a large graduate music program that therefore also has many small classes in addition to applied music. Furthermore, private teaching offers some great advantages besides the obvious instructional ones, not the least of which is the relationship that develops between teacher and student, the extra counseling that results from that relationship, and even the assistance students receive in placement and career follow-up. It is probable, although not provable, that music students receive a better and more satisfying college education than most because of music faculties' insistence on private tutelage. The truth of that statement depends, of course, on the competence and conscientiousness of the studio teacher. The quality of a given music student's college education may be more dependent on one teacher than is true in any other discipline.

Music faculty members share with those of every other discipline on a campus the problem that they are rarely prepared in any formal way for college teaching. They, like all others, rely almost entirely upon observation of their own professors for preparation. Those in the field of music education are exceptions, of course, because they do have, at the undergraduate level, some formal preparation for teaching, but most other teachers teach as they were taught. This lack of training presents a particular problem when young faculty members are expected to teach in areas outside their own specialization. Many instrumentalists, for example, are appointed to faculties because the college needs an oboe teacher or a double bass teacher or some other specialty, but there are not enough oboe or double bass students to fill the teaching load. What is assigned? Usually teaching loads are filled with subject areas that it is assumed all musicians can teach—music appreciation (by whatever title) and elementary music theory. The assumption that any musician can teach such subjects well is, of course, a faulty one. Imagine the case of the young oboist, who had baccalaureate and master's degrees from a conservatory, a few years of performing experience as an orchestral player, and a doctorate in performance from a university, where he held an assistantship in oboe. His first full-time college teaching position is in a small state college where the need is for someone to teach one section of music theory to freshmen, one or two sections of an introductory music course for nonmajors, and (most of all) for someone who can attract oboe players for the college band program. He is an excellent performer and appears to be the type of person who will be attractive to prospective students. It is likely that the college will give only scant consideration, at best, to his lack of experience with music theory or music appreciation before appointing him, because the need for oboists is so critical. He is delighted to accept the appointment and is confident that he can fulfill the commitment more than adequately. He also, of course, is thinking about his ability to attract and teach oboists because that has been his entire professional orientation. He does not face the fact that teaching oboe will be no more than one-third or one-fourth of this assignment. The shock comes when he realizes how much time is required to prepare for the music theory and appreciation classes, particularly when he has had no help in establishing exactly what those courses are supposed to accomplish, no experience in dealing with music students at the level of those in his theory class, and certainly no experience in teaching students who display as little interest in anything as those in his required appreciation classes. It is easy enough for him to concoct examinations to measure the achievement of the theory students, but he has no idea how or what to measure in the appreciation class, except what is suggested in the textbook (over which he had no choice because it had already been ordered when his appointment was made). His year is a miserable one, partly because of his lack of preparation for teaching theory and appreciation and partly because he is too proud to ask for assistance.

The example is not far-fetched. Some young people emerge from such an experience and go on to become excellent teachers. They are usually the ones who have caring colleagues or department chairpersons and who are conscientious enough to ask questions about how they can improve. Some survive long enough to find a position that allows them to teach fulltime in their specialty. Others succumb and either leave the field or stay in it as mediocre or poor, and probably unhappy, teachers. The fault lies with advanced graduate programs that admittedly exist to prepare professionals for college teaching and that may do that very well in one area of specialization but fail to provide even a single seminar that would help young people face the realities of the situation. Under the circumstances it is amazing that the level of college teaching is as high as it is. A cynic might say that it has more to do with the capacity of learners than the capability of teachers.

Some comment should be made about music instruction in higher education with regard to credentials. One observes a difference between "research" and "teaching" institutions in their attitude toward credentials required for tenured status, and in some cases for initial appointment as well. The research institution that has a strong performance program in music is less likely to insist on the earned doctorate for performance faculty (and perhaps others as well) than the teaching institution. This may be attributed to insecurity on the part of the latter, or it may be that large research institutions have more diversity and more autonomy of disciplinary units, thereby reducing the reliance on institution-wide rules. Whatever the reasons, some institutions do themselves a serious disservice by slavish adherence to a requirement that performers hold the doctorate before they are considered for tenure. Although the earned doctorate in performance or composition can be of great value to the individual as a faculty member, and although it does ensure a certain comprehensive knowledge of literature and of the field as a whole, it is but one means of proving one's competence. Musicologists and theorists need the doctorate because they cannot easily prove their competence with activities outside the academic realm, but a significant career as a performing professional, particularly over a period of years and with varied experiences, may be better background for college teaching in performance than the earned doctorate. There is no substitute for sensitive musicianship in helping a young person to achieve it, and an institution that bars musicians from tenure simply because of the lack of a specific credential is very shortsighted.

Administration

Charles Leonhard describes the methodological process of administration as that which "provides the setting for learning." We will discuss some of the structures within which music functions in higher education, comment upon some of the physical and budgetary needs for music instruction, and reflect on the responsibilities of music administration for supervision of instruction.

People are sometimes confused about the difference between a collegiate music department, a school of music, and a college of music. The differences are not clear in many cases because, like nearly everything else having to do with the nomenclature of higher education in the United States, nothing is standardized. The terms *department, school,* and *college* do not reflect differences in size but, rather, relationships with other units within a college or university. Typically, a department is headed by a chairperson and is part of a larger unit within the institution, such as a college of arts and sciences or a college of fine arts. A department chairperson, therefore, usually reports to a dean, who in turn reports to an academic vice-president. The term *school* usually refers to a professional unit for a single discipline, as opposed to a college, which would typically house several disciplines. Schools are usually headed by deans or directors—a dean if that person reports directly to the vice-president, a director if the school is part of a larger professional unit, such as a college of fine arts. There are a few colleges of music in the United States—they are equivalent to professional schools in which the dean reports directly to a vice-president.

The important difference in structure is not in the title of the unit but in the allocation of resources and determination of policies and practices related to such important matters as tenure, promotion, and faculty appointments. Music units that have relative autonomy, that is, those in which the administrator reports directly to a vice-president for academic affairs, usually have an advantage in all of these matters. One less administrative layer means one less level to which music's special needs must be interpreted. A music school that can avoid sending its tenure and promotion cases through an arts and sciences college committee, for example, will usually have a much freer hand in determining its own future through the qualifications of its faculty. (It also must therefore shoulder a heavier responsibility in maintaining quality.) In budgetary allocations, the general rule is "the closer to the source, the better." Each level through which budgets pass will of necessity extract its own reserve categories, leaving less for those down the line. Therefore, unless the unit of which music is a part has an exceptionally strong spokesperson, one who is considerably more effective than the music administrator, the music school that is parallel in structure to other colleges and professional schools will have a better opportunity for adequate funding than one that is imbedded in a larger college. There are some notable exceptions, but most of these are in older institutions in which the history, tradition, and prestige of the music program have more effect on budget allocations than does the structure of the institution.

Music has some physical needs for adequate instruction that are well known to musicians but always seem to need special interpretation for those outside the field. The acoustical properties of teaching space, for example, are critical, yet many (perhaps most) new college music buildings are built with inadequate acoustical integrity. Architects and budget administrators must be convinced that the extra cost, which may be as much as 35–50% higher than for other instructional space, is necessary. The height of ceilings for rehearsal rooms, a quiet ventilating system that does not transmit sound from room to room, soundproofing within rooms for proper acoustical ambiance—all these are extremely important for music instructional space. One of the music administrator's responsibilities is to provide physical facilities with such properties, yet, in these times, the opportunity for new space, and even for improvement of space, is rare.

Equipment needs are well known. Music schools need pianos, good ones and lots of them, and they need sundry other instruments as well. They need double basses and harps, percussion galore, contrabassoons and bass clarinets, bass flutes and soprano saxophones, piccolo trumpets and descant horns, and a whole raft of sousaphones for the marching band. They may also need sackbuts and krummhorns, and perhaps kotos and a gamelan. Those needs are relatively well understood. The new needs (not really so new anymore) are for digital synthesizers, 32-channel mixers, 16-track recorders, and banks of microcomputers to drive this equipment and to assist with instruction. According to HEADS, accredited music schools in the United States each spent an average of nearly $28,000 during 1982–1983 on equipment, and the large publicly supported schools (over 400 majors) spent an average of $57,600, including purchases, leases and rentals, and maintenance (NASM, 1984, Music Chart 25). That figure is perhaps not extreme when compared with the needs of the sciences, but it is high when compared with equipment expenses for other arts and humanities. On some campuses it is difficult to convince central administrators that such needs for music are justified.

Another need that often requires special explanation is the music library. Larger music schools have their own branch libraries, but in many institutions that is not possible, either because of campus-wide library policy or simply because of the extra funding required for staffing a branch facility. Even if the college's main library is next door to the music department, a problem of convenience and access may exist, not because of the lack of physical proximity of the library to music faculty and students, but because music materials may be scattered throughout the library. Reference works may all be on the first floor, for example, with periodicals in another location and music books and scores in another. If there is a collection of recordings and a listening center, these may be on yet another floor. In this instance the student must engage in a scavenger hunt to prepare a simple term paper.

Music materials—books, periodicals, scores, and recordings—should be located together in a library. It is difficult enough to persuade undergraduate music students to use the library without making it an obstacle course for them. On some campuses books and periodicals are housed in one facility and scores and recordings in another, presumably because a wise librarian years ago decided that the acquisition of scores and recordings was the business of the music department, not the library. Thus, books and periodicals are housed in the library and scores and recordings in the music building. That arrangement is irritating, but the situation is impossible when scores are housed in one building and recordings in another, and this occurs on no small number of campuses.

Listening facilities in libraries and classrooms are another matter of critical interest to music faculty and students. There are many problems, security being one. Any piece of electronic equipment tends to acquire feet with which to walk away (sometimes even in the middle of the day). Nevertheless, the maintenance of good listening equipment is extremely important, and it is rather disturbing to note that in many institutions one visits, this maintenance has not been given adequate attention. Classrooms should be equipped with both turntables and cassette tape decks as well as with amplifiers and speakers that provide a high quality of sound. Fully equipped rooms would also include a reel-to-reel tape deck; but these are very expensive and seem less important with the vast improvement in the quality of cassette tapes and decks. In small music departments that have limited funds, provision for listening centers is even more of a problem than classroom equipment. Equipment maintenance, staffing, maintenance of the recordings, copyright law, and so on are all worries. If the listening center can be properly staffed, that is, with knowledgeable and responsible people for enough hours during the week, the best arrangement is a behind-the-desk operator to play recordings and feed them to listening carrels equipped with cassette decks. The lids of the decks can be secured with screws so that the tape can be removed only by using a screwdriver. This arrangement prevents illegal copying of tapes, a violation of the copyright law. On the first listening, the student makes a cassette recording of the entire piece, then has hands-on access to the cassette for analysis purposes. This procedure works very well and is less expensive over the long term than replacing recordings at the rate necessary when students handle them directly; but it may prove to be too costly in the short term for smaller music departments. There is, it appears, no satisfactory solution to this problem without funds; but good listening facilities are essential to a viable music program.

There are several reasons to suggest that the administration of music programs in higher education may be somewhat more complicated than that of most other disciplines. The balance of instrumentation required for a program of quality, the detailed planning required for the presentation of performances, the complexities of budget that naturally accompany ensemble activities, and the role of music departments as the presenters of culture in their communities, all contribute to the complications of the music administrative task. Even if it could be argued that any discipline has its peculiarities and special problems, one thing seems certain: Music schools and departments demand continuity and strength of leadership if they are to be successful. The collegial practice of electing chairpersons for two- or three-year terms, or of rotating the chair on a biennial or triennial basis, is usually not satisfactory in music. That is not to say that music administrators should not be evaluated on a periodic basis, or that faculty members should not have a voice in their selection, but in music, much more is at stake than the assignment and scheduling of classes and appointing of committees that many academics associate with departmental leadership. Part of the reason for this unique responsibility is that music is an area of extreme specialization that calls for long-range planning and the utmost in coordination. Administrators who are either reluctant to lead or nervous about their futures will probably not take the strong stands that are often necessary for such planning and coordination.

Evaluation of performance is one area of music administration that may be less problematic than in many other disciplines. Although it is not true for all components of the curriculum, of course, student progress in musical performance—applied music, ensembles, even perhaps intern teaching—is certainly more directly observable than the learning that takes place in mathematics or history. Both the analysis-evaluation process and any discussions that are held for the purpose of improving instruction are more easily conducted, because the results are observable not only by the supervising administrator but also by faculty colleagues and other students. The same is true of the evaluation of faculty members' research activities when the principal creative activity is performance. How many other faculty members on a university campus subject themselves to such open public scrutiny as performing faculty musicians? This practice leads to a certain amount of tension at times, but the observableness of music activities makes the music administrator's task both more challenging and more rewarding.

One of the natural follow-ups to the analysis and evaluation of instructional activities is faculty development. The term *faculty development* is used as a euphemism for retraining, for renewal, for rejuvenation, sometimes for reassignment of faculty members to other duties. As inoffensive as the term *faculty development* seems, it remains a curiosity in that almost no faculty member believes that he or she needs to be "developed." However, any one of us from time to time needs an opportunity to gain a fresh perspective on our subject matter, on our teaching practices, perhaps on ourselves. Faculty sabbaticals, which were once as much a part of the stereotype of academic life as ivy on the walls, provided that opportunity. Today, it seems that fully paid sabbatical leaves are nearly as rare as ivy-covered walls, although many institutions grant almost unlimited numbers of partial sabbaticals. Others have cooperative arrangements with like institutions for a semester or a year. Exchanges may be less practicable in music than in some other disciplines, however, because of the difficulty in matching exact specializations. Institutions that have programs abroad have the advantage of being able to assign faculty members to teach in those programs occasionally, which usually results in a change of teaching assignment as well as location. Perhaps the most effective approaches to faculty development, although they are seldom thought of in those terms, are those that support travel for participation in professional meetings and programs of master classes or short-term residencies by guest artist performers or scholars. Travel to professional meetings, which seems to be less and less supported by institutions as funds become tighter, is extremely important, not only for keeping faculty members abreast of developments in their fields, but also for keeping them acquainted on a personal basis with people in the field. Both are important. Visits to campus by guest performers and scholars are usually planned for the benefit of students, but often the benefit is almost as great to faculty members. In one way, funds spent for this purpose are more cost-effective than those spent for faculty travel because one visiting expert can stimulate several faculty members and numbers of students.

Procedures for assigning faculty loads in music have been afforded too little thought and imagination, at least until the last five years. Two three-credit-hour courses, although they may be relatively equal in terms of the time and effort required of students, are not necessarily equal in the time and effort required of faculty members. And certainly credit hours are not a sufficient measure in calculating ensemble or applied music assignments. Collective bargaining and other factors that have effected greater formalization of various procedures in higher education have also forced closer examination of fairness and equitability in the assignment of faculty loads. Some institutions are now considering, course by course and activity by activity, the amount of faculty effort required, using such factors as size of class (which ranges from one to several hundred), level of instruction (lower division, upper, or graduate), instructional mode (lecture, seminar, laboratory, etc.), type of assignments and examinations to be graded (essays, term papers, regular written assignments), whether or not a graduate assistant is assigned, and number of contact hours per week or semester. Such systems can do much to ensure equitability, but there will probably always exist the feeling on the part of applied faculty that they work harder than classroom teachers, and vice versa.

Evaluation

Evaluation is a natural, integral part of the education process that becomes increasingly important as resources become scarcer and as institutions seek better definitions of their missions and better measures of their effectiveness. These brief comments will refer to evaluation of faculty and to evaluation, both internal and external, of programs.

The evaluation of faculty is conducted for only one purpose—to improve faculty effectiveness. Even when the evaluation is for determination of salary increments, the real purpose is to improve faculty performance. Therefore, the important factors are the assurance of fairness in the process, agreement about criteria between those being evaluated and those conducting the evaluation, and effective means of conveying information gained or judgments made to those affected. Faculty members should have the opportunity to discuss and approve both the criteria and procedures by which they are evaluated. They should also have the opportunity to participate in the process as peers. If they do, and if the process is conducted in a relatively open manner, the results can be productive. If any of those factors is missing, serious morale problems can develop.

As is true of many procedures in higher education, the faculty evaluation process has become somewhat more formalized in recent years, at least in many institutions. Where it was once conducted unilaterally by a dean or department chairman, many institutions now involve students, faculty committees, and perhaps more than one level of administration. Where the evaluation was once a subjective, holistic judgment, the more common practice now is to render independent judgments from several individuals or groups about the effectiveness of faculty members as teachers, as researchers (or composers or performers), and in the area of service. The trend is toward greater objectivity in the interest of fairness.

Of the three areas of faculty activity—teaching, research or creative efforts, and service—teaching is by far the most difficult to evaluate. The long-term effectiveness of a given teacher's efforts is nearly impossible to judge from observation of a single year's activity, and teaching results are much more difficult to summarize in writing than research or service activities. Many institutions use student evaluations of teaching, although some do not include those results in determining annual salary increments. Where student evaluations are used, they are often regarded suspiciously, particularly if they are very critical. They are especially suspect when used in one-to-one situations such as applied music, because they are seldom very discriminating in those cases. In fact, student evaluations are probably most useful when they are highly positive and therefore reinforce a strong self-concept on the part of the teacher.

Peer evaluations of teaching, even though they are usually totally subjective, are perhaps the most valid. That is particularly true when the group is not too large. In a faculty unit of 5 to 25 members, particularly if the group is relatively homogeneous (e.g., a theory-composition, or music education, faculty), most teachers tend to know quite well how others are performing in the classroom or studio. How they know this is a bit of a mystery, although applied faculty usually hear each others' students in auditions and jury examinations. Some institutions schedule classroom observations by peers or by administrators for each faculty member (or in some cases only for nontenured faculty). The value of this technique is dubious, if only because the classroom situation under such circumstances can hardly be normal.

If faculty members are asked to summarize their teaching effectiveness in writing, experienced people can list the accomplishments of their former students. One can question to what extent those former students are solely the product of one particular faculty member, and in addition, the young member is at a great disadvantage here because he or she has not had time to develop such a list. There are simply no easy or totally satisfactory methods for evaluating teaching effectiveness, yet for most faculty members in music, teaching constitutes more than 70% of their total assignment.

Program evaluation is done both internally and externally in the great majority of institutions. For clarification here, internal evaluations are those that are conducted entirely by people within the institution and by procedures designed within. External evaluations are those conducted by outside agencies such as accrediting bodies, state coordinating boards, or by evaluators invited from outside the institution. Internal evaluation may be instigated by the music unit itself, or it may be ordered by the central administration of the institution. It may be done informally and on a relatively continuous basis, or it may be formal and conducted on a regular 5- or 10-year schedule as institutional policy. An aggressive music administration may stimulate evaluation of specific programs within the school or department on a frequent basis, but that will depend, of course, upon the attitude and willingness of the faculty. In some institutions the graduate school mandates regular program review of graduate programs as a means of quality control. However done and for whatever purpose, internal program evaluation can cause more consternation among a college faculty than evaluations conducted by external groups, the reason being that internal reviews are often more threatening.

Internal evaluations are especially perceived as threatening if they are called for without clear understanding on the part of the faculty as to their purpose or if the department has experienced difficulties such as loss of enrollment. It is usually assumed that more is to be lost than gained as a result of such an evaluation. The problem caused by a threatened faculty, aside from the obvious one of morale, is that an evaluation can seldom be a thorough and effective one if faculty members are not open and honest in conducting it. For that reason, many internal evaluations that are specially called are a waste of time and may cause more harm than good. That is not true of regularly scheduled program reviews because they are usually not regarded as suspiciously by faculty members, who are the key to the success of any program evaluation.

Program evaluation conducted by outside evaluators, particularly when they are peers, that is, music educators who understand both the needs of the profession and the limitations of institutions, are an essential element in the development and maintenance of quality. External evaluators may be invited directly by the institution, they may be arranged for by professional groups or associations such as the National Association of Schools of Music or the Council of Graduate Schools, or if the evaluation is for the purpose of accreditation, the evaluators are assigned (with veto power on the part of the institution) by NASM. Consultants or evaluators from outside have many advantages over local reviewers, most of them obvious. An outsider has the advantage of a fresh and objective perspective, and he or she will usually have an opportunity to speak as an expert, both to music faculty and students and to personnel in central administration, simply by virtue of being from outside.

The accreditation process is intended to ensure quality in education. It is criticized by some as being too lax and by others as being too restrictive, but it is nevertheless accepted by most people in higher education, and by the general public, as the best available means for ensuring quality, insofar as that can be done. Specialized accreditation in music is conducted by the National Association of Schools of Music, which is one of the oldest and largest of all the specialized accrediting bodies in the United States. NASM's criteria for accreditation are established by vote of the entire body of more than 500 accredited music departments and schools, all evaluation visits are conducted by representatives of accredited schools, and all accreditation decisions are made by commissions of such representatives who are elected by their peers. Thus, accreditation in music is totally a peer-review process.

Accreditation reviews are probably the most thorough external evaluations to which most music departments subject themselves. A thorough self-study is required, and it is suggested that this be conducted with full faculty participation. Schools are asked to examine the why, what, and how of every aspect of their curricula and procedures. Institutions that conduct the self-study conscientiously find this a very valuable process, even though a time-consuming one. Assigned evaluators, two or three in number and usually from institutions of similar nature, spend two days on campus, visiting classes and rehearsals, interviewing faculty, students, and administrators, and reviewing transcripts and other records. Their report is submitted, along with the self-study document prepared by the institution, to the appropriate NASM accrediting commissions (undergraduate, graduate, etc.), which render judgments about accredited status and recommendations for improvement.

Accreditation for music departments is probably the most effective form of external evaluation for several reasons. First, the criteria used in the evaluation are quite specifically stated, and the fact that they have been established by a national group lends to them a certain weight and prestige. Second, because the review is by an external group, a faculty and student body tend to rally round the flag—they want to present the best side of themselves and they usually want to unify in doing so. Third, accreditation in music is for the most part a matter of prestige—loss of music accreditation in most cases does not bring a loss of funding or eligibility of students to be licensed, as is the case in some professional fields. It is therefore less threatening than some internal reviews, and it is certainly less threatening than accreditation in fields such as engineering, law, or medicine. Finally, and perhaps most important, accreditation as an evaluative process is both more thorough and less expensive than engaging consultants to conduct a review, because accrediting evaluators and commissions do their work as volunteers. The only cost of the evaluation, other than that which the institution invests in the self-study, is for actual expenses.

It is interesting to contemplate the gains in prestige and public confidence made by higher education in music in the United States over the past 30 years. In the 1950s it was assumed that musicians, particularly performers and composers and, to some extent, historians, needed to complete their education in Europe to hold a high status in the profession. That is no longer true. In fact, many Europeans now recognize that the best educational opportunities in music are in the United States. And certainly Asians are streaming to this country for their higher education in music. The reasons for this trend are probably two: The fact that our voluntary, peer-review process to ensure quality has allowed and encouraged change and up-dating of curricula (as compared with state ministries of education, which tend to stifle change), and the fact that U.S. music schools are comprehensive, combining the study of performance and composition with theoretical and historical studies and the preparation of teachers.

Music in American higher education may face some difficult times over the next decade and a half. The adjustment to smaller enrollments, the scarcity of financial resources, and the need to modernize curricula to embrace our increasingly diverse cultures may tax our imagination. However, for the most part our methodology is proven, and our philosophy of providing the utmost educational opportunity for all is right. Furthermore, music is more and more accepted as an important discipline and our mission is becoming better understood on American campuses. As in any other venture, the future is bright if we look forward to our challenges rather than dwelling on our problems.

16 The School and College Band: Wind Band Pedagogy in the United States

Craig Kirchhoff

The current condition of wind band pedagogy in the United States must be viewed with an understanding of the historic role of the band in society and in the educational setting. The *Random House Dictionary of the English Language* defines the band as "a musical group, usually employing brass, percussion, and often woodwind instruments, that plays especially for marching or open-air performances." Similarly, *Webster's New World Dictionary of the American Language* (2nd College Edition) defines the band as "a group of musicians playing together, especially upon wind and percussion instruments (a dance band)." Definitions such as these are misleading, limiting, and not entirely representative of the role the wind band seeks to fulfill in society. The public image of the band is influenced by its history as a functional ensemble whose purpose was to fulfill service-oriented roles. Throughout history the band has perpetuated and reinforced this public image by its close relationship with athletics, military events, and public ceremonies. My intention in this chapter is not to deny the history of the wind band and its traditional roles, but to put these roles in their proper perspectives to arrive at a methodology that encompasses deliberate efforts to bring about musical learning in school and college bands.

Richard Franco Goldman (1962) precisely marks the origin of the wind band as 1789 with the formation of the National Guard Band in Paris. In terms of size, function, and repertoire the National Guard Band is the ancestor of the modern wind band. Military bands existed in the 16th and 17th centuries primarily as groups of trombones and cornets. The regimental band of the 18th century played on its feet and moved from place to place with wind instruments that were loud and portable. In the 19th century, however, "bands developed whose connections with the military were more

remote, and which concentrated on purely concert-giving activities" (Goldman, 1962, p. 189).

The peak of popularity of professional bands in the United States was
reached about 1910, with many bands touring and attracting large and loyal
audiences. Until 1925 the entire band movement was a professional and military undertaking with an emphasis entirely upon entertainment or fulfilling
ceremonial roles. After 1925 the school band movement developed significant momentum, and the majority of wind band activity in this country
shifted to the public schools and colleges. With this shift came the dilemma
that is still perplexing instrumental music education today: the choice between an activity-oriented program and an aesthetic-oriented program.

Program Development

Program development involves making decisions about appropriate objectives. The band-conducting profession gives the appearance of great vitality; however, in the face of declining budgets and a renewed emphasis on
basic education, in some instances at the expense of the arts, serious difficulties loom on the horizon for instrumental music education. Bennett
Reimer's (1970) commentary on music education, in general, applies to the
current state of the band-conducting profession:

> It is difficult to find another field as active, so apparently healthy, so venerable
> in age and widespread in practice, which at the same time is so worried about
> its inherent value. The profession gives the appearance, a very accurate ap-
> pearance, of tremendous vitality and purposefulness and goodness of inten-
> tion, while at the same time the nagging doubt exists whether it all makes
> much difference at all. (p. 3)

One of the problems facing instrumental music education today is the failure of many instrumental teachers to embrace the values and principles of
aesthetic music education. Eugene Corporon (n.d.), director of bands at
Michigan State University, suggests that four issues must be addressed if we
are to develop a guiding philosophy for public school band programs:

> 1. Should the purpose of the band program be to educate the students
> within the program or to entertain those outside of the program?
> 2. Should the band program provide the students within the program ed-
> ucational or service-related experiences?
> 3. Should the band program be a process oriented endeavor or should it re-
> volve around a resultant product?
> 4. Should the band program serve the needs of individuals within the pro-
> gram or should it exploit those individuals to further its reputation? (p. 3)

The current pedagogy has resulted in a variety of goals and intentions and a diversity of results. Bennett Reimer (1970) makes the following assessment of school performance programs:

> Unfortunately for the children engaged in performance, unfortunately for the performance program and for music education, and unfortunately for the general level of musical sensitivity of the American culture, the evidence on effects of performance experience in the schools does not seem to bear out the assumption about its aesthetic efficacy. Research tends to indicate that there is little if any relation between school performance activities and subsequent tastes or preferences for music. Even involvement in music making activities after high school graduation seems to be only marginally related to the level of involvement while in school. (p. 130)

Robert Mager (1968) interprets learning as follows:

> Learning is for the future; that is, the object of instruction is to facilitate some form of behavior at a point after the instruction is completed. The likelihood of the student putting his knowledge to use is influenced by his attitude for or against the subject; things disliked have a way of being forgotten. People influence people. Teachers and others do influence attitudes toward subject matter—and learning itself. One objective toward which to strive is that of having the student leave your influence with as favorable an attitude toward your subject matter as possible. In this way you will help maximize the possibility that he will remember what he has been taught, and will willingly learn more about what he has been taught. (p. 11)

Mager's interpretation of learning and Reimer's comments have serious implications for the current state of band pedagogy. Too many instrumental programs have not addressed the essential goal of music education: that students graduating from their programs leave with a desire for continued involvement in musicmaking, and an undying appetite for great music, and become active supporters and consumers of the fine arts. Therefore, the major purpose and focus of any instrumental music program should be to educate students musically where opportunities are provided for the expressive power of music to be felt. Charles Leonhard states in Chapter 11 of this volume the following regarding the importance of expressive import in music education:

> The strength of music as an art and the reason every society has nurtured and valued its music lie in the strong appeal of music to the life of feeling and to the imagination. The potential strength and value of the music education program lie in the development of responsiveness to the expressive import of music. Bereft of its expressive function and its aesthetic quality, music has

nothing unique to offer to the education of children, young people, or adults. With consistent emphasis on its expressive function, however, music education can fill a unique role in the development of the human potential of people of all ages. This should be the dominant objective, the overriding end toward which we strive and toward which the entire program is directed. (p. 187)

Activity-oriented instrumental programs focus on those objectives that can often be achieved in other educational settings. Such objectives include winning, entertainment, development of discipline, cooperation, and teamwork. Music and its expressive nature are casual by-products at best. The activity-oriented program discourages meaningful learning for the future by emphasizing short-term rewards and focusing on the product rather than the process. In my opinion, too many school band programs in this country are activity oriented. Despite the fact that the United States can boast of the most skilled and professional-sounding school bands in the world, too many students have failed to experience music's true value and significance.

The first step in program development is to make a decision regarding educational objectives. Why so many instrumental teachers fail to succeed in this first crucial step can only be surmised. The tradition and the history of the band, its public image, and peer, parental, and music industry pressure for teachers to succeed, compete, and conform are among the many factors that contribute to this philosophical breakdown. Many colleges and universities are failing to prepare music education students adequately to incorporate an aesthetic-oriented approach rather than an activity-oriented program in their teaching. Perhaps most critically, many public school administrators lack an informed understanding of the purpose and the intent of an instrumental music program within the total school curriculum. Too much abuse is heaped upon the instrumental programs in our schools by uninformed administrators who view the band program only as a public relations tool or service organization.

The strongest recommendation I can make is to insist that teachers and administrators alike endorse an instrumental music education philosophy that emphasizes music and its expressive capacities and student learning for the future. State certification rules requiring candidates for administrative certificates to take arts related courses can only improve their understanding of the role of the music program within the school curriculum.

Ensembles commonly found in the high school band curriculum include marching bands, pep bands, concert bands or wind ensembles, and jazz ensembles. Some schools are fortunate to have an expanded curriculum that includes courses in music theory, conducting, and chamber music; however, these schools are in the minority.

Renewed emphasis on basic education, increased college entrance requirements in the areas of English, mathematics, science, and foreign language, and reduction in the number of class periods during the academic day have eroded the elective potential that was available to students in the past. Consequently, students are often faced with the dilemma of having to enroll in courses that meet at the same time as their music elective. These factors, in combination with the trend of declining enrollment, have significantly decreased the pool of students who are interested in and able to participate in high school instrumental music programs. Also of concern are staffing reductions in many school systems, which have severely limited the amount of time teachers are able to spend either in classes or in private lessons. Consequently, students not able to afford private instrumental lessons have little opportunity to study their instrument in depth outside of the school band rehearsal.

Current Trends

The key to maintaining an instrumental program is balance. I am concerned about several trends that have gained momentum over the past 5 to 10 years. The greatest concern is the increased emphasis on the marching band and the proliferation of marching band contests throughout the country. The high school marching band has always been associated with the traditional high school instrumental program. Those band conductors who adhere to an aesthetic music education philosophy use the marching band as a vehicle to prepare students for the remainder of the year. Musicianship is stressed and expected. Concepts such as tone quality, intonation, rhythm, pitch, balance, and blend can be taught, reinforced, and used as the bases of further growth. Furthermore, the public relations advantages that can be achieved by an outstanding high school marching band can provide momentum for the entire music program within a school district. There is no doubt that by-products of ensemble musical experience such as discipline, cooperation, and social interaction can contribute to the success of the entire academic year. Unfortunately, the allurements of promoters, peer and parental pressure, and the urgings of the music industry have brought the marching band and the importance of the marching band contest to an unparalleled fervor in the history of bands in this country.

An increased emphasis on competition has reinforced the attitude that music education emphasizes the short-term reward of winning rather than the long-term goal of lifetime enjoyment and aesthetic pleasure. In many states marching band contests commence as early as August and continue weekly through December. It is not unusual to find high school bands competing throughout the summer as well. Not unexpectedly, the band director burn-out rate has increased significantly, with many teachers succumbing to the lure of fund raising or other occupational ventures before completing their seventh year of service. More critically, a smaller percentage of graduating seniors is taking advantage of music opportunities in college or seeking performance outlets after the completion of their high school careers.

A parallel development, with the increased emphasis on competition, has been the emergence of the "corps-style" band. This phenomenon has caused significant polarization within the profession. In my opinion the proliferation of the marching band contest and the increasing emphasis on the corps band approach pose a serious menace to the integrity and future of instrumental education. In some aspects, the corps-style band has raised the standard of performance and the level of sophistication of the marching band. Percussion sections and auxiliary units have reached new heights in performance technique and complexity. Charting and show design techniques have made quantum leaps in sophistication and complexity, and bands are executing music and drill design with a higher level of proficiency than ever before.

Progress, however, has not been achieved without sacrifice. It is not unusual to find high school marching bands rehearsing and perfecting one basic show during the entire season for the purpose of entering and winning competitions. Often, music and marching preparation is begun in the preceding spring, continued through summer, refined in band camp in July, and put to the test from August to December. The result is that students are spending inordinate amounts of time on a severely limited amount of music that offers little stylistic variation or aesthetic worth. The concomitant effect is that students are not developing sufficient reading and technical skills and are not exposed to a sufficient range of music from different periods. There is little attempt to develop comprehensive musicianship and a true love of music and musicmaking through the study of worthwhile musical literature. Consequently, many band programs are graduating students who are musically illiterate, technically deficient, and aesthetically bankrupt.

Another aspect of the corps band philosophy that has affected band programs is the negative impact it is having on woodwind playing. The decrease in the number of students studying woodwind instruments and the general decline of performance standards for these instruments is of great concern to many instrumental music educators. It would be unfair to lay the entire blame for this upon the corps-style marching band; however, several factors lead me to believe that its influence is significant. First, there has been a trend to eliminate woodwinds from the marching field in favor of brass and percussion. Woodwind performers are often encouraged to transfer to a brass instrument or are encouraged and expected to perform in the auxiliary units. With the increase of time spent in marching band endeavors there has been a proportional decrease in the amount of time woodwind players are spending learning their instruments. Woodwind players may be performing on their instruments only from December until late April or May, when it is again time to begin preparations for the next marching contest season. It is logical, under those circumstances, for students to lose interest in these instruments. With the emphasis placed upon the brass, percussion, and auxiliary units, performing on a woodwind instrument carries little status and is consequently less desirable and, perhaps, even unpopular.

The evolution of the corps band concept has also resulted in the use of specialized instruments for the marching field that were previously the domain of the drum and bugle corps. Bell front French horns and over-the-shoulder tubas are the most obvious examples. The result has been that students spend an increased amount of time performing on instruments that are foreign to the mainstream of musicmaking in this country and abroad. There is little doubt that a partial reason for the performance deficiencies of tuba and French horn players in some high school programs can be attributed to this trend.

The increased emphasis upon marching band and marching band contests has meant that greater numbers of students are leaving high school band programs literally overloaded and burned out. They have been victims of an educational curriculum that has placed its entire emphasis on the short-term reward of winning. They have been exploited unknowingly, to perpetuate a tradition of winning to further enhance the reputation of either their band director or their school. Vince Lombardi was a great man and a great coach. Unfortunately, his belief and philosophy that "winning is the only thing" has become the credo for too many band directors and administrators. Whereas winning may have everything to do with sports, it has nothing to do with art and aesthetic education. Winning does not necessarily mean that much musical learning has taken place.

The marching band is not the only group that stands in the way of students' achieving an aesthetic music education. The jazz ensemble and the concert band have also been guilty. To overemphasize either of these performance mediums at the expense of the entire curriculum is as educationally empty as is a total emphasis on the marching band. The jazz ensemble is in the unenviable position of being vulnerable to exploitation because of its unique popularity, status, and almost universal appeal. An overemphasis on the visibility of the jazz ensemble and the high level of peer status attached to being a member of this ensemble has contributed, in some degree, to the decline in woodwind performance and interest in those brass instruments not usually associated with the ensemble, such as French horn and tuba.

The jazz ensemble can provide opportunities to explore many facets of musical style and creative musicianship through improvisation for students who are uniquely gifted in this performance medium. Too many conductors, however, emphasize one style of jazz performance that is determined more by the popularity of the most current jazz artists and jazz-rock ensembles or the limits of their own past experience than the dictates of good teaching philosophy. The element of improvisation, the gateway to true self-expression, is usually poorly taught, leaving students with no real understanding of the art. Most public school band directors are poorly equipped to teach jazz as a real art form. Those teachers lacking extensive experience as jazz performers are literally unprepared to cope with the medium. Unfortunately, few colleges, universities, and conservatories offer or encourage enrollment in jazz pedagogy courses that could promote a better pedagogical approach to the performance practices of this art form.

To restate my hypothesis, the key to the successful aesthetic instrumental music program is balance. The concert band or wind ensemble must function as the focal point of the entire program and provide the central music experiences for the wind and percussion performer. The concert band or wind ensemble is the only ensemble within the band program that has a repertoire of original and borrowed literature that spans music history from the Renaissance to the present. The band conductor who uses this ensemble to win contests in lieu of providing students with a broad exposure to the music of different styles and periods is as fraudulent, educationally, as the conductor who uses the marching band for the same purposes.

In my opinion, many conductors are not covering sufficient amounts of repertoire. The academic year begins and sometimes ends with the preparation of three or four pieces from the concert repertoire that will be performed at contest in April or May. Students rarely understand the true musical essence of these works, concentrating only on details in order to achieve a highly polished, sanitized, and probably misunderstood performance of the work. The results of such a scenario are similar to the results produced by the band program that performs one marching band show for the entire season. Students have difficulty reading because they spend an inordinate amount of time performing a few pieces and thus have little opportunity for sight-reading. Second, the emphasis is on the final product; the entire motivational focus is toward the short-term goal. Students may learn a great deal about specific technical aspects of their instruments to negotiate the part in front of them; however, they may learn very little about the music and much less about the composer and the aesthetic principles behind the music. There is little learning for their future lives available to them.

Equally at fault are those conductors who concentrate on one style of composition to the exclusion of others. The conductor who programs only the most difficult and latest contemporary music is cheating his students to the same degree as the conductor who programs only pop music or lighter fare. The key to a successful concert band program is mastering the art of programming. Too many band conductors have not given serious consideration to this matter. Often, program decisions are made on a whim rather than on the basis of a carefully planned curriculum. Many conductors are concerned with what is new rather than what is good and, therefore, ignore much of the standard repertoire of the wind band. Too many students have passed through high school programs with no exposure to the music of Gustav Holst, Ralph Vaughan Williams, Gordon Jacob, or even Clare Grundman or John Phillip Sousa.

Programming is one of the most important things we do as music educators. Despite this fact, most teacher education curricula are inadequate in this regard. Few university curricula require specialized repertoire courses for students intending to be elementary, junior high, and senior high school band conductors. Programming is usually discussed peripherally in an instrumental methods course or an administrative course for the high school instrumental teacher. Consequently, the novice band conductor is usually unprepared to make informed, intelligent, and aesthetic decisions regarding repertoire. More often than not, repertoire decisions are based upon that conductor's high school and college band experiences. Usually, this music proves to be too difficult. Often, the new teacher will rely upon the advice of the local music dealer. In many instances, this advice could be sound and educationally justifiable. More often than not, the advice is based upon what is hot, what is selling, and what works. Unfortunately, what is hot, what is selling, and what works does not always constitute repertoire having substantive musical value. Too many band conductors permit the music dealer to program their concerts rather than taking that responsibility on their own shoulders.

It is the responsibility of the universities, the colleges, and the conservatories to provide each potential band conductor with criteria for selecting music based upon sound aesthetic principles. It is also the responsibility of the universities, colleges, and conservatories to provide students with a thorough knowledge of the standard repertoire of the wind band at all educational levels. Students must be taught the basic formulas and theorems of effective programming. The art of programming is a skill that improves with experience; however, the basic architectural skills needed to program aesthetically satisfactory and educationally viable concerts must be acquired at the college level. I would urge all colleges and universities to reevaluate their curricula to see to it that these basic needs are being met. More likely than not, music education degree programs will be unable to absorb additional credits into the curriculum. At the very least, repertoire courses must be offered on an elective basis. To continue to ignore this basic need will result in music publishers and music dealers—the music market-place and not conductors—programming concerts.

One of the continuing problems in instrumental music is the proliferation of music of questionable value. This is especially prevalent at the junior high school and middle school levels. What constitutes good music as opposed to bad music, and what are the criteria that can serve as guidelines for selecting music of appropriate content and aesthetic worth? Bennett Reimer (1970) provides insight into this matter in his discussion of how music education can fulfill the major function of aesthetic education.

> First, the music used in music education, at all levels and in all aspects of the program, should be music which contains, in its created aesthetic qualities, conditions which can give insight into human feeling. Not every bit of music used in teaching will plumb the depths of the human psyche, nor be a masterpiece of aesthetic excellence. The criteria for selection of music are 1) genuine expressiveness, 2) the possibility of at least some of the expressiveness being shared by the particular students being taught, 3) the impetus for discovering new shades of feeling through discovering new aesthetic qualities in the piece, and 4) the addition of some further ability to share the insight in a wider variety and complexity of music. (p. 53)

The great challenge for the future is to seek out composers of great skill who are willing to write music for school-level instrumental ensembles. Worthwhile music for the junior high school and middle school medium may be the most difficult to write because of the need to cater to the technical limitations of young players and the formidable danger of being trapped into providing clichés and formulas of writing. Due to the efforts of Boosey and Hawkes, Carl Fischer, and other publishing companies there is considerable optimism for seeing higher quality music in the future for these ensembles. Band conductors must understand, however, that some publishers will continue to publish music of questionable quality if it continues to be marketable. The responsiblity for ensuring a better wind repertoire for our students is clearly on the shoulders of the band-conducting profession, not the publishing industry.

Another consideration to be addressed under the area of program development is chamber music. Few schools are fortunate enough to have a chamber music program in the curriculum. I urge, however, that chamber music opportunities be continually provided for students even if it is outside of the official curriculum offerings. Chamber music can be a special reward and a rich learning experience for the gifted performer who needs special challenges and growth experiences to remain motivated. For the gifted musician who may be headed to college as a music major, the opportunity to coach a chamber ensemble could be the most complex musical learning experience of his or her high school career. It can also be a great learning experience for those players who must develop greater rhythmic independence and individual accountability for their parts. Chamber music can develop rhythmic skills, acute sensitivity to intonation, and the ability to listen and communicate musically. District and regional solo and ensemble festivals are among the most important and beneficial music activities, and the band conductor should encourage students to participate in the activities. The ability to create opportunities for chamber music performance as an integral part of the band program is limited only by one's lack of imagination and creativity. Chamber music could be included as "preconcert music" before each band concert or during intermission. A concert could be performed with smaller chamber ensembles set up in various locations within the concert hall to fill the time during stage changes with music. The possibilities are endless. Chamber music participation can foster a high level of enthusiasm and musicianship and, consequently, a better band program.

Instruction: The Conductor and Teacher

All that has been discussed thus far revolves around the educational and musical quality of the teacher. The success of each teacher in his or her classroom or rehearsal hall is dependent upon many factors; the most important of these factors may be his or her love of music and love of people. The teacher's love of music will ensure that the music has been performed with understanding and that the objective items of musicmaking such as rhythm, balance, intonation, tone quality, and dynamics are in order. The teacher's love of people will ensure that his or her students will become independent and highly motivated musicians. The majority of students who participate in public school bands will not become professional musicians. Instead, they will become consumers, listeners. It is our responsibility to teach them to listen well and to help them enjoy it. Indeed, if the purpose of learning is to facilitate a desired behavior after the instruction has been completed, the power of the teacher's personality and style of teaching may have an even greater effect upon the student than all the information accumulated in the learning process.

Robert Mager (1968) divides learning attitudes into two categories: approach response and avoidance response. Approach response

> is action that indicates a moving toward the subject (an object, activity, or situation) about which you are interested in making a tendency statement. . . . The more strongly [students] are attracted to a subject the more obstacles they will overcome to come into contact with it and stay in contact with it. (p. 11)

Approach responses develop from positive experiences. Avoidance response is action taken by students to avoid contact with conditions that produce adverse consequences. These consequences can be outlined as pain, fear, anxiety, frustration, humiliation, embarrassment, boredom, and physical discomfort. Mager states that "people learn to avoid things they are hit with" (p. 11).

Many successful band conductors accomplish their goals using techniques associated with avoidance response. This style of teaching may be the result of our heritage and history as a military organization, or it may be the residual effects of such conductors as Fritz Reiner and Arturo Toscanini, who were tyrannical and dictatorial in their approach to musicmaking. Because these conductors were successful, others imitated their styles and believed that this was the correct approach to adopt when working with students in the public schools and universities. Although this style of teaching is not nearly as common now as it was 10 or 15 years ago, too many band conductors still use intimidation and maintain a negative learning atmosphere in their rehearsals. The conductor Bruno Walter (1961) may provide insight into a more humane approach to musicians:

> In general, however, it can be said that a violent manner of dealing with people will either be defeated by their resistance or result in their intimidation. On the other hand, the milder methods of psychological empathy, persuasion, and moral intermediation will have an encouraging and productive effect. . . . A moral danger which, at the same time, is an artistic one lies for the conductor in the power he has over others—if it be given to him, that is. It is in his interest as a human being, as well as in that of his musical achievements, to resist the temptation to misuse it. Tyranny can never bring to fruition artistic or, for that matter, human gifts; subordination under a despot does not make for joy in one's music making; intimidation deprives the musician of the full enjoyment of his talent and proficiency. . . . The conductor should strive to encourage every sign of emotional participation in the orchestra; he should explore and employ to the fullest degree the capacities of his collaborators; he should excite their full interest, advance their musical talents; in short, he should exert a beneficial influence on them. In this way, the orchestra will not be a subjugated, that is, artistically inhibited, mass of people, but a harmoniously attuned, live unity of individuals who will gladly follow the conductor's guidance; the work of art in all its facets will receive its due, and the conductor will have at his disposal an instrument from which his soul will sound forth. . . . Selflessness, . . . with an equal investment of personal dynamism, [should characterize the conductor who] wishes to convince, help, advise and teach; such an ego does not prey upon others, but seeks to give itself to that other one, the composer, and to those others, the players, and thus to wield influence as an educator; it means to do justice to the manifoldness of the works. (pp. 120–124)

Bruno Walter's comments have significance for the current state of band conducting. To intimidate students can only lead to negative reactions to, if not a complete fear of, music and their conductor. If we are endeavoring to create an appreciation and love of great music for the long term, we cannot afford to teach by intimidation. The conductor must possess confidence, poise, and impulse of will. It is also imperative that the conductor possess an understanding of group psychology and motivational techniques. Bruno Walter writes that "he who cannot deal with people or exert his influence on them is not fully qualified for this profession" (1961, p. 124). It is imperative to remember, however, that it is not what we say but how we say it that has the greatest impact for the future.

Teaching: The Expressive Challenge

Perhaps the weakest link in the current pedagogy is the inability of many instrumental music conductors to achieve the expressive challenge that is inherent in every good piece of music. Charles Leonhard states the importance of musical expressiveness for education in Chapter 11 of this volume:

> Expressive import is the humanizing force in music; it is the source of the human values in music education. . . . The time has come for music educators to return to the basics of music education, the true fundamentals of music: emphasis on the expressive import of the music we involve our students in and the cultivation of responsiveness to that import. (pp. 189–90)

The essential problem is a misunderstanding of the fundamental role of the conductor. The conductor is, first and foremost, a teacher. Just as the primary role of the music education program is to promote "feelingful thought and thoughtful feeling, processes in which the imagination is freed, is stimulated and takes flight" (Leonhard, p. 190), the primary role of the conductor is to reveal the expressive nature of the music and to be the composer's representative.

Miriam Tait (1982) a member of the School of Dance faculty at California State University, Fullerton, expressed the following about the art of conducting:

> Like mime, conducting is the language that goes beyond words. It is more than the art of providing the beat. It must give shape to the tone, the mood, the mystery, and the very essence of the composition's expression. THE MUSICIAN UNLOCKS THE SOUND FROM THE PAGE, THE CONDUCTOR UNLOCKS THE MAGIC . . . the magic that not only lies at the core of the musical score, but the magic that is in the heart and breath of each member of the ensemble. If the

music is to have a soul, a sense of feeling, then so must its conductor. If feelings are embraced and made manifest by the conductor, they become contagious. (p. 2)

To reveal the magic in the score one must have a thorough grasp of the music at hand and understand the importance of interpreting the intentions of the composer. Far too many conductors study only the road signs, that is, the time changes, dynamic variations, tempo changes, and cues. Stanley De-Rusha (1984) describes the role and responsibility of the conductor:

> The process of score analysis is one of research, discovery, and decision-making. Score analysis is not [merely] knowing time changes, dynamic variations, new entrances, etc. These are the details needed to navigate, not conduct. To be brief, score analysis involves research into the composer, his background, his style and compositional procedures, and his other works. Such research can give the conductor clues to what one might expect in the score as well as the opportunity to hear the composer's other works written for any medium.
>
> In score analysis, discovery comes from looking with the intent to find something specific. The archeologist digs knowing what it is he might find; the conductor, too, asks questions of the score knowing what those answers may be—form, harmonic rhythm, thematic material and development, texture, density, motives, materials, rows and such. With the knowledge discovered, the conductor then decides *what* is important and *how* the music is to be performed.
>
> The conductor does not suppose that the composer has written every nuance of interpretation into the printed score. On the contrary, the composer has given the conductor, his interpreter, the most specific information he can with our present system of notation—and this leaves the majority of the subtle decisions to the musicians, filtered, of course, through the conductor's experience. Vincent Persichetti once said to me, "I write my music for musicians and they know what to do with it." What is obvious to the composer is often that which needs to be discovered by the conductor. With knowledge of the score from [the] score analysis in hand, the conductor is ready to rehearse the work and reveal the magic of the music to the performer. (p. 30)

Coming to terms with the essential aesthetic and expressive nature of the work is the key responsibility of the conductor. The key to developing comprehensive musicianship in students is to share these insights and to rehearse in a manner in which the expressive power of the music can be felt. One might refer to the "second theme" rather than to "letter A"; or say, "let's begin at the recapitulation" rather than calling out a rehearsal letter or number. Likewise, the whole of the work should be rehearsed rather than just the detail. The key to resolving this issue is to rehearse details as they affect the music, not as ends in themselves.

The detail is important only as it applies to the whole. The correct rhythm is important only as it applies to the direction and contour of the phrase or to the flow of the music. Balance is important only as it applies to what the conductor has decided is most important in the music, not as an end in itself. Wrong notes need to be corrected only as they interrupt the tonal idea of the composer. (DeRusha, 1984, p. 30)

An obstruction to the goal of rehearsing music to achieve its inherent expressiveness is that many public school bands are performing literature that is too difficult for them. Consequently, most of the energies of the players and conductors alike are focused on achieving correct notes and rhythms. This results in the "fix-it" approach to rehearsing—the method of rehearsing used by the majority of band conductors in the country today. The fix-it approach consists of proceeding through a piece of music until an error occurs. The rehearsal is interrupted until the problem is solved. The rehearsal then proceeds to the next error, where the same kind of interruption occurs again. This style of rehearsing emphasizes the importance of *correctness*. There is an assumption that if the music is correct it is good music.

Without question, good performance is characterized by "correct" playing, i.e., good ensemble, balance, blend, intonation, and tone quality. A great performance transcends those important details; it depends precisely [upon] "how" the music is performed. Even with the most elementary of performers, this goal is still attainable. (DeRusha, 1984, p. 31)

The technical demands of the music should be well within the reach of the ensemble. It is far more beneficial to have players focusing most of their energies on the music and listening to each other rather than focusing most of their energies on the notes. This is not to say that groups should not be technically challenged and stretched—they should be. The goal should be to stretch them *musically*. The greatest learning can take place when they are focusing on the music, with a minor part of their time and energies spent on correcting wrong notes and rhythms.

The conductor, consequently, is much more than the keeper of the pulse and the repairman of the objective items of musicmaking. The conductor's most important responsibility is to unlock the magic of each work for the players and to be their guide to the expressive nature of the music by insisting they use their listening skills and their imaginations.

Our conducting courses at the college and university level often fail to focus attention on the real responsibility of the conductor. Most conducting courses teach technique and emphasize correctness at the expense of being expressive and representing the composer. Much work must be done to elevate the general level of band conducting in the public schools above mere timebeating. The effort must start with the colleges and universities, who must reevaluate the focus of their conducting courses. The profession, as a whole, needs to provide experiences for public school teachers to encourage their growth in the area of conducting. Conducting symposiums sponsored by state organizations or universities can do much to improve the state of the art. Good conducting does make a difference.

The Band Contest

Unfortunately, the band contest has become the means of assessment most often used by administrators to evaluate the effectiveness of an instrumental music program. In some school districts the rating achieved by ensembles is used by the administration and by the community as a barometer of their educational success or failure. More acceptable processes that determine to what extent the objectives are being achieved in an instrumental music education program are generally ill-defined and nonstandardized from school to school.

There is little doubt that the band contest has helped to raise and maintain performance standards of public school bands in this country. One of the problems with the band contest, however, is that it overemphasizes the objective items of performance and de-emphasizes creative and aesthetic musicmaking. Therefore, the goal and motivational energy of the ensemble are focused on eliminating errors, achieving correctness, and winning or receiving a Division I award. Categories evaluated on a typical judging form include tone quality, intonation, balance and blend, rhythm, articulation, and dynamics. At the bottom of the form is that issue called musicianship, which often receives little or no attention. Complicating the situation is the fact that many judges are not properly trained or qualified to judge. Some deal entirely with objective items without consideration of the musical accomplishments, or lack thereof, of an ensemble. Some deal only with interpretational aspects of the performance and penalize the ensemble if the interpretation does not match their own or does not follow slavishly what is indicated in the score. Some judges are totally negative and avoid giving suggestions for improvement; some simply sit and wait for the next mistake. And some are totally incompetent because they do not have the depth of musicianship or the experience to make a valid musical judgment. Judging is a complex task and a special responsibility that should be entrusted to our best teachers. Not everyone who teaches has the unique ability to judge band contests in a fair and constructive manner. State organizations need to upgrade and refine their criteria for selecting judges and providing continuing seminars in the art of adjudication to ensure uniformly high standards of judging.

If one is fortunate enough to perform for a panel of three competent and consistent judges, however, the majority of the comments will be addressed to the objective categories with small attention to the musical issues at hand. This style of judgment, almost out of necessity, dictates a style of rehearsing in which the elimination of error is the prime objective. Thus, if one is to be successful at a contest or the district festival, achieving correctness through the fix-it approach to rehearsing is nearly unavoidable. Subsequently, there is little time to spend on the expressive aspects of the music, and the entire rehearsal procedure is oriented to "lining it up" and "tuning it up." As indicated previously, correct musicmaking does not necessarily equate with great musicmaking. It is through great musicmaking that feelings expand geometrically, because the expressive nature of the music was explored in rehearsal; conductor, players, and audience alike share in a spontaneous-sounding, creative performance. Performers will often forget what a great performance sounded like. What they will never forget, however, is how it felt. "How it felt" is the key issue if we are hoping to give our students something memorable to grasp onto for their futures.

I am not proposing that band contests and band festivals be dismantled. I am merely stating that they are ineffective tools for evaluation if they are used as the only method of evaluation. Similarly, band contests should not be the only motivation for playing well. Perhaps alternatives to the band festival or contest should be investigated. In lieu of participating in a band contest every year, another activity could be substituted as a focal point. Inviting a respected guest clinician to evaluate and rehearse the band may accomplish the same objectives that going to a contest does, and it can, at the same time, provide the additional stimulation of working with a musician who may further expand and elaborate the expressive meaning of the music. A field trip to visit the school or department of music at a major university might provide several attractive options in addition to contests. Or a field trip to hear a symphony orchestra in concert or in rehearsal could provide students with a unique perspective about musicians and musicmaking. Again, the potential for creating situations that can foster the musical growth of our students is limited only by our lack of imagination.

Summary

In many respects, instrumental programs in this country are models for the international music community. The United States has produced the finest secondary school and collegiate wind bands in the world. A growing repertory of original works by some of the world's leading composers is an indication of the increased status the wind band has achieved in the mainstream of music. One wonders, however, why the increase of leisure time in American society has not resulted in a commensurate growth and proliferation of community bands and other instrumental activities outside of the school environment. A continuing reevaluation of educational values and attitudes about wind music and bands must occur if we are to reach the goal of achieving an aesthetic music education for the thousands of students who become novice musicians every fall.

The universities, colleges, and conservatories must take the lead and establish a sound philosophy and methodology for their students. College curricula must be revised and improved if future teachers are to meet the challenge of providing an aesthetic music education for their students. School systems must examine their curricula, and many administrators must change their perceptions and expectations to ensure that their instrumental programs are balanced and provide meaningful musical experiences for their students.

Perhaps it is time to view the marching band as an extracurricular activity. This represents a radical orthodoxy; however, we are failing to attract and keep the most talented and gifted students in our band programs. Is it because they cannot see redeeming value in spending an inordinate amount of time and energy in the pursuit of an activity that has little meaning for their futures? Most important perhaps, universities, colleges, conservatories, and public schools must cooperate to provide forums for the continued growth of members of the profession. The issue of our continued growth may be the most difficult and important professional challenge. If we cannot meet it, instrumental music education in our schools will never reach the potential we all envision for it.

17 The Orchestra and American Education

William LaRue Jones

One of the significant differences between music education in America and that of our students' young counterparts in Europe is the opportunity given to any person by our public school programs to be introduced to a musical instrument as part of his or her general education. This public school instruction, along with that of our colleges and universities, has helped to create unparalleled opportunities for personal involvement in the creative and re-creative processes of musical performance. As general music programs developed in our schools, so did instrumental and vocal ensembles; and some of our educational institutions were showcasing excellent orchestras and bands as well as exemplary vocal programs in the early part of the 20th century.

Orchestras first made their appearance in America as a result of increased wealth of many citizens of the Eastern seaboard and their need for increased cultural and social activities, which were associated with meaningful leisure time. A strong desire to emulate what were considered to be fashionable and proper European customs compelled the American colonists to import selected cultural activities and to seek the services of conservatory-trained European musicians. The musicians, in turn, came to America seeking increased personal and professional gain. Imported European artists were responsible for introducing colonial Americans to the music of their European contemporaries—Handel, Haydn, Stamitz, and so forth. America's own young composers, conductors, and performers were ignored—a syndrome with repercussions that continue to be felt in this country today.

Most American professional orchestras that began during the last half of the 19th century and the early 20th century were filled with European musicians as well as European conductors and have remained so until relatively recent times. We now find very few American communities with populations of 50,000 or more that cannot boast of a good high school, college, or community orchestra, or, in many cases, a professional orchestra. Some communities have all these types of orchestras. The opportunities to learn to play an instrument that began in elementary school now continue to exist through community ensembles and provide possibilities for life-long involvement in music.

Orchestral Education Today

Basically, orchestras can be placed in five categories:

1. Public or private school
2. College or conservatory
3. Civic or community
4. Youth
5. Professional

Although there is a definite commonality among categories, each has its own constituency and mission, and each serves a unique role in society.

The school orchestra is the introductory vehicle, which offers students the opportunity to begin what could become a life-long venture. Elementary, junior high, and senior high school orchestra programs are purposefully educational in design, serving those who live within the boundaries of a particular school district. The repertoire is specifically edited and graded to match and reinforce the developmental stages of the students. Performance opportunities are provided periodically—for an audience mainly of peers and parents—as a culmination of numerous growth-oriented rehearsals. The school music program is supported financially by local taxes with occasional fund-raisers held by members and their parents (sales of candy, fruit, cheese, etc.) helping to underwrite special trips or activities.

It is important here to mention the instructional program that has become the most revolutionary development in modern string education—the Talent Education program formulated by Dr. Shinichi Suzuki. Dr. Suzuki, a distinguished Japanese violinist and teacher, introduced the concept of teaching violin to very young children (2 1/2 to 3 years old) based on what he referred to as the mother tongue principle. He realized that all people who are not limited by mental or physical disabilities can master their native languages long before they can read or write. In much the same way that a parent teaches a young child to associate names with people or objects, Dr. Suzuki repeated patterns or phrases of music on his violin to be imitated by the child on his or her small violin.

One other distinguishing feature of Talent Education is that the parents have the explicit roles of motivator and surrogate teacher during the home practice period between classes. Many "Suzuki teachers" will not accept a student if at least one parent will not commit himself or herself to the program in these ways. Dr. Suzuki states: "Most children will not practice spontaneously. It is for parents and teachers to cause them to *want* to practice. Helping to create an inner drive is not compulsion; it is motivation [caused by guiding] . . . children into the proper performance of these responsibilities" (Mills and Murphy, 1973, p. 64).

This approach, introduced in America during the 1960s, has stimulated a tremendous growth in the number of string players in the country. It has also meant that school string teachers must be much more flexible and imaginative when Suzuki-trained students begin to enter grade school or junior high school orchestras. It is not uncommon for a 10-year-old who has had seven years of experience on his or her instrument to be placed in a string class with other fifth graders who are being introduced to an instrument for the first time.

The other approach, in general use since the early part of the century, involves the student with written music almost from the beginning. The basic design of this system is the conservatory (class) or apprentice-type (private) lessons, where sight-reading is the mark of independent musicianship, along with the same high level of individual proficiency in tone production, technical facility, intonation, and expressive nuance expected of Suzuki Talent Education students. Ensemble skills are developed in both systems; but the conservatory system is set up to educate students to respond to conducting gestures almost from the beginning. Of the three systems noted here, the conservatory system is the most orchestral, because the student is expected not only to develop individual musicianship, including solo performance capabilities, but also to adjust her or his performance to the guidance of a conductor and the responses of other players.

There have been several exemplars of the conservatory method: Paul Rolland, Gilbert Waller, Joseph T. Maddy, J. Frederick Müller, and Elizabeth Green are noted teachers who have educated others through their classes, workshops, and publications. Jacquelyn A. Dillon and Casimer B. Kriechbaum, Jr., have also applied the conservatory method to schools (1978). Samuel Appelbaum's analyses of the playing techniques and teaching principles of master studio teachers and world-class string performers are excellent records of the best of recent practice in apprentice-type string education.

The collegiate orchestra represents the culmination of the educational experience. It serves students drawn to a specific institution from an unlimited boundary who are seeking academic degrees in areas of their specific interests. Repertoire includes works from both standard and avant-garde orchestral literature, with the majority of the students being introduced to the works for the first time. Rehearsals extended over a period of several weeks usually culminate in a performance attended by the collegiate community, supportive alumni, and townspeople. The collegiate mission is to provide the best educational opportunities possible to those students who have enrolled at that particular institution. Some institutions, particularly music conservatories, consider their mission to be preprofessional musical training with little or no liberal education emphasis in the curriculum.

The civic or community orchestra is predominantly an adult organization that represents an opportunity for people who live within commuting distance of rehearsals to participate in the orchestral experience on an avocational basis. Its purpose is to serve members through once-a-week rehearsals, normally in a pleasurable social setting with a serious focus. Usually a series of concerts (typically four or five each season) is presented for the edification of members and is attended by circles of friends and close relatives. Most often repertoire is standard orchestral literature, tending toward the less adventuresome and catering to the conservative tastes of the nonprofessional members. The civic or community orchestra's budget is usually quite moderate in amount; its financial base is provided by limited local community fund-raising and dues paid by members. There are situations, however, such as in Rochester, Minnesota, and Meridian, Mississippi, where city taxes underwrite some or most of the organization's budget. In Rochester, the music director is hired by the city as is the police chief and fire chief.

The professional orchestra basically has one mission: to present the orchestral literature with the highest possible skill and musical insight. The orchestra is expected to employ, on a full-time or guest soloist basis, the finest instrumental performers available on the world market and to present on a regular basis showcase performances of the world's great orchestral literature. Although the members of the professional orchestra are also involved in public relations activities, their primary responsibility is for the high-quality production of a marketable product: well-performed music to be "purchased" by the consumer. This primary emphasis on the product, along with the fact that professional musicians are paid (usually) a living wage and amateurs are not, differentiates the thrust of the professional ensemble from that of the amateur ensemble.

Youth symphonies by definition are organizations devoted to providing musically gifted, talented, and highly motivated young people the opportunity to explore the world's finest orchestral repertoire through rehearsals and performances. There are basically four types of youth orchestras. They can be divided by administrative structure and financial support sources:

1. The youth orchestra operated by the local school district draws the top students from each of its school orchestras—an all-city concept. Cities that have such orchestras include Lincoln, Nebraska; Houston, Texas; Albuquerque, New Mexico; Mobile, Alabama. The budget is usually underwritten by the school district, which provides rehearsal and performance facilities, large equipment (percussion, piano, etc.), and often underwrites the salaries of the conductor and coaches.

2. The university-sponsored youth symphony program operates structurally in much the same way as the local school district program except that it serves an additional role as a recruiting tool or preparatory division for the university. Examples of such programs are the Wisconsin Youth Symphony Orchestras (University of Wisconsin—Madison) and the Greater Boston Youth Symphony Orchestra (Boston University). Most of the orchestra's physical needs are supplied by the university, and often the conductor and coaches are members of the faculty. In most instances, both the local school district orchestras and the university-sponsored structures use a parent board, which helps to facilitate the orchestra's public relations, concert, and social activities.

3. Professional orchestras that sponsor youth symphonies (i.e., the Atlanta Symphony Youth Orchestra, St. Louis Youth Symphony, Pittsburgh Youth Symphony, and Duluth Youth Symphony) use a variety of administrative structures. Some have a very loose nonadministrative relationship with the local professional orchestra and mainly draw upon its resources for artistic leadership. Some are the sponsored activity of the women's auxiliary of the parent organization, and others represent an educational adjunct of a wing of the main board of directors (i.e., the Alabama Youth Symphony, Birmingham). Music staff, again, is usually drawn from the professional orchestra, and its budget is a line item of the main budget. Fund-raising is held to a minimum to avoid conflicts with the activities of the professional board.

4. The fourth structure and perhaps the one that most closely resembles the professional structure administratively is the independent youth symphony. The Greater Twin Cities Youth Symphonies (GTCYS) of Minneapolis and Saint Paul, Minnesota, and the Huntsville (Alabama) Youth Orchestra, provide examples of this type of youth orchestra.

Organization and Teaching: The GTCYS Approach

Of the four types mentioned above the most complex is the fourth. Because it has become a model for youth orchestras of its type, the GTCYS approach will be discussed in some detail. With small variations this description applies to others as well.

Governance of GTCYS is by a 30-member board of directors that sets policy and is responsible for the fiscal solvency of the organization. Under the corporation's regulations and by-laws, the board hires a music director–administrator who is directly responsible for the artistic direction as well as the day-to-day operation of the structure. The music director of GTCYS has three full-time administrative assistants who are involved in the various aspects of record keeping, financial recording, public relations, communications, library maintenance, and other tasks.

The GTCYS, as a structure, operates eight full orchestras over a September-through-May season, a three-orchestra summer program in June and July, and a week-long summer retreat (The Orchestral Institute of America). This program serves approximately 1,000 young people annually from elementary through high school age. In addition to the four full-time staff members, there are seven assistant conductors, a stage manager, and five part-time rehearsal assistants.

The annual budget is in excess of a quarter of a million dollars, approximately 30% of which must be raised through grants and contributions from foundations, corporations, businesses, and individuals. Student members pay $200 (1987–1988) in tuition per season. Each GTCYS orchestra is an independent unit, although all operate within the same philosophy, rules, and regulations. None is advertised nor represented to students as preparatory to another, and each has its own conductor, repertoire, and performance opportunities. Collectively GTCYS orchestras perform approximately 60 concerts annually.

The basic methodology used by GTCYS, which is now beginning to be emulated by other orchestras, is its placement procedure. Audition teams are made up of members of the two professional orchestras, the Minnesota Orchestra and the Saint Paul Chamber Orchestra. Teams of professional players audition students on their own instruments. Following the four days of auditions, the GTCYS conductors meet as a group to evaluate the audition results and to staff the orchestras. Successful auditionees are placed in like-instrument-proficiency groupings that become repertoire levels. Age is not a serious consideration.

Once the orchestra rosters are complete, each conductor prepares a seating chart based on the audition evaluation. Students are not seated in order of strongest to weakest but are paired in such a way as to make each stand strong. That is, a student with excellent pitch scores but low rhythm scores is paired with someone with advanced rhythmic skills but low pitch scores on the audition. There are no designated principals or concertmasters and a rotational seating system is used with violins being divided equally among first and second parts. Rotation provides students the opportunity to experience performing in the front, middle, and back of the section and to experience the inherent ensemble and aural problems each seat offers. Likewise, in the winds, there are no designated firsts or seconds; parts are passed around. If there are solo lines each student learns the parts and the conductor decides who will play them, with each student having the opportunity to play the solos in rehearsals. The solos are often rotated among players when there are successive concerts.

Challenges are strictly forbidden in all circumstances. Contrary to the belief that challenges prepare students for the real world, they simply pit student against student and negate the underlying peer support necessary for establishing strong ensembles. There is not a professional orchestra anywhere that allows challenges for seating between its members. No one challenges the concertmaster, nor the fourth desk outside, for that matter. Auditions for openings must not be misconstrued as or equated with challenges. Some form of rotating seat assignments in the string sections, excluding the first desk, however, is a growing practice in professional orchestras.

Challenges are a school phenomenon and are the result of attempting to justify a hierarchy of chairs in bands or orchestras by applying techniques common in athletics, where certain players are designated to be "starters" or "first string" players. The main disadvantage of challenges is that they place undue stress on interpersonal relationships and function to undermine efforts to establish a well-balanced, cooperative ensemble. After all, if each part were not important, the composer would not have taken the trouble to write it.

In professional orchestras such as the Chicago Symphony and the Philadelphia Orchestra, rotation of string sections is considered to be an important stimulant and motivational factor. No one wishes to be stuck in the back of the orchestra simply because he or she was the last one hired, advancing only through attrition and seniority. Rotation is a positive solution to an old orchestral motivation problem.

How does a conductor motivate people to practice if the fear factor and the embarrassment penalty (of losing one's seat) are removed? The answer lies in the preparation, stimulation, and pacing of orchestra rehearsals.

First, orchestra rehearsals are not the times for the conductor to be learning the music. Truly significant insights can be offered to students only if the teacher is familiar with the material and is prepared.

Preparation means score study—making decisions as to how to help the players achieve uniformity of style and the interpretive concept that the particular period of the piece dictates. Preparation means knowing the tonal language used by the composer and how the rhythms employed carry the tonal ideas. It means understanding the form of the piece and how it implies approaches to melodic phrasing or harmonic balance or tone color or textural shifts. Preparation means having already determined the tempi of a work and how they relate to the *melos* of the music, and it means having decided what gestures most clearly convey all of the above to an ensemble without having to say a word.

Knowledge is useless unless it can be tried, tested, and converted to effective action. In order to make use of the insight we have attained, we must find or create a receptive situation through which to work. Simply having an orchestra is not enough. We must find ways to convey our knowledge in a most productive and lasting manner. Therefore, the attention and concerted efforts of the orchestra must be maintained. This desired behavior demands that two closely related concepts come to the fore: stimulation and rehearsal pacing.

No one can be stimulating all of the time. Sometimes the most diligently prepared efforts can become laborious. If one is prepared and rehearsals still bog down, it is usually the result of poor pacing. The ability to keep the rehearsal moving and keep players mentally involved goes beyond musical preparedness and requires that the conductor actively communicate his or her awareness of the orchestra members' needs.

The following rehearsal outline based on a one-and-a-half-hour rehearsal is suggested for young ensembles. Time frames can be adjusted to suit any length of rehearsal.

REHEARSAL PACING

Min. 0–10	Tune Play 5–10 minutes *full* orchestra prior to working sections.
10–45	Do majority of small detail work at this time, i.e., intonation, phrasing, rhythmic subtleties (students are still fresh and alert; concentration highest of entire rehearsal). Intermingle sections of tutti playing every few minutes to maintain constant focus, not attending to any one section of the orchestra for too long. Keep comments short and to the point.
45–52	Short break (approximately 7 minutes)
52–70	Check tuning Play tutti for approximately 5 minutes (focus) before any sectionalizing. Do less detail work at this point and more clarification—repetition of passages, double-checking previous instructions, etc.
70–85	Introduce something new or unfamiliar for sight-reading purposes—tutti work.
85–90	Close with an "upper"—something that has been rehearsed earlier, or a section that will help positive reinforcement of the learning experience and group dynamics.

It is important to remember that we must always educate rather than train. For the young musician, it is difficult to connect techniques with their practical applications unless the need can be immediately demonstrated. Scales for scales' sake, rhythmic drills, and similar "musical calisthenics" are seldom meaningful enough in isolation for practical retention. But immediate association of those desired techniques using illustrations within the orchestra's music brings about an awareness of these connections and allows for positive reinforcement through successive rehearsals and performances of this music.

Along with the aforementioned knowledge of the score and decisions made before the rehearsal regarding style, tempi, melodic-harmonic balances, texture and rhythmic phrasing, and so forth there must be an analysis of the strengths and weaknesses of the orchestra. This analysis is crucial for prerehearsal planning. Having determined the composer's intent and the particular ease or difficulty an ensemble may have in achieving that intent bears heavily on rehearsal pacing. The ability to pace rehearsals consistently, allowing for maximum individual as well as ensemble growth, establishes the ideal situation for the positive reinforcement. Such reinforcement goes beyond words of praise and this ensures, through important practical application, that the words used by the conductor do not lose their impact.

Professional orchestra rehearsals at their best do not follow the outline above; however, good pacing and effective teaching are important attributes of the best professional conductors, along with superior musicianship, mastery of the score being rehearsed, and clear gestures. All conductors, regardless of the level or purpose of the ensemble must aspire to the skills of the best professional conductors. In educational situations the need to provide developmental experiences for young players adds curricular planning to the responsibilities of conductors; it does not provide an excuse for poor rehearsing or poor conducting technique.

Orchestras in the 1980s

Orchestras in all categories seemed to flourish in the United States during the 1960s and 1970s, reaching a peak about 1980. To supplement local funds, large amounts of money came from the National Endowment for the Arts, state arts agencies, major oil companies (Texaco, Mobil, Exxon), and an array of foundations and businesses who discovered that the arts were big business—a vital part of the very much sought after "quality of life." The 1980s, however, find a number of orchestras, ranging from school to professional programs, falling by the wayside. School programs are fighting declining enrollment, severe budget constraints, shifting priorities in education, and the general attitude that school arts are expendable.

Professional orchestras are confronted with rising costs in administrative and artistic operations and with the inability to pass the cost along to the ticket-purchasing consumer. As the musician's union becomes stronger, orchestra administrators have less flexibility in marketing the orchestras and are limited by the number of services allowed per week, the types of services acceptable, constraints on touring, and so on. At the same time, the base pay and fringe benefits of the players have increased dramatically.

Recently, these difficulties have been compounded by the cuts in federal and state funding for human services. The same foundations, corporations, businesses, and individuals who were previously supporters of arts activities are now being asked to divert their contributable income to agencies dealing with basic human needs (food for the hungry, housing for the homeless, etc.) in order to take up the slack between reduced governmental aid and the need for humanitarian assistance. As a direct or indirect result of these trends, we have witnessed some professional orchestras falling on hard times, incurring large budget deficits or suspending operations altogether (e.g., the Kansas City Philharmonic and the Miami Symphony).

The increases in numbers and quality of young string players in the 1960s and 1970s were explained in a variety of ways. Some believed that the school and youth orchestra picture looked very bright.

> Because of the large number of potential students, the improved teaching methods, and the disenchantment by a large part of the student population with the regimentation of bands, the potential for many large and excellent [school-youth] orchestra programs is greater than it has ever been in the past. (Dillon and Kriechbaum, 1978, p. 281)

College or university and community orchestras should benefit from these increases; but they are in strong competition for orchestral instrument players, especially in strings and double reeds. Good high school players are recruited heavily by colleges. At the community level, a better quality of support for professional orchestras should develop as these students graduate and join their communities' leadership structures; however, it is too early to tell whether this is happening widely.

The orchestral picture, in the mid-1980s, is indeed changing. There is a need for reevaluation, reassessment, and perhaps realignment among arts producers and suppliers, educators, artists, and arts consumers. We all have a tremendous responsibility to see that music continues to be expressed through live performances by living, breathing, feeling human beings—not just packaged in video discs and as industrial background music. We are both the privileged ones and the ones with the burden—the teachers and performers who have the developed talents and sensitivities to understand and appreciate the incredible treasure of the arts. We must use all our talents to perpetuate them.

18 Growing Awareness: Notes from the Piano Studio

Amanda Penick

Private teaching allows for personal observations, comments, and interaction, which distinguish this instruction from classroom learning. Its justification, therefore, is in providing individual direction in learning according to specific needs through expanding the awareness of the student.

Awareness, or "consciousness-of," can for this purpose be defined as having a revelation absorbed into the musical blood stream through the visual, tactile, or aural sense. Students are born not with awareness but only with the capacity for it, which the teacher must stretch and deepen so that the student may learn to perceive, hear, and feel in an ever-increasing circle.

This teaching requires imaginative suggestions, generous use of imagery, and the ability to translate symbols or mental concepts into the appropriate sensation; but after all, these are the same responses necessary in performing music itself.

Quite often, in briefly hearing young students from different studios in the area, I am struck by their dissimilar levels of awareness. For example, I recently worked with two students from different teachers. They were similar in talent and performance level, but on the second lesson I made the following evaluations:

1. The more aware student had accomplished more in practice; he had absorbed both musical and technical suggestions. The other student had made negligible progress because he was less conscious of right from wrong and was frustrated that his practice, consisting of "over and over playing," had not been productive. A student's accomplishment is proportionate to his level of awareness.

2. The more aware student was actively enthusiastic toward progress and was engrossed in his music as well as in the music of others. The second student's passivity caused by lack of awareness of what or how he played will

eventually destroy his initial hope and enthusiasm. Surely a circular equation is applicable at this point: Increased awareness = productive practice = accomplishment = motivation = increased awareness.

3. The more aware student had the light of understanding and a shining eagerness in his eyes. The second student's eyes were downcast and glazed. The eyes, to me, are the truest indicators of realization of learning.

We, as teachers, *must* open the doors to awareness for our students and lead them in an active pursuit of accomplishment. Their eyes must see rather than merely look; in their physical approach to the piano, they must feel rather than mechanize; and their ears must hear rather than just listen.

Visual Awareness

Vision in depth refers to actively looking rather than passively seeing details, and growth in visual awareness can be described as a development in both depth and peripheral vision.

An experiment was once conducted in an aesthetics class composed of fine-arts majors from different fields. The studio art professor wished to prove that art majors who had been broadening their visual awareness saw in greater detail; after chatting briefly with the class, he left the room, asking that the color of each detail of his appearance be jotted down. The experiment proved that the eye of the art majors recorded 15 details to each 1 of the nonart majors. His concluding point was that this high level of awareness was gathered from training and was not an inherent part of talent.

In the private music studio, efforts toward such expanded vision can be equally productive. A student's study of the printed page of music should result in an ever-increasing number of details absorbed at sight and in less time. For example, an effective test of conceptual note learning that demonstrates a student's awareness can be given by having the student study (without playing) a measure for 30 seconds then play all remembered details. He or she can gradually become able to play such passages from memory and even extend the amount covered. Each day of practice on a piece should result in additional visual details gleaned from the score:

1. What is the overall form?
2. What sections are the same? What sections are different? How?
3. What is the meter? Key?
4. What is the meaning of each term used?
5. What is the basic dynamic plan?
6. What is the basic harmonic plan?
7. Does the title suggest a character or way of playing?
8. Does the composer's name suggest a style of playing?

Eventually the student should develop visual memory of all or part of the printed score.

Absorption of visual details is a most important part of awareness expansion, and the development of conceptual note learning and other printed details on the score greatly facilitates learning and sight-reading music.

Visual awareness at the keyboard is another aspect of importance, not only necessary for sight-reading and theory but for correct placement and accuracy in performing. Visualization of a specific chord mentally followed by the playing of the chord with closed eyes is an indication of the visual level that can be reached. Visualization of an octave span in order more successfully to identify intervals in ear training is another example.

The extension of peripheral vision is also possible, and experiments have indeed proved that exercises composed of extending intervals in contrary motion can develop the ability to encompass visually a wider range on the keyboard. From the very beginning of study, repertory for students must include pieces exploring the entire keyboard. Fortunately, today's composers for the young child offer attractive selections to develop visual awareness, and the student is no longer restricted to the two-octave range of past elementary material.

Physical Awareness

The growth or stretching of physical awareness is made possible through learning to recall the physical sensations necessary for a specific passage. The teacher guides the student toward the correct "feel" for such technical concepts as runs, leaps, rotation, trills, arpeggios, repeated notes, and the like. This approach is similar to the ideo-kinetics theory advanced a generation ago, in which students, instead of thinking in terms of what hands and fingers are preparing to do, think instead in terms of interpretive rendering.

The Liszt *Mephisto Waltz* is a tour de force in virtuosity in that most all of the technical features are employed one after another, if not simultaneously, so the performer must "trigger" one specific sensation after another with no rest in between. This piece is obviously for the most physically aware; most private teaching consists of helping the student to become aware of each feature individually spaced throughout his or her study. If the student is not guided toward the appropriate sensations, such as where the impulse is generated, how many notes can be covered under one impulse, or how the hand and arm must feel during performance, all technical study will be virtually useless because the sensation cannot be remembered and repeated. Physical awareness should be considered to be a form of choreography at the keyboard. The following suggestions serve as examples of easily transferable sensations:

1. As early as the first lesson, a student must learn how it feels to sit correctly at the keyboard. The correct position and height are essential to allow the body to move freely in a lateral motion, and body weight must be properly distributed. Tension in shoulders and neck is the result of incorrect seating, and the playing mechanism is affected by incorrect body weight. A small child's feet must be supported on a stool until they can comfortably reach the floor for weight balance.

2. Students should incorporate the feeling of horizontal movements at the keyboard with these movements guided by the upper arm so that fingers and wrist become more often than not an extension of the arm. The sensation of playing a glissando or an easily rolled chord is the proper horizontal movement, which can be adapted to scales and arpeggios. Most students, unfortunately, conceive of piano playing as a vertical pressing down of the fingers, which produces stiffness and a brittle sound. Abby Whiteside, eminent teacher of a generation ago, commented that pianistic stiffness was a result of three errors: holding down notes, pressing down notes, and reaching for notes—all done by the fingers alone. She added that as long as the fingers do all of the work at the keyboard, the upper arm, or large muscles, cannot assist. Her "full arm stroke" was designed for incorporating the entire arm as a unit in producing tone, a sensation initiated by the upper arm; the stroke is similar in feeling to raising and lowering a window shade. (See Whiteside, 1929.)

3. Students should feel in touch with the keys. This tactile sensation prevents unnecessary efforts involved in quick releases as in staccato notes. Once the student feels the effort expended in quick lifting, he or she is invariably surprised, having assumed that greater effort was necessary to play a note than to lift it. The sensation of riding a key up in release is valuable.

4. Students can play with greater ease if the elbow can work with guiding the hand in playing. So often the elbows are locked into the body very tensely. Creating the sensation of a "floating elbow" (as in floating in salt water) is an effective aid to awareness. Using the imagery of elbows being supported by puppet strings extended from the ceiling is another possibility. Reminders from the teacher to "stay picked up in the elbows" will be helpful to students while playing.

5. Passages played in the air, away from the keyboard but in the correct choreography, can facilitate awareness through eliminating the physical tension a student creates in the very process of note playing. The effortlessness of air playing convinces the student of the excessive effort he or she has employed when in contact with the keys.

6. Learning the correct sensation of playing a passage under the pulse impulse is essential for playing rapid figuration. The pianist feels himself or herself playing one impulse, but along with it he or she has tucked in all remaining notes within the pulse.

7. Physical sensations providing color in sound such as "stroking" the key, "ringing" the note, and "pouncing as a cat" are all easily acquired elements of awareness for the student's physical storehouse.

These are only a few examples of the many physical requirements for pianists. All problems can be solved through awareness if the teacher can diagnose incorrect physical movements, which often can be seen, and imaginatively translate the correct movement into a transferable sensation. Reminders are a part of teaching until the student's mechanism has naturalized the sensation, for bad habits die hard; but most often the student is quick to acquire that which feels, and is, easier. Too many teachers ignore the student's technical approach to the keyboard in their effort to teach notation and advance in repertory; they wait until problems affect performance before becoming concerned, by which time, of course, habits have become ingrained. Through guidance into physical awareness from the first lesson, the student learns from his or her initial impression that which is correct and easiest.

Aural Awareness

Finally, and most important of all, is the development of aural awareness. Language learning through the aural sense is the primary experience from infancy until the child learns to read and write, and if music is the universal language, we, as teachers, must nurture and expand the child's aural efforts from the first lesson on.

Aural awareness can be defined as directed listening, and the most respected teachers will agree that their "method" is getting students to listen to themselves. Theodor Leschetizky, one of the most famous teachers of all, said that to involve a student in hearing three successive notes played beautifully was for him real teaching. (See Gerig, 1975.)

Aural awareness can be divided into two classifications for discussion: theoretical awareness and awareness of sound.

Theoretical Awareness

Picture if you will, a child coming into a lesson and the teacher, trying to incorporate theoretical concepts into the student's musical training, asks to *see* his or her theory homework, which consists of a series of written exercises. The teacher reads through the assignment then checks the answers and grades the paper. Sadly, this is an all too familiar pattern that is not only unappealing but nonproductive for the student, who never makes the association of mental concepts into sound as incorporated into music. The teacher, however, feels productive in his or her efforts.

Several years ago, in preparation for a thesis on the importance of developing the ear, a graduate student in piano pedagogy mailed to private teachers in the state a questionnaire on the frequency of their attention given to developing the theoretical aural awareness of students. A similar questionnaire was given to university undergraduate music majors enrolled in theory. An interesting analysis revealed that 98% of all teachers answered that they frequently (at almost every lesson) worked on theory, and 61% of the students felt that their precollege theoretical training was inadequate. Unfortunately, the low test scores of entering freshmen on the Aliferis test (melodic, intervallic, and rhythmic elements) strongly corroborate the students' feelings.

A "sound before sight" procedure is necessary in this form of aural learning. If, for example, the teacher wishing to introduce the interval of a fifth at a lesson would begin by playing it and commenting on its inherent distinctive qualities, awareness would result. Imagery is a valuable tool in teaching, and this fifth could perhaps be compared with the sounds of Indian drums. Next, the student might play the fifth, harmonically and then melodically. This could be followed by the student's finding fifths all over the keyboard, singing fifths in order to provide that most important vocal association, recognizing fifths in comparison with other sounded intervals, and finally finding them on the page of music. Now the student has expanded his or her awareness, and this "sound before sight" approach has allowed him or her to perceive the individual quality of each interval based on sound.

The use of the voice in learning music at any level or age cannot be too strongly stressed, for not only is the voice an additional aural instrument, but it is the definitive method of understanding and absorbing melodic lines in music. Almost all music for piano, through the 19th century at least, is based on vocal melody, and no pianist can simulate this vocal line on the keyboard without an awareness of singing. The playing of fingers one and five on an octave is far easier than the spacing and effort expended in the singing of it. Pianists must learn to emulate these relative efforts expended in sounding intervals. One enterprising teacher actually used boxes, and students climbed to the various intervals in order to feel their relative physical exertion.

The playing of scales, arpeggios, and cadences likewise falls too often into the dull routine of a pianist's preparation because of their arbitrary inclusion as something that "has to be done." The student must be shown how to listen to cadences in order to hear the chords moving one into another, building to the greatest point of tension, and finally resolving on the tonic. Scales and arpeggios must be played as melodic studies as well as theoretical exercises. All exercises are relatively ineffective without aural musical involvement.

Young children are eager to begin study when they have, somewhere, sat at a piano and made sounds, perhaps rocking back and forth on only two notes with total fascination and wonder. Learning to play the piano should not and must not diminish or extinguish this enthusiasm for making sound. Aural awareness will need to be developed at an early age if it is to be trusted or used by the student in later years, and the ear will stretch as the learning expands.

Awareness of Sound

The second category of aural awareness is defined as attentive listening to sound. From the very first lesson, a student should begin to recognize and listen for the best and most appropriate quality of sound and learn to distinguish this from harsh and unpleasant tone. Even as the student begins those tentative first steps toward note finding or notational learning, he or she must be guided in listening for sound and in learning the relationship between touch and sound. Through listening and watching the teacher play one note, the student can soon match the quality. The use of imagery is particularly valuable in helping students in sound. Small sound, yes; the young pianist like the young singer should never be allowed to force tone. As muscles develop, sound will grow.

Fine aural awareness is the result of years spent stretching and absorbing the many levels and details of textured sound. If it is true that only a small portion of the brain's capacities is ever developed, it is certainly equally true of the ear, and no musician ever hears all that it is possible to hear. This is an encouraging belief in that all musicians, regardless of age and level of artistry, can enjoy continuous expansion of aural awareness.

How does tonal awareness deepen? By consistently adding to what is already heard. The ear must learn to encircle sound, to dart between the beats, voices, and harmonies. It must carry sound through dots, bar lines, and the piano's "dying" sustaining tone. It must hold sound, shape sound, and connect sound. It must imagine sound.

The following list can serve as a growth chart of listening elements and advances in difficulty:

1. Quality of sound. Effective and appropriate tone is the most important feature of beautiful piano playing.

2. Simple balance. Learning how to subordinate simple accompaniments to melody begins as soon as the student plays with both hands together. As in all coordinative requirements, it is most effectively executed slowly and in exaggeration at the beginning. Holding the arms at slightly different levels is helpful so that the arm playing the accompaniment is held higher, resulting in less weight reaching the fingers.

3. Giving inflection to melody. The musical sentence is inflected in the same manner as the spoken sentence in which the voice moves to the important word. When we go up we get louder; going down we soften and we let the harmony guide us through tension and resolutions. These are fundamental principles to use in shaping. Again, singing the phrase with the student is essential as well as playing along with him or her and shaping the phrase in the air.

4. Using accompaniment to support melodic shading. So often the melody alone cannot provide enough directional shaping. The accompaniments, although subordinate, must also have musical and supportive shape.

5. Balance of more than one voice in one hand. In chords, in the right hand, the top tone must be highlighted over the other tones. Have the student use this procedure: play the top tone first and follow softly with the other notes. Notice the greater weight given to the top. Now holding the hand in the same way, play the chord notes simultaneously. This process can be reversed for left hand chords so the bass note can be featured.

6. Listening through sound. Students' ears must be directed to hearing on the subdivision of the beat after a note is played so that he or she can successfully hear the note throughout its duration and hear it connect with the next note.

7. Listening to and for the pedal. Because the pedal is a mechanism, it is most often used in an unconscious way without regard for its effect on the sound of music. Pedal should not be added to music until decisions of when, why, and how are made. The pedal should then be listened to and used with utmost accuracy. Various levels of the pedal are necessary in playing, with shallow depths desirable in soft passages. The foot must move quietly so changes do not produce a vertical accent or sound. The pedal is not a crutch to cover weaknesses; it is intended to enhance the sound of music, and its incorporation should be as imperceptible as possible.

8. Varying sound for stylistic purposes. The sounds and textures of a Mozart sonata are quite different from those necessary for Debussy, for example. This high level of distinction is based on many listening elements as well as experience in hearing music. Listening to recordings of Mozart's symphonies, operas, and quartets will certainly enhance a pianist's stylistic awareness in playing a Mozart sonata.

9. Varying color for contrast within a piece. Experimentation at the piano through listening to sounds will result in certain solutions for color changes. For example, an opaque color is produced when all tones are of the same level. A transparent color is the result of much tonal difference between voices. A dark color can be produced by exaggerating the low voices, and the list could continue. Important here is the need to "prehear" the desired color change in preparation for it.

10. Varying sound simultaneously. If possible, sound should be varied through its phrasing differences. It is practical also to conceive of voices as having the tonal properties of different instruments.

11. Listening to several voices individually and yet collectively as in a Bach fugue. This is the most demanding level in awareness and calls upon all previously mentioned elements in combination. We can "listen to" these voices parading through our consciousness but to "hear" them individually demands stereophonic aural awareness and a very slow tempo. This listening is the perfect example of progression in aural awareness toward stretching the ear.

Pianists tend to hear more completely when the music is soft and slow and the texture is thin. Music with these qualities should be chosen for a student first learning to listen. Later, selected music will stretch his or her ear to hear faster, bigger, thicker textures. The pianist does not hear low as well as high ranges; he does not hear the ends of phrases as well as the middle. He does not hear short notes as well as long, or weak beats as well as strong ones. The teacher's work of directing listening to these specific weaknesses is similar to teaching a singer to increase his or her vocal range.

It is said that rhythm is "felt." This is true, but feeling is a result of hearing, and the ear must be aware of rhythm in order to place the beats in the music. Students must increase their awareness in order to hear unsounded beats existing in dots, sustained notes, and rests. They must learn to hear the weak side of beats and the inner moving of large pulses; this ability will make it possible to avoid rushing. It is so often true that the pianist hears sound only on the attack of the beat and fails to listen for the residual sound's subordinate beats; this causes a clipped or shortened duration of the beat. Poor or weak rhythm is unheard rhythm.

In broadening aural awareness the teacher will need to provide imagery consistently of what the music sounds like, provide directed or specific spots of listening, and learn to stretch his or her own awareness in order to hear the student more objectively. The teacher's objectivity is often as questionable as the student's, for both want to hear what they are thinking. It can be a revelation to listen with closed eyes to music as though for the first time, away from the score and identity of the performer. This is the most lucid way to judge the effectiveness of performance awareness and to realize that all mental concepts must be "auralized" to be heard.

Students are, of course, at different levels: They are of different temperaments and abilities. Some, it is true, have a greater capacity for awareness than others; and some have a greater affinity for one of the three mentioned awareness areas than another. Two facts, however, remain unchanged. First, all students can grow in awareness as long as they are involved in music, and they will become more motivated as well as more effective as a result. Second, any growth of awareness must be initiated and directed by the teacher. Lessons consisting of correcting fingering, rhythm, and notes may be necessary and even productive, but too often, correcting is the sum total of the lesson. Correcting is not teaching. If time is spent at each lesson moving up a step in awareness, pointing out some previously unheard, unfelt, or unseen idea, students will want to play and will be able to play with more accuracy. They will show in their eyes a shining delight in discovery, which is the telling and rewarding sign that the goal was accomplished. That is real teaching.

Part IV
Postscript

19 The Alabama Project: Its Impact and Its Future

Roosevelt Shelton, Joan Vold, Mai Kelton, James Rogers, Johnny Jacobs, William Timmons, Joy Driskell-Baklanoff, and others

A poster that states "Don't let school interfere with your education" sets into play one of the great tragedies of professional development in music education: Music teachers are generally dedicated people who have an active love affair with music by way of their own aesthetic experience. They are also busy people, and being too active could become our profession's fatal flaw.

Many schools list music as a "basic" on one document and on another include the elimination of music programs as a possible means to cut costs. Music in these schools enjoys a somewhat tenuous existence, providing teachers with a major motivation to become busy people. The Alabama Project explored the concepts of the music teacher as a transmitter of culture, a preacher, a policeman, a propagandist, an institutor, a distributor, a provider of space, and a seeker of funds. Music educators are often content to remain busy at these somewhat more technical tasks of teaching and never enter the realm of theory.

Serious questions as to the direction, future, and even the continued existence of music education in America have been raised by the Alabama Project. Only by confronting the weaknesses in the current status of music education can we, as music educators, hope to gain strength and begin to plant the seeds of change that will bring forth positive actions for the future of musical literacy in our society. Often the words *value* and *society* were found together. We as a society must become vocal about the value of music if the nation's artistic potential is to be reached, and it is most often the music educator in his or her local community who must lead this effort.

299

The Alabama Project at the National Level

Several times throughout the year, references were made to the Tanglewood Symposium and to other events in the history of 20th-century American music education to which the Alabama Project was likened. Educators had come from every region of the nation to present papers, and they represented 15 of the country's major universities as well as other important institutions, such as the National Endowment for the Arts. The focus extended even beyond the national boundaries by the inclusion of two educators, Malcolm Tait and J. H. Kwabena Nketia, whose cultural roots lie outside the United States. As participants, all shared in making the Alabama Project happen, and in so doing each one became necessarily a part of the larger community of music educators who may be catalysts for change and growth in American music education.

The Alabama Project at the Personal Level

As doctoral candidates in music education, we felt the effect of the residencies primarily through the individual conferences. From each one we received incomparable encouragement and support.

Those attending all four symposia have dealt with the how's, what's, and why's of music's place in the development of fully functioning individuals. The effect these sessions have had on us personally was twofold: They have reinforced our belief that the arts cannot exist in a vacuum, and they have helped us understand the problems of developing a common set of professional goals and standards for American music educators to live by.

Finally, the Alabama Project has served as a catalyst for our own developing research interests. Having the opportunity to see and hear most of the revered authorities in our profession grapple with our most complex issues has intensified our commitment to shedding some light on the problems of developing musical self-expression in others. Why do we now find ourselves genuinely admiring these gadflies? Because behind their diverse approaches to answering the questions that profoundly affect our profession, we saw a genuine love affair with music and education—a love affair that they feel compelled to share. Nevertheless they are firmly grounded in the ways real people learn and experience music. We will remember Malcolm Tait's advice after our philosophy symposium: "Stick with the children; they're the ones who have the answers!"

Probably the most important effect that the project has had on us is that it has forced us to reconsider in great detail the process of educating people musically. Why do we educate people in music? Are the methods even important? What are the benefits to the individual and society if we do our jobs well?

These are by no means easy questions, and it is not right to assume that all of us have even heard them. What is most important is that these questions and others be considered. If the main effect of the project is that it has stimulated us to think about them, then we might truly say that the Alabama Project was a success.

Prospects for the Future

The Alabama Project should be used as a model for future ventures in music education. Certainly, at The University of Alabama in future years, when the endowed chair is to be administered by the music education department, a number of the speakers may profitably share that chair. The format used in 1984–1985 could be used again.

Other institutions of higher education should form projects based on the Alabama Project. An ongoing forum, perhaps through the Music Educators National Conference (MENC), should continue to focus on not only the "how" but also the "why" in music education in America. As our society continues to change, we must constantly reflect on the underlying values that form our attitudes and shape the ways we go about our work. We help each other grow as we share the quest for a theory of music education in America in the years ahead.

In order for there to be a healthy learning environment where all members of a community can find a satisfying mode of artistic self-expression, there must be common commitment and respect among members of the artistic community (e.g., professional and amateur performers, music teachers, critics, promoters, philosophers, patrons). Without this common core of acceptance, elitism will undermine the growth of all forms of arts education.

At least one pattern of differences and two patterns of similarities have emerged from the Alabama Project. Each has had a positive effect on the graduate students who regularly participated in all its aspects.

The keynote speakers introduced us to four distinct ways of thinking that are current and vital in music education and doubtless will continue to be important in the next decade. The typical graduate student is acquainted with his or her own way of thinking, knowing, and doing, and it often becomes the *only* way of thinking, knowing, and doing. This is a pitfall of which those doctoral students involved with the project have, fortunately, been made abundantly aware.

More important, however, are two continuous patterns iterated by the project speakers. These include:

1. Music must come first within the musical teaching-learning process. Although much emphasis has been placed on the aesthetic value of music in the past two decades, the time is now right for renewed attention by educators to this essential theme.

2. Music educators must be sensitive to music in its sociocultural context, and this should include all the world's music. "Music is culture," said Nketia at the philosophy symposium, and he amply illuminated this point. Music educators at all levels must expand the universe of musical experience for their students. We have come, again, to believe that the emphasis on music in society—all societies, cultures, and ethnic groups—will be a pivotal point for the future of music education.

Five years from now we will look back and say that the Alabama Project was an effort to make a significant change in the status of music education in American society. Perhaps not many opportunities remain.

References

American Association of School Administrators (AASA). (1959). *Your AASA in 1958–59: Official report*. Washington, DC: AASA.

American Symphony Orchestra League (ASOL). (1984). *Orchestra education programs: A handbook and directory of education and outreach programs*. Washington, DC: ASOL.

Andress, B. (1980). *Music experience in early childhood*. New York: Holt, Rinehart & Winston.

Apel, Willie, (Ed.). (1972). *Harvard dictionary of music* (2nd ed.). Cambridge, MA: Harvard University Press.

Applebaum, E. (1972). A practice of narrowing options. *Music Educators Journal, 58*(7), 43–45.

Arabadzhev, S. (1978). Suggestive effect of music and aphorisms on fluency in tests of creativity. *Studia Psychologica, 10*, 170–177, 188.

Arieti, S. (1976). *Creativity: The magic synthesis*. New York: Basic Books.

Arnstein, D. (1966). Shaping the emotions: The sources of standards for aesthetic education. *Journal of Aesthetic Education, 1*(1), 45–69.

Art for the sake of . . . children. (1984, November 16). *Time*, p. 14.

Association for Classical Music (ACM). (1984). *Survey of students' attitudes toward classical music*. New York: Association for Classical Music. (News release.)

Bamberger, J. (1974). *What's in a tune?* (Report No. LOGO-13). Boston: M.I.T., Artificial Intelligence Lab. (ERIC Document Reproduction Service No. ED 118 369)

Barkan, M., Chapman, L., Kern, E. J. (1970). *Guidelines: Curriculum development for aesthetic education*. St. Louis: Central Midwestern Regional Educational Laboratory.

Barnes, H. E. (Ed.). (1947). *An introduction to the history of sociology*. Chicago: University of Chicago Press.

Baudo, J. (1982). The effectiveness of jazz education on the enhancement of the characteristic traits associated with creativity in music: Implications for curriculum planning. *Dissertation Abstracts International, 43*(10), 3252A. (University Microfilms No. 8303085)

Beall, G. H. (1981). *Music as experience*. Dubuque, IA: C. Brown.

Beall, G. H. (1982). Music education in adolescence: A problem in perspectives. In R. Colwell (Ed.), *Symposium in music education*. Urbana: University of Illinois Press.

Beardslee, D., & O'Dowd, D. (1960). *College student images of a selected group of professions and occupations*. Cooperative Research Project No. 562 (8142) with the United States Office of Education. Washington, DC: Department of Health, Education and Welfare.

Benner, C. H. (1976). Implications of social change for music education. In *Challenges in music education: Proceedings of the XI International Conference of the International Society for Music Education*. Perth: Department of Music, University of Western Australia with the Music Board of the Australia Council.

Bennett, S. (1975). Learning to compose: Some research, some suggestions. *Journal of Creative Behavior, 9*(3), 205–210.

Benson, W. (1967). *Creative projects in musicianship*. Washington, DC: Music Educators National Conference.

Benson, W. (1973). The creative child could be any child. *Music Educators Journal, 59*(8), 38–40.

Bierstedt, R. (1957). *The social order: An introduction to sociology.* New York: McGraw-Hill.

Birge, E. B. (1937). *History of public school music in the United States.* Philadelphia: Oliver Ditson.

Bolin, Mary J. (Ed.). (1984). *A closer look at recent reports concerning the present status of education in the United States.* Unpublished manuscript prepared for MENC Eastern Division Symposium.

Boston School Committee. (1838, December 5). Report of Special Committee. *Boston Musical Gazette, 1,* n. 16.

Boyer, E. (1983). *High school: A report of the Carnegie Foundation for the Advancement of Teaching on secondary education in America.* New York: Harper & Row.

Bradley, I. (1974). Development of aural and visual perception through creative processes. *Journal of Research in Music Education, 22* (3), 234–240.

Brameld, T. (n.d.). *Culture: Philosophical perspectives.* Unpublished manuscript, Boston University.

Brameld, T. (1950). *Education for the emerging age.* New York: Harper.

Brameld, T. (1955). *Philosophies of education in cultural perspective.* New York: Holt, Rinehart & Winston.

Brameld, T. (1956). *Toward a reconstructed philosophy of education.* New York: Dryden Press.

Brameld, T. (1962). *Philosophy of education as philosophy of religion.* Unpublished lectures, Meadville Theological School, Chicago.

Bronowski, J. (1978). *The visionary eye: Essays in the arts, literature, and science.* Cambridge, MA: MIT Press.

Broudy, H. S. (1958). A realistic philosophy of music education. In Nelson B. Henry (Ed.), *Basic Concepts in Music Education.* 57th yearbook, Part 1, National Society for the Study of Education. Chicago: University of Chicago Press, 62–87.

Broudy, H. S. (1966). Aesthetic education in a technical society: The other excuses for art. *Journal of Aesthetic Education, 1*(1).

Brown, E. (1968). A study of the application of creativity in the teaching of secondary school music. *Dissertation Abstracts International, 29*(5), 1553A. (University Microfilms No. 68-15219)

Bruner, J. S. (1979). *On knowing: Essays for the left hand.* Cambridge, MA: Belknap Press, Harvard University Press.

Buber, M. (1947). *Between man and man.* Translated by Ronald Gregor Smith. London: Routledge & Kegan Paul.

Buckner, R. T. (1974). A history of music education in the black community of Kansas City, Kansas. *Dissertation Abstracts International, 35,* 4219A. (University Microfilms No. 75-157)

Burgess, A. (1983). *This man and music.* New York: McGraw-Hill.

Burns, J. M. (1978). *Leadership.* New York: Harper & Row.

Carpenter, L. W. (1969). The Stephen Foster Memorial, 1931–1969: A socio-cultural force in a rural community. *Dissertation Abstracts International, 31,* 1306A. (University Microfilms No. 70-16321)

Castaldo, J. (1969). Creativity can end our musical isolationism. *Music Educators Journal, 56*(3), 36–38.

Castellano, J. (1969). Music composition in a music therapy program. *Journal of Music Therapy, 6,* 12–14.

Chapman, L. (1982). *Instant art, instant culture: The unspoken policy for American schools.* New York: Teachers College Press, Columbia University.

Cheyette, I. (1977). Developing the innate musical creativity of children. *Journal of Creative Behavior, 11*(4), 256–260.

Cheyette, I., & Cheyette, H. (1969). *Teaching music creatively in the elementary school.* New York: McGraw-Hill.

Choate, R. A. (Ed.). (1968). *Documentary Report of the Tanglewood Symposium.* Reston, VA: Music Educators National Conference.

Cleall, C. (1981). Notes toward the clarification of creativity in music education. *Psychology of Music, 9*(1), 44–47.

CMP 3. (1966). *Experiments in musical creativity.* Washington, DC: Music Educators National Conference.

Coates, J. (1978). *Proceedings of the conference: Research in the Arts.* Washington, DC: Walters Gallery and National Endowment for the Arts.

Coates, P. (1983). Alternatives to the aesthetic rationale for music education. *Music Educators Journal, 68*(7), 31–32.

Coleman, S. (1922). *Creative music for children.* New York: Putnam.

College Entrance Examination Board (CEEB). (1981). *The basic academic competencies.* Princeton, NJ: Educational EQuality Project.

College Entrance Examination Board (CEEB). (1983). *Academic preparation for college: What students need to know and be able to do.* (Report of the Educational EQuality Project of the CEEB.) New York: College Board Publications.

College Music Society (CMS). (1983). *Directory of music faculties in colleges and universities, U.S. and Canada, 1982–84.* Boulder, CO: College Music Society.

Corporon, E. (n.d.). *Towards a guiding philosophy for the University of Northern Colorado band program.* Unpublished manuscript, University of Northern Colorado, Greeley.

Cox, E. (1966). A functional approach to creative experiences in music in the elementary school. *Dissertation Abstracts International, 27*(12), 4277A. (University Microfilms No. 67-06519)

Crawford, J. D. (1972). The relationship of socioeconomic status to attitude toward music and home musical interest in intermediate grade children. *Dissertation Abstracts International, 34,* 351A-352A. (University Microfilms No. 73-9752)

Dahlenberg, W. J. (1967). Music in the culture of Miami: 1920–1966. *Dissertation Abstracts International, 28,* 2708A. (University Microfilms No. 68-346)

Dallman, R. (1970). A survey of creativity in music through composition in elementary schools of Colorado. *Dissertation Abstracts International, 31*(2), 6644A. (University Microfilms No. 71-14523)

Davies, P., & Grant, W. (1963). Music composition by children. In (Eds.) *Music in Education: Proceedings of the 14th symposium of the Calston Research Society* (pp. 108–123). London: Butterworth.

Davison, A. (1926). *Music education in America.* New York: Harper.

DeGrazia, S. (1962). *On time, work, and leisure.* New York: Twentieth Century Fund.

Dennis, M. (1972). Music composition by children. *International Society for Music Education Journal, 2,* 20–21.

DeRusha, S. (1984). The rehearsal technique. *College Band Directors National Association Journal, 1*(1), 30–31.

Dewey, J. (1916). *Democracy and education.* New York: Macmillan.

Dewey, J. (1937). Philosophy. In *Encyclopedia of the social sciences* (Vol. 2). New York: Macmillan.

Dewey, J. (1957). *Reconstruction in philosophy* (enlarged edition). Boston: Beacon

Press. (Originally published 1920)

Dillon, J., & Kriechbaum, C. (1978). *How to design and teach a successful school string and orchestra program.* San Diego: Kjos West/Neil A. Kjos, Jr.

Dobbins, B. (1980). Improvisation: An essential element of musical proficiency. *Music Educators Journal, 66*(5), 36–41.

Dodson, T. (1979). A comparison and evaluation of the effects of a creative-comprehensive approach and a performance approach in acquisition of music fundamentals by college students. *Dissertation Abstracts International, 40*(4), 1941A.

Doig, D. (1941). Creative music: I. Music composed for a given text. *Journal of Educational Research, 35,* 262–275.

Doig, D. (1942a). Creative music: II. Music composed on a given subject. *Journal of Educational Research, 35,* 344–355.

Doig, D. (1942b). Creative music: III. Music composed to illustrate given music problems. *Journal of Educational Research, 36,* 241–253.

Downey, R. A. (1974). Factors influencing leadership for community musical activities in the state of Colorado. *Dissertation Abstracts International, 35,* 4220A. (University Microfilms No. 75-88)

Driskell, J. (1985). *Traditional Black music and musicians in rural Alabama and northeast Mississippi, 1940–1982: An ethnomusicological analysis.* Unpublished doctoral dissertation, University of Alabama.

Dumazedier, J. (1967). *Toward a society of leisure?* New York: Free Press.

Dumazedier, J. (1974). *The empirical sociology of leisure.* Amsterdam: Elsevier.

Duncan, H. D. (1957). Sociology of art. In H. Becker & A. Boskoff (Eds.), *Modern sociological theory in continuity and change* (pp. 482–497). New York: Dryden.

Dunlap, J. E., Jr. (1975). The relationship of musical achievement as measured by the Colwell *Music Achievement Test* to socio-economic status, race, community size, and the presence of the father in the home in seventh grade general music classes in Arkansas and Mississippi. *Dissertation Abstracts International, 36,* 2466A. (University Microfilms No. 75-19880)

Dykema, P. G., & the Committee on Resolutions. (1950). The child's bill of rights in music. Report of the committee to the Biennial Convention of the Music Educators National Conference. *Proceedings of the Thirty-First Annual Meeting, St. Louis.* Washington, DC: Music Educators National Conference.

Eagle, C. (1983, February). A creative view of creativity. In *Loyola Symposium VI,* Loyola University of New Orleans.

Education Commission of the States (ECS). (1983). *Action for excellence: Report of the Task Force on Education for Economic Growth.* Denver: Education Commission of the States.

Eisner, E. (1982). *Cognition and curriculum.* New York: Longman.

Elliot, C. (1983). Behind the budget crisis, a crisis of philosophy. *Music Educators Journal, 70*(2), 36–37.

Fain, S. S. (1956). *A study of the community symphony orchestra in the United States, 1750–1955.* Unpublished doctoral dissertation, University of Southern California.

Farmilo, N. (1981). The creativity, teaching style, and personality characteristics of the effective elementary music teacher. *Dissertation Abstracts International, 42,* 591A–592A. (University Microfilms No. 8117057)

Farruggia, J. A. (1969). A study of factors that influence instrumental music dropouts in two small towns and two large city high schools in the state of California. *Dissertation Abstracts International, 31,* 1307A-1308A. (University Microfilms No. 70-15336)

Feinberg, S. (1973). A creative problem-solving approach to the development of perceptive music listening in the secondary school music literature class. *Dissertation Abstracts International, 34*(2), 806A-807A. (University Microfilms No. 73-18722)

Feinberg, S. (1977). Creative problem-solving and the music listening experience. *Journal of Creative Behavior, 11*(3), 158–164.

Flohr, J. (1979). Musical improvisation behavior of young children. *Dissertation Abstracts International, 40*(10), 5355A. (University Microfilms No. 8009033)

Flohr, J. (1983, February). A longitudinal study of music improvisation. In *Loyola Symposium VI*, Loyola University of New Orleans.

Forbes, J. M. (1974). The music program of Berea College (Kentucky) and the folk-music heritage of Appalachia. *Dissertation Abstracts International, 35*, 2746A. (University Microfilms No. 74-25202)

Ford Foundation. (1974). *The finances of the performing arts: Survey of the characteristics and attitudes of audiences for theatre, opera, symphony, and ballet in 12 U.S. cities.* New York: Ford Foundation.

Forrai, K. (1983). Cultural impact of the Kodály presentation in early childhood education. *Bulletin of the International Kodály Society, 2*, 18–20.

Fowler, C. B. (1964). *A reconstructionist philosophy of music education.* Unpublished doctoral dissertation, Boston University.

Fowler, C. B. (1966). Discovery method: Its relevance for music education. *Journal of Research in Music Education, 14*(2), 126–134.

Fowler, C. B. (1975, February). The arts—getting it all together. *Musical America,* 8–9.

Fowler, C. B. (Ed.). (1984). *Arts in education/education in arts: Entering the dialogue of the 80's.* Washington, DC: National Endowment for the Arts.

Fox, L., & Hopkins, T. (1936). *Creative School Music.* New York: Silver Burdett.

Freeman, J. (1977). Social factors in aesthetic talent. *Research in Education, 17*, 63–76.

Freundlich, D. (1978). *The development of musical thinking: Case studies in improvisation.* Unpublished doctoral dissertation, Harvard University.

Fridman, R. (1973). The first cry of the newborn: Basis for the child's future musical development. *Journal of Research in Music Education, 21*(3), 264–269.

Galloway, M. (1972). Let's make an opera: A happening with 120 young children. *Journal of Creative Behavior, 6*(1), 41–48.

Gamble, J. (1981). The effects of relaxation training and music upon creativity. *Dissertation Abstracts International, 42*(8), 3399B. (University Microfilms No. DDJ82-02082)

Gardner, D. P. (1984). Unpublished lecture. David P. Gardner Graduate Lecture in the Humanities and Fine Arts, University of Utah.

Gardner, H. (1982). *Art, mind, and brain.* New York: Basic Books.

Gardner, H. (1983a). Artistic intelligences. *Art Education, 36*(6), 2.

Gardner, H. (1983b). *Frames of mind: The theory of multiple intelligences.* New York: Basic Books.

Gaylin, W. (1979). *Feelings, our vital signs.* New York: Harper & Row.

Gerber, L. (1982). Music in early childhood: Postscript and preview. In R. Colwell (Ed.), *Symposium in music education.* Urbana: University of Illinois Press.

Gerig, R. (1975). *Famous pianists and their technique* (3rd ed.). Washington, DC: Robert B. Luce.

Gilbert, J. P. (1980). An assessment of motor music skill development in young children. *Journal of Research in Music Education, 28*(3), 167–175.

Gilbert, J. P. (1982). Preferences of elderly individuals for selected music education experiences. *Journal of Research in Music Education, 30*(4), 247–253.

Gilman, R. (1976, August 1). [Review of Arieti's *The magic synthesis.*] *New York Times*, Sec. 7, p. 4.

Goetze, M. (1985). *Factors affecting accuracy in children's singing.* Unpublished doctoral dissertation, University of Colorado.

Goldman, R. F. (1961). *The wind band.* Westport, CT: Greenwood.

Goleman, D. (1984, October 23). Nightmares are linked to creativity in new view. *New York Times*, C1, C2.

Goodlad, J. (1984). *A place called school: Prospects for the future.* New York: McGraw-Hill.

Gorder, W. (1976). An investigation of divergent production abilities as constructs of musical creativity. *Dissertation Abstracts International, 37*(1), 177A. (University Microfilms No. DDJ76-16136)

Gorder, W. (1980). Divergent production abilities as constructs of musical creativity. *Journal of Research in Music Education, 28*(1), 34–42.

Gordon, E. E. (1979a). *The assessment of music aptitude of very young children.* Unpublished manuscript. (Available from Edwin E. Gordon, Temple University, Philadelphia, PA 19122.)

Gordon, E. E. (1979b). *Primary measures of music audiation. Manual.* Chicago: G.I.A. Publications.

Gordon, E. E. (1980). *Developmental music aptitudes among inner-city primary children.* Unpublished manuscript. (Available from Edwin E. Gordon, Temple University, Philadelphia, PA 19122.)

Gould, G. (1983). *Glenn Gould/by himself and his friends.* Garden City, NY: Doubleday.

Graf, M. (1947). *From Beethoven to Shostakovich: The psychology of the composing process.* New York: Philosophical Library.

Graham, R. M. (1972). Seven million plus need special attention, who are they? *Music Educators Journal, 58*(8), 22–23.

Grant, F. H. (1963). *Foundations of music education in the Cleveland public schools.* Unpublished doctoral dissertation, Western Reserve University.

Greene, C. M. (1968). The scope and function of music in the community colleges under the supervision of the State University of New York. *Dissertation Abstracts International, 30*, 751A. (University Microfilms No. 69-11298)

Greene, M. (1985). Imagination releases us; it is the health of every human being. *Learning in New York.* Albany: New York State Education Department.

Greenhoe, M. (1972). Parameters of creativity in music education: An exploratory study. *Dissertation Abstracts International, 33*(4), 1766A. (University Microfilms No. 72-27467)

Gronlund, N. E. (1978). *Stating objectives for classroom instruction* (2nd ed.). New York: Macmillan.

Guilford, J. P. (1967). *The nature of human intelligence.* New York: McGraw-Hill.

Guilford, J. P. (1968). *Intelligence, creativity, and their educational implications.* San Diego, CA: Knapp.

Haack, P. A., & Heller, G. N. (1983). Music education and community in nineteenth-century Kansas Euterpe, Tonnies, and the Academy on the Plains. *Journal of Research in Music Education, 31*(2), 115–132.

Hammond, P. G. (1974). Music in the urban revivalism in the northern United States, 1800–1835. *Dissertation Abstracts International, 35*, 2319A. (University Microfilms No. 74-22660)

Harris, R. (1942). The basis of artistic creation in music. In M. Anderson, R. Carpenter, & R. Harris, *The Bases of Artistic Creation* (pp. 19–29). New Brunswick, NJ: Rutgers University Press.

Harvey, R. G. (1975). The procedural and financial activities of selected community symphony orchestras in central and northern California. *Dissertation Abstracts International, 36,* 17A. (University Microfilms No. 75-14439)

Henry, N. (Ed.) (1958). *Basic Concepts in Music Education.* 57th yearbook, Part 1, National Society for the Study of Education. Chicago: University of Chicago Press.

Hitler, A. (1939). *Mein Kampf.* New York: Reynal & Hitchcock.

Hoenack, P. (1971). Unleash creativity—let them improvise. *Music Educators Journal, 57*(9), 33–36.

Holderried, E. (1969). Creativity in my classroom. *Music Educators Journal, 55*(7), 37–39.

Holman, F. L. (1973). An analysis of research pertaining to the intellectual abilities of lower socioeconomic status children and implications for teacher and learning processes involved in the development of musicality. *Dissertation Abstracts International, 34,* 3450A. (University Microfilms No. 73-30185)

Hooper, P., & Powell, E. (1970). Influence of musical variables on pictorial connotations. *Journal of Psychology, 76*(1), 125–128.

Howe, R. M. (1952). *Interrelated arts for the college and community.* Unpublished doctoral dissertation, George Peabody College for Teachers.

Jenkins, J. M. D. (1976). The relationship between maternal parents' musical experience and the musical development of two- and three-year-old girls. *Dissertation Abstracts International, 37,* 7015A. (University Microfilms No. 77-11111)

Jensen, E. (1969). Creativity and its sources. *Music Educators Journal, 55*(7), 34–36.

Johnson, A. C., et al. (n.d.). *Older Americans: The unrealized audience for the arts.* Madison: Center for Arts Administration, University of Wisconsin, Madison.

Jones, R. M. (1968). *Fantasy and feeling in education.* New York: New York University Press.

Judd, T. (1979). Towards a neuromusicology: The effects of brain damage on music reading and musical creativity. *Dissertation Abstracts International, 40*(8), 4017B. (University Microfilms No. DDJ80-03941)

Kaltsounis, B. (1973). Effect of sound on creative performance. *Psychological Abstracts, 33*(3), 737–738.

Kaplan, B. (1981). *An investigation of the use of the "Primary Measures of Music Audiation" as an indicator of developmental music aptitude in rural Alabama.* Paper presented at the Auburn University Conference on Educating the Gifted Rural Child, Birmingham, AL, April. (Available from Barbara Kaplan; College of Education; Auburn University; Auburn, AL 36830)

Kaplan, B. (Ed.). (1985). *The Kodály concept; A bibliography for music education.* Monograph No. 1 in the series Kodály, A Dynamic Tradition. Whitewater, WI: Organization of American Kodály Educators.

Kaplan, M. (1966). *Foundations and frontiers of music education.* New York: Holt, Rinehart & Winston.

Kaplan, M. (1970). We have much to learn from the inner city. *Music Educators Journal, 56*(5), 39–42.

Kaplan, M. (1972a). A new language for a new leisure. *Bulletin of the Association of Departments of English, 33,* 76–84.

Kaplan, M. (1972b). Leisure in the design profession. *Lifestyle 2000: Designing for the third millennium*. Chicago: American Iron and Steel Institute.

Kaplan, M. (1974). Report of the UNESCO conference, project #3155: Cultural innovations in technological and post-industrial societies, Tampa, Florida, October 28–31, 1973. *Arts in society, 11*(3), 382–413.

Kaplan, M. (1976). The Kodály movement: Cross-cultural issues, ethnicity. *Kodály Envoy, 3*(1), 13–15.

Kaplan, M. (1978). *Leisure: Perspectives on education and policy.* Washington, DC: National Education Association.

Kaplan, M. (1979). *Leisure: Lifestyle and lifespan.* Philadelphia: Saunders.

Kaplan, M. (1982). *Leisure: Theory and policy.* Springfield, IL: Charles C. Thomas. (Originally published 1975, New York: Wiley.)

Karma, K. (1976). The ability to structure acoustic material as a measure of musical aptitude: III. Theoretical refinements. *Research Bulletin, 47,* 1–32. Institute of Education, University of Helsinki.

Keenan, J. (1984, December 10). Trapped in a musical elevator. *Time,* p. 110.

Kemp, A. (1981a). The personality structure of the musician, I. *Psychology of Music, 9*(1), 3–14.

Kemp, A. (1981b). The personality structure of the musician, II. *Psychology of Music, 9*(2), 69–75.

Kemp, A. (1982). The personality structure of the musician, III. *Psychology of Music, 10*(1), 48–58.

Keyes, N. (1969). *Study of the values of original composition in the training of public school music teachers* (Report No. BR-8-F-023). Kansas State Teachers College, Emporia. (ERIC Document Reproduction Service No. ED 031 507)

Khatena, J. (1971). Evaluation and the creative potential in music. *Gifted Child Quarterly,* Spring, 19–22.

Klapahouk, M. (1968). The dream of Franz Schubert: Relations between the dream and artistic creativity. *Encephale, 57,* 51–97.

Klotman, R. (1976). The musician in education: 2025 A.D. In A. Motycka (Ed.), *Music education for tomorrow's society: Selected topics* (pp. 19–20). Jamestown, RI: GAMT Music Press.

Knieter, G. (1983). Aesthetics for art's sake. *Music Educators Journal, 69*(7), 33–35, 61–64.

Kodály, Z. (1974). Hungarian music education. In F. Bonis (Ed.), *Selected writings of Zoltán Kodály* (pp. 152–155). Budapest: Corvina. (Originally published 1945)

Koestler, A. (1967). *The act of creation.* New York: Dell.

Kratus, J. (1983). Musical characteristics of children's original songs. In P. Tallarico (Ed.), *Contributions to symposium/83: The Bowling Green State University symposium on music teaching and research* (pp. 125–152). Bowling Green, Ohio: Bowling Green State University.

Kratus, J. (1985a). Rhythm, melody, motive, and phrase characteristics of original songs by children aged five to thirteen. *Dissertation Abstracts International, 46*(11), 3281A. (University Microfilms No. 8600883)

Kratus, J. (1985b). The use of melodic and rhythmic motives in the original songs of children aged 5 to 13. *Contributions to Music Education, 12,* 1–8.

Kyme, G. (1967). *A study of the development of musicality in the junior high school and the contribution of musical composition to this development* (Report No. CRP-H-254). University of California, Berkeley. (ERIC Document Reproduction Service No. 015 532)

Lang, R. (1976). The identification of some creative thinking parameters common to the artistic and musical personality. *British Journal of Educational Psychology, 46,* 267–279.

Langer, S. (1953). *Feeling and form: A theory of art.* New York: Scribner.

Langer, S. (1957). *Problems of art.* New York: Scribner.

Lasch, C. (1978). *The culture of narcissism.* New York: Norton.

Lasch, C. (1984). The degradation of work and the apotheosis of art. In D. Shetler (Ed.), *The future of musical education in America* (pp. 11–19). Rochester: Eastman School of Music Press.

Lasker, H. (1971). *Teaching creative music in secondary schools.* Boston: Allyn & Bacon.

Lasker, H. (1973). Why can't they compose? *Music Educators Journal, 59*(8), 41–45.

Lathom, W. (n.d.). *The role of music therapy in the education of handicapped children and youth.* Alexandria, VA: National Association for Music Therapy.

Lax, M.E. (1966). *A study to determine the factors that influence the dropouts from the instrumental music programs in moving from one school level to another in selected Detroit public schools.* Unpublished doctoral dissertation, Wayne State University.

Lazarsfeld, P. (1970). *Main trends of research in the social and human sciences.* Paris: UNESCO; The Hague: Mouton.

LeBlanc, A. (1979). Generic style music preferences of fifth-grade students. *Journal of Research in Music Education, 27*(4), 255–270.

LeBlanc, A. (1981). Effects of style, tempo, and performing medium on children's music preference. *Journal of Research in Music Education, 29*(2), 143–156.

LeBlanc, A. (1982). An interactive theory of music preference. *Journal of Music Therapy, 19,* 28–45.

LeBlanc, A. (1987). The development of music preference in children. In J. C. Peery, I. W. Peery & T. W. Draper, (Eds.), *Music and child development* (pp. 137–157). New York: Springer.

LeBlanc, A., & Cote, R. (1983). Effects of tempo and performing medium on children's music preference. *Journal of Research in Music Education, 31*(1), 57–66.

LeBlanc, A., & McCrary, J. (1983). Effect of tempo on children's music preference. *Journal of Research in Music Education, 31*(4), 283–294.

LeBlanc, A., & Sherrill, C. (1986). Effect of vocal vibrato and performer's sex on children's music preference. *Journal of Research in Music Education, 34*(4), 222–237.

Lee, R. (1931, December 20). Dimitri Shostakovich, in the *New York Times,* X8. (Interview in Moscow, December 5, 1931)

Lee, R. T. (1970). A study of teacher training experiences for prospective inner-city instrumental music teachers. *Dissertation Abstracts International, 31,* 4202A-4203A. (University Microfilms No. 71-4660)

Lehman, P. (1984). The last word: Who says music is basic? *Music Educators Journal, 71*(2), 80.

Leibowitz, L. (1978). The relationship of continuation in applied music study to musical aptitude, creativity, and scholastic average in four New York City high schools. *Dissertation Abstracts International, 40*(1), 147A. (University Microfilms No. DDJ79-11249)

Leonhard, C. (1966). The next ten years in music education. *Bulletin of the Council for Research in Music Education, 7,* 13–23.

Leonhard, C., & House, R. (1972). *Foundations and principles of music education* (2nd ed.). New York: McGraw-Hill. (Originally published 1958)

Letts, R. (1972). Creative musicianship and psychological growth: Bases in some theories of personality, creativity, instruction, aesthetics, and music, for a music curriculum for the late twentieth century. *Dissertation Abstracts International, 31*(1), 278A. (University Microfilms No. 72-19867)

Ling, S. (1974). Missing: Some of the most exciting creative moments of life. *Music Educators Journal, 40*(3), 93–95.

Lorentzen, B. (1970). Electronic music means switched-on creativity. *Music Educators Journal, 57*(3), 56–57.

Lowery, J. (1980). The effect of three creativity instructional methods on the creative thinking of gifted elementary school children. *Dissertation Abstracts International, 41*(10), 4360A. (University Microfilms No. DDJ81-08262)

Lowry, W. M. (Ed.). (1984). *The arts and public policy in the United States: Background papers for the 67th American Assembly, Columbia University.* Englewood Cliffs, NJ: Prentice-Hall.

Lundberg, G., Komarovsky, M., & McIllney, N. (1934). *Leisure, a suburban study.* New York: Columbia University Press.

Macarov, D. (1980). *Work and welfare: The unholy alliance.* Beverly Hills: Sage Library of Social Research.

McClellan, L. (1977). The effects of creative experiences on musical growth. *Dissertation Abstracts International, 39*(1), 16A. (University Microfilms No. DDJ78-10090)

Madsen, C. (1977). Creativity and music education: Comparing two methods of teaching junior high school general music. *Dissertation Abstracts International, 41*(2), 539A. (University Microfilms No. DDJ77-16809)

Mager, R. (1962). *Preparing instructional objectives.* Palo Alto, CA: Fearon.

Mager, R. (1968). *Developing attitude for learning.* Belmont, CA: Fearon.

Mandelbaum, J. (1978). A study of the relationship of an in-service program in music and movement to provide opportunities for creativity in selected kindergartens. *Dissertation Abstracts International, 39*(8), 4883A. (University Microfilms No. DDJ78-24095)

Mark, M. L. (1982). The evolution of music education philosophy from utilitarian to aesthetic. *Journal of Research in Music Education, 30*(1), 15–21.

Marsh, M. (1970). *Explore and discover music: Creative approaches to music education in elementary, middle, and junior high schools.* New York: Macmillan.

Martindale, D. (1960). *The nature and types of sociological theory.* Boston: Houghton Mifflin.

Merriam, A. P. (1964). *The anthropology of music.* Chicago: Northwestern University Press.

Merritt, G. T. (1967). A study and report on the organization, implementation, and evolution of three programs in music education under Title I of the Elementary and Secondary Education Act of 1965 in New York City during 1966. *Dissertation Abstracts International, 28,* 3705A. (University Microfilms No. 68-2434)

Meyer, L. B. (1960). Universalism and relativism in the study of ethnic music. *Ethnomusicology, 4*(2), 49–54.

Meyer, L. B. (1961). *Emotion and meaning in music.* Chicago: University of Chicago Press, Phoenix Books. (Originally published 1956)

Mills, E., & Murphy, T. (1973). *The Suzuki concept.* Berkeley: Diablo Press.

Modugno, A. (1971). Electronic creativity in the elementary classroom. *Today's Education, 60*(3), 62–64.

Moore, D. L. (1973). A study of the pitch and rhythm responses of five year old children in relation to their early musical experiences. *Dissertation Abstracts International, 34,* 6690A-6691A. (University Microfilms No. 74-9488)

Moorehead, G., & Pond, D. (1978). *Music for young children.* Santa Barbara, California: Pillsbury Foundation for the Advancement of Music Education.

Morris, V. C. (1961). *Philosophy and the American school.* Boston: Houghton Mifflin.

Mumford, L. (1973). *In the name of sanity.* Westport, CT: Greenwood. (Originally published 1954)

Mursell, J. (1934). *Human values in music education.* New York: Silver Burdett.

Mursell, J. (1953). *Music education: Principles and programs.* Morristown, NJ: Silver Burdett.

Music Educators National Conference (MENC). (1981). *Documentary report of the Ann Arbor Symposium: Applications of psychology to the teaching and learning of music.* Reston, VA: Music Educators National Conference.

Music Educators National Conference, National Executive Board. (1984). Religious music in the schools. *Music Educators Journal, 71*(3), 28.

Naisbitt, R. (1982). *Megatrends.* New York: Warner Books.

National Association of Schools of Music (NASM). (1984). *Higher Education Arts Data Services (HEADS), Data Summary: Music 1982–1983.* Reston, VA: NASM.

National Association of Schools of Music (NASM). (1985). *1985–1986 Handbook.* Reston, VA: NASM.

National Center for Educational Statistics (NCES). (1984). *Course offerings and enrollments in the arts and the humanities at the secondary school level.* Arlington, VA: Evaluation Technologies.

National Commission on Excellence in Education (NCEE). (1983). *A nation at risk: The imperative for educational reform.* Washington, DC: U.S. Government Printing Office.

National Endowment for the Arts (NEA). (1985). *Audiences—overview: 1987–1991 planning document.* Unpublished manuscript, National Endowment for the Arts, Washington, DC.

Neulinger, J. (1981). *To leisure: An introduction.* State College, PA: Venture.

Obenshain, K. (1974). An information-processing approach to the assessment of creative ability in college music majors. *Dissertation Abstracts International, 35*(5), 2777A. (University Microfilms No. DDJ74-23819)

O'Brien, J. (1972). Stop the conveyor belt—the kids want to get off. *Music Educators Journal, 58*(9), 25–29.

O'Brien, J. (1974). Use of a factored biographical inventory to identify differentially gifted adolescents. *Psychological Reports, 35,* 1195–1294.

Ortega y Gassett, J. (1932). *The revolt of the masses.* New York: Norton.

Ozick, C. (1974, December). Culture and the present moment. *Commentary,* p. 6.

Parsons, T. (1949). *The structure of social action.* New York: Free Press.

Parsons, T., Shils, E., Naegele, K., & Pitts, J. (Eds.). (1961). *Theories of society: Foundations of modern sociological theory.* New York: Free Press.

Payne, D. (1974). Use of a factored biographical inventory to identify differentially gifted adolescents. *Psychological Reports, 35,* 1195–1294.

Perdue, B. (Ed.). (1983). *Directory: Alabama public school music educators.* Montgomery: Alabama State Department of Education.

Peyre, H. (1962). *Anxiety and the creative process.* Paper presented at Wayne State University, Detroit. (Privately distributed)

Pfeil, C. (1972). Creativity as an instructional mode for introducing music to nonmusic majors at the college level. *Dissertation Abstracts International, 33*(5), 2415A. (University Microfilms No. 72-30028)

Phillips, K. (1983). Utilitarian vs. aesthetic. *Music Educators Journal, 69*(7), 29–30.

Pieper, J. (1962). *Leisure, the basis of culture.* London: Faber & Faber. (Originally published 1952)

Plato. *Republic, III: The collected dialogues of Plato.* E. Hamilton & C. Huntington (Eds.). New York: Norton.

Plummeridge, C. (1980). Creativity and music education—the need for further clarification. *Psychology of Music, 8*(1), 34–40.

Pond, D. (1980). The young child's playful world of sound. *Music Educators Journal, 66*(7), 39–41.

Pond, D. (1981). A composer's study of young children's innate musicality. *Bulletin of the Council for Research in Music Education, 68,* 1–12.

Prall, D. W. (1967). *Aesthetic analysis.* New York: Thomas Y. Crowell, Apollo Edition. (Originally published 1936)

Prevel, M. (1976). Helping children build their own music. In F. Calloway (Ed.), *Challenges in Music Education* (pp. 64–78). Perth: Department of Music, University of Western Australia.

Prevel, M. (1979). Emergent patterning in children's musical improvisations. *Canadian Music Educator, 15,* 13–15.

Putsch, H. (Ed.). (1984). AICA survey of current trends in art education. In *Art education in the schools: Strategies for action.* Washington, DC: Alliance of Independent Colleges of Art.

Rabin, M. J. (1968). History and analysis of the Greater Boston Youth Symphony Orchestra from 1958–1964. *Dissertation Abstracts International, 29,* 2295A. (University Microfilms No. 69-1416)

Rainbow, E. (1981). A final report on a three-year investigation of the rhythmic abilities of pre-school aged children. *Bulletin of the Council of Research in Music Education, 66–67,* 181–183.

Read, H. (1945). *Education through art.* New York: Pantheon Books.

Reimer, B. (1970). *A philosophy of music education.* Englewood Cliffs, NJ: Prentice-Hall.

Reimer, B. (1971). Aesthetic behaviors in music. In *Toward an aesthetic education* (pp. 65–87). Washington, DC: Music Educators National Conference.

Revesz, G. (1954). *Introduction to the psychology of music.* Norman: University of Oklahoma Press.

Rexroth, K. (1963). The institutionalization of revolt, the domestication of dissent. *Arts in Society, 2*(2), 120–126.

Reynolds, M. C. (1976). Official actions of the delegate assembly of the Council for Exceptional Children. In *Exceptional Children, 43* (September), 43.

Rhodes, E. A. (1971). A comparative study of selected contemporary theories of creativity with reference to music education in the secondary schools. *Dissertation Abstracts International, 31*(9), 5610B. (University Microfilms No. 71-06602)

Richardson, C. (1983). Creativity research in music education: A review. *Bulletin of the Council for Research in Music Education, 74,* 1–21.

Richta, R. (Ed.). (1969). *Civilization at the crossroads.* Prague: Czech Academy of Sciences.

Roderick, J. (1965). An investigation of selected factors of the creative thinking ability of music majors in a teacher training program. *Dissertation Abstracts International, 26*(1), 409. (University Microfilms No. 65-07156)

Rummler, R. (1973). Direct involvement through contemporary composition. *Music Educators Journal, 60*(4), 22–25.

Salvatore, S. (1984, October 23). In W. Broad, Scientists bet on new design. *New York Times,* C1, C8.

Sanders, S. (1977). Effects of musical stimuli on creativity. *Psychological Record, 27*(2), 463–471.

Schafer, M. (1976). *Creative music education.* New York: Schirmer.

Schantz, A. P. (1983). *A new statement of values for music education based on writings of Dewey, Meyer, and Wolterstorff.* Unpublished doctoral dissertation, University of Colorado.

Schrader, S. F. (1968). A history of the University Musical Society of Ann Arbor, Michigan: 1872–1892. *Dissertation Abstracts International, 30,* 359A. (University Microfilms No. 69-12234)

Schubert, D. (1977). Family constellation and creativity: Firstborn predominance among classical music composers. *Journal of Psychology, 95*(1), 147–149.

Schwadron, A. (1967). *Aesthetics: Dimensions for music education.* Washington, DC: Music Educators National Conference.

Schwadron, A. (1969). Structural meaning and music education. *Journal of Aesthetic Education, 3*(4), 109–122.

Schwadron, A. (1971). On words and music: Toward an aesthetic conciliation. *Journal of Aesthetic Education, 5*(3), 91–108.

Schwadron, A. (1972). On play and music: A critique. *Journal of Aesthetic Education, 6*(4), 11–27.

Schwadron, A. (1973). Are we ready for aesthetic education? *Music Educators Journal, 60*(2), 37–39, 87.

Schwadron, A. (1974). Comparative aesthetic perspectives in the philosophy of music education. *Journal of the Indian Musicological Society, 5*(2), 5–12.

Schwadron, A. (1976). Comparative music aesthetics and education: Observations in speculation. In A. Motycka (Ed.), *Music education for tomorrow's society: Selected topics* (pp. 21–29). Jamestown, RI: GAMT Music Press.

Schwadron, A. (1982). Music education and teacher preparation: Perspectives from the aesthetics of music. *Journal of Musicological Research, 4,* 175-192.

Schwadron, A. (1984). World musics in education. In *1984 Yearbook, International Society for Music Education* (pp. 80–86). Nedlands, Western Australia: International Society for Music Education.

Schwadron, A. (1985). *National education commission reports and music education.* Unpublished address to the general assembly, Southern Division, Music Educators National Convention, Mobile, Alabama, March 28.

Seifert, L. (1975). Children as music makers. In *Annual Report, High/Scope Foundation.* Ypsilanti, MI: High/Scope Foundation.

Sheftel, S. (1982). *Mozart: A psychoanalytic study.* Unpublished doctoral dissertation, University for Experimenting Colleges and Universities.

Sherman, R. (1971a). Creativity and the condition of knowing in music, Part 1. *Music Educators Journal, 58*(2), 18–22.

Sherman, R. (1971b). Creativity and the condition of knowing in music, Part 2. *Music Educators Journal, 58*(3), 59–61.

Simon, R. G. (1968). The propriety of the study of sacred music in the public schools of Greeley, Colorado: A community survey. *Dissertation Abstracts International, 29,* 1920A. (University Microfilms No. 68-14738)

Simonton, D. (1977). Creative productivity, age, and stress: A biographical time-series analysis of 10 classical composers. *Journal of Personality and Social Psychology, 35,* 791–804.

Simpson, A., & Simpson, J. (Eds.). (1983). *Sociology: Contemporary readings.* Itasca, NY: F. E. Peacock.

Simpson, D. (1970). The effect of selected musical studies on growth in general creative potential. *Dissertation Abstracts International, 30*(2), 502A. (University Microfilms No. 69-13081)

Skura, M. (1980, Spring). Creativity: Transgressing the limits of consciousness. *Daedalus,* p. 130.

Snow, C. (1959). *The two cultures and the scientific revolution.* Cambridge: Cambridge University Press.

Sorokin, P. (1947). *Society, culture, and personality.* New York: Harper.

Southwestern Regional Educational Laboratory (SWRL). (1984). *The tide of educational quality and the current situation of fine arts instruction.* Los Alamitos, CA: SWRL Educational Research and Development.

Steinel, D. (Ed.). (1984). *Music and music education: Data and information.* Reston, VA: Music Educators National Conference.

Stephens, R. (1974). Creativity in the classroom. *Elements: Translating Theory into Practice, 5*(8), 1–2.

Stewart, T. W. (1984). *The University of California adopts revised statement for electives in the visual and performing arts.* Typescript report distributed by the Office of Academic Interinstitutional Programs, University of California, Los Angeles.

Stolnitz, J. (1960). *Aesthetics and philosophy of art criticism: A critical introduction.* Boston: Houghton Mifflin.

Storr, A. (1975). Creativity in music. *Psychology of Music, 3*(2), 9–16.

Stringer, P. (1965, October 7). The art student's personality. *New Society,* pp. 4–5.

Sudano, G., & Sharpham, J. (1981). Back to basics: Justifying the arts in general education. *Music Educators Journal, 68*(3), 48–50.

Sullivan, H. F. (1975). A descriptive study of the musical, academic, and social characteristics of selected students in a suburban high school in New York State. *Dissertation Abstracts International, 36,* 169A. (University Microfilms No. 75-14175)

Sunderland, J. T. (1974). *Older Americans and the arts: A human equation.* Washington DC: National Council on Aging and John F. Kennedy Center for the Performing Arts.

Swanner, D. (1985). Relationships between musical creativity and selected factors including personality, motivation, musical aptitude, and cognitive intelligence as measured in third grade children. *Dissertation Abstracts International, 46*(12), 3646A. (University Microfilms No. AAD86-01941)

Swanwick, K. (1974). Music and the education of the emotions. *British Journal of Aesthetics, 14*(2), 134–141.

Szalai, A. (Ed.). (1972). *The use of time: Daily activities of urban and suburban populations in twelve countries.* The Hague: Mouton.

Tait, M. (1982). *Conducting clinic.* Unpublished manuscript. Music Educators National Conference, San Antonio, TX, February.

Tait, M., & Haack, P. (1984). *Principles and processes of music education: New perspectives.* New York: Teachers College Press.

Tapley, I. B. (1976). An evaluation of musical training in auditory perception for first grade children. *Dissertation Abstracts International, 37,* 6336A. (University Microfilms No. 77-8227)

Tarratus, E. (1964). Creative processes in music and the identification of creative music students. *Dissertation Abstracts International, 25*(11), 6679A. (University

Microfilms No. 65-03927)

Teague, W. (1984). *A plan for excellence: Alabama's public schools.* Montgomery: Alabama State Department of Education.

Tellstrom, A. T. (1971). *Music in American education, past and present.* New York: Holt, Rinehart, & Winston.

Thackray, R. (1965). *Creative music in education.* London: Novello.

Thomas, R. (1970). *Manhattanville Music Curriculum Project: Final Report* (Report No. BR6-1999). Purchase, NY: Manhattanville College of the Sacred Heart. (ERIC Document Reproduction Service No. ED 045 865)

Thompson, D. (1980). Vocal improvisation for elementary students. *Music Educators Journal, 66*(5), 69–71.

Torrance, E. (1969). Originality of imagery in identifying creative talent in music. *Gifted Child Quarterly, 12*(1), 3–8.

Trollinger, L. (1979). A study of the biographical factors of creative women in music. *Dissertation Abstracts International, 40*(5), 2533A. (University Microfilms No. DDJ79-24039)

Trollinger, L. (1981). Responses of high and low creative women musicians to undergraduate music courses: Anxiety, boredom, avoidance, and pleasure. *Journal of Creative Behavior, 15*(4), 257–264.

Trollinger, L. (1983, February). Creativity: Basic concepts and recent developments. In *Loyola Symposium VI.* Loyola University of New Orleans.

Tuttle, T. (1976). What is this thing called creativity? *Triad, 26*(5), 26.

Ultan, L. (1984). Music in our schools: A question of values. *College Music Symposium 24,* n. 1.

Vander Schoot, A. (1983). Cultural specific factors in the realization of Kodály's philosophy outside of Hungary. *Bulletin of the International Kodály Society, 2,* 20–23.

Vaughan, M. (1971). Cultivating creative behavior in children. *Dissertation Abstracts International, 32*(10), 5833A. (University Microfilms No. 72-11056)

Vaughan, M. (1973). Cultivating creative behavior. *Music Educators Journal, 59*(8), 35–37.

Vaughan, M. (1977). Musical creativity: Its cultivation and measurement. *Bulletin of the Council for Research in Music Education, 50,* 72–77.

Vaughan, M., & Myers, R. (1971). An examination of musical process as related to creative thinking. *Journal of Research in Music Education, 19*(3), 337–341.

Viscott, D. (1970). A musical idiot savant: A psycho-dynamic study, and some speculations on the creative process. *Psychiatry: Journal of the Study of Interpersonal Processes, 33*(4), 494–515.

Vulliamy, G., & Shepherd, J. (1983). A sociological approach to pop music in teaching: A response to Swanwick. *International Journal of Music Education, 2*(1), 6–9.

Walls, C. (1973). The identification of musical concepts by elementary children from contrasting racial groups and socioeconomic environments. *Dissertation Abstracts International, 34,* 4828A. (University Microfilms No. 74-3340)

Walsh, M. (1984, September/October). Chaos and opportunity: New music today. *Vantage Point,* pp. 22–26.

Walter, B. (1961). *Of music and music-making,* trans. Paul Hamburger. New York: Norton.

Watkins, A. (1966). Music composition by the non-professional. *Music Director, 19,* 3–4.

Watson, T. W. (1968). A study of musical attitudes and their relationship to environment among rural socio-economically deprived students in central Oklahoma. *Dissertation Abstracts International*, 29, 1247A. (University Microfilms No. 68-14214)

Weber, M. (1958). Science as a vocation. In H. H. Gerth & C. W. Mills (Eds.), *From Max Weber: Essays in sociology*. New York: Oxford University Press.

Webster, P. (1976). Identifying the creative musician. *Triad*, 26(6), 32–35.

Webster, P. (1977). A factor of intellect approach to creative thinking in music. *Dissertation Abstracts International*, 38(6), 3136A. (University Microfilms No. DDJ77-2619)

Webster, P. (1979). Relationship between creative behavior in music and selected variables as measured in high school students. *Journal of Research in Music Education*, 27(4), 227–242.

Webster, P. (1983). An assessment of musical imagination in young children. In P. Tallarico (Ed.), *Contributions to symposium/83: The Bowling Green State University symposium on music teaching and research*, pp. 100–123. Bowling Green, OH: Bowling Green State University.

Webster, P. (1987). Conceptual bases for creative thinking in music. In J. C. Peery, I. W. Peery, & T. W. Draper (Eds.), *Music and child development*. New York: Springer.

Welwood, A. (1980). Improvising with found sounds. *Music Educators Journal*, 66(5), 72–77.

Wermuth, R. F. (1971). Relationship of musical aptitude to family and student activity in music, student interest in music, socioeconomic status, and intelligence among Caucasian and Negro middle school students. *Dissertation Abstracts International*, 32, 4054A. (University Microfilms No. 72-4689)

Whalam, W. (1975). *Why sing? A conversation about music*. Corte Madera, CA: Chandler & Sharp.

Whiteside, A. (1929). *The pianist's mechanism*. New York: Schirmer.

Wiggins, J., Renner, K., Clore, G., & Rose, R. (Eds.). (1971). *The psychology of personality*. Reading, MA: Addison-Wesley.

Williams, P. (1977). Musical creativity: An interdisciplinary approach from Troy to Carthage, from Virgil to Berlioz. *Creative Child and Adult Quarterly*, 2(3), 148–150.

Willman, R. (1944). An experimental investigation of the creative process in music. *Psychological Monographs*, 57(1).

Young, W. (1976). *A synthesis of recent research on the child voice*. Paper presented at the meeting of the Organization of American Kodály Educators, Pittsburgh, PA, February.

Zimmerman, G. (1973). A danger to musical art. *Music Educators Journal*, 60(2), 68–69.

Zimmerman, M. P. (1970). Percept and concept: Implications of Piaget. *Music Educators Journal*, 56(6), 49–50, 147.

Zimmerman, M. P. (1982). Developmental processes in music education. In R. Colwell (Ed.), *Symposium in Music Education*. Urbana: University of Illinois Press.

Contributors

Gretchen H. Beall, University of Colorado, Boulder
Gordon Epperson, University of Arizona, Tucson
Charles B. Fowler, Writer and consultant, Washington, D.C.
J. Terry Gates, State University of New York at Buffalo
Robert Glidden, Florida State University, Tallahassee
Richard M. Graham, University of Georgia, Athens
Merilyn Jones, University of Alabama, Tuscaloosa
William LaRue Jones, Greater Twin Cities Youth Symphonies, Minneapolis, Minnesota
Barbara Kaplan, Auburn University; Auburn, Alabama
Max Kaplan, Writer and consultant, Auburn, Alabama
Craig Kirchhoff, Ohio State University, Columbus
Albert LeBlanc, Michigan State University, East Lansing
Charles Leonhard, University of Illinois, Urbana (retired)
Michael L. Mark, Towson State University; Towson, Maryland
Amanda Penick, University of Alabama, Tuscaloosa
Abraham Schwadron, University of California at Los Angeles (deceased)
Malcolm Tait, West Chester State University; West Chester, Pennsylvania
Peter Webster, Case-Western Reserve University, Cleveland

Index

Absolute expressionism: Schwadron on, 100–101; Leonard Meyer and, 110 (n. 12)
Acculturation, 105–06
ACM. *See* Association for Classical Music
Administration: defined, 186; and music in higher education, 248–49
Adolescents: music education for, 220–21
Aesthetic: knowing, 93; properties (listing of), 93; commitment, 96, 104–05; discrimination, 177
Aesthetic education: in performance classes, 92–95; and philosophical aesthetics, 96–97; meaning of term, 96–97; measurement in, 99; aesthetic illiteracy, 105; terms descriptive of, 109 (n. 6); and score preparation, 283–84
Aesthetic experience: and qualitative living, 86; functions of, in society, 103–05; aesthetic response, 158–59; benefits of, 163
Aesthetic inquiry: pedagogical questions for, 93–94; and historical contexts of musical works, 94–95; need for, 156
Aesthetic-musical-educational complex: Schwadron's description of, 95–96
Aesthetics: meanings in music, 97–98; role in music education, 187–91
AICA. *See* Alliance of Independent Colleges of Art
Alabama: musical culture in, 47; school music in, 47–48
Alabama Project, ix–xi, 3, 5, 108, 239, 299–302; Symposia, ix–x; publications, x–xi; Symposium II, 32; and professional leadership, 65
All-American Youth Orchestra: audition expectations, 175
Alliance of Independent Colleges of Art (AICA): on staffing changes (c. 1984), 142
Amadeus (Broadway musical), 203
American Association of School Administrators: on the arts in the school curriculum (c. 1959), 123
American Symphony Orchestra League (ASOL), 135
Andress, Barbara, 217
Ann Arbor Symposium, 156, 199
Appelbaum, Samuel: contribution to string pedagogy, 279

Applications of Research in Music Behavior, edited by Madsen and Prickett, xi
Apprentice approach: defined, 279
Aptitude. *See* Music aptitude
Arieti, Sylvano: reviewed by Gilman, 22
Art music: and music preference, 41
Arts: research in, 7; social roles and functions of, 11–18; unique roles in education, 104–05; in school curriculum, 123; in American culture, 133–41; demand for, 138–39
Arts eduction: Schwadron on current difficulties of, 85–86; Adolph Hitler on, 113; benefits of, 190–91
Arts teacher: societal roles and functions, 18–20; training of, 20; and social change, 30, 137. *See also* Music teacher
ASOL. *See* American Symphony Orchestra League
Association for Classical Music (ACM), 136
Atlanta Music Club, 10
Auburn University: and Alabama Project, xi; study of music aptitude in elementary schools (1980), 48–58
Auditions: in youth symphonies, 175, 282–83
Aural awareness: and musical performance, 291–95
Ausubel, David, 205
Awareness of sound: as attentive listening, 293–95; program objectives for, 293–95

Bachelor of Music degree: developments in, 242–44
Band: philosophy of, 260; contest, 274–75. *See also* Jazz ensemble; Marching band
Bartók, Béla, 3
Barzun, Jacques, 171
Beall, Gretchen H., ix, 182
Behavioral objectives: usefulness of, 194–95
Behavioral terms: related to musical sensitivity, 166
Behavior management: *Goss* vs. *Lopez,* 224
Benner, Charles: on comprehensive musicianship, 64
Blacks: as creative segment of society, 16–17
Boston School Committee (1838), 111
Boston University 31
Boyer, Ernest, 143; on arts education, 191

320

LIBRARY.
ST. LOUIS COMMUNITY COLLEGE
AT FLORISSANT VALLEY.